Prentice Hall
LITERATURE
Timeless Voices, Timeless Themes

Adapted Reader's Companion
Teacher's Edition

Hall

Upper Saddle River, New Jersey
Glenview, Illinois
Needham, Massachusetts

ISBN 0-13-063104-3

2 3 4 5 6 7 8 9 10   05 04 03 02

Acknowledgments

Grateful acknowledgment is made to the following for permission to reprint copyrighted material:

Miriam Altschuler Literary Agency
"Treasure of Lemon Brown" by Walter Dean Myers from *Boy's Life Magazine,* March 1983. Copyright © 1983, by Walter Dean Myers.

AMG
"A Christmas Carol: Scrooge and Marley" by Israel Horovitz, an adaptation of Charles Dickens's *A Christmas Carol.* Copyright © 1994 by Fountain Pen, Inc. All rights reserved.

Arte Publico Press
"Maestro" by Pat Mora is reprinted with permission from the publisher of *Borders* (Houston: Arte Publico Press-University of Houston, 1986).

Susan Bergholz Literary Services, New York
"Four Skinny Trees" from *The House on Mango Street.* Copyright © 1984 by Sandra Cisneros. Published by Vintage Books, a division of Random House, Inc., and in hardcover by Alfred A. Knopf in 1994. All rights reserved.

Curtis Brown Ltd.
"Ribbons" by Laurence Yep, copyright © 1992 by Laurence Yep from *American Girl,* Jan/Feb 1992.

Brandt & Hochman Literary Agents, Inc.
"The Third Wish" from *Not What You Expected: A Collection of Short Stories* by Joan Aiken. Copyright © 1974 by Joan Aiken.

Delacorte Press, a division of Random House, Inc.
"The Luckiest Time of All" from *The Lucky Stone* by Lucille Clifton. Copyright © 1979 by Lucille Clifton. All rights reserved.

Don Congdon Associates, Inc.
"All Summer In A Day" by Ray Bradbury, published in *The Magazine of Fantasy and Science Fiction,* March 1, 1954. Copyright © 1954, renewed 1982 by Ray Bradbury.

Farrar, Straus & Giroux, Inc.
"The Cat Who Thought She Was a Dog and the Dog Who Thought He Was a Cat" from *Naftali the Storyteller and His Horse, Sus* by Issac Bashevis Singer. Copyright © 1973, 1976 by Isaac Bashevis Singer.

M.W. Farrell, executrix for the Estate of Juliet Piggot Wood
"Popocatepetl and Ixtlaccihuatl" from *Mexican Folk Tales* by Juliet Piggott. Copyright © 1973 by Juliet Piggott.

Golden Books Family Entertainment
"The Bride of Pluto" (retitled "Demeter and Persephone") from *Golden Treasury of Myths and Legends* by Anne Terry White. Copyright © 1959 Western Publishing Company, Inc. All rights reserved.

G.P Putnam's Sons, a division of Penguin Putnam, Inc.
"Two Kinds" by Amy Tan from *The Joy Luck Club.* Copyright © 1989 by Amy Tan. "Our Finest Hour" from *The Osgood Files* by Charles Osgood. Copyright © 1986, 1987, 1988, 1989, 1990, 1991 by Charles Osgood.

Harcourt, Inc.
Excerpt from *In Search of Our Mother's Gardens: Womanist Prose,* copyright © 1983 by Alice Walker. "Seventh Grade" from *Baseball in April and Other Stories,* copyright © 1990 by Gary Soto.

HarperCollins Publishers, Inc.
"How the Snake Got Poison" from *Mules and Men* by Zora Neale Hurston. Copyright © 1935 by Zora Neale Hurston. Copyright renewed 1963 by John C. Hurston and Joel Hurston. From *An American Childhood* by Annie Dillard. Copyright © 1987 by Annie Dillard.

John Hawkins & Associates Inc.
"My Furthest-Back Person—The African" by Alex Haley, published July 16, 1972, by *The New York Times Magazine.* Copyright © 1972 by Alex Haley.

Bill Hilgers, Esq., for the Estate of Barbara Jordan
"All Together Now" by Barbara Jordan, originally published in *Sesame Street Parents,* July/August 1994.

(Acknowledgments continue on page 374)

Contents

To the Teacher ix

Part 1: Selection Adaptations With Excerpts of Authentic Text . . 1

Interacting With the Text 2

Unit 1: Independence and Identity

**The Cat Who Thought She Was a Dog and
the Dog Who Thought He Was a Cat** Isaac Bashevis Singer 4
Two Kinds Amy Tan 11
My Furthest-Back Person Alex Haley 21
A Day's Wait Ernest Hemingway 31
Was Tarzan a Three-Bandage Man? Bill Cosby 39

Unit 2: Common Threads

from **In Search of Our Mothers' Gardens** Alice Walker 46
Seventh Grade Gary Soto 54
Melting Pot Anna Quindlen 63
The Hummingbird That Lived Through Winter William Saroyan 71

Unit 3: What Matters

The Third Wish Joan Aiken 79
The Charge of the Light Brigade Alfred, Lord Tennyson 88
The Californian's Tale Mark Twain 94
Four Skinny Trees Sandra Cisneros 105

Unit 4: Meeting Challenges

The Night the Bed Fell James Thurber 111
All Summer in a Day Ray Bradbury 120
The Highwayman Alfred Noyes 129
Amigo Brothers Piri Thomas 138

Unit 5: Just For Fun

Our Finest Hour Charles Osgood 149

Cat on the Go James Herriot 156

The Luckiest Time of All Lucille Clifton 165

How the Snake Got Poison Zora Neale Hurston 172

Unit 6: Short Story

Rikki-tikki-tavi Rudyard Kipling 178

After Twenty Years O. Henry 188

Papa's Parrot Cynthia Rylant 196

Ribbons Laurence Yep 203

The Treasure of Lemon Brown Walter Dean Myers 212

Unit 7: Nonfiction

I Am a Native of North America Chief Dan George 222

All Together Now Barbara Jordan 229

How to Enjoy Poetry James Dickey 235

The Chase *from* **An American Childhood** Annie Dillard 242

Unit 8: Drama

A Christmas Carol: Scrooge and Marley
Dramatized by Israel Horovitz Charles Dickens

Act I, Scenes 1 and 2 250

Act I, Scenes 3, 4, and 5 260

Unit 9: Poetry

The Cremation of Sam McGee Robert Service 270

Annabel Lee Edgar Allan Poe 277

Maestro Pat Mora 283

The Village Blacksmith Henry Wadsworth Longfellow 288

Unit 10: Legends, Folk Tales, and Myths

Popocatepetl and Ixtlaccihuatl Juliet Piggott 294

The People Could Fly Virginia Hamilton 303

Demeter and Persephone Anne Terry White 311

Icarus and Daedalus Josephine Peabody 319

Part 2: Selection Summaries With Alternative Reading Strategies **327**

Unit 1: Independence and Identity

The Cat Who Thought She Was a Dog and the Dog Who Thought He Was a Cat Isaac Bashevis Singer 329

Two Kinds Amy Tan 330

from **Song of Myself** Walt Whitman 331

I'm Nobody Emily Dickinson 331

Me Walter de la Mare 331

My Furthest-Back Person Alex Haley 332

The Third Level Jack Finney 332

A Day's Wait Ernest Hemingway 334

Was Tarzan a Three-Bandage Man? Bill Cosby 335

Oranges Gary Soto 335

Unit 2: Common Threads

from **In Search of Our Mothers' Gardens** Alice Walker 336

Seventh Grade Gary Soto 337

Melting Pot Anna Quindlen 337

Fable Ralph Waldo Emerson 338

If– Rudyard Kipling 338

Thumbprint Eve Merriam 338

Mother to Son Langston Hughes 339

The Courage That My Mother Had Edna St. Vincent Millay 339

The Hummingbird That Lived Through Winter William Saroyan 339

Unit 3: What Matters

The Third Wish Joan Aiken 340

A Boy and a Man *from* **Banner in the Sky** James Ramsey Ullman 341

from **Into Thin Air** Jon Krakauer 341

The Charge of the Light Brigade Alfred, Lord Tennyson 342

The Enemy Alice Walker 342

St. Crispian's Day Speech *from* **Henry V** William Shakespeare 342

The Californian's Tale Mark Twain 343

Valediction Seamus Heaney 343

Stopping by Woods on a Snowy Evening Robert Frost 344

Miracles Walt Whitman 344

Four Skinny Trees Sandra Cisneros 344

Unit 4: Meeting Challenges

The Night the Bed Fell James Thurber 345

All Summer in a Day Ray Bradbury 346

The Highwayman Alfred Noyes 347

The Real Story of a Cowboy's Life Geoffrey C. Ward 347

Amigo Brothers Piri Thomas 348

The Walk Thomas Hardy 348

Justin Lebo Phillip Hoose 348

The Rider Naomi Shihab Nye 348

Unit 5: Just For Fun

Our Finest Hour Charles Osgood 349

Cat on the Go James Herriot 350

The Luckiest Time of All Lucille Clifton 351

in Just– E.E. Cummings 351

The Microscope Maxine Kumin 351

Sarah Cynthia Sylvia Stout Would Not Take the Garbage Out
Shel Silverstein 351

Father William Lewis Carroll 351

Zoo Edward D. Hoch 352

The Hippopotamus Ogden Nash 352

How the Snake Got Poison Zora Neale Hurston 352

Unit 6: Short Story

After Twenty Years O. Henry 353

Rikki-tikki-tavi Rudyard Kipling 354

Papa's Parrot Cynthia Rylant 355

Suzy and Leah Jane Yolen 356

Ribbons Laurence Yep 357

The Treasure of Lemon Brown Walter Dean Myers 357

Stolen Day Sherwood Anderson 358

Unit 7: Nonfiction

How to Enjoy Poetry James Dickey 359

No Gumption Russell Baker 360

The Chase *from* **An American Childhood** Annie Dillard 360

Nolan Ryan William W. Lace 361

Rattlesnake Hunt Marjorie Kinnan Rawlings 362

from **Barrio Boy** Ernesto Galarza 362

I Am a Native of North America Chief Dan George 362

All Together Now Barbara Jordan 362

Unit 8: Drama

A Christmas Carol: Scrooge and Marley
Dramatized by Israel Horovitz Charles Dickens
Act I 363
Act II 364
The Monsters Are Due on Maple Street Rod Serling 365

Unit 9: Poetry

The Cremation of Sam McGee Robert Service 366
Washed in Silver James Stephens 366
Winter Nikki Giovanni 366
Seal William Jay Smith 367
The Pasture Robert Frost 367
Three Haiku Matsuo Bashō 367
Annabel Lee Edgar Allan Poe 368
Martin Luther King Raymond R. Patterson 368
Full Fathom Five William Shakespeare 369
Onomatopoeia Eve Merriam 369
Maestro Pat Mora 369
The Village Blacksmith Henry Wadsworth Longfellow 370
Fog Carl Sandburg 370
Life Naomi Long Madgett 370
Loo-Wit Wendy Rose 370

Unit 10: Legends, Folk Tales, and Myths

Popocatepetl and Ixtlaccihuatl Juliet Piggott 371
The People Could Fly Virginia Hamilton 372
The Lion and the Statue Aesop 372
The Fox and the Crow Aesop 372
All Stories Are Anansi's Harold Courlander 372
Phaëthon, Son of Apollo Olivia E. Coolidge 373
Demeter and Persephone Anne Terry White 373
Icarus and Daedalus Josephine Peabody 373

Answers: Part 1 . . . . **375**

Answers: Part 2 . . . . **399**

To the Teacher

As you face the challenge of heterogeneous classes, you will find a wide variety of abilities and strengths among your students. This book is aimed at special education students who have difficulty with their grade-level textbook. You can use it to keep your classes reading the same selections, but getting the instruction and reading support at the appropriate level. This book provides extended support for those students who need more guidance with reading strategies, literary analysis, and critical thinking skills.

Factors that Affect Reading Success

There are four key factors that influence students' ability to achieve reading success. These factors, alone and in combination, determine how well a student will learn, grow, and succeed as a reader. To understand the students in your classroom, consider these factors:

(a) **Kinds of Learners** Consider each student's background, previous learning experiences, and special needs. In addition to students who read fluently at grade level, you may find a mix of the following learning characteristics in your classroom:

- *Students who speak a language other than English at home*   Unlike their fully fluent counterparts, these students often speak English only at school. This situation leaves them limited hours in which to learn the grammar, vocabulary, idioms, and other intricacies of English.

- *Students who have recently moved to this country*   These students may be highly capable students without the specific language skills to function academically in English.

- *Students with learning disabilities*   These students may have cognitive, behavioral, social, or physical challenges that make reading more difficult.

(b) **Kinds of Skills and Instruction** Students' reading ability is influenced by the skills they bring to the task. Students must master the skills of decoding, activating and building prior knowledge, and making connections among experiences and new information. Other factors include a student's knowledge of the English language and vocabulary, and a student's ability to apply reading comprehension strategies.

Active reading, including the practice of summarizing, questioning, setting a purpose, and self-monitoring, is key to successful reading. For those students who have not yet developed such skills, your classroom instruction is critical. You should model such skills and encourage students to practice them.

Through practice, students should be able to internalize the strategies of active reading.

(c) **Kinds of Texts** Just as students and their backgrounds and skills vary, so do the texts presented in a language arts curriculum. The grade-level language arts classroom curriculum traditionally addresses fiction, nonfiction, poetry, and drama. Each of these forms presents unique challenges to students. Each writer and selection also presents challenges in the difficulty of the concepts addressed or in the coherence of the writing. For example, you may find that students are more comfortable with narratives than with expository writing. Focused reading strategies that you model and reinforce can help students tackle texts that are more dense or difficult for them to master.

(d) **Classroom Environment** The classroom environment affects everything and everyone within it. Research suggests that students learn best in a friendly, respectful setting categorized by these criteria:

- Students feel a sense of safety and order.
- They feel comfortable taking risks.
- They understand the purpose and value of the tasks presented.
- Students have high expectations and goals for learning.
- They feel accepted by their teachers and peers.

Students performing below grade level may be especially self-conscious. Therefore, these criteria are key to helping students take full advantage of the opportunities the classroom affords. Set up your classroom as a caring yet on-purpose environment that helps students achieve.

Researchers encourage teachers to be truthful with students about the work it will take to build and master abilities in the language arts. Tell your students that improving reading, writing, speaking, and listening takes a great deal of practice. You need to be prepared to provide direct instruction, guided practice, specific feedback, coaching, and more. Then, encourage your students to understand their responsibilities as active, self-directed learners as well.

The Special Education or Special Needs Student

Most likely, your classroom has a number of special education or special needs students—young people who begin the year three or more years below grade level and yet do not qualify for special education services. Special education and special needs students have difficulty in organizing and categorizing new information during instruction. They may have trouble in the following areas:

Memory

- ordering or arranging information
- classifying information
- grasping a main idea or "big picture"
- using long-term memory to make meaningful connections or connecting to prior knowledge

Attention

- focusing attention on the most important elements of a presentation or a selection

By presenting specific focused strategies and interactive review and extension activities, you can provide these students with full access to the language arts curriculum.

Another category of deficiency in special education readers is the ability to apply learning strategies to a variety of situations. Special education and special needs students often have these weaknesses:

Learning Strategies

- a lack of effective or efficient strategies for completing academic tasks such as taking notes, responding to literature, or writing a focused paragraph
- a limited set of learning strategies from which to draw
- difficulty in self-monitoring—they often don't know which strategies to use or when a strategy is not working

Many of these students are underprepared; their deficiencies are generally based on their lack of experience, not on any biological difference. When these students learn effective strategies, they can improve their academic performance. Teachers need to provide direct instruction to explicitly show them how, when, and why to use each strategy.

Overview of Components for Universal Access

The *Prentice Hall Literature: Timeless Voices, Timeless Themes* program includes an array of products to provide universal access. Fully integrated, these materials help teachers identify student needs or deficiencies and teach to the varying levels in a classroom, while providing the quality that literature teachers expect.

As your main resource, the *Annotated Teacher's Edition* provides a lesson plan for every selection or selection grouping. In addition to teaching notes and suggestions, it also includes cross-references to ancillary material. Customize for Universal Access notes help teachers direct lessons to the following groups of students: special needs students, less proficient readers, English learners, gifted and talented students, and advanced readers. In addition to teaching notes and suggestions, it also includes cross-references to ancillary material such as the *Reader's Companion*, the *Adapted Reader's Companion*, and the *English Learner's Companion*.

The **Teaching Guidebook for Universal Access** gives you proven strategies for providing universal access to all students. In addition to its general teaching strategies and classroom management techniques, this component explains how the parts of the Prentice Hall program work together to ensure reading success for all student populations.

The **Reading Diagnostic and Improvement Plan**—part of the Reading Achievement System— provides comprehensive diagnostic tests that assess students' mastery of reading skills. The book also includes charts that help you map out an improvement plan based on students' performance on the diagnostics.

You can use the **Basic Reading Skill: Comprehensive Lessons for Improvement Plan**—also part of the Reading Achievement System— to give instruction and practice that bring students up to grade level, enabling them to master the skills in which they are deficient. For each skill covered, you'll find the following materials:

- lesson plan with direct instruction
- teaching transparency
- blackline master for student application and practice

The **Reader's Companion** and **Reader's Companion Teacher's Edition** are consumable components of the Reading Achievement System. The books contain the full text of approximately half of the selections from the student book. Questions prompt students to interact with the text by circling, underlining, or marking key details. Write-on lines in the margins also allow for students to answer questions. You can use this book in place of the student book to help students read interactively. In addition, a summary and a reading-skill worksheet support every selection grouping in the student book.

The ***Adapted Reader's Companion*** and ***Adapted Reader's Companion Teacher's Edition*** are another set of consumable components of the Reading Achievement System. These books use the same format and contain the same selections as the *Reader's Companion*. However, the selections are abridged and appear in a larger font size. The questions are targeted toward special education students. You can use this book as a supplement to or in place of the student book for certain selections to enable special education students to experience the same literature and master the same skills as on-level students. These components also contain a summary and a reading-skill worksheet to support every selection grouping in the student book.

The ***English Learner's Companion*** and ***English Learner's Companion Teacher's Edition*** are a third set of consumable components of the Reading Achievement System. These books use the same format and contain the same selections as the *Reader's Companion*. Again, the selections are abridged and appear in a larger font size. The questions are targeted toward English learners. You can use this book as a supplement to or in place of the student book for certain selections to enable English learners to experience the same literature and master the same skills as students who are native English speakers. These components also contain summaries in English, Spanish, Chinese, Vietnamese, Cambodian, and Hmong, along with a reading-skill worksheet to support every selection grouping in the student book.

Listening to Literature Audiotapes and CDs These components feature professional recordings of every selection in the student book. To support student reading, you can play the selections, in part or in full, before students read them.

Spanish/English Summaries Audio CD Audio summaries in both English and Spanish are provided for every selection. You can play these selection summaries for struggling readers, special education students, and English learners before they read the actual texts.

Basic Language Skills: Reteaching Masters With the reteaching masters, you can provide basic-level instruction and practice on grammar and language skills.

Interest Grabber Videos These videos are an optional enrichment resource designed to provide background for a selection or otherwise motivate students to read the selection. There is a video segment for every selection or selection grouping in the student book.

About the Adapted Reader's Companion

The *Adapted Reader's Companion* is designed to support your special education or special needs students. Its two parts offer different levels of support.

Part 1: Selection Adaptations with Excerpts of Authentic Text

Part 1 will guide special education or special needs students as they interact with half the selections from *Prentice Hall Literature: Timeless Voices, Timeless Themes.* This range of selections includes the more challenging selections, the most frequently taught selections, and many examples of narrative and expository writing. Part 1 provides pre-reading instruction, larger print summaries of literature selections with passages from the selection, and post-reading questions and activities.

The **Preview** page will help your students get the general idea of the selection and therefore be better equipped to understand it. Both written and visual summaries preview the selections before students read the adapted versions.

The **Prepare to Read** page is based on its parallel in *Prentice Hall Literature: Timeless Voices, Timeless Themes.* It introduces the same literary element and reading strategy addressed in the textbook, and provides a graphic organizer to make the information more accessible.

The **selection** pages present the text in a larger font size. Interspersed among blocks of authentic text, the companion also provides summaries of episodes or paragraphs to make the selections more accessible to your students.

The **side notes** make active reading strategies explicit, asking students to look closely at the text to analyze it in a variety of ways. Notes with a *Mark the Text* icon prompt students to underline, circle, or otherwise note key words, phrases, or details in the selection. Notes with write-on lines offer students an opportunity to respond in the margin to questions or ideas. These notes offer focused support in a variety of areas:

Literary Analysis notes provide point-of-use instruction to reinforce the literary element introduced on the Preview page. By pointing out details or events in the text in which the literary element applies, these notes give students the opportunity to revisit and reinforce their understanding of literature.

Reading Strategy notes help students practice the skill introduced on the Preview page. These notes guide students to understand when, how, and why a strategy is helpful.

Stop to Reflect notes ask students to reflect on the selection or on a skill they are using. By encouraging students to solidify their own thinking, these notes help to develop active reading skills.

Reading Check notes help students confirm their comprehension of a selection. These notes help to make explicit a critical strategy of active reading.

Read Fluently notes provide students with concrete, limited practice reading passages aloud with fluency.

Background notes provide further explanation of a concept or detail to support students' understanding.

The ***Review and Assess*** questions following the selection ensure students' comprehension of the selection. Written in simple language, they assess students' understanding of the literary element and the reading strategy. In addition, they offer a scaffolded guide to support students in an extension activity based on either a writing or a listening and speaking activity in the *Student Edition* of the grade-level textbook.

Part 2: Selection Summaries with Alternative Reading Strategies

Part 2 contains summaries of all selections in *Prentice Hall Literature: Timeless Voices, Timeless Themes.* These summaries can help students prepare for reading the selections. Alternatively, the summaries may serve as a review tool.

This section also includes alternative reading strategies to guide students as they read selections. The strategies may be useful for reviewing selection events and ideas or to reinforce specific reading strategies for students.

How to Use the *Adapted Reader's Companion*

When you are planning lessons for heterogeneous classes, this companion reader offers you an opportunity to keep all the students in your class reading the same selection and studying the same vocabulary, literary element, and reading strategy but getting the support they need to succeed. Here are some planning suggestions for using the book in tandem with the grade-level volume of *Prentice Hall Literature: Timeless Voices, Timeless Themes.*

Use the *Annotated Teacher's Edition* and the *Student Edition* of the grade-level textbook as the central text in your classroom. The *Annotated Teacher's Edition* includes *Customize for Universal Access* notes throughout each selection. In addition, it identifies when use of the *Adapted Reader's Companion* is appropriate.

TEACHING SELECTIONS INCLUDED IN PART ONE

PRE-TEACH with the Full Class

Consider presenting the* Interest Grabber *video segment. This optional technology product can provide background and build motivation.

Preview the selection. To help students see the organization of a selection, or to help them get a general idea of the text, lead a quick text pre-reading or "text tour" using the textbook. Focus student attention on the selection title, the art accompanying the text, and any unusual text characteristics. To build connections for students, ask them to identify links between the selection and other works you have presented in class, or to find connections to themes, activities, or other related concepts.

Build background. Use the Background information provided in the *Student Edition.* Whether explaining a historical time period, a scientific concept, or details about an idea that may be unfamiliar to students, this instruction presents useful information to help all students place the literature in context.

Focus vocabulary development. The *Student Edition* includes a list of vocabulary words included in the selection or selection grouping. Instead of attempting to cover all of the vocabulary words you anticipate your students will not know, identify the vocabulary that is most critical to talking and learning about the central concepts. However, for the words you do choose to teach, work to provide more than synonyms and definitions. Using the vocabulary notes in the *Annotated Teacher's Edition,* introduce the essential words in more meaningful contexts: for example, through simple sentences drawing on familiar issues, people, scenarios, and vocabulary. Guide students in internalizing the meanings of key terms through these familiar contexts and ask them to write the definitions in their own words. Look at these examples of guided vocabulary instruction:

Point out the word *serene* and explain that it means "calm or peaceful." Then, provide the following scenarios and ask students to determine whether the situations are *serene* or not: an empty beach at sunset *(yes);* a playground at recess (no). You might also ask students to provide their own examples of *serene* situations.

Point out the word *intervals* and explain that it means "the period of time between two events or point of time." Ask students to identify the interval between Monday and Wednesday *(two days)* and the interval between one Monday and the next Monday *(one week).*

You might also take the opportunity to teach the prefix *inter-,* meaning "between." Then, discuss with students the following group of words:

interview (a meeting between two or more people);
interstate (between two or more states);
international (between nations);
intervene (to come between two sides in a dispute).

Introduce skills. Introduce the *Literary Analysis* and *Reading Strategy,* using the instruction in the *Student Edition* and the teaching support in the *Annotated Teacher's Edition.*

Separate the class. As average level students begin reading the selection in the *Student Edition,* have special education and special needs students put their textbooks aside. Direct these students to the *Adapted Reader's Companion* for further pre-teaching.

PRE-TEACH for Special Education Students Using the *Adapted Reader's Companion*

Reinforce the general idea. Use the selection and visual summaries presented on the first page of every selection in the *Adapted Reader's Companion.* These summaries will give students a framework to follow for understanding the selection. Use these tools to build familiarity, but do not use them as a replacement for reading.

Present audio summaries. The *Spanish/English Summaries Audio CD* can reinforce the main idea of a selection.

Reinforce skills instruction. Next, use the *Prepare to Read* page to reinforce the *Literary Analysis* and *Reading Strategy* concepts. Written in simpler language and in basic sentence structures, the instruction will help students better grasp these ideas.

Provide decoding practice. Because many special education students lack strategies for decoding bigger words, give them guided practice with the vocabulary words for the selection. Using the list, model a strategy for decoding polysyllabic words. First, show students how to break the word into parts and then put the parts back together to make a word.

> For the word *mimic,* ask students to draw a loop under each word part as they pronounce it.
>
> *mim ic   fright en ing*

Using this strategy, you can encourage students to look for familiar word parts and then break the rest of the word down into its consonant and vowel sounds. By building this routine regularly into your pre-teaching instruction, you reinforce a key reading skill for your students.

Prepare for lesson structure. To build students' ability to complete classroom activities, examine your lesson to see what types of language functions students will need to participate. Look at these examples:

> If students are being asked to make predictions about upcoming paragraph content in an essay, review the power of transition words that act as signals to meaning. Rather than teaching all transitions, limit your instruction to the ones in the passages. Identify the key transition words and point out their meaning. In addition, teach students some basic sentence patterns and verbs to express opinions. Model for students statement patterns such as:
>
> *I predict that . . .*
>
> *Based on this transition word, I conclude that . . .*

TEACH Using the *Adapted Reader's Companion*

As average achieving students in your class read the selection in the textbook, allow special education and special needs students to read the adapted version in the *Adapted Reader's Companion.* Whenever possible, give these students individualized attention by pairing them with aides, parent volunteers, or student peers.

Set purposes and limits. To keep students focused and motivated, and to prevent them from becoming overwhelmed as they read a selection, clearly establish a reading purpose for students before assigning a manageable amount of text. Once you identify a focus question or a purpose, revisit the question occasionally as students read. You can do this with a brief whole-group dialogue or by encouraging students in pairs to remember the question. In addition, your effective modeling will also provide the scaffolding for students to begin internalizing these strategies for effective reading.

Model your thinking. Describe and model strategies for navigating different kinds of text. Use the questions raised in the side notes as a starting point.

Then, explain how you arrive at an answer. Alternatively, ask a student to explain his or her responses to classmates.

Reinforce new vocabulary. Present key words when they occur within the context of the reading selection. Review the definition as it appears on the page. Then, make the words as concrete as possible by linking each to an object, photo, or idea.

Build interactivity. The side notes in the *Adapted Reader's Companion* are an excellent way to encourage student interactivity with the selections. To build students' ability to use these notes, model several examples with each selection. These are not busy work; they are activities that build fluency and provide the scaffolding necessary for student success.

Whenever possible, get students physically involved with the page, using *Mark the Text* icons as an invitation to use highlighters or colored pencils to circle, underline, or number key information. In addition, some students may find that using a small piece of cardboard or heavy construction paper helps to focus and guide their reading from one paragraph or page to the next.

Vary modes of instruction. To maintain student attention and interest, monitor and alternate the mode of instruction or activity. For example, alternate between teacher-facilitated and student-dominated reading activities. Assign brief amounts of text at a time, and alternate between oral, paired, and silent reading.

Monitor students' comprehension. As students use the side notes in the margins of the *Adapted Reader's Companion*, build in opportunities to ensure that students are on purpose and understanding. Consider structured brief conversations for students to share, compare, or explain their thinking. Then, use these conversations to praise the correct use of strategies or to redirect students who need further support. In addition, this is an excellent chance for you to demonstrate your note-taking process and provide models of effective study notes for students to emulate.

Reinforce the reading experience. When students read the selection for the first time, they may be working on the decoding level. If time allows, students should read the selection twice to achieve a greater fluency and comfort level.

REVIEW AND ASSESS Using the *Adapted Reader's Companion*

Reinforce writing and reading skills. Assign students the extension activity in the *Adapted Reader's Companion*. Based on an activity presented in the grade-level text, the version in the *Adapted Reader's Companion* provides guided, step-by-step support for students. By giving students the opportunities to show their reading comprehension and writing skills, you maintain reasonable expectations for their developing academic competence.

Model expectations. Make sure that students understand your assessment criteria in advance. Provide models of student work, whenever possible, for them to emulate, along with a non-model that fails to meet the specified assessment criteria. Do not provide exemplars that are clearly outside of their developmental range. Save student work that can later serve as a model for students with different levels of academic preparation.

Lead students to closure. To achieve closure, ask students to end the class session by writing three to five outcome statements about their experience in the day's lesson, expressing both new understandings and needs for clarification.

Encourage self-monitoring and self-assessment. Remember to provide safe opportunities for students to alert you to any learning challenges they are experiencing. Consider having students submit anonymous written questions (formulated either independently or with a partner) about confusing lesson content and process. Later, you can follow up on these points of confusion at the end of class or in the subsequent class session.

EXTEND Using the *Student Edition*

Present the unabridged selection. Build in opportunities for students to read the full selection in the grade-level textbook. This will allow them to apply familiar concepts and vocabulary and stretch their literacy muscles.

Play an audio reading of the unabridged selection. Use the *Listening to Literature Audiotapes* or *CDs.* Students may benefit from reading along while listening to a professional recording of the selection. Encourage students to use their fingertips to follow the words as they are read.

Invite reader response. When students have finished reviewing the selection—whether in the companion or in the grade-level textbook—include all students in your class in post-reading analysis. To guide an initial discussion, use the Respond question in the *Thinking About the Selection* in the textbook. You will find that questions such as the following examples will provide strong springboards for classroom interaction:

> **Respond :** What advice would you have given the mother and daughter? Why?

> **Respond:** What questions would you like to ask the writer about his experience?

> **Respond:** Do you find the boy's actions courageous, touching, or silly? Explain your answer.

Encourage students to explain their answers to these questions by supporting their ideas with evidence from the text or their own lives. In addition, invite students to respond to classmates' ideas. These questions will lead students from simply getting the gist of a selection to establishing a personal connection to the lesson content.

Direct student analysis with scaffolded questions. When you are ready to move students into the Review and Assess questions, let your average achieving students use the instruction and questions in the grade-level textbook. At the same time, encourage special education and special needs students to use the questions in the *Adapted Reader's Companion.*

- Questions in the companion, written in more simple language and providing more explicit support, will be more accessible to these students. Students will be applying concepts and practicing strategies at their own level.

- Some special education or special needs students may be prepared to answer questions in the grade-level text. The two-part questions in the *Thinking About the Selection* section are written to build and support student analysis. First, students use lower-level thinking skills to identify information or to recall important details in a selection. For the second part, students use a higher-level thinking skill based on the answer to the first part.

Look at these examples of scaffolded questions from the grade-level textbook:

(a) Recall: Why does the boy tell his father to leave the sickroom?
(b) Infer: What does this reveal about the boy?

(a) Recall: Why does the boy think he will die?
(b) Infer: What is the meaning of the title?

Revisit and reinforce strategies. Recycle pre- and post-reading tasks regularly, so students can become more familiar with the task process and improve their performance. If they are constantly facing curricular novelty, special education and special needs students never have the opportunity to refine their skills and demonstrate improved competence. For example, if you ask them to identify a personality trait of an essential character in a story and then support this observation with relevant details in an expository paragraph, it would make sense to have them write an identical paragraph in the near future about another character.

Show students how to transfer skills. Consider ways in which students can transfer knowledge and skills gleaned from one assignment/lesson to a subsequent lesson. For example, discuss with students the ways in which they can apply new vocabulary and language strategies outside of the classroom. In addition, demonstrate the applicability of new reading and writing strategies to real-world literacy tasks. Include periodic writing tasks for an authentic audience other than the teacher: another class, fellow classmates, local businesses, family, etc.

Offer praise and encourage growth. Praise students' efforts to experiment with new language in class, both in writing and in speaking.

USING PART TWO

For selections that are not presented as adaptations in Part One, use the summaries and activities in Part Two to support your special education or special needs students.

PRE-TEACH

In addition to the pre-teaching strategies listed on page xvi, consider these strategies to accommodate special education or special needs students:

Provide students with a "running start." Use the selection summaries provided in the *Adapted Reader's Companion.* These summaries will give students a framework for understanding the selection to follow.

Build interest. To take full advantage of the summaries, ask students to write one or two questions that the summaries raise in their minds. Share these questions in a discussion before reading the full text.

TEACH

As your students read the full selection in the textbook, provide special education and special needs students with support and individualized attention by pairing them with aides, parent volunteers, or student peers. In addition to the suggestions on page xviii, consider these additional strategies.

Model your thinking for side-column questions. To help these students practice the *Literary Analysis* skill and the *Reading Strategy*, use the questions raised in the side notes as a starting point. If students have difficulty answering the questions, review the concept for students and model your thinking process. Look at these examples of modeling explicit thinking:

Reading Strategy: Making Inferences

Remind students that, in a work of fiction, a writer expects readers to make connections with what they already know or have read in an earlier passage. Show students how to make inferences based on the side-column question and the appropriate text. Look at this passage from a selection as an example:

> "Mary, you oughta write David and tell him somebody done opened his letter and stole that ten dollars he sent," she said.

> "No mama. David's got enough on his mind. Besides, there's enough garden foods so we won't go hungry."

Then, use language like this to model your thinking process:

I'm not sure who the characters are talking about. There hasn't been any David mentioned in the story. What's this about an envelope? First, I ask myself what information there is in the passage. Mama sounds like she cares about this person; it's probably a friend or a family member. David sends money to the family, so he must be in another place. I'll ask myself what I know from what I've already read. Do I know anything about characters who live far away? Earlier, Mama said the father worked in Louisiana so that he could support the family. Could David be the father? I think so! He probably sends his wages back to Mississippi. That's the part about the envelope! Somebody opened up one of the letters and took the money.

Reading Strategy: Interpreting Poetic Language

In poetry, writers may describe an event in very different language from what they might use in writing an essay. Students can increase their understanding of poetry by learning to interpret poetic language. To help them, use the side notes and any marked texts to model your thinking process. Look at this example based on the following poetic lines:

> You crash over the trees,
>
> you crack the live branch—
>
> the branch is white,
>
> the green crushed,

Then, use language like this to model your thinking process:

I am not sure exactly what is being described in the last two lines. What do the colors mean? Why is the branch white? What is the author referring to by "green crushed"? I'll start by figuring out what I do know. This poem is about a storm. From the second line, I can figure out that lightning or wind has struck the tree and cracked a branch. Green is the color of leaves. When a storm cracks a branch, it may fall to the ground. The leaves are crushed by the fall; this must be "the green crushed." But branches aren't white; they're brown or gray. However, if they're cracked open, the wood inside is white. The storm has cracked the branch and exposed its white insides.

Use the Reading Check *questions in the* Student Edition. Consider pairing students, working with small groups, or setting brief instructional time for *Reading Check* questions that appear with every selection. These recall-level questions can be answered based on information in the text. Ask students to point to their answers in the selection before returning to reading.

REVIEW AND ASSESS

In addition to the suggestions on page xix, consider these additional strategies:

Build tests using the computer test bank. The computer test bank allows you to sort questions by difficulty level. Use this feature to generate tests appropriate to special education and special needs students.

Part 1

Selection Adaptations With Excerpts of Authentic Text

Part 1 will guide and support you as you interact with selections from *Prentice Hall Literature: Timeless Voices, Timeless Themes*. Part 1 provides summaries of literature selections with passages from the selection.

- Begin with the Preview page in the *Adapted Reader's Companion*. Use the written and visual summaries to preview the selections before you read.

- Then study the Prepare to Read page. This page introduces skills that you will apply as you read selections in the *Adapted Reader's Companion*.

- Now read the selection in the *Adapted Reader's Companion*.

- Respond to all the questions along the sides as you read. They will guide you in understanding the selection and in applying the skills. Write in the *Adapted Reader's Companion*—really! Circle things that interest you. Underline things that puzzle you. Number ideas or events to help you keep track of them. Look for the **Mark the Text** logo for help with active reading.

- Use the Review and Assess questions at the end of each selection to review what you have read and to check your understanding.

- Finally, do the Writing or the Speaking and Listening activity to extend your understanding and practice your skills.

Interacting With the Text

As you read, use the information and notes to guide you in interacting with the selection. The examples on these pages show you how to use the notes as a companion when you read. They will guide you in applying reading and literary skills and in thinking about the selection. When you read other texts, you can practice the thinking skills and strategies found here.

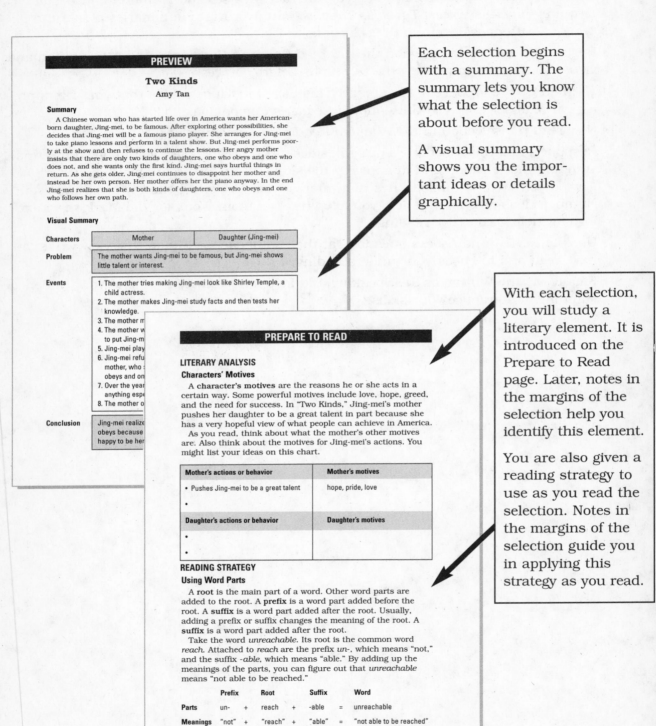

PREVIEW

Two Kinds
Amy Tan

Summary

A Chinese woman who has started life over in America wants her American-born daughter, Jing-mei, to be famous. After exploring other possibilities, she decides that Jing-mei will be a famous piano player. She arranges for Jing-mei to take piano lessons and perform in a talent show. But Jing-mei performs poorly at the show and then refuses to continue the lessons. Her angry mother insists that there are only two kinds of daughters, one who obeys and one who does not, and she wants only the first kind. Jing-mei says hurtful things in return. As she gets older, Jing-mei continues to disappoint her mother and instead be her own person. Her mother offers her the piano anyway. In the end Jing-mei realizes that she is both kinds of daughters, one who obeys and one who follows her own path.

Visual Summary

Characters	Mother	Daughter (Jing-mei)
Problem	The mother wants Jing-mei to be famous, but Jing-mei shows little talent or interest.	
Events	1. The mother tries making Jing-mei look like Shirley Temple, a child actress. 2. The mother makes Jing-mei study facts and then tests her knowledge. 3. The mother m... 4. The mother w... to put Jing-m... 5. Jing-mei play... 6. Jing-mei refu... mother, who s... obeys and on... 7. Over the yea... anything espe... 8. The mother o...	
Conclusion	Jing-mei realize... obeys because... happy to be her...	

PREPARE TO READ

LITERARY ANALYSIS

Characters' Motives

A **character's motives** are the reasons he or she acts in a certain way. Some powerful motives include love, hope, greed, and the need for success. In "Two Kinds," Jing-mei's mother pushes her daughter to be a great talent in part because she has a very hopeful view of what people can achieve in America.

As you read, think about what the mother's other motives are. Also think about the motives for Jing-mei's actions. You might list your ideas on this chart.

Mother's actions or behavior	Mother's motives
• Pushes Jing-mei to be a great talent	hope, pride, love
•	
•	
Daughter's actions or behavior	**Daughter's motives**
•	
•	

READING STRATEGY

Using Word Parts

A **root** is the main part of a word. Other word parts are added to the root. A **prefix** is a word part added before the root. A **suffix** is a word part added after the root. Usually, adding a prefix or suffix changes the meaning of the root. A **suffix** is a word part added after the root.

Take the word *unreachable*. Its root is the common word *reach*. Attached to *reach* are the prefix *un-*, which means "not," and the suffix *-able*, which means "able." By adding up the meanings of the parts, you can figure out that *unreachable* means "not able to be reached."

	Prefix		Root		Suffix		Word
Parts	un-	+	reach	+	-able	=	unreachable
Meanings	"not"	+	"reach"	+	"able"	=	"not able to be reached"

Each selection begins with a summary. The summary lets you know what the selection is about before you read.

A visual summary shows you the important ideas or details graphically.

With each selection, you will study a literary element. It is introduced on the Prepare to Read page. Later, notes in the margins of the selection help you identify this element.

You are also given a reading strategy to use as you read the selection. Notes in the margins of the selection guide you in applying this strategy as you read.

Two Kinds
Amy Tan

The mother in this story was born in China. She fled during the communist revolution of 1949. She lost everything in the revolution: her parents, her first husband, her two baby daughters, her family home. But in America she married again and had a new daughter, Jing-mei. It is Jing-mei who tells the story:

◆ ◆ ◆

My mother believed you could be anything you wanted to be in America. You could open a restaurant. You could work for the government. . . . You could become rich. You could become instantly famous.

◆ ◆ ◆

Jing-mei's mother decides that her daughter can be a prodigy, or supertalented child. First, she plans to make Jing-mei a movie star and has Jing-mei's hair cut just like the popular child actress Shirley Temple's. Then, the mother gets a better idea: She makes Jing-mei study books and magazines and tests her on the facts. When Jing-mei's performance is disappointing, her mother gives up on that idea too.

◆ ◆ ◆

Two or three months had gone by without any mention of my being a prodigy again. And then one day my mother was watching *The Ed Sullivan Show* on TV. . . .

◆ ◆ ◆

On the show, a young Chinese girl is playing the piano. When she is done, she

---

Vocabulary Development

prodigy (PRAH di gee) *n.* a child of unusually high talent

◆ **Reading Check**

What does Jing-mei's mother believe anyone can be in America? Circle three answers.

◆ **Reading Strategy**

Super- is a prefix meaning "over; above; beyond normal." Circle the three **word parts** in the word *supertalented.* Then, complete this sentence: A *supertalented* child is a child who _____

_____

_____

Text set in a narrow margin provides a summary of selection events or details.

Text set in a wider margin provides the author's actual words.

Use write-on lines to answer the questions. You may also want to use the lines for your own notes or for questions you have.

When you see this symbol, follow the directions to underline, circle or mark the text as indicated.

Questions after every selection help you think about the selection. You can use the write-on lines or charts to answer the questions.

REVIEW AND ASSESS

1. How does Jing-mei disappoint her mother in the story? Answer by circling the word or phrase in parentheses that best completes each sentence:

   The mother wants Jing-mei to be (famous, beautiful, contented, sent away).

   But Jing-mei can only be (brilliant, pleading, a child, herself).

2. What does the mother say are the two kinds of daughters?

   Kind 1: _____ Kind 2: _____

3. In the end, what does Jing-mei realize about the kind of daughter she is? _____

   _____

4. **Reading Strategy:** For each word on the right, add up the meanings of the word parts to figure out the meaning of the word. Write the meaning on the line below the word.

	Prefix		Root		Word
	un-	+	like		= unlike
Meanings	"not"	+	"similar to"		= _____
	Root		**Suffix**		**Word**
	child	+	-ish		= childish
Meanings	"young person"	+	"like"		= _____

5. **Literary Analysis:** Fill out this chart by putting at least one **motive** in the second column of each item.

Mother's actions or behavior	Mother's motives
• pushes Jing-mei to be famous	_____
• arranges for a talent show	_____
• offers to give Jing-mei the piano	_____

The Cat Who Thought She Was a Dog and the Dog Who Thought He Was a Cat

Isaac Bashevis Singer

Summary

Jan Skiba lives in a small hut with his wife, his daughters, a dog, and a cat. They are poor, but they don't really notice. Even the dog and cat get along, for they do not realize that they are different from each other. Then one day the Skibas buy a mirror. For the first time, they see what they look like. They notice flaws in their appearance and begin to long for changes in their lives. The dog and cat realize that they are different and begin to fight. Finally, Jan decides that the mirror is no good. He returns it, and the family returns to normal.

Visual Summary

What are things like at first?	What happens after the family buys a mirror?	What happens after Jan gets rid of the mirror?
Skiba family • very poor • live in a small hut	Jan Skiba • dislikes his thick lips and buck teeth	Burek the dog • again thinks he is a cat • plays with Kot
Burek the dog • thinks he is a cat • plays with Kot	Marianna Skiba • thinks missing tooth makes her ugly	Kot the cat • again thinks she is a dog • plays with Burek
Kot the cat • thinks she is a dog • plays with Burek	Skiba daughters • dislike something about their looks	Skiba daughters • make good marriages
	Burek the dog • gets angry at his reflection • fights with Kot	Skiba family • returns to normal
	Kot the cat • becomes confused • fights with Burek	

LITERARY ANALYSIS
The Moral of a Story

A **moral** is a message about how people behave or how they should behave. The events in many stories point to a moral.

Example 1: Suppose you read a story about someone who works hard and does well in life. The moral of that story might be: "Hard work is often rewarded."

Example 2: Suppose you read a story about a lion who is kind to a mouse. The moral of that story might be: "Be kind to those who are weaker than you."

Singer's story has more than one moral. To figure out the morals, answer these questions:

1. What does the story show about the importance of owning things?
2. What does the story show about the importance of a person's looks?
3. What does the story show are the most important things in life?

READING STRATEGY
Clarifying Word Meanings

When you read, you will often come across words you aren't sure about. How can you figure out their meaning? One way is to look at nearby words and sentences, which often help make the meaning clear. For example, Singer's story uses the word word *mimic*, which you may not know. But the next sentence gives you an example of how Burek the dog and Kot the cat *mimic* each other. From it, you can tell that to mimic must mean "to imitate" or "to act like someone else."

Filling out a chart like this might help you with other unfamiliar words in the story.

Unfamiliar Word	Burek and Kot . . . tried to mimic each other.
Nearby Words	When Burek barked, Kot tried to bark along, and when Kot meowed, Burek tried to meow too.
Meaning of Word	to imitate; to act like someone else

The Cat Who Thought She Was a Dog and the Dog Who Thought He Was a Cat

Isaac Bashevis Singer

◆ Reading Strategy

Circle the words that help you understand the meaning of *peasant*.

Jan Skiba was a <u>peasant</u>, or poor farmer. He lived in a tiny hut far from town with his wife Marianna and their three daughters. The Skibas were so poor that they didn't own very much. In fact, they didn't even own a mirror. But they did have a dog named Burek and a cat named Kot. The animals had been born within a few days of each other. Even though the family was poor, Jan Skiba never let the dog and the cat go hungry.

◆ ◆ ◆

◆ Stop to Reflect

The Skibas are very poor, but they still find food for the dog and cat. What do these actions show about them?

Write your ideas on these lines.

_____

_____

_____

_____

_____

_____

_____

_____

Since the dog had never seen another dog and the cat had never seen another cat and they saw only each other, the dog thought he was a cat and the cat thought she was a dog. True, they were far from being alike by nature. The dog, like most dogs, barked and went after rabbits. The cat, like most cats, meowed and <u>lurked</u> after mice. But . . . Burek and Kot lived on good terms, often ate from the same dish, and tried to mimic each other.

◆ ◆ ◆

◆ Reading Strategy

Circle the words in the bracketed passage that help you understand the meaning of *peddler*. Then, write the meaning here.

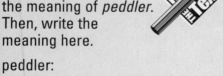

peddler:

_____

_____

In those days, <u>peddlers</u> traveled from door to door, buying and selling things. Because the Skibas were poor, peddlers never stopped at their house—the Skibas had nothing to buy or sell. Then one day a peddler did stop. He had jewelry, kerchiefs and other trinkets to sell.

◆ ◆ ◆

Vocabulary Development

lurked (lerkd) *v.* waited quietly

But what <u>enthralled</u> the women of the house most was a mirror set in a wooden frame.

◆   ◆   ◆

The peddler agreed to let them give him a small amount of money each month until the mirror was paid for. After he left, the Skibas kept looking in the mirror. They saw problems they had never noticed before.

◆   ◆   ◆

Marianna was pretty but she had a tooth missing in front and she felt that this made her ugly. One daughter discovered that her nose was too <u>snub</u> and too broad; a second that her chin was too narrow and too long; a third that her face was sprinkled with freckles. Jan Skiba too caught a glimpse of himself in the mirror and grew displeased by his thick lips and teeth, which <u>protruded</u>. . . .

◆   ◆   ◆

The women ignored their chores and kept looking in the mirror. The first daughter kept pinching her nose to try to make it narrower. The second kept pushing her chin to try to make it shorter. The third wondered if she could go to the city and buy something to remove her freckles. Her mother thought of visiting a city dentist and getting a new tooth. But all this would cost more than they could afford.

◆   ◆   ◆

◆ **Reading Check**

What happens when the Skibas look in the mirror? Circle the answer.

◆ **Stop to Reflect**

The characters are using a mirror for the first time. Do their reactions to their looks seem believable to you? Write *yes* or *no*, and then explain your opinion.

_____

_____

_____

_____

◆ **Reading Check**

Use numbers to label what the three daughters do. Use *1* for the first daughter, *2* for the second, and *3* for the third.

Vocabulary Development

enthralled (in THRAWLD) *v.* fascinated; excited; charmed
snub (SNUB) *adj.* short and turned up
protruded (proh TROO did) *v.* stuck out

Mark
the
Text

◆ Literary Analysis

What does Jan Skiba now think is important in life? Complete this **moral** based on what Jan thinks.

_____ is/are

more important than _____

_____ .

◆ Literary Analysis

What does the priest think is important in life? Complete this **moral** based on what the priest says.

_____

_____ is/are

more important than _____

_____

_____ .

For the first time the Skiba family deeply felt its poverty and <u>envied</u> the rich.

◆ ◆ ◆

The dog and cat also became unhappy. They now saw themselves in the mirror and realized they were different. They began biting and clawing each other until they had to be separated.

◆ ◆ ◆

When Jan Skiba saw the <u>disruption</u> the mirror had created in his household, he decided a mirror wasn't what his family needed.

◆ ◆ ◆

Jan thought they should look at things like the sun and the moon. He returned the mirror to the peddler in exchange for kerchiefs and slippers. Without the mirror in the house, things went back to being the way they had been. The cat and the dog stopped fighting because, once again, the cat thought she was a dog and the dog thought he was a cat. The daughters quit worrying about what was wrong with their looks.

◆ ◆ ◆

When the village priest heard what happened, he pointed out that a glass mirror shows only the outside of a person. The real image of a person comes from his or her being willing to help family and, if possible, others. This real image shows what is on the inside— the person's soul.

Vocabulary Development

envied (EN veed) *v.* was jealous of
disruption (dis RUP shun) *n.* a confused situation; a situation that does not go smoothly

---

1. Write three words that describe the Skibas' life when the story opens.

   1. _____ 2. _____ 3. _____

2. Complete this chart that lists the problems each character has after looking in the mirror.

Jan Skiba	lips too thick, teeth stick out
Marianna Skiba	
first daughter	
second daughter	
third daughter	
Burek	realizes he is not a cat
Kot	

3. Why does Jan give back the mirror?

   _____

   _____

4. **Reading Strategy:** A *trinket* is a small, pretty item that is not worth very much money. In paragraph 3 (page 6) of the story, which words help you understand the meaning of *trinket*?

   trinket: _____

   _____

5. **Reading Strategy:** Use the words near *glimpse* in paragraph 3 (page 7) to help you figure out the meaning of *glimpse*.

   glimpse: _____

   _____

(Continued)

6. **Literary Analysis:** Put a check in front of each sentence that you think is a **moral** of this story.

____ What makes people unhappy is not doing without things but wanting more than they have.

____ Beautiful people have an easy life.

____ Never buy something you cannot afford.

____ It is better to look at the world and not be so interested in looking at yourself.

____ You show your true self by your actions, not your appearance.

Writing

A **fable** is a simple story that teaches a moral. Usually it has animal characters who act like human beings. Write down your ideas for a fable about Burek the dog and Kot the cat. Explain how they will act and what will happen to them. Start by stating what the moral of the fable will be.

Moral:

_____

_____

_____

Ideas:

_____

_____

_____

_____

Two Kinds
Amy Tan

Summary

A Chinese woman who has started life over in America wants her American-born daughter, Jing-mei, to be famous. After exploring other possibilities, she decides that Jing-mei will be a famous piano player. She arranges for Jing-mei to take piano lessons and perform in a talent show. But Jing-mei performs poorly at the show and then refuses to continue the lessons. Her angry mother insists that there are only two kinds of daughters, ones who obey and ones who do not, and she wants only the first kind. Jing-mei says hurtful things in return. As she gets older, Jing-mei continues to disappoint her mother and, instead, be her own person. Her mother offers her the piano anyway. In the end Jing-mei realizes that she is both kinds of daughters, one who obeys and one who follows her own path.

Visual Summary

Characters	Mother	Daughter (Jing-mei)
Problem	The mother wants Jing-mei to be famous, but Jing-mei shows little talent or interest.	

Events	1. The mother tries making Jing-mei look like Shirley Temple, a child actress.
	2. The mother makes Jing-mei study facts and then tests her knowledge.
	3. The mother makes Jing-mei take piano lessons with Mr. Chong.
	4. The mother wants to show off her daughter and gets Mr. Chong to put Jing-mei in a talent show.
	5. Jing-mei plays badly in the talent show.
	6. Jing-mei refuses to continue piano lessons and fights with her mother, who says that there are two kinds of daughter, ones who obey and ones who do not.
	7. Over the years, Jing-mei is true to herself but does not do anything especially well.
	8. The mother offers her the piano for her thirtieth birthday.

Conclusion	Jing-mei realizes that she is both kinds of daughter, one who obeys because she needs the approval of others and one who is happy to be herself.

LITERARY ANALYSIS

Characters' Motives

A **character's motives** are the reasons he or she acts in a certain way. Some powerful motives include love, hope, greed, and the need for success. In "Two Kinds," Jing-mei's mother pushes her daughter to be a great talent in part because she has a very hopeful view of what people can achieve in America.

As you read, think about what the mother's other motives are. Also think about the motives for Jing-mei's actions. You might list your ideas on this chart.

Mother's actions or behavior	Mother's motives
• Pushes Jing-mei to be a great talent •	hope, pride, love
Daughter's actions or behavior	**Daughter's motives**
• •	

READING STRATEGY

Using Word Parts

A **root** is the main part of a word. Other word parts are added to the root. A **prefix** is a word part added before the root. A **suffix** is a word part added after the root. Usually, adding a prefix or suffix changes the meaning of the root.

Take the word *unreachable*. Its root is the common word *reach*. Attached to *reach* are the prefix *un-*, which means "not," and the suffix *-able*, which means "able." By adding up the meanings of the parts, you can figure out that *unreachable* means "not able to be reached."

	Prefix		Root		Suffix		Word
Parts	un-	+	reach	+	-able	=	unreachable
Meanings	"not"	+	"reach"	+	"able"	=	"not able to be reached"

Two Kinds
Amy Tan

The mother in this story was born in China. She fled during the communist revolution of 1949. She lost everything in the revolution: her parents, her first husband, her two baby daughters, her family home. But in America she married again and had a new daughter, Jing-mei. It is Jing-mei who tells the story:

◆　◆　◆

My mother believed you could be anything you wanted to be in America. You could open a restaurant. You could work for the government. . . . You could become rich. You could become instantly famous.

◆　◆　◆

Jing-mei's mother decides that her daughter can be a <u>prodigy</u>, or <u>supertalented</u> child. First, she plans to make Jing-mei a movie star and has Jing-mei's hair cut just like the popular child actress Shirley Temple's. Then, the mother gets a better idea: She makes Jing-mei study books and magazines and tests her on the facts. When Jing-mei's performance is disappointing, her mother gives up on that idea too.

◆　◆　◆

Two or three months had gone by without any mention of my being a prodigy again. And then one day my mother was watching *The Ed Sullivan Show* on TV. . . .

◆　◆　◆

On the show, a young Chinese girl is playing the piano. When she is done, she

---

Vocabulary Development

prodigy (PRAH di gee) *n.*　a child of unusually high talent

What do Jing-mei and the piano player on TV have in common? Write your answer on the lines below.

_____

_____

_____

What is Jing-mei's first reaction to the idea of taking piano lessons? Circle the answer.

What does the mother say is her **motive** in wanting Jing-mei to take piano lessons? Circle the answer.

Read fluently the paragraph that begins "I soon found out." Then, circle the problem the piano teacher has.

makes a sweeping <u>curtsy</u> in her fluffy white dress. The mother decides that Jing-mei will take piano lessons too. She speaks with Mr. Chong, a retired piano teacher who lives in the same apartment building. She agrees to clean his apartment if he will give lessons to Jing-mei.

◆　◆　◆

When my mother told me this, I felt as though I had been sent to hell. I whined and then kicked my foot a little when I couldn't stand it anymore.

"Why don't you like me the way I am? I'm not a genius! I can't play the piano. And even if I could, I wouldn't go on TV if you paid me a million dollars!" I cried.

My mother slapped me. "Who ask you be genius?" she shouted. "Only ask you be your best. For your sake. You think I want you be genius? Hnnh! . . ."

◆　◆　◆

Jing-mei secretly nicknames the piano teacher Old Chong and begins taking lessons from him. She does not do very well, for there is a serious problem.

◆　◆　◆

I soon found out why Old Chong had retired from teaching piano. He was deaf. . . .

Our lessons went like this. He would open the book and point to different things, explaining their purpose: "Key! <u>Treble</u>! <u>Bass</u>! No sharps or flats. So this is C major! Listen now and play after me!"

Vocabulary Development

curtsy (KERT see) *n.*　a polite action in which a female bends her knees and lowers her body

treble (TRE bul) *n.*　the higher sounds in music

bass (BAYS) *n.*　the lower sounds in music

And then he would play the C scale a few times, a simple chord, and then, as if <u>inspired</u> by an old, <u>unreachable</u> itch, he gradually added more notes and running <u>trills</u> and a pounding bass until the music was really something quite grand.

I would play after him, the simple scale, the simple chord, and then I just played some nonsense that sounded like a cat running up and down on top of garbage cans. Old Chong smiled and applauded and then said, "Very good! But now you must learn to keep time!"

◆　◆　◆

Jing-mei never mentions Old Chong's problem to anyone. She continues to take lessons from him. One day she hears her mother talking to Lindo Jong, a close family friend whom Jing-mei calls her aunt. Lindo brags about her daughter Waverly, a chess <u>champion</u>.

◆　◆　◆

"She bring home too many trophy. . . . You lucky you don't have this problem," said Auntie Lindo with a sigh to my mother.

And my mother squared her shoulders and bragged: "Our problem worser than yours. If we ask Jing-mei wash dish, she hear nothing but music. It's like you can't stop this natural talent."

◆　◆　◆

A few weeks later, Jing-mei's mother gets Old Chong to plan a talent show in which Jing-mei and others will perform. Jing-mei is supposed to learn by heart a

---

Vocabulary Development

inspired (in SPī rd) *v.* influenced; aroused; caused to create

trills (TRILZ) *n.* musical sounds that go rapidly back and forth between the same notes

champion (CHAMP ee un) *n.* someone who has won many games or contests

---

◆ **Reading Strategy**

Unreachable means "not able to be reached." Circle the prefix and suffix in the word. Below, explain what those **word parts** mean.

un-: _____

-able: _____

◆ **Reading Check**

Circle the words that show that Jing-mei's playing is not very good. Why does Mr. Chong praise her? Answer here:

_____

_____

◆ **Stop to Reflect**

Does Lindo really think Jing-mei's mother is lucky? Explain your answer.

_____

_____

◆ **Literary Analysis**

What is the mother's main **motive** for arranging the talent show? Circle the letter of the correct answer.

(a) her need to forget past sadness

(b) her love of music

(c) a parent's pride and need to brag

Now circle the word in the bracketed paragraph that points to this answer.

piece called "<u>Pleading</u> Child" from a work
called *Scenes from Childhood*. But she has
trouble practicing.

◆ ◆ ◆

The part I liked to practice best was the
fancy curtsy: right foot out, touch the rose on
the carpet with a pointed foot, sweep to the
side, left leg bends, look up and smile.

◆ ◆ ◆

Jing-mei's parents invite all their friends
and relatives to the show, including Auntie
Lindo and Waverly the chess champion.
After some other children dance, sing, recite
poems, and play tunes, it is Jing-mei's turn.

◆ ◆ ◆

And I started to play. It was so beautiful. I
was so caught up in how lovely I looked that at
first I didn't worry how I would sound. So it
was a surprise to me when I hit the first wrong
note and I realized something didn't sound
quite right. And then I hit another and another
followed that. A chill started at the top of my
head and began to trickle down. . . .

◆ ◆ ◆

After the awful performance, the whole
room is quiet except for Old Chong, who
cheers loudly. Jing-mei leaves the stage and
returns to her seat in shame. When the show
is over, people in the audience talk together
before leaving.

◆ ◆ ◆

Waverly looked at me and shrugged her shoulders. "You aren't a genius like me," she said. . . .
And if I hadn't felt so bad, I would have pulled
her braids and punched her stomach.

◆ ◆ ◆

As Jing-mei and her parents return
home, Jing-mei's mother says nothing. She

Vocabulary Development

pleading (PLEED ing) *adj.* asking; begging

seems to be in a state of shock. Yet two days later, she expects Jing-mei to begin practicing the piano again. But Jing-mei has had enough.

◆ ◆ ◆

"I'm not going to play anymore. . . . Why should I? I'm not a genius."

◆ ◆ ◆

Her mother insists that Jing-mei play, but Jing-mei refuses.

◆ ◆ ◆

"No!" I said, and I now felt stronger, as if my true self had finally <u>emerged</u>. So this was what had been inside me all along.

"No! I won't!" I screamed.

◆ ◆ ◆

As her mother drags her to the piano, Jing-mei begins to cry.

◆ ◆ ◆

"You want me to be someone that I'm not!" I sobbed. "I'll never be the kind of daughter you want me to be!"

"Only two kinds of daughters," she shouted in Chinese. "Those who are <u>obedient</u> and those who follow their own mind. Only one kind of daughter can live in this house. Obedient daughter!"

"Then I wish I wasn't your daughter. I wish you weren't my mother," I shouted. As I said these things I got scared. It felt like worms and toads and slimy things crawling out of my chest, but it also felt good, as if this awful side of me had <u>surfaced</u> at last.

"Too late change this," said my mother shrilly.

I could sense her anger rising to its breaking point. I wanted to see it spill over. And that's

◆ **Stop to Reflect**

Do you think this is really Jing-mei's true self? Circle *yes* or *no*. Then, explain your answer on the lines below.   yes   no

_____

_____

_____

_____

_____

_____

◆ **Reading Check**

According to the mother, what are the two kinds of daughters? Circle them, and number them *1* and *2*.

◆ **Literary Analysis**

Circle the sentence that helps explain Jing-mei's **motive** for making these very hurtful remarks to her mother. Also circle the feeling or emotion that is part of the motive for both her and her mother's behavior here.

Vocabulary Development

emerged (ee MERGD) *v.* came out

obedient (oh BEE dee ent) *adj.* doing what others say; obeying

surfaced (SER fisd) *v.* came to the top; showed itself

REVIEW AND ASSESS

1. How does Jing-mei disappoint her mother in the story? Answer by circling the word or phrase in parentheses that best completes each sentence:

   The mother wants Jing-mei to be (famous, beautiful, contented, sent away).

   But Jing-mei can only be (brilliant, pleading, a child, herself).

2. What does the mother say are the two kinds of daughters?

   Kind 1: _____ Kind 2: _____

3. In the end, what does Jing-mei realize about the kind of daughter she is? _____

   _____

4. **Reading Strategy:** For each word on the right, add up the meanings of the word parts to figure out the meaning of the word. Write the meaning on the line below the word.

	Prefix		Root	Word
	un-	+	like	= unlike
Meanings	"not"	+	"similar to"	= _____

	Root		Suffix	Word
	child	+	-ish	= childish
Meanings	"young person"	+	"like"	= _____

5. **Literary Analysis:** Fill out this chart by putting at least one **motive** in the second column of each item.

Mother's actions or behavior	Mother's motives
• pushes Jing-mei to be famous	_____
• arranges for a talent show	_____
• offers to give Jing-mei the piano	_____

(Continued)

Daughter's actions or behavior	Daughter's motives
• agrees to take piano lessons	_____
• refuses to take any more piano lessons	_____
• says hurtful words to her mother	_____

Writing

Imagine that the same story was told by Jing-mei's mother instead of Jing-mei. What thoughts and feelings would the mother describe? Write at least two thoughts or feelings for each item on this list.

- the mother's thoughts or feelings about America

_____

_____

- the mother's thoughts or feelings about her daughter being famous

_____

_____

- the mother's thoughts or feelings about the talent show

_____

_____

- the mother's thoughts or feelings when she and Jing-mei have their big fight after the show

_____

_____

- the mother's thoughts or feelings years later

_____

_____

My Furthest-Back Person
(The Inspiration for *Roots*)

Alex Haley

Summary

Alex Haley tells how he traced his family's roots to Africa. Checking government records from just after the Civil War, he was excited to find that relatives he'd heard about had actually lived. He then began checking his grandmother's story of the family's "furthest-back person" in America. Some of the strange words she had used turned out to be from an African language. Also *Kin-tay*, the name she called the "furthest-back person," turned out to be the old West African family name *Kinte*. Traveling to Africa, Haley found his distant Kinte relatives and heard the family history from a traditional oral historian. Piecing together all his research, he confirmed his grandmother's story: His "furthest-back person" in America was Kunta Kinte, a 16-year-old African kidnapped near the Gambia River in 1767, shipped to Annapolis, Maryland, and sold into slavery.

Visual Summary

Starting Point: Grandmother's stories of relatives include the family's "furthest-back person" in America, a man named Kin-tay, who was kidnapped in Africa, brought to 'Naplis, and sold into slavery.

Research in America

1. Census records confirm 1800s relatives
2. Cousin Georgia repeats story of furthest-back relative Kin-tay
3. Professor identifies strange African words; one is Gambia River
4. Dr. Curtin identifies Kin-tay as old African family name Kinte
9. Records in Maryland show arrival and sale of 98 slaves Sept./Oct. 1767

Research in Africa

5. Gambians confirm terms are Gambia River and Kinte
6. Traditional storyteller tells of Kinte family history and disappearance of 16-year-old Kunta in time of "king's soldiers"

Research in England

7. Records show soldiers sent mid-1767 to protect Britain's James Fort on Gambia River
8. Shipping records show British ship with 140 slaves left Gambia for Annapolis on July 5, 1767

Conclusion: Research confirms that Haley's family's "furthest-back person" in America was Kunta Kinte, a kidnapped Gambian brought to Annapolis, Maryland, in 1767, and sold into slavery.

LITERARY ANALYSIS

Personal Essay

An **essay** is a short piece of nonfiction writing on a particular topic. In a **personal essay**, the topic is usually an experience in the writer's life. The writer shares thoughts about what happened and shows why it was important. The style of the writing is conversational, as if the writer were talking to you.

As you read Haley's essay, answer these questions.

1. What personal experience is Haley's essay about?
2. What are his thoughts and feelings about the experience?
3. Why is the experience so important to him?

READING STRATEGY

Breaking Down Long Sentences

Sometimes it is hard to follow a long sentence. It helps if you **break down long sentences** and think about how the different parts are related.

Step 1. Put lines between groups of words that you think work together. There is no one right way to divide a sentence—just divide it into groups of words that seem best to you.

Step 2. Think about what the different groups of words are saying. Then, underline the key group or groups that tell you what happened. This sample sentence from the essay is divided into five groups with key words underlined:

After about a dozen microfilmed rolls, | <u>I was beginning to tire,</u> | when in utter astonishment | <u>I looked upon the names of Grandma's parents:</u> | Tom Murray, Irene Murray . . .

Step 3. Decide what the other groups of words in the sentence tell you. To show their relationship to the other groups of words, you might create a chart like the one below.

Sentence Part	What the Part Tells
After about a dozen microfilmed rolls	tells when first thing happened
I was beginning to tire	first thing that happened (key group)

My Furthest-Back Person
(The Inspiration for *ROOTS*)
Alex Haley

As a boy, Alex Haley often sat on his grandmother's front porch, listening to her stories of family history going back to the days of slavery. The "furthest-back person" she spoke about was an African who was kidnapped from his homeland, shipped to Annapolis, Maryland, and sold as a slave. Years later, in 1965, Haley walked past the National <u>Archives</u> in Washington, D.C. His grandmother's stories came to mind, and he decided to go inside. In the main reading room, where people do research, he spoke with the man at the desk.

◆ ◆ ◆

I wouldn't have dreamed of admitting to him some curiosity hanging on from boyhood about my slave <u>forebears</u>. I kind of bumbled that I was interested in <u>census records</u> of Alamance County, North Carolina, just after the Civil War.

◆ ◆ ◆

The records were stored on rolls of microfilm that Haley viewed on a special machine.

◆ ◆ ◆

After about a dozen microfilmed rolls, I was beginning to tire, when in utter astonishment I looked upon the names of Grandma's parents: Tom Murray, Irene Murray . . . older

---

Vocabulary Development

archives (AR kīvz) *n.* a place where records are stored
forebears (FOHR bayrz) *n.* relatives who came before; ancestors
census (SEN sus) **records** *n.* official lists of people living in a particular area

---

Circle three words in these bracketed sentences that contribute to the conversational style of this **personal essay**. Why do you think the author uses italics in the second sentence? Write your answer on these lines.

_____

_____

_____

_____

sisters of Grandma's as well—every one of them a name that I'd heard countless times on her front porch.

It wasn't that I hadn't believed Grandma. You just *didn't* not believe my Grandma. It was simply so <u>uncanny</u> actually seeing those names in print and in official U.S. government records.

◆ ◆ ◆

Having seen proof of some of his grandmother's stories, Haley grew more curious about the family's "furthest-back person." Since his grandmother was no longer alive, he went to visit his elderly Cousin Georgia in Kansas City, Kansas.[1]

◆ ◆ ◆

◆ Reading Strategy

Use lines to break this bracketed sentence into parts. Then, circle the key part that tells what happened.

Wrinkled, bent, not well herself, she was so overjoyed, repeating to me the old stories and sounds. . . . "Yeah, boy, that African say his name was '*Kin-tay*'; he say the banjo was '*ko*,' an' the river '*Kamby Bolong*,' an' he was off choppin' some wood to make his drum when they grabbed 'im!"

◆ ◆ ◆

Haley now realized that the strange words in the story must be from an African language. But he had no idea which one. So he met with Dr. Jan Vansina, a professor in Wisconsin who had studied African languages. Vansina recognized that some of the words were from a West African language called Mandinka.

◆ ◆ ◆

Among Mandinka stringed instruments, Dr. Vansina said, one of the oldest was the "<u>kora</u>."

◆ Stop to Reflect

What word used earlier by Cousin Georgia does Dr. Vansina think was a short version of *kora*? _____

What did Georgia say it meant?

_____

Based on your answers, circle whether this sentence is true or false: A banjo is a stringed musical instrument.

true   false

Vocabulary Development

uncanny (un CAN ee) *adj.*   strange; weird

---

1. **Kansas City, Kansas:** A smaller city near Kansas City, Missouri.

"*Bolong*," he said, was clearly Mandinka for "river." Preceded by "*Kamby*," it very likely meant "<u>Gambia</u> River."

◆   ◆   ◆

Vansina phoned another expert on Africa, Dr. Philip Curtin. Curtin said that "*Kintay*" was how you pronounced "*Kinte*," the name of a <u>clan</u> going back to the old African kingdom of Mali, near where the Gambia River flows.

◆   ◆   ◆

I knew I must get to the Gambia River.

◆   ◆   ◆

Haley traveled to the African nation of Gambia and told his family's story to many people in the capital. They felt that the key to finding more information was in the name "Kinte."

◆   ◆   ◆

Then they told me something I would never ever have <u>fantasized</u>—that in places in the back country lived very old men, commonly called *griots*, who could tell centuries of the histories of certain very old family clans. As for *Kintes*, they pointed out to me on a map some family villages, Kinte-Kundah, and Kinte-Kundah Janneh-Ya, for instance.

◆   ◆   ◆

Not long afterward, Haley traveled with others into the back country to meet a griot named Kebba Kanga Fofana. As the group headed up the Gambia River, they passed the ruins of an old British fort called James Fort. There, for two centuries, Africans had been loaded onto ships and brought to the Americas as slaves.

Vocabulary Development

clan (CLAN) *n.*   a group of people with a common ancestor
fantasized (FAN tuh sizd) *v.*   dreamed; imagined

◆ **Read Fluently**

Try saying the words *Kamby* and *Gambia* so that they sound alike. Can you see why the professor thinks the river is the Gambia? Circle your answer:

yes   no

◆ **Stop to Reflect**

Where do you think Haley will go next? Circle the letter of your answer.

(a) Washington, D.C.

(b) Kansas City, KS

(c) Wisconsin

(d) Africa

Explain your answer.

_____

_____

_____

◆ **Reading Strategy**

Use lines to break this bracketed sentence into parts. Then circle two parts that give information about what *griots* are. To show you understand the sentence, explain what a *griot* is on these lines.

griot:

_____

_____

_____

_____

_____

_____

◆ ◆ ◆

Then we continued upriver to the left-bank village of Albreda, and there put ashore to continue on foot to Juffure,[2] village of the griot.

◆ ◆ ◆

The griot recited the history of the Kinte clan, which he knew by heart. Every few sentences he would pause for his words to be translated into English. He told of the clan's beginnings in Old Mali. He spoke of one clan member, Kairaba Kunta Kinte, who came to Gambia and settled right there in Juffure. Kairaba's youngest son, Omoro, had about 30 "rains," or years, when he married a woman named Binta Kebba. Omoro and Binta had four sons.

◆ ◆ ◆

"About the time the king's soldiers came, the eldest of these four sons, Kunta, when he had about 16 rains, went away from his village, to chop wood to make a drum . . . and he was never seen again. . . ."

◆ ◆ ◆

When Haley heard this, he grew very excited. The details matched the story his grandmother had always told! Learning how the stories matched, the griot and other villagers welcomed Haley as a long-lost relative. Haley was deeply moved.

◆ ◆ ◆

Let me tell you something: I am a man. But I remember the sob surging up from my feet, flinging up my hands and <u>bawling</u> as I had not done since I was a baby. . . . If you really knew the <u>odyssey</u> of us millions of black Americans, if you

Vocabulary Development

bawling (BAWL ing) *v.* crying loudly
odyssey (AH duh see) *n.* a very long journey

---

2. **Juffure** (joo foo ray)

really knew how we came in the seeds of our <u>forefathers</u>, captured, driven, beaten, inspected, bought, branded, chained in <u>foul</u> ships, if you really knew, you needed weeping . . .

◆   ◆   ◆

Haley decided to write the story of his family, which he felt was like the story of so many African Americans. But he needed more details. What ship had brought Kinte to America? Since the griot had spoken of he arrival of "king's soldiers," Haley went to Britain to continue his research. In British government records he found what he was looking for.

◆   ◆   ◆

<u>Feverish</u> searching at last identified . . . "Colonel O'Hare's Forces," <u>dispatched</u> in mid-1767 to protect the then British-held James Fort whose ruins I'd visited.

◆   ◆   ◆

So if Kinte was caught soon after British soldiers came to Gambia, the ship bringing him to America must have sailed around then. Haley began checking British shipping records for 1767.

◆   ◆   ◆

And then early one afternoon I found that a *Lord Ligonier* under a Captain Thomas Davies had sailed on the Sabbath of July 5, 1767. Her cargo: 3,265 elephants' teeth, . . . 800 pounds of cotton, 32 ounces of Gambian gold and 140 slaves; her <u>destination</u>: "Annapolis."

◆ Stop to Reflect

If Haley finds out the name of the ship, to what city in the Americas do you think the ship will have sailed? Why?

Write your answer here:

_____

_____

_____

Vocabulary Development

forefathers (FOHR fa therz) *n.* ancestors

foul (FOWL) *adj.* filthy and disgusting

feverish (FEE ver ish) *adj.* very excited; frantic

dispatched (dis PATCHD) *v.* sent

destination (des tuh NA shun) *n.* the place being traveled to

◆ Stop to Reflect

How many Africans died
on the trip from Gambia
to Annapolis? _____
out of _____

What does this tell
you about conditions on the
slave ship?

_____

_____

_____

_____

◆ Literary Analysis

Based on the other details
in this **personal essay**,
circle three words in
the newspaper ad
that you think would
make Haley especially
angry.

Back in America, Haley visited the
Annapolis Historical Society. He found
records of the arrival of the *Lord Ligonier* on
Sept. 29, 1767. Only 98 slaves had survived
the trip, but one of them must have been
16-year-old Kunta Kinte. Haley also found, on
microfilm, a copy of the *Maryland Gazette*
for Oct. 1, 1767. On page 2, the newspaper
announced a sale:

◆ ◆ ◆

"from the River GAMBIA, in AFRICA . . . a
<u>cargo</u> of choice, healthy SLAVES . . ."

Vocabulary Development

cargo (CAR goh) *n.* the load carried by a ship

1. Who was Kunta Kinte in relation to Alex Haley and his family?

_____

_____

_____

2. What apparently happened to Kinte in 1767, when he was about 16?

_____

_____

_____

3. List five items of information Haley found in his research. Also write the person or organization that supplied the information and the place where he found it. An example is done for you.

Information	Person or Organization	Place
census records of grandmother's parents and sisters	National Archives	Washington, DC
_____	_____	_____
_____	_____	_____
_____	_____	_____
_____	_____	_____

4. **Reading Strategy:** Draw lines to break this sentence from the essay into smaller parts. Then, show that you understand the sentence by answering the following questions.

   Then we continued upriver to the left-bank village of Albreda, and there put ashore to continue on foot to Juffure, village of the *griot*.

(Continued)

Where did the travelers leave their boat?

_____

Who or what was Juffure?

_____

5. **Literary Analysis:** Why are the experiences in Haley's **personal essay** so important to him? Give two reasons.

1. _____

_____

2. _____

_____

Writing

Haley's book *Roots* is based on his and his family's experiences in this essay. Like all authors, he had to persuade a publisher to publish *Roots*. What do you think he said? Write your ideas on a separate paper. Your ideas should include answers to the questions below. Many of the questions can have more than one answer, so you decide what *you* would have said if you were Haley.

- What is the main topic of the book? _____
- When and where will the book begin? _____

_____

- Who is the first main person the book will be about? _____

_____

- What will the book show about slavery? _____

_____

- Why will the book be important to African Americans? _____

_____

_____

A Day's Wait

Ernest Hemingway

Summary

When Schatz has the flu, his father calls the doctor. The doctor says that Schatz's temperature is 102 degrees. Later that day, Schatz asks about his temperature. He is very quiet and worried, and his father cannot understand why. Finally, Schatz asks when he is going to die. His father says he is not that ill and will not die. Schatz says that boys at school in France told him a person could not live with a temperature of 44 degrees. His father then realizes that Schatz has been waiting to die all day, ever since he heard the doctor. The father explains that in France they use a different kind of thermometer. On that thermometer a normal temperature is 37 degrees. On the thermometer the doctor used, normal is 98 degrees. Schatz is very relieved by the explanation.

Visual Summary

A Day's Wait: The story takes place in one day			
Early Morning to 11 AM			
Schatz comes down with flu. →	Father calls doctor. →	Doctor says temperature is 102 degrees. →	Father tries to read to Schatz.
11 AM to Late Afternoon			
Schatz sends father away. →	Father goes hunting. →	Father returns to house. →	Father learns Schatz wouldn't see anyone all day.
Late Afternoon to Early Evening			
When Schatz asks about dying, father says Schatz won't die. →	Schatz says in France such high temperature meant certain death. →	Father explains that Schatz confused two types of thermometers. →	Father realizes Schatz has spent all day in bed expecting to die.

LITERARY ANALYSIS

Internal Conflict

Most stories center on a **conflict**, or struggle between two forces. Sometimes the struggle is an **internal conflict**, taking place in the character's mind.

For example, in "A Day's Wait," Schatz struggles between his desire to be brave and his fear and worry about his illness. We see Schatz's tension in his own words and behavior.

"I don't worry," he said, "but I can't keep from thinking."

"Don't think," I said. "Just take it easy."

"I'm taking it easy," he said and looked straight ahead. He was evidently holding tight on to himself about something.

As you read "A Day's Wait," pay careful attention to Schatz's words and actions. Look for signs that he is going through an internal conflict.

READING STRATEGY

Identifying Word Roots

A **root** is the main part of a word. Other parts are added to word roots. Some of the roots in English words come from other languages, especially Latin and Greek. You can often get an idea of a word's meaning if you know the meaning of its Latin or Greek root.

Study this chart of Latin and Greek roots, their meanings, and examples of words in which they appear. Look for these roots in "A Day's Wait."

Root	Meaning	Word with Root	Word's Meaning
-vid- *or* -vis-	see	evidently	in a way that is easily seen; clearly
-medic-	doctor	medicine	something a doctor recommends to fight an illness
-therm-	heat	thermometer	an instrument that measures heat

A Day's Wait
Ernest Hemingway

In "A Day's Wait," a father tells the story of an amazing day in the life of his nine-year-old son. As the story opens, the son comes into the bedroom, where his parents are sleeping. The boy does not look or act like he feels well. He is pale and shivering. He looked as though it ached to move.

◆   ◆   ◆

"What's the matter, Schatz?"[1]
"I've got a headache."
"You better go back to bed."
"No, I'm all right."

◆   ◆   ◆

The father tells his son to go back to bed. But when he comes downstairs, the boy is dressed and sitting by the fire. His son looks sick and miserable. When he feels his son's forehead, it's obvious the boy has a <u>fever</u>. The doctor comes to check on the boy and takes his temperature. When the father asks what it is, the doctor states that it is one hundred and two. Downstairs, the doctor identifies the boy's illness as influenza, or flu. He leaves three kinds of medicine for the boy to take at different times throughout the day. The father returns to the boy's room after writing down the doctor's <u>instructions</u>. The boy lay still. The father noticed that his son's face was pale with dark circles under his

1. **Schatz** (SHAHTZ): A loving nickname that comes from the German word for "treasure" or "dear."

◆ **Reading Check**

Circle three details that show that Schatz looks ill.

◆ **Stop to Reflect**

Circle what the father tells Schatz to do and what Schatz does instead. Why do you think Schatz does not obey his father? Write your answer here:

_____

_____

_____

_____

_____

◆ **Reading Strategy**

The Latin root -*struct*- means "build." To *instruct* is "to build knowledge step by step; to teach." What do you think *instructions* are? Write the meaning.

instructions:

_____

_____

_____

Mark the Text

eyes. Despite the fact that the boy seems <u>detached</u> and listless, the father offers to read to him from a book about pirates. While he was reading, the boy lay still, but did not seem to be listening.

◆ ◆ ◆

"How do you feel, Schatz?" I asked him.
"Just the same, so far," he said.

◆ ◆ ◆

The father sits at the foot of the bed, looking at the book himself. He is waiting until it is time to give the boy more of the <u>prescribed</u> medicine. The boy's father notices that his son has a strange look on his face. He suggests to his son that he sleep until it's time for the <u>capsules</u> that are his next dose of medicine. The boy, however, wants to stay awake.

◆ ◆ ◆

After a while he said to me, "You don't have to stay in here with me, Papa, if it bothers you."
"It doesn't bother me."
"No. I mean you don't have to stay if it's going to bother you."

◆ ◆ ◆

The father thinks his son is feeling light-headed from being sick and taking medicine. After he gives his son the prescribed medicine late in the morning he leaves for a while.

When he leaves the house, the father goes hunting for quail, a type of bird that is usually hunted with the help of a dog. The dog that the father takes with him is a young

◆ **Stop to Reflect**

What might Schatz think will bother his father later? Write your guess here:

_____

_____

_____

◆ **Stop to Reflect**

The father enjoys outdoor sports like hunting. Do you think this has anything to do with the way his son behaves in the story? Circle *yes* or *no*:

        yes   no

Then, explain your opinion here:

_____

_____

_____

_____

Vocabulary Development

detached (dee TACHD) *adj.* not connected to
prescribed (pree SCRĪBD) *adj.* ordered in writing
capsules (CAP soolz) *n.* medicine enclosed in small containers that a person can swallow like pills

Irish setter. The two slide along the frozen creek. Then the dog drives some quail from the bushes. Since it is so icy, it isn't easy to shoot at the flying birds. But the father still manages to kill two. He and the dog then return to the house.

While the father is gone, the boy doesn't let anyone come near him. He warns everyone not to come in the room because they must not get what he has. The father ignores what the boy says and goes in. He finds him in exactly the position he left him in.

◆ ◆ ◆

I took his temperature.
"What is it?"
"Something like a hundred," I said. It was one hundred and two and four tenths.
"It was a hundred and two," he said.
"Who said so?"
"The doctor."

◆ ◆ ◆

The father assures his son that his temperature is all right and nothing to worry about. He also suggests that the boy just take it easy and gives him another dose of medicine. The boy <u>evidently</u> isn't taking it easy because he asks whether taking the medicine will do any good. The father reassures his son and sits down and starts reading aloud from the pirate book again. And again, the boy doesn't pay attention. So the father stops.

◆ ◆ ◆

"About what time do you think I'm going to die?" he asked.

Vocabulary Development

evidently (ev uh DENT lee) *adv.* clearly

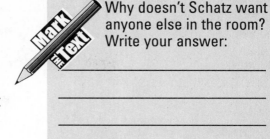

Why doesn't Schatz want anyone else in the room? Write your answer:

_____

_____

_____

_____

Now circle the words that show you the answer.

◆ Literary Analysis

Circle two details in the bracketed paragraph that show Schatz is going through an **internal conflict**. Then, complete this sentence to show what you think the conflict is about: Schatz's inner struggle seems to be between

_____

_____

and

_____

_____.

"What?"

"About how long will it be before I die?"

"You aren't going to die. What's the matter with you?"

◆ ◆ ◆

As the father talks with his son, he realizes that the boy has been waiting all day to die—ever since he overheard the doctor say that his temperature was one hundred and two. The boys at his school in France, told him that a person can't survive a fever of forty-four <u>degrees</u>. The boy believes that he is dying because his temperature is a hundred and two. When the father discovers the cause of his son's worry, he explains the difference between thermometers and their temperature readings. Thirty-seven degrees is a normal temperature on the kind of thermometer that the boys at school were talking about.

◆ ◆ ◆

"Are you sure?"

"Absolutely," I said. "It's like miles and kilometers.[2] You know, like how many kilometers we make when we do seventy miles in the car?"

"Oh," he said.

But his gaze at the foot of the bed relaxed slowly. The hold over himself relaxed too, finally, and the next day it was very <u>slack</u> and he cried very easily at little things that were of no importance.

◆ Reading Strategy

Circle the two words in the bracketed passage that contain the Greek **root** -*meter*-, which means "measure." Since the Greek root -*therm*- means "heat," what do you think a *thermometer* measures?

_____

◆ Literary Analysis

Circle one or two words that tell you what happened to Schatz's **internal conflict**, or inner tension. Why do you think he cries easily the next day? Write your answer here:

_____
_____
_____
_____

Vocabulary Development

degrees (duh GREEZ) *n.* the units of measure that show heat or body temperature

slack (SLAK) *adj.* loose

---

[2]**kilometers** (KIL oh MEET erz): Units for measuring distance used instead of miles in many other nations, including France. A kilometer is 1000 meters or about 5/8 of a mile.

1. In the story, what does Schatz confuse? Circle the letter of the correct answer.

   (a) kilometers in France and miles in America

   (b) kilometers in France and degrees in America

   (c) thermometers in France and America

   (d) school in France and America

2. Why does his mistake cause Schatz to think he will die? Write your answer on the lines.

   _____

   _____

3. Write two words that describe the father in this story.

   1. _____ 2. _____

4. **Literary Analysis:** Explain Schatz's internal conflict by choosing four words from the Word Box to complete the sentence. Then, in the columns, list examples from the story to illustrate the words you chose.

Word Box: brave   mean   noisy   scared   spoiled   unselfish   worried

Schatz is (A) _____ and (B) _____ , BUT he tries to be

(C) _____ and (D) _____ .

Examples of (A) and (B)	Examples of (C) and (D)
_____	_____
_____	_____
_____	_____
_____	_____
_____	_____

(Continued)

5. **Reading Strategy:** Use the meaning of each **word root** to help you explain the meaning of the word in which it appears. Write the meanings of the word on the lines provided.

Root	Meaning of Root	Word	Meaning of Word
-vid-	see	evidently	
-scrib-	write	prescribed	
-tach-	stick; connect	detached	

Listening and Speaking

Work in a group of four students. Take turns explaining the mistake Schatz made and listening to the explanations of your classmates. After you listen to an explanation, give feedback on how it might be improved. Use these questions as a guide.

Yes   No

1. Was the explanation clear and easy to understand?   _____ _____
   If not, what changes might improve it?

_____

_____

2. Was the information right?   _____ _____
   If not, which details need to be corrected?

_____

_____

3. Was the speaker's voice clear?   _____ _____
   Was he or she interesting to listen to?   _____ _____
   If not, what could be improved?

_____

_____

Was Tarzan a Three-Bandage Man?

Bill Cosby

Summary

When Bill Cosby was young, he and his friends tried to act cool by imitating their sports heroes. Bill's mother pokes fun at him for walking funny to copy famous ball players. She scolds him for putting bandages on his face to imitate champion boxers. Cosby now realizes it might have been better to imitate the boxers who gave injuries rather than those who received them.

Visual Summary

Cosby and Friends' Actions	Cosby's Mother's Reaction	Adult Cosby's Reaction
• Copy walk of Jackie Robinson, fastest man in baseball • Copy walk of football player Buddy Helm • Imitate boxers like Sugar Ray Robinson by wearing a bandage above an eye	• Pokes fun by questioning Robinson's shoes and whether walk slows speed • Pokes fun at how son twists his legs to copy these men's walks • Suggests son is being stupid and needs better role models; makes him remove his bandage	• Pokes fun by saying walk was painful • Pokes fun by suggesting the behavior made little sense

LITERARY ANALYSIS

Anecdote

An **anecdote** is a short account of an interesting incident in a person's life. Usually it is something that happened to the author. In "Was Tarzan a Three-Bandage Man?" the author tells an anecdote from his own childhood.

One reason Bill Cosby tells his anecdote is to entertain. His childhood actions are very funny, and so are his mother's comments about them:

> "Why you walkin' like that?" said my mother one day.
> "This is Jackie Robinson's walk," I proudly replied.
> "There's somethin' wrong with his shoes?"
> "He's the fastest man in baseball."
> "He'd be faster if he didn't walk like that. . . ."

As you read the anecdote, think about Cosby's purposes in telling it. Focus on these questions:

- What is funny or entertaining about the anecdote?
- Why do you think the events are important to the author?
- What general points do you think he is trying to make about life or human behavior?

READING STRATEGY

Using Context Clues

The **context** is the situation or surroundings in which a word appears. Often a word's context will give you clues to its meaning. For example, read this passage from the selection.

> In fact, they were such heroes to me and my friends that we even <u>imitated</u> their walks. When Jackie Robinson, a pigeon-toed walker, became famous, we walked pigeon-toed. . . .

The term *imitated* may be unfamiliar, but the context gives clues to its meaning. The first sentence says that Cosby and his friends *imitated* the heroes' walks. The next sentence says that Jackie Robinson was a pigeon-toed walker and that they too "walked pigeon-toed." From this context, you can tell that *imitated* must mean "copied."

Was Tarzan[1] a Three-Bandage Man?

Bill Cosby

Bill Cosby recalls events when he was young, in the late 1940's. Then, <u>athletes</u> were sports stars even before they started to <u>incorporate</u> themselves by selling products. One of the biggest sports heroes of the time was Jackie Robinson, the first African American to play in major-league baseball. Bill and his friends were so impressed with Robinson and other sports heroes that they copied the way the athletes walked.

◆   ◆   ◆

When Jackie Robinson, a pigeon-toed[2] walker, became famous, we walked pigeon-toed, ...

"Why you walkin' like that?" said my mother one day.

"This is Jackie *Robinson's* walk," I proudly replied.

◆   ◆   ◆

Bill's mother is both amused and annoyed by her son's behavior. When he explains that Robinson is the fastest man in baseball, she remarks that he'd be faster if he walked normally. Bill finds that walking pigeon-toed is a painful form of <u>locomotion</u>.

When football season starts, Bill tries to walk like Buddy Helm, a football player. His mother asks more questions. This time she asks why he's walking bowlegged.[3]

Vocabulary Development

athletes (ATH leetz) *n.*   someone who is good at sports

incorporate (in CORP uh rayt) *v.*   to form a business

---

1. **Tarzan** (tar ZAN): a popular movie hero who swung from vines in the jungle.
2. **pigeon-toed** (PIJ un tohd) *adj.*   having the toes or feet turned in toward each other.
3. **bowlegged** (BOH leg id) *adj.*   having legs that are curved outward.

◆ Literary Analysis

Circle a funny remark that adds to the humor of this **anecdote**. What do you find funny about Bill's actions here? Write your answer on the lines.

_____

_____

_____

_____

_____

_____

_____

◆ Reading Strategy

What do you think *locomotion* means? Circle the letter of the answer.

(a) moving from one place to another

(b) a subway train

(c) a baseball game

(d) feeding food to birds in the park

Now circle the **context clues** that helped you figure out the meaning.

What do you think *emulate* means?

emulate: _____

Now circle the **context clues** that helped you figure out the meaning.

Cosby continues his anecdote by explaining that prizefighters, or boxers, like Sugar Ray Robinson were bigger heroes than baseball and football stars. The way to <u>emulate</u> a fighter was to wear a Band-Aid. Since boxers often had cuts around their eyes, the Band-Aid needed to be worn on the face. Bill and his friends hoped that people would understand that they were worshipping boxers and not trying to cover up their acne.

Of course, Bill's mother asks what the bandage over his eye is for. His muttered reply of "nuthin" doesn't impress her.

◆ ◆ ◆

"Now that's a new kinda stupid answer. That bandage gotta be coverin' somethin'—besides your entire brain."

◆ ◆ ◆

◆ **Read Fluently**

Read the bracketed quotation aloud. What tone would be best to use for the mother's comment about the brain? Circle the answer.

cheerful   sad

hopeful   sarcastic

Bill explains that the Band-Aid is just for show and that he wants to look like Sugar Ray Robinson. His mother thinks Bill means Robinson, the baseball player. Bill explains that it's a different Robinson. Then his mother asks if he's going to imitate the Swiss Family Robinson next. They were children's book characters who had to live all alone on an island after their ship was lost at sea. Bill wants to know if the Swiss Family Robinson is a family that lives in the projects.[4] Bill's mother suggests that if he read more books instead of walking funny or wearing bandages that he'd know who they are.

◆ **Stop to Reflect**

Why does the mother ask if Bill will imitate the Swiss Family Robinson?

(a) The Swiss family all wore bandages.

(b) She wants Bill to face hardships as the Swiss family did on the island.

(c) Bill has imitated two other Robinsons, so she suggests an even sillier possibility.

(d) The book about the Swiss family is her son's favorite book.

---

4. **projects** (prah jektz): inexpensive apartment houses in poor neighborhoods.

Bill's mother thinks he should copy a person like Booker T. Washington[5] instead of an athlete. Bill doesn't know who this particular Washington is so he asks, "Who does he play for?" His mother doesn't answer him, but tells him that he can't wear the bandage.

♦ ♦ ♦

" . . . You take off that bandage right now or I'll have your father move you up to stitches."

♦ ♦ ♦

The next morning, Bill tells his friends Fat Albert, Junior, and Eddie that his mother won't let him wear a bandage.

♦ ♦ ♦

"What's wrong with that woman?" said Fat Albert. "She won't let you do *nuthin'*."

♦ ♦ ♦

One of Bill's other friends tells him that it's okay that he can't wear the bandage—the tough guys wear two bandages—one is not enough anyway. The boys discuss what being a two-bandage man might be about. Eddie decides he "wouldn't want to mess with no two-bandage man."

Bill Cosby goes on to recall that the toughest guys wore the largest bandages. He finds it all very funny and ridiculous now.

♦ ♦ ♦

Our hero worshipping was backwards: we should have been emulating the men who had caused the *need* for bandages.

5. **Booker T. Washington** (1856-1915): A famous African American educator who stressed the importance of education.

◆ Stop to Reflect

Why do you think she mentions Booker T. Washington as someone to imitate?

_____

_____

_____

◆ Reading Check

What is the mother threatening to have the father do in the underlined passage? Circle the answer.

(a) remove the bandage

(b) hit Bill if he doesn't start behaving

(c) tell jokes that keep Bill in stitches

What does she mean by "move you up"?

_____

_____

_____

_____

◆ Literary Analysis

Circle the main point about young people's behavior that Cosby makes near the end of his **anecdote**.

1. Why do Bill and his friends imitate the sports stars?

_____

_____

2. Label each statement about the mother *T* if it seems true or *F* if it seems false.

_____ The mother thinks Bill's behavior is silly.

_____ The mother is a friend of Jackie Robinson's mother.

_____ The mother thinks Bill's feet will fall off.

_____ The mother has a good sense of humor.

_____ The mother knows the names of all the popular sports heroes.

3. Explain what is funny about Eddie's fear of "two-bandage men."

_____

_____

4. What do you think the anecdote's title means?

_____

_____

5. **Reading Strategy:** Circle the **context clues** that help you figure out the meaning of *acne*. Then, circle the letter of the meaning.

   People with *acne* walked around that way too, but we hoped it was clear that we were worshipping good fists and not bad skin.

   Acne means (a) a skin condition (b) a type of boxing (c) on tiptoes (d) height

6. **Literary Analysis:** List examples that show each of Cosby's three purposes in telling this **anecdote**.

- **Purpose: to tell a funny, interesting story** (list three examples)

1. _____

2. _____

3. _____

- **Purpose: to describe something important to him** (list one example)

_____

_____

- **Purpose: to make a point about life or people's behavior** (list two examples)

1. _____

2. _____

Writing

Should young people make heroes of sports stars? On a separate sheet, write a paragraph expressing your opinion about this question. First, follow these four steps:

1. List your ideas in a two-column chart like this one.

Why it might be good to make heroes of sports stars	Why it might not be good
_____	_____
_____	_____

2. Study your chart and decide where you stand.
3. Open your paragraph with a statement of your opinion. For example, you might say, "I believe (or I do not believe) that young people should make heroes of sports stars."
4. Explain your opinion by giving reasons, examples, and other details. List them here.

_____

_____

from In Search of Our Mothers' Gardens
Alice Walker

Summary

   Alice Walker praises her mother and other African American women like her. Walker sees her mother as an artist whose talents helped make Walker the writer she is today. Her mother revealed her artistic talent in the stories she told and in the flower gardens she grew. Being poor and working hard all her life did not stop her from taking time to grow these lovely gardens. Walker admires how black women of her mother's generation managed to "hold on" despite the difficulty of their lives. From these women, Walker has inherited a respect for strength as well as a love of beauty.

Visual Summary

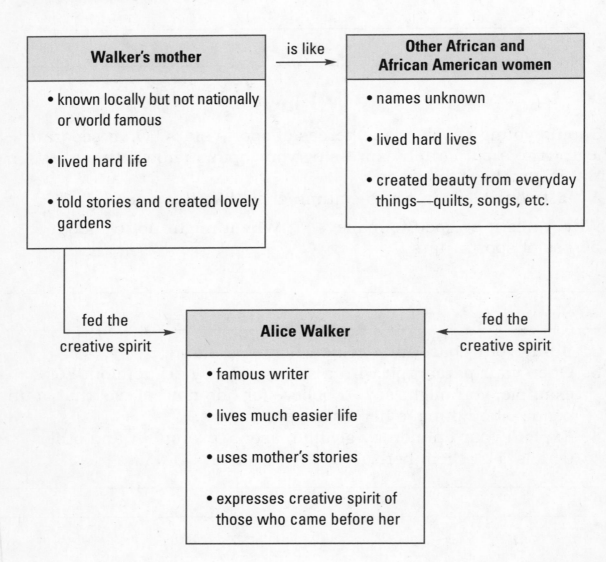

LITERARY ANALYSIS

Tribute

A **tribute** is a piece of writing that expresses thanks or admiration to a special person. It includes details about that person's life. It also explains why the person is important to the writer.

"In Search of Our Mothers' Gardens" is Alice Walker's tribute to her mother. In it, Walker considers what she as a writer owes to her mother. She provides many specific details about her mother's life to show why she admires her mother:

> She planted ambitious gardens—and still does—with over fifty different varieties of plants. . . . Whatever she planted grew as if by magic, and her fame as a grower of flowers spread over three counties.

As you read Walker's tribute, focus on these questions:
- What does Walker admire about her mother?
- In what ways does the mother contribute to Walker's own creative life as a writer?

READING STRATEGY

Recognizing Word Roots

A **root** is the main part of a word. Other parts are added to root words. Many English words have roots that come from Latin and Greek. Learning some of these common roots will help you understand whole groups of words.

For example, consider the Latin root *-herit-*, which means "heir." (An *heir* is someone who has property or something else passed down to him or her. For example, a daughter may be the *heir* to her father's money or her mother's temper.) Once you know the root, you have an idea of the meanings of the whole group of words that contain it.

English Words with the Latin Root *-herit-* ("heir")	
inherit:	to have property or something else passed down to you
inheritance:	the property or other things that are passed down to you
heritage:	the cultural or family traditions passed down to you
disinherit:	to take away someone's right to have property passed down

Was the working day really just what the mother did in the fields? Write *yes* or *no*, and explain your answer.

_____

_____

_____

_____

_____

Now, circle the words in the bracketed sentences that helped you answer.

Mark the Text

The **root** *-spir-* in *spirit* means "breath." Since breath is associated with life, what do you think *spirit* means? Circle the letter.

(a) life force; soul

(b) a drawing of the human body

(c) loss of hope

(d) a bad cough

Which of these African Americans do you think Walker is most likely to refer to right after the underlined phrase?

(a) prize-winning author Toni Morrison

(b) a poor woman who made quilts

(c) opera star Leontyne Price

(d) ballet star Arthur Mitchell

Explain your answer:

_____

_____

from In Search of Our Mothers' Gardens
Alice Walker

Now a famous writer, Alice Walker came from a poor farm family in Georgia. Her mother was weighed down with household chores and back-breaking farm work all her life. She canned vegetables and fruits. She sewed all of the clothes the family wore, even her brother's overalls. She also sewed the towels, sheets, and quilts they used.

◆ ◆ ◆

During the "working" day, she <u>labored</u> beside—not behind—my father in the fields. Her day began before sunup, and did not end until late at night.

◆ ◆ ◆

It would seem that Walker's mother had no time to be creative. And yet, it is to her mother that Walker looks when she wants to understand her own creative <u>spirit</u>.

◆ ◆ ◆

But when, you will ask, did my overworked mother have time to know or care about feeding the creative spirit?

The answer is so simple that many of us have spent years discovering it.

◆ ◆ ◆

To answer that question, Walker feels that we must look <u>high—and low</u>. She thinks that looking just in high places for her mother's kind of creative spirit is not enough. Among the places Walker herself looks is one of the famous Smithsonian Institution museums in Washington, D.C., where she finds a beautiful quilt made a hundred years

Vocabulary Development

labored (LAY berd) *v.* worked

ago by an <u>anonymous</u> black woman in Alabama. The quilt is unusual. It is so valuable that it's beyond price. To Walker, the woman who made the quilt is one of her grandmothers, an artist who left her mark in one of the few ways possible for her at the time.

◆　◆　◆

And so our mothers and grandmothers have, more often than not anonymously, handed on the creative spark, the seed of the flower they themselves never hoped to see; or like a sealed letter they could not plainly read.

◆　◆　◆

Walker knows that her mother won't have her name on any work of art or piece of writing either. Yet so many of the stories that Walker writes are her mother's stories.

◆　◆　◆

Only recently did I fully realize this: that through years of listening to my mother's stories of her life, I have absorbed not only the stories themselves but something of the manner in which she spoke.

◆　◆　◆

Walker explains that her mother's creative spark also expressed itself in another way. Besides telling stories, she also created beautiful flower gardens. No matter how poor or plain a house the family was forced to live in, Walker's mother always decorated it with flowers.

◆　◆　◆

She planted <u>ambitious</u> gardens—and still does. . . . Before she left home for the fields,

◆ **Literary Analysis**

Does this **tribute** praise only Walker's mother? Write *yes* or *no:* _____

Then, circle the words that point to your answer.

◆ **Literary Analysis**

Read the bracketed passage. What does the writer realize about her mother's gifts to her? Write your ideas on these lines.

_____

_____

_____

_____

Vocabulary Development

anonymous (a NAHN i mus) *adj.* with no known name; unknown

ambitious (am BISH us) *adj.* involving a lot of work or effort

---

What do the details about the mother in this part of the tribute show the mother to be like? Circle the letter of the term that best describes her here.

(a) lazy

(c) lifeless

(b) creative

(d) sad and hopeless

Circle the letter of the choice that best completes this sentence: Walker considers her mother's garden to be

_____.

(a) a wild place that no one can control

(b) an overgrown place that needs care

(c) a work of art and creation of beauty

(d) a dream world no one understands

Circle the words that helped you answer.

she watered her flowers, chopped up the grass, and laid out new beds. . . .

Whatever she planted grew as if by magic, and her fame as a grower of flowers spread over three counties.

◆　◆　◆

Walker revisits her memories of people coming from all over to see her mother's garden. They are drawn to the flowers and trees that bloom profusely. They admire her mother's ability to turn any soil into a magnificent garden—her art. Many ask for cuttings from the flowers so they can take a piece of the beauty home with them.

Her mother's creativity in the garden drew on color and design. But the garden also showed the work needed for their care: her mother had to divide clumps of bulbs,[1] plant, dig a cold pit,[2] replant, and prune the flowers and trees. Strangers still come by the house in Georgia and ask to stand or walk in Walker's mother's garden.

Walker observes that when her mother is at work in her garden, her face brightens and she seems fully alive. The work she does in the garden is for her soul—she creates her own conception of beauty. Even though her

---

Vocabulary Development

profusely (pro FYOOS lee) *adv.* in great number; freely; plentifully

creativity (KREE ay TIV i tee) *n.* imagination; artistic talent

prune (PROON) *v.* to cut off branches of a plant

conception (kon SEP shun) *n.* idea

---

1. **bulb:** a short thick underground stem covered by thick fleshy leaves that stores the food for a shoot to grow. Tulips and daffodils grow from bulbs.
2. **cold pit:** a hole in which small plants are placed at the beginning of spring.

mother has been <u>hindered</u> and had her work <u>intruded upon</u> by daily responsibilities, she has created her art every day of her life.

◆ ◆ ◆

This ability to hold on, even in very simple ways, is work black women have done for a very long time.

◆ ◆ ◆

Walker's mother values life and all it has to offer—the bad as well as the good. She has passed her attitude down to her children. Walker is moved by her mother's example and writes a poem to her. Walker does not feel that her poem is enough, but she thinks it is something of a tribute—to honor the woman who brought beauty and creativity into her life, and who <u>literally</u> covered holes in the wall with sunflowers.

Walker thinks of other proud women in Africa more than two hundred years ago. She wonders if they struggled to express themselves. Maybe they sang or painted bright colors on their hut walls. Perhaps the mother of Phillis Wheatley, the first African American poet in America, was a poet too. Walker realizes her own desire to write comes from the efforts of her mother and of black women who came before her. These nameless women, living in hard times, still managed to create something beautiful out of the simple things around them.

◆ ◆ ◆

Guided by my heritage of a love of beauty and a respect for strength—in search of my mother's garden, I found my own.

Vocabulary Development

hindered (HIN derd) *adj.* held back
literally (LIT er uh lee) *adv.* actually

◆ **Reading Strategy**

The **root** -*trud*- means "push." What do you think "intruded upon" means?

(a) helped   (b) interrupted

(c) being an artist (d) praised

How does the root point to the meaning?

_____

_____

◆ **Read Fluently**

Read the bracketed passage of the summary aloud. What image does it give you of the kind of person the mother was? Circle the letter of the best answer.

(a) silly and wasteful

(b) vague; unable to concentrate

(c) happy, careless, and sloppy

(d) creative, comforting, and hopeful

◆ **Reading Check**

Mark the Text

Circle the two values or attitudes that Walker believes are part of her heritage from her mother. What do the last ten words mean? Circle the letter.

(a) By exploring her mother's creative spirit, she found the source of her own.

(b) While traveling to Georgia, she saw interesting things to write about.

(c) She has now become a gardener just like her mother.

(d) She was moved to learn her mother had named a rose bush "Alice Walker."

1. To whom does Walker feel she and other African American women owe their creative spirit?

   _____

2. Check the statements that apply to Alice Walker's mother.

   ____ She spent most of her life in poor neighborhoods in large cities.

   ____ She and her husband worked hard on their farm.

   ____ No matter how plain their house, she always planted a garden.

   ____ People from counties all around came to hear her wonderful stories.

   ____ She made a lovely quilt that hangs in the Smithsonian Institution in Washington, D.C.

3. What main point is made about the story of the quilt in Washington? Circle the letter of your answer.

   (a) Poor people have little time to be creative.

   (b) Poor people can still be creative with everyday things.

   (c) Fame is a terrible thing; it is better for no one to know your name.

   (d) Making quilts is a difficult and tiring household chore.

4. What does the mother's garden seem to represent to Walker? Circle the letter of your answer.

   (a) a work of art where her mother expresses her personal ideas of beauty

   (b) her cultural heritage as an African American

   (c) a place where creative spirit is nurtured or cared for

   (d) all of the above

5. **Literary Analysis:** Based on this **tribute**, list at least four qualities or talents that Walker admires in her mother.

1. _____

2. _____

3. _____

4. _____

6. **Reading Strategy:** Complete the chart below by writing another word with each root and explaining its meaning.

Root	Meaning	Word	Meaning	Word	Meaning
-liter-	letter	literally	To the letter; actually		
-nym-	name	anonymous	With no known name		
-magni-	large	magnitude	large and impressive		

Listening and Speaking

Alice Walker feels that a person can be creative in everyday activities like gardening. Give a **how-to** speech to classmates. In your speech, explain how to do an everyday activity or chore. Try to pick one that you think can be creative.

- Choose an activity or chore that you know.
- Identify the activity or chore at the beginning of your speech. You might say something like, "I am explaining how to _____."
- When you give your speech, explain the activity in steps your classmates can follow. Use words like *first, second, third,* or *next, then, last* to make the order clear.
- On another piece of paper, list the steps in the activity. Then, put a number next to each to show the order in which the steps must be done.

Seventh Grade

Gary Soto

Summary

On his first day of seventh grade, Victor signs up for French because Teresa is taking the class. He hopes Teresa will be his girlfriend this year. In the hallway, he runs into his friend Michael, who is also trying to attract girls. Teresa is in Victor's homeroom but not in his other classes except for French. In their first French class, Victor embarrasses himself by pretending to speak the language. The French teacher is not fooled, but Teresa is. Impressed, she asks Victor to help her with French during the year. Victor happily heads for the library to take out some French textbooks.

Visual Summary

Setting	**Place:** a school in Fresno, California **Time:** the first day of seventh grade

Problem	Victor doesn't know how Teresa feels about him.

Goal	Victor wants Teresa to be his girlfriend this year.

Events
- Victor knows Spanish but signs up for French because Teresa is taking the class.
- In homeroom, Victor makes sure Teresa notices him but is awkward when she says "Hi."
- When his English teacher asks for a noun that names a person, Victor says "Teresa."
- In French class, Victor pretends to know French, though the teacher soon realizes he doesn't.
- Victor is embarrassed and runs off quickly when the bell rings but then must return for a book.

Climax	Teresa is impressed that Victor knows French and asks if he can sometimes help her study. The teacher hears them talking but does not give away Victor's secret.

Conclusion	Victor agrees to help Teresa with French and heads for the library to take out some French books.

LITERARY ANALYSIS

Tone

The **tone** of a work is the attitude the writer expresses. For example, the tone could be serious or humorous. It could be happy or angry or sad. In "Seventh Grade," Gary Soto uses a sympathetic tone to describe Victor and his problems. Soto's tone is also amused at times, as he gently pokes fun at Victor.

His brown face blushed. Why hadn't he said, "Hi, Teresa," or "How was your summer?" or something nice?

As Teresa walked down the hall, Victor walked the other way, looking back, admiring how gracefully she walked, one foot in front of the other.

As you read, look for details that convey Soto's amused but sympathetic tone. List them on a chart like this one.

Sympathetic Tone	Amused Tone
Victor blushes and wonders why he didn't say "something nice"	Victor admires how gracefully Teresa walks, "one foot in front of the other"

READING STRATEGY

Identifying Idioms

An **idiom** is an expression that means something different from the words that make it up. For example, this sentence from "Seventh Grade" uses the idiom *bump into*:

He wanted to leave when she did so he could <u>bump into</u> her and say something clever.

To *bump* is to knock against someone or something. *Bump into* is an idiom that means "meet in a casual or unplanned way."

As you read "Seventh Grade," list other idioms from the story on a chart like this one.

Idiom	What Separate Words Mean	What Idiom Means
bump into	knock against; knock into	meet casually or unexpectedly

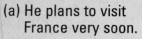
Seventh Grade
Gary Soto

It was the first day of seventh grade for Victor Rodriguez. When he signed up for classes, Victor had a choice about which language to study. Taking Spanish would probably have been easy, since he was of Mexican background. But he signed up for French instead. Victor thought he might like to visit France someday to see the sights and people. He also knew that a girl named Teresa was taking French. He hoped they'd be in the same class.

◆ ◆ ◆

Teresa is going to be my girl this year, he promised himself as he left the gym full of students in their new fall clothes. She was cute.

◆ ◆ ◆

Victor ran into his friend Michael Torres, who looked very strange.

◆ ◆ ◆

"How come you're making a face?" asked Victor.

"I ain't making a face. . . . This *is* my face."

◆ ◆ ◆

Michael explained that he had changed his expression over the summer, after he saw a copy of the men's magazine *GQ*. All of the male models were with beautiful women and had the same look on their faces—in all of the pictures they would <u>scowl</u>. Michael figured that the scowl must somehow be attractive so he decided to copy it.

◆ ◆ ◆

Vocabulary Development

scowl (SKOWL) *v.* to lower the eyebrows and corners of the mouth in an angry or annoyed look

---

"What classes are you taking?" Michael said, scowling.

"French. How 'bout you?"

"Spanish. I ain't so good at it, even if I'm Mexican."

"I'm not either, but I'm better at it than math, that's for sure."

◆ ◆ ◆

As Victor headed to his homeroom, he wondered about Michael's idea. Could making a face make him seem handsome? He tried it and felt silly, until he noticed a girl looking at him. Maybe scowling worked.

◆ ◆ ◆

In homeroom, . . . Victor sat calmly, thinking of Teresa, who sat two rows away, reading a paperback novel. This would be his lucky year. She was in his homeroom, and would probably be in his English and math classes. And, of course, French.

◆ ◆ ◆

When the bell rang, most of the students raced to their first class. But Teresa stayed to talk to the homeroom teacher. Victor lingered too. If he left at the same time Teresa did he could talk to her. He wanted to say something clever to her. So he waited and watched Teresa on the sly.

◆ ◆ ◆

As she turned to leave, he stood up and hurried to the door, where he managed to catch her eye. She smiled and said, "Hi, Victor."

He smiled back and said, "Yeah, that's me." His brown face blushed. Why hadn't he said, "Hi, Teresa," or "How was your summer?"

◆ ◆ ◆

Vocabulary Development

lingered (LING erd) *v.* was slow to leave; continued to stay

---

◆ **Read Aloud**

Read the bracketed conversation aloud. Then, jot down a few things it tells you about Michael and Victor.

Michael:

_____

_____

_____

Victor:

_____

_____

_____

◆ **Think Ahead**

Do you think everything Victor expects to happen *will* happen? Explain here:

_____

_____

_____

◆ **Reading Strategy**

Sly means "sneaky." What do you think the **idiom** "on the sly" means?

on the sly:

_____

Circle another idiom in the next paragraph. Explain its meaning here:

_____

_____

_____

_____

_____

_____

◆ Stop to Reflect

Do you think the scowling works the way Michael thinks it does? Explain your opinion on these lines.

_____

_____

_____

_____

◆ Literary Analysis

Circle at least two details in this passage that you think contribute to Soto's sympathetic, understanding tone.

Victor watched Teresa as she headed toward her next class. He thought she looked graceful as she walked. As it turned out, Teresa was not in Victor's English class. The English teacher began reviewing parts of speech. Victor was called on for an example of a noun that names a person.

◆ ◆ ◆

"Teresa," Victor said <u>automatically</u>.

Some of the girls giggled. They knew he had a crush on Teresa. He felt himself blushing again.

◆ ◆ ◆

After English, Victor had math and then social studies. Teresa was in neither class. At lunchtime, he went to the cafeteria and sat with Michael. Michael practiced his scowl and was excited when some girls noticed him.

Victor wasn't interested in Michael's scowl because he was thinking about Teresa. He didn't see her in the cafeteria. It was possible that she had brought her lunch from home and was eating outside. He decided to go out to the bag lunch area and check it out. Victor opened his math book and pretended to read from it. With his eyes lowered, he looked to the left and didn't see her. Then he looked for her to the right.

◆ ◆ ◆

Still no sign of her. He stretched out lazily in an attempt to disguise his snooping.

Then he saw her. . . . Victor moved to a table near her and daydreamed about taking her to a movie.

◆ ◆ ◆

Vocabulary Development

automatically (aw toh MA tic lee) _adv._ without pausing or thinking

Victor and Teresa went to French class separately. There, the teacher, Mr. Bueller, said hello in French and asked if anyone knew the language. Wanting to impress Teresa, Victor raised his hand, The teacher asked him a question in French. Victor didn't really know French, so he didn't understand the question. What made it worse was that he couldn't answer in French.

◆   ◆   ◆

. . . He tried to bluff his way out by making noises that sounded French.

"La me vave me con le grandma," he said uncertainly.

◆   ◆   ◆

Mr. Bueller asked Victor to speak up.

◆   ◆   ◆

Great rosebushes of red bloomed on Victor's cheeks. . . . He felt awful. Teresa sat a few desks away, no doubt thinking he was a fool.

◆   ◆   ◆

Victor mumbled something else that he thought might sound like French.

◆   ◆   ◆

"Frenchie oh wewe gee in September."

◆   ◆   ◆

But Mr. Bueller realized Victor didn't know French, and turned back to the rest of the class. Mr. Bueller continued with the lesson, but Victor could no longer concentrate. Victor was completely embarrassed and miserable.

When the bell rang, Victor raced from the room, but realized he had forgotten his math book. He had to go back. Mr. Bueller was still there, erasing the board. Teresa was there too. Victor was terrified she would learn the truth.

◆   ◆   ◆

© Pearson Education, Inc.

◆ **Reading Check**

What is funny about Victor's remarks in French? Write your answer:

_____

_____

_____

_____

Circle the words before these remarks that told you what was funny about them.

In exchange for Victor's help in French, what subject could Teresa help Victor with? Write it here: _____

What do you predict will happen when Victor helps Teresa with French?

_____

_____

_____

_____

Circle the words that show what caused the "rosebushes" on Victor's face in the first place and what causes them now. Why does Soto call them rosebushes? Circle the answer.

(a) Victor has broken skin, just like you'd get from thorns on a rosebush.

(b) Victor's cologne is sweet smelling, like a rose.

(c) The whole situation is romantic.

(d) Roses are usually red or deep pink, like Victor's cheeks.

Why does Victor go to the library for French textbooks?

_____

_____

_____

"I didn't know you knew French," she said. "That was good."

◆　◆　◆

Victor tried to send a message to Mr. Bueller with his eyes. Victor silently begged his teacher not to let Teresa know that he didn't know French. Mr. Bueller seemed to get Victor's message. Better yet, he seemed to understand the situation. He said nothing. Victor's situation brought back Mr. Bueller's own embarrassing moments from his own past. As Mr. Bueller thought about a time when he had tried to impress a new girl-friend, Teresa asked Victor if he would help her with her French.

◆　◆　◆

"Sure, anytime," Victor said. "I won't be bothering you, will I?" "Oh, no. I like being bothered."

◆　◆　◆

The two left together and stopped out-side Teresa's next class. She smiled and said "Bonjour," the term for "good day" that Mr. Bueller had taught them.

◆　◆　◆

"Yeah, right, *bonjour*," Victor said. . . . The rosebushes of shame on his face became bou-quets of love. Teresa is a great girl, he thought. And Mr. Bueller is a good guy.

◆　◆　◆

Victor's happiness caused him to sprint to his next two classes. After he left school that day, he raced to the public library. He was in a hurry to check out some French textbooks so he could help Teresa with her French.

◆　◆　◆

He was going to like seventh grade.

Vocabulary Development

sprint (SPRINT) *n.* a race or run at full speed

1. Write a reason for each of these story events.

Event	Reason
Victor signs up for French.	_____
Victor is slow to leave homeroom.	_____
Victor goes outside during lunch.	_____
Victor pretends to know French.	_____
Victor gets French books at the library.	_____

2. List at least three times in the story when Victor feels embarrassed or ashamed.

   1. _____

   2. _____

   3. _____

3. What impression does the story give of seventh grade? Answer by completing this sentence.

   Seventh grade is a time of _____

   _____

   _____

4. **Literary Analysis:** List six details from the story that illustrate Soto's amused but understanding tone.

Amused	Understanding
_____	_____
_____	_____
_____	_____

(Continued)

5. **Reading Strategy:** On the lines below, define these **idioms** from the story.

making a face:

_____

_____

catch her eye:

_____

_____

Writing

Victor is just starting seventh grade. On a separate paper, write a paragraph about seventh grade that might be helpful to someone like Victor. Explain what seventh grade is like by comparing and contrasting it to sixth grade.

- List several similarities and differences between sixth and seventh grade. They can be about schoolwork, social life, or any other similarity or difference that you think is important.

6th grade	7th grade
_____	_____
_____	_____
_____	_____
_____	_____

- Make a general statement about how seventh grade is like or unlike sixth grade. For example: Seventh grade is like sixth grade, only more fun. Or: Seventh grade is much harder than sixth grade. Or: In seventh grade, you are on your own more than in sixth grade. _____

_____

- Use your general statement to open your paragraph. Then, support that statement with some of the similarities and differences you listed.

Melting Pot
Anna Quindlen

Summary

The author describes her New York City neighborhood as a mixture of different ethnic and social groups. She sees the idea of the American melting pot existing where she lives, but only on a person-to-person level. In groups, the people often don't get along, but as individuals they usually do.

Visual Summary

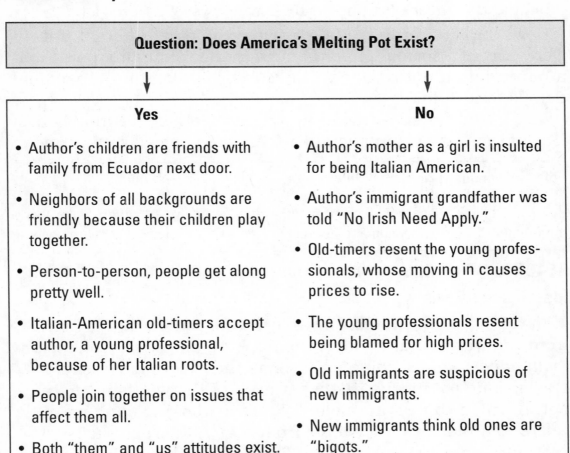

Question: Does America's Melting Pot Exist?

Yes

- Author's children are friends with family from Ecuador next door.

- Neighbors of all backgrounds are friendly because their children play together.

- Person-to-person, people get along pretty well.

- Italian-American old-timers accept author, a young professional, because of her Italian roots.

- People join together on issues that affect them all.

- Both "them" and "us" attitudes exist.

No

- Author's mother as a girl is insulted for being Italian American.

- Author's immigrant grandfather was told "No Irish Need Apply."

- Old-timers resent the young professionals, whose moving in causes prices to rise.

- The young professionals resent being blamed for high prices.

- Old immigrants are suspicious of new immigrants.

- New immigrants think old ones are "bigots."

- Looked at in broad strokes, the neighborhood is a pressure cooker of groups who don't always mix well.

Conclusion: Melting pot exists person to person but not group to group

LITERARY ANALYSIS

Tone

Tone is the attitude a writer expresses in a work. For instance, the writer's tone might be serious or lighthearted, angry or joyful, happy or sad. In "Melting Pot," Anna Quindlen uses an informal tone to explore her subject. To understand how she creates that tone, read this passage:

> It took awhile. Eight years ago we were the new people on the block. . . . We thought we could feel people staring at us from behind the sheer curtains on their windows. We were right.

Now, think about how the passage would be different if it were part of a formal paper about America's melting pot. Such a paper would not be likely to use informal language, personal details, and humor.

As you read Quindlen's essay, look for more details that convey her informal tone. You might list them on a chart like this one.

Informal Language	Personal Details	Humor
It took awhile; on the block	personal experiences eight years ago; how she and her family felt	"We were right"—the neighbors are nosey

READING STRATEGY

Identifying Idioms

An **idiom** is an expression that means something different from the words that make it up. An example is the expression *melting pot*, which Quindlen uses as the title of her essay. A real *melting pot* means just what each of the words mean, a pot in which things are melted. But the idiom *melting pot* refers to a place where people from many different backgrounds come together in a unified way. With people from all over the world coming to its shores and becoming American citizens, the United States itself is often called a *melting pot*.

Idiom	What Separate Words Mean	What Idiom Means
melting pot	a container in which things are heated until they melt	a country or an area where people of many backgrounds join or blend together

Melting Pot
Anna Quindlen

In Anna Quindlen's New York City neighborhood, there are people who came to America from all over the world. Right now, her children are next door having dinner with a family from the Spanish-speaking nation of Ecuador.

♦ ♦ ♦

The father speaks some English, the mother less than that. The two daughters are <u>fluent</u> in both their native and their adopted languages but the youngest child, a son, a close friend of my two boys, speaks almost no Spanish.

♦ ♦ ♦

The boy's parents want him to speak English instead of Spanish because he is an American, living in an American city. Quindlen isn't surprised at how the parents feel because her mother was raised as an American—speaking English—among Italians in her family.

Yet Quindlen wonders if America really is a melting pot where people of different backgrounds join together. Her mother was called nasty names when she was a girl—simply for being Italian American. When Quindlen's Irish grandfather first came to America and looked for work, signs said "No Irish Need Apply." Quindlen still sees dislike and suspicion among different groups in

---

Vocabulary Development

fluent (FLOO ent) *adj.* able to write or speak easily and smoothly

---

© Pearson Education, Inc.

Number the four
neighborhood groups in
this paragraph 1, 2, 3,
and 4. What do the
details here suggest
about people in
general?

(a) They usually get along.

(b) They find change difficult.

(c) They welcome newcomers.

(d) They are all bigots.

Why do you think the old-timers
find the author different from
the other young professionals
moving into the neighborhood?

_____

_____

her neighborhood. For instance, the old-timers are suspicious of the new moneyed professionals. They think they are taking over. At the same time the professionals think that everyone in the neighborhood blames them for rising rents. In fact, they are the ones that are moving in and having to pay the high rents.

♦   ♦   ♦

The old immigrants are suspicious of the new ones. The new ones think the old ones are bigots.

♦   ♦   ♦

Yet on a person-to-person level, members of all these groups usually get along. Quindlen herself is friendly with neighbors of many backgrounds simply because her children play with theirs. She recalls that their friendliness didn't happen overnight. When she and her family moved in they thought people were watching them. The old-timers of the neighborhood were, indeed, watching them.

♦   ♦   ♦

Eight years ago we were the new people on the block.

♦   ♦   ♦

Quindlen recalls her first New York apartment in an old Italian American neighborhood where young professionals were moving in. Though she too was a young professional, the old-timers accepted her because of her Italian background.

♦   ♦   ♦

Vocabulary Development

professionals (pro FESH uh nuhlz) *n.* people whose jobs require advanced education and training
bigots (BIG ots) *n.* very narrow-minded, prejudiced people

I remember sitting . . . with a group of half a dozen elderly men, . . . watching a glazier[1] install a great spread of tiny glass panes to make one wall of a restaurant.

♦ ♦ ♦

The men were convinced that the window panes soon would be broken and the restaurant wouldn't last. Despite their predictions, the restaurant became busy and successful. Two years later, all but three of the men had moved or died. The remaining men still sat and watched the restaurant. But now they <u>dolefully</u> watched people waiting in line to eat there. Quindlen even ate at the restaurant. However, the old men didn't have hard feelings toward Quindlen because she ate there. They said she wasn't one of "them."

♦ ♦ ♦

It's an argument familiar to members of almost any <u>embattled</u> race or class: I like you, therefore you aren't like the rest of your kind, whom I hate.

♦ ♦ ♦

The neighborhood where Quindlen now lives has also changed. Not only young professionals but also many new immigrant groups have arrived. She doesn't think change comes easy to people in America. However, she notes that change is constant. Some people deal with it better than others. The antiques store used to be the butcher shop—the butcher now sits sadly outside the pizzeria[2] because his shop is gone. Quindlen

Literary Analysis

Do you think the writer likes or dislikes the men in the bracketed passage? Explain your answer.

_____

_____

_____

_____

Vocabulary Development

dolefully (DOHL ful lee) *adv.* sadly; glumly
embattled (em BAT ld) *adj.* in conflict; forced to fight

. **glazier** (GLA zher) *n.* a person who cuts and installs glass.
2. **pizzeria** (PEETS uh REE uh) *n.* pizza shop.

Label the three views of squid—as calamari, as sushi, and as bait—with the letter of the group who views the squid that way:
(a) Italian American old-timers; (b) young professionals; (c) groups who would never eat squid and would only use it to catch other fish. How does the sentence about the squid contribute to the tone of the selection? Circle the letter or your answer.

(a) It is the author's personal experience.

(b) It expresses strong personal feeling.

(c) It uses informal language.

(d) It adds humor.

Think about how the underlined idioms are used in the selection. Then, circle the correct meaning of the idiom from the two choices given.

1. drawn in broad strokes: swimming very hard or described in a general way

2. pressure cooker: a very tense place or a place where groups blend

3. oil and water: two things that go together or two things that don't mix easily

sees the changes reflected in the types of stores and the items they sell.

♦ ♦ ♦

About a third of the people in the neighborhood think of squid as calamari,[3] about a third think of it as sushi,[4] and about a third think of it as bait.

♦ ♦ ♦

Quindlen thinks the neighborhood has reached a nice mix. People get along, even if there are still some tensions.

♦ ♦ ♦

Drawn in broad strokes, we live in a pressure cooker: oil and water, us and them.

♦ ♦ ♦

The groups of people are still different. And their differences can cause problems. At times, however, people from all the different groups gather together to complain about things they have in common. If they can agree, they can get along.

♦ ♦ ♦

We melt together, then draw apart. I am the granddaughter of immigrants, a young professional—either an interloper or a longtime resident. . . . I am one of them, and one of us.

Vocabulary Development

interloper (IN ter LOP er) *n.* someone who intrudes on another's rights or territory

---

3. **calamari** (KAL uh MAR ee) *n.* squid cooked as food, especially in Italian dishes.
4. **sushi** (SOO she) *n.* Japanese rice cakes cooked with vegetables and seafood, including squid.

1. On the lines, explain what people mean when they call America a melting pot.

_____

_____

_____

_____

2. According to Quindlen, when is her neighborhood most like a melting pot? Put a check in front of the correct answer.

____ It is most like a melting pot when people deal with each other person-to-person.

____ It is most like a melting pot when people deal with each other group-to-group.

3. On the lines below, list the main groups in conflict in the neighborhood. Choose from these groups: old-timers, old immigrants, new immigrants, young professionals.

_____ vs. _____

_____ vs. _____

4. Explain how Anna Quindlen belongs to at least three of the four groups listed in item 3.

_____

_____

_____

_____

_____

(Continued)

5. **Reading Strategy:** Read this sentence from the selection. Then, explain the meaning of the underlined **idiom**.

The old-timers are angry because they think the new moneyed professionals are <u>taking over</u> their town.

taking over: _____

6. **Literary Analysis:** List two examples of each of these four kinds of details that convey Quindlen's informal **tone**.

personal experiences:

1. _____ 2. _____

personal feelings:

1. _____ 2. _____

informal language:

1. _____ 2. _____

humor:

1. _____ 2. _____

Listening and Speaking

Imagine that a neighborhood group is trying to solve a problem between two residents. With other students, role-play the meeting of such a group.

- Think of a situation or problem that has two sides—for example, a disagreement over building something, where one person wants to build it and one person doesn't.
- Two students, both pretending to be local residents, should present each side of the issue.
- The rest of your group should act as the neighborhood group's board members. The board should ask the residents questions to learn more information. The board should then discuss the situation among themselves and try to come up with a solution to the problem.

The Hummingbird That Lived Through Winter

William Saroyan

Summary

Old Dikran, an Armenian immigrant to California, is nearly blind. One cold winter day, he finds a hummingbird. Though the bird is near death, he nurses it back to health and lets it go. The narrator is not sure if the bird survives the rest of winter. However, the next summer, the narrator sees many hummingbirds. Old Dikran says that each of them is the hummingbird they saved.

Visual Summary

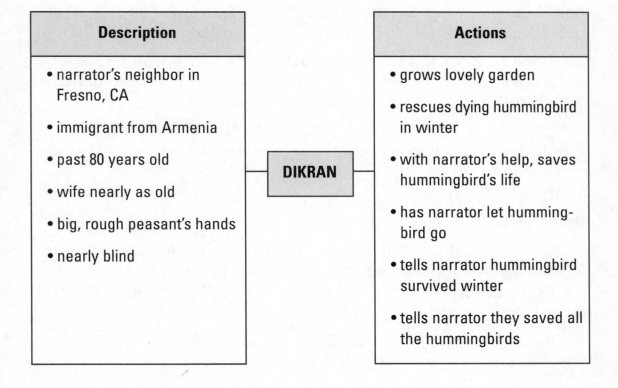

Description	Actions
• narrator's neighbor in Fresno, CA • immigrant from Armenia • past 80 years old • wife nearly as old • big, rough peasant's hands • nearly blind	• grows lovely garden • rescues dying hummingbird in winter • with narrator's help, saves hummingbird's life • has narrator let hummingbird go • tells narrator hummingbird survived winter • tells narrator they saved all the hummingbirds

DIKRAN

LITERARY ANALYSIS

Symbol

A **symbol** is something that conveys an idea or meaning beyond what it actually is. For example, a dove actually is a bird. However, it often conveys the idea of peace. When it does, it is a symbol.

A symbol does not always stand for just one thing. Sometimes a symbol can stand for several ideas at once. Sometimes the same symbol means different things to different readers.

To understand what a symbol means, you need to look at the details about it. In Saroyan's story, the hummingbird is a symbol. It has been near death, but later it takes on a new life:

It spun about in the little kitchen, going to the window, coming back to the heat, suspending, circling as if it were summertime and it had never felt better in its whole life.

As you read, list all the details about the hummingbird. Then, decide on its meaning as a symbol.

READING STRATEGY

Using Word Parts

One way to figure out the meaning of an unfamiliar word is to look for a part you recognize. The familiar part can give you a clue to the meaning of the whole word. For example, consider the word *guardian* in the story.

Plants, bushes, trees—all strong, in sweet black moist earth whose <u>guardian</u> was old Dikran.

As you read the story, underline unfamiliar words and circle the parts that help you figure out their meanings. Keep track of the words and their meanings on a chart like this one.

Unfamiliar Word	Familiar Part	Meaning of Part	Probable Meaning of Word
guardian	guard	to watch over; to take care of	someone who watches over; a caretaker

The Hummingbird That Lived Through Winter

William Saroyan

Old Dikran (DEEK ran) was once a peasant, or poor farmer, in the southeastern European nation of Armenia. After fleeing hardship in his homeland, he settled with his wife in a California neighborhood where many other Armenian Americans live. The boy who tells the story lives just across the street and is also of Armenian background. He recalls a winter day when his neighbor old Dikran made an unusual discovery.

◆ ◆ ◆

There was a hummingbird once which in the wintertime did not leave our neighborhood in Fresno, California.

◆ ◆ ◆

As the narrator, the boy begins to tell the story. Dikran and his wife are about eighty years old. Old Dikran can hardly see. The couple keep a neat house—inside and outside. Dikran has a wild and wonderful garden with all kinds of plants, bushes and trees. He looks after his garden with care. Everything that flies in the sky comes to this place. It is a special spot in the poor neighborhood in which they live. Dikran loves the creatures that came to his garden.

One of these creatures from the sky is a hummingbird that has managed to survive into winter. This is unusual, because hummingbirds are creatures of summer who do not take to winter's cold.

◆ ◆ ◆

One freezing Sunday, in the dead of winter, as I came home from Sunday School, I saw old Dikran standing in the middle of the street.

◆ ◆ ◆

◆ **Stop to Reflect**

Many immigrants choose to live in areas where others from their homeland have settled. List one reason this is a good idea and one reason it is not.

Good Point:

_____

_____

_____

Bad Point:

_____

_____

_____

◆ **Reading Check**

What sort of garden does Dikran have? Circle the words that tell you.

Then, circle the things below that you think come to his garden.

birds   butterflies   airplanes

bees   helicopters   balloons

Read aloud the explanation of
what a hummingbird is in the
bracketed paragraph. What
other questions do you have
about the bird's appearance or
behavior? Write one:

_____

_____

_____

_____

Circle three details
describing a humming-
bird in summer and
box three contrasting
words that describe
the bird now. Based
on these contrasts, what might
the hummingbird be a **symbol**
of? Circle the letter of your
answer.

(a) the joys of both summer and
winter

(b) luck or good fortune

(c) the wonder and beauty of
nature

(d) the fragile or delicate nature
of life

Dikran holds out his hand to the boy.
Speaking in Armenian, he asks the boy what
is in his hand. The boy looks and tells Dikran
that it's a hummingbird. Dikran is not familiar with the English word and too blind to
see the bird itself. The boy describes a hummingbird to old Dikran. He tells him it is the
little summer bird with wings that beat fast.
He says it "stands in the air" before it
"shoots away." He also tells Dikran that the
bird is dying.

Because Dikran's wife is still at church,
he asks the boy to help him care for the bird.
He has the boy look at the bird again and
report its condition.

◆ ◆ ◆

It was a sad thing to <u>behold</u>. This wonderful
little creature of summertime in the big rough
hand of the old peasant. Here it was the cold of
winter, absolutely helpless and <u>pathetic</u>, not
<u>suspended</u> in a <u>shaft</u> of summer light.

◆ ◆ ◆

Again, the boy tells the old man that the
bird is dying. Old Dikran gently blows warm
breath on the bird he cannot see. He speaks
to the bird in Armenian, reassuring the bird
that it is not long until summer.

He heads for his kitchen, where he has
the boy warm some honey on the stove and
put the honey in his hand. Soon the hummingbird begins to recover. The dying bird is
showing new signs of life.

◆ ◆ ◆

Vocabulary Development

behold (bee HOLD) _v._ to see
pathetic (pa THET ic) _n._ causing pity, sorrow, or sympathy;
very sad
suspended (sus PEND ed) _adj._ hanging in the air
shaft (SHAFT) _n._ a column of light; a beam

The warmth of the room, the <u>vapor</u> of the warm honey—and, well, the will and love of the old man.

◆ ◆ ◆

As the hummingbird begins to eat the honey, Old Dikran declares that it will live. He urges the boy to stay and watch what happens. The boy is amazed by the change in the bird.

◆ ◆ ◆

It spun about in the little kitchen, going to the window, coming back to the heat.

◆ ◆ ◆

The bird circles and flies as though it is outside on a summer's day. It also seems far from dying now. The old man sits in his plain chair, paying careful attention to what is happening, even though he cannot see. The boy describes the bird's behavior.

◆ ◆ ◆

When the bird was <u>restless</u> and wanted to go, the old man said, "Open the window and let it go."

◆ ◆ ◆

The boy is unsure. He asks whether the bird will live if it goes outside. Old Dikran announces that the bird is alive now. He points out to the boy that it wants to go outside. Then he commands the boy to open the window for it to fly out.

When the boy opens the window, the bird seems to test the cold air a bit and then flies off. The boy closes the window and talks a little more with Dikran before going home. Dikran continues to claim that the hummingbird lived through winter. The boy isn't so sure.

◆ **Literary Analysis**

Circle at least one detail in this passage that suggests the hummingbird may be a **symbol** of hope.

◆ **Reading Strategy**

The word part -*less* often means "without." Draw a line to break the word *restless* into two parts. Then, use the **word parts** to help you figure out the meaning of the full word. Write it here.

restless:

_____

_____

Vocabulary Development

vapor (VAY pur) *n.* mist or steam floating in the air

Do you think the hummingbird will live? Make a prediction and then explain it.

_____

_____

_____

◆ **Stop to Reflect**

What do you think Dikran means in the last paragraph of the story? Write your ideas on these lines.

_____

_____

_____

_____

When summer comes, the boy sees hummingbirds about but can't tell them apart. Finally he again asks Dikran if the bird lived. Dikran tells the boy to look around. He then asks the boy if he sees the bird.

◆ ◆ ◆

"I see humming*birds*," I said.

"Each of them is our bird," the old man said. "Each of them, each of them," he said swiftly and gently.

1. On the lines, list three things that Dikran or the boy do for the ailing hummingbird.

   - _____

   - _____

   - _____

2. Why do you think Dikran wants the bird freed even though the winter cold might kill it?

   _____

   _____

3. Put a check in front of each statement that you think applies to Dikran.

   ____ He can barely see.

   ____ He is very wealthy.

   ____ He loves and respects nature.

   ____ He respects the freedom of living things.

   ____ He has a dark, negative view of the future.

4. **Literary Analysis:** Check the ideas on the left that you think the hummingbird might be a **symbol** of. Then, on the right, explain why the bird might be a symbol of each idea you checked.

Checklist of Possible Symbols	Explanation
____ hope or renewal	
____ the fragile or delicate nature of life	
____ youth and old age	
____ the beauty and wonder of nature	
____ human selfishness and greed	

(Continued)

5. **Reading Strategy:** Use the **word parts** to help you explain the meaning of these words from the story.

hummingbird:

_____

helpless:

_____

heartbreaking:

_____

Writing

A **database** is a catalog of information for use on a computer. Prepare a database of at least ten works about birds or other animals.

- Include the same information for each work, and put it in the same place. Follow this model.

Model Database Record
Title of Work:

Type of Work:	Encyclopedia ☐	Quality:	Excellent ☐
	Book ☐		Good ☐
	Magazine ☐		Poor ☐
	Other ☐		

Summary:

- For *Type of Work*, indicate whether the work is a movie, book, story, poem, or true story. Try to list at least two examples of each of these types.

- For *Quality*, indicate whether you think the work is excellent, good, fair, or poor.

- For *Summary*, tell what the work is about in a sentence or two.

The Third Wish

Joan Aiken

Summary

One evening, while driving through a forest, Mr. Peters discovers a swan tangled in a bush. He frees the swan, who turns into a little man, the King of the Forest. The King agrees to grant Mr. Peters three wishes and gives him three leaves to wish on. He warns that people who use wishes often end up worse off than before. Mr. Peters wants very little, and he is aware of the trouble wishes often bring. But he is lonely, so he decides to wish for a beautiful wife. His wish is granted with the arrival of Leita, a former swan, whom he then marries. But Leita misses her swan's life and her swan sister Rhea. And in time Mr. Peters realizes that Leita will never be happy as a human being. So he uses his second wish to turn her back into a swan. He and the two swans remain close. Those who know his situation are surprised that he never uses his third wish to ask for another wife. But he says that two wishes are enough for him, and that he prefers to stay true to Leita. One morning he is found dead with a smile on his face and a leaf and white feather in his hands.

Visual Summary

1

It is a spring evening.
Mr. Peters is driving through the forest.

2

Mr. Peters hears a noise.
He rescues a swan tangled in bushes.
The swan turns into the King of the Forest.
He gives Mr. Peters three magical leaves that will grant three wishes.
Mr. Peters wishes for a wife.
The next day he gets a wife who was once a swan.
She loves him but desperately misses her old life and swan sister.

3

Mr. Peters uses his second wish to turn his wife back into a swan.

4

The wife joins her swan sister.
The two stay close with Mr. Peters.
He says two wishes are enough and won't wish for another wife.

5

Mr. Peters is found dead in bed with a smile on his face and the third leaf and a white feather in his hands.

LITERARY ANALYSIS

Modern Fairy Tale

Fairy tales are stories that often include one or more of these:

- imaginary creatures, such as fairies, elves, giants, and ogres (monsters)
- animals with unusual abilities, such as being able to talk
- wishes that come true and other magic
- mysterious and fantastic events

Most fairy tales take place a long time ago and were written long ago as well. But in more recent times, some writers have created **modern fairy tales**. They combine the elements of fairy tales with aspects of modern life. In "The Third Wish," for example, Mr. Peters meets a magical creature in the forest. He meets that creature while driving through the forest in a car.

As you read, list the elements of this modern fairy tale on a chart like the one below. On the left, list elements like those in a regular fairy tale. On the right, list the details about modern life from "The Third Wish."

Fairy-Tale Elements	Modern Elements
Mr. Peters encounters the magical King of the Forest.	Mr. Peters drives a car through the forest.

READING STRATEGY

Clarifying Word Meanings

Often when you are reading, you will come across words with confusing or unclear meanings. To **clarify word meanings**, or make their meanings clear to you, look for clues in nearby words and sentences. Take this example from "The Third Wish":

The only thing that troubled him was that he was a little lonely, and had no <u>companion</u> for his old age.

The word *companion* may be unfamiliar, but the surrounding words and phrases give clues to its meaning. They indicate that a *companion* will stop the man from being lonely. So *companion* probably means "someone to be with" or "someone who keeps you company."

The Third Wish
Joan Aiken

One evening in early spring, Mr. Peters was driving through the forest. As he came to a stretch of empty road, he heard an odd cry.

◆ ◆ ◆

He left his car and climbed the mossy bank beside the road. . . . As he neared the bushes he saw something white among them which was trying to <u>extricate</u> itself; coming closer he found that it was a swan that had become entangled in the thorns growing on the bank of the canal.

◆ ◆ ◆

When he tried to help, the swan hissed and pecked at him. Still, Mr. Peters managed to untangle it.

◆ ◆ ◆

. . . And in a moment, instead of the great white bird, there was a little man all in green with a golden crown and long beard, standing by the water.

◆ ◆ ◆

The little green man did not seem grateful to be rescued. Instead, he spoke in a threatening way.

◆ ◆ ◆

"You think that because you have rescued—by pure good <u>fortune</u>—the King of the Forest from a difficulty, you should have some fabulous reward."

"I expect three wishes, no more and no less," answered Mr. Peters. . . .

"Three wishes he wants, the clever man! Well, I have yet to hear of the human being who made any good use of his three wishes—they mostly

---

◆ **Reading Strategy**

Circle the letter of the correct meaning of *extricate*.

(a) untangle   (b) scratch

(c) grow thickly   (d) entertain

Now, circle the nearby word or words that helped you figure out the meaning of *extricate*.

◆ **Literary Analysis**

This **modern fairy tale** includes an imaginary creature similar to those in old fairy tales. Circle the words that show this creature is something like an elf. What fantastic and mysterious fairy-tale event has happened to him?

_____

_____

_____

◆ **Literary Analysis**

Think about Mr. Peters's behavior in this **modern fairy tale**. Why does he expect three wishes? Do characters in regular fairy tales usually know what to expect? Write your answers on the lines.

_____

_____

_____

end up worse off than they started. Take your three wishes then"—he flung three dead leaves in the air—"don't blame me if you spend the last wish undoing the work of the other two."

◆ ◆ ◆

Mr. Peters caught the leaves and put them in his briefcase. He spent some time thinking about what his wishes should be. He knew the stories of wishes being granted only to bring trouble to those who made them. He wanted to avoid that. Besides, he didn't need many things.

◆ ◆ ◆

The only thing that troubled him was that he was a little lonely, and had no companion for his old age. He decided to use his first wish and to keep the other two in case of an emergency. . . .

◆ ◆ ◆

Holding one of the leaves, Mr. Peters looked at the forest all around him and made his wish:

◆ ◆ ◆

"I wish I had a wife as beautiful as the forest." A tremendous quacking and splashing broke out on the surface of the water. He thought that it was the swan laughing at him.

◆ ◆ ◆

Mr. Peters ignored the noise, returned to his car, and went to sleep in it. When he awoke, it was morning.

◆ ◆ ◆

Coming along the track towards him was the most beautiful woman he had ever seen, with eyes as blue-green as the canal, hair as dusky as the bushes, and skin as white as the feathers of swans.

"Are you the wife that I wished for?" asked Mr. Peters.

"Yes, I am," she replied. "My name is Leita."

◆ ◆ ◆

◆ **Reading Check**

Circle and number the two reasons that Mr. Peters decides to wish for a wife.

Mark the Text

◆ **Literary Analysis**

What **fairy-tale** event happens to Mr. Peters?

_____

_____

_____

_____

Leita and Mr. Peters drove to a nearby church to get married. He then took her to his home in a lovely valley. She was especially glad to see a river nearby.

◆ ◆ ◆

"Do swans come up there?" she asked.
"Yes. I have often seen swans there on the river," he told her, and she smiled.

◆ ◆ ◆

Leita was a good and loving wife. But as time passed, Mr. Peters saw that she was not really happy. She wandered around outside and sometimes disappeared with no explanation. One evening he saw her down by the river, hugging a swan and crying. Tears rolled from the swan's eyes too.

◆ ◆ ◆

"Leita, what is it?" he asked, very troubled.
"This is my sister," she answered. "I can't bear being separated from her."
Now he understood that Leita was really a swan from the forest, and this made him very sad because when a human being marries a bird it always leads to sorrow.

◆ ◆ ◆

He offered to use his second wish to give Leita's sister human form. Then the two sisters could be companions.

◆ ◆ ◆

"No, no," she cried. "I couldn't ask that of her."
"Is it so very hard to be a human being?" asked Mr. Peters sadly.
"Very, very hard," she answered.
"Don't you love me at all, Leita?"
"Yes, I do. I do love you," she said, and there were tears in her eyes again. "But I miss the old life in the forest. . . ."

◆ ◆ ◆

Mr. Peters then offered to turn Leita back into a swan again. But she refused.

◆ ◆ ◆

◆ **Stop to Reflect**

Why do you think Leita likes living near the river and asks this question? _____

_____

_____

_____

◆ **Literary Analysis**

A character in an old fairy tale would probably not have this thought. Why would a character in a **modern fairy tale** know this?

(a) He knows more about science.

(b) He knows more about nature.

(c) He knows more about marriage.

(d) He knows more about what happens in fairy tales.

"No, I could not be as unkind to you as that. I am partly a swan, but I am also partly a human being now. I will stay with you."

Poor Mr. Peters . . . did his best to make her life happier, taking her for drives in the car, finding beautiful music for her to listen to on the radio, buying clothes for her and even suggesting a trip around the world. But she said no to that; she would prefer to stay in their own house near the river.

◆ ◆ ◆

Mr. Peters built his wife a special seat down by the river so that she could spend more time with her sister. But Leita still continued to grow thin and pale. One night her husband found her weeping in her sleep and calling out:

◆ ◆ ◆

"Rhea! Rhea! I can't understand what you say! Oh, wait for me, take me with you!"

Then he knew that it was hopeless and she would never be happy as a human. He stooped down and kissed her goodbye, then took another leaf from his notecase, blew it out of the window, and used up his second wish.

◆ ◆ ◆

Mr. Peters used his second wish to turn Leita back into a swan. He brought her down to the river. After resting her head lightly on his hand, she flew away. Mr. Peters heard a nasty laugh behind him and turned to find the old King there.

◆ ◆ ◆

"Well, my friend! You don't seem to have managed so wonderfully with your first two wishes, do you? What will you do with the last? Turn yourself into a swan? Or turn Leita back into a girl?"

"I shall do neither," said Mr. Peters calmly. "Human beings and swans are better in their own shapes."

◆ ◆ ◆

After that, Mr. Peters was often seen spending time with two swans. One swan wore a gold chain just like a chain he had given Leita. Some people were a little afraid of him. Others were amazed at how happy he seemed. Sometimes people who knew his story would ask why he didn't use his last wish for another wife.

◆　◆　◆

"Not likely," he would answer <u>serenely</u>. "Two wishes were enough for me. . . . I've learned that even if your wishes are granted they don't always better you. I'll stay faithful to Leita."

◆　◆　◆

One autumn night, people heard the sad song of two swans at Mr. Peters' home.

◆　◆　◆

In the morning Mr. Peters was found peacefully dead in his bed with a smile of great happiness on his face. In his hands, which lay clasped on his breast, were a <u>withered</u> leaf and a white feather.

Did Mr. Peters ever use his third wish? Write *yes* or *no*: _____

Now, circle the detail in the last paragraph that tells you the answer to this question.

Vocabulary Development

serenely (suh REEN lee) *adv.*　peacefully
withered (WITH erd) *adj.*　dried up; wrinkled

1. What does Mr. Peters do to get the three wishes? Write your answer on the line.

   _____

2. What seems to be the attitude of the King of the Forest? Circle the best answer.

   (a) He seems grateful to be rescued.

   (b) He seems fed up with granting wishes and makes fun of human beings.

   (c) He feels deep sympathy and pity when Mr. Peters loses his wife.

   (d) He is devoted to nature and all its creatures.

3. Why do you think Mr. Peters was smiling when he died? Answer on the lines below.

   _____

   _____

4. Which of these points do you think the story makes? Check more than one.

   _____ We are never comfortable when we try to be what we are not.

   _____ Love will always be enough to keep a marriage together.

   _____ Love sometimes means letting go so that the person you love can do what makes him or her happy.

   _____ It is selfish and wrong to wish for things.

   _____ What we wish for does not always turn out the way we expected.

   _____ There are many different kinds of love.

5. **Literary Analysis:** List at least three details in each column to show that the story displays the elements of a **modern fairy tale**.

Fairy-Tale Elements	Details of Modern Life
_____	_____
_____	_____
_____	_____
_____	_____

6. **Reading Strategy: Clarify word meanings** by using nearby words to figure out the meaning of each underlined word. Then circle the letter of the correct meaning from the choices given.

- *He left his car and climbed the mossy* <u>bank</u> *beside the road.*

   bank:
   (a) a place where money is kept (c) a roadway
   (b) to save money in such a place (d) the side of a road or waterway

- *Coming along the track towards him was the most beautiful woman he had ever seen, with eyes as blue-green as the canal, hair as* <u>dusky</u> *as the bushes, and skin as white as the feathers of swans.*

   dusky:
   (a) plain   (b) blue-green   (c) dark   (d) light

Writing

Choose "Cinderella," "Jack and the Beanstalk," "Little Red Riding Hood," or any other fairy tale you know. Then, in a paragraph or two, retell it as a modern fairy tale.
- Keep the basic plot, but make the events and settings more modern. For example, instead of a ball, Cinderella might go to a line dance or a night club.
- Keep the main characters, but make their backgrounds and experiences more modern. For example, Little Red Riding Hood might be a fourth-grade student.
- Keep the fairy-tale elements, though you can change details about them. For example, Jack would still grow a beanstalk from magic beans, but he might order them over the Internet.

The Charge of the Light Brigade
Alfred, Lord Tennyson

Summary

Six hundred lightly armed British troops on horseback attack an enemy position. Since the enemy are heavily armed with cannon, the British soldiers know that something was wrong with their orders. Still, they follow their orders bravely, as good soldiers do. Many are killed, but their courage will be honored always.

Visual Summary

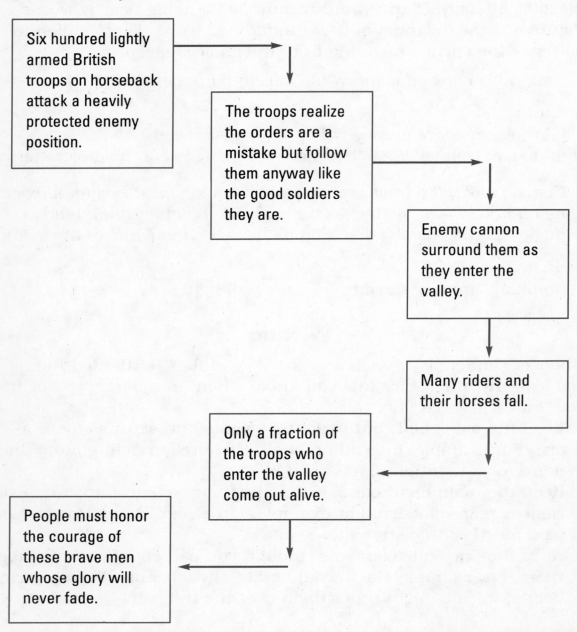

Six hundred lightly armed British troops on horseback attack a heavily protected enemy position.

The troops realize the orders are a mistake but follow them anyway like the good soldiers they are.

Enemy cannon surround them as they enter the valley.

Many riders and their horses fall.

Only a fraction of the troops who enter the valley come out alive.

People must honor the courage of these brave men whose glory will never fade.

LITERARY ANALYSIS

Repetition

Repetition is the repeated use of the words or sounds. Poets use repetition to add to the music of their poems. Repetition also stresses ideas and helps create a mood or atmosphere. Read aloud these famous lines about the soldiers in "The Charge of the Light Brigade":

> *Theirs not to make reply,*
> *Theirs not to reason why,*
> *Theirs but to do and die.*

The repetition in this example helps create the musical rhythm in the poem. It also stresses the idea that the soldiers had no say in the decision to attack.

As you read, look for other examples of repetition. List them on a chart like this one.

Example of Repetition	What It Does
theirs not to/theirs not to/ theirs but to	adds to musical rhythm; stresses the idea that the soldiers have no say in the decision to attack

READING STRATEGY

Using Word Parts

You can use **word parts** to help you understand the meanings of related words. For example, take these lines from "The Charge of the Light Brigade":

> *Half a league, half a league,*
> *Half a league <u>onward</u>,*

You may not know what *onward* means, but you probably recognize its parts. The word part -*ward*- appears in common words like *forward*, *toward*, and *backward*. -*ward*- clearly has something to do with movement. One meaning of *on* is "ahead" (as in "move *on* to the next topic"). So you can figure out that *onward* probably means "move ahead; go forward."

As you read, look for other words whose parts are familiar. Figure out what they mean from their parts.

The Charge of the Light Brigade
Alfred, Lord Tennyson

Circle examples of **repetition** in these lines. What sound is Tennyson most likely trying to imitate with his repeated rhythms? Circle the letter of your answer.

(a) the sound of horses' hooves

(b) the sound of beautiful music

(c) the sound of the sea

(d) the sound of army helicopters

British poet Alfred, Lord Tennyson, writes here about the Battle of Balaklava in the Crimean War. Britain and Russia fought that war in the 1850s. In this battle, 600 lightly armed British troops attacked an area held by heavily armed Russian troops.

◆ ◆ ◆

Half a league,[1] half a league,
Half a league onward,
All in the valley of Death
    Rode the six hundred.
"Forward, the Light Brigade![2]
Charge for the guns!" he said:
Into the valley of Death
    Rode the six hundred.

◆ Read Fluently

Read the quotation aloud in a tone you think would be appropriate. Who is speaking these words? Circle the letter of your answer.

(a) the commanding officer

(b) the enemy's commanding officer

(c) the king of England

(d) each soldier, speaking together

"Forward, the Light Brigade!"
Was there a man <u>dismayed</u>?
Not though the soldier knew
    Someone had <u>blundered</u>:
Theirs not to make reply,
Theirs not to reason why,
Theirs but to do and die,
Into the valley of Death
    Rode the six hundred.

◆ Stop to Reflect

Why don't the soldiers question the orders?

(a) They aren't smart enough.

(b) They agree with the orders.

(c) They hate the enemy and want to attack as soon as possible.

(d) Good soldiers do not question orders.

---

1. **league** (LEEG) *n.* three miles.
2. **light brigade** (LĪT bri GAYD) *n.* lightly armed troops on horseback.

Vocabulary Development

dismayed (dis MAYD) *adj.* upset; afraid; without confidence

blundered (BLUN derd) *v.* made a foolish mistake

Cannon to right of them,
Cannon to left of them,
Cannon in front of them
 Volleyed and thundered. . . .
Stormed at with shot and shell,
While horse and hero fell,
They that had fought so well
Came through the jaws of Death,
Back from the mouth of Hell,
All that was left of them,
 Left of six hundred.

When can their glory fade?
O the wild charge they made!
 All the world wondered.
Honor the charge they made!
Honor the Light Brigade.
 Noble six hundred!
 ◆ ◆ ◆

 Six hundred British troops rode into battle that day. Three quarters of them were
killed. The charge was a terrible mistake. But
the men who fought so bravely are forever
remembered because of this famous poem.

◆ **Reading Check**

Did any of the six
hundred soldiers
survive? Circle the
answer.

 yes *no*

How do you know? Circle the
words in the text that tell you.

Vocabulary Development

volleyed (VAHL eed) *v.* fired together

1. Put a check in front of each statement that accurately describes the soldiers' situation.

_____ They are riding into battle on horses.

_____ They are lightly armed, while the enemy is heavily armed.

_____ They greatly outnumber the enemy.

_____ They have no idea what they are facing.

_____ They are attacking because someone made a mistake and ordered them to.

2. With what attitude do the soldiers make their charge? Circle the letter of the best answer.

(a) They go forward bravely without question.

(b) They are full of questions for those who ordered the attack.

(c) They fear the enemy and hold back as long as possible.

(d) They feel a violent hatred for the enemy and cannot wait to fight.

3. What happens to the soldiers making the attack? Write your answer on the lines.

_____

_____

_____

4. How does the speaker of the poem seem to feel about the soldiers? Circle the letter of the correct answer.

(a) He is worried that they will be forgotten.

(b) He is proud of their bravery.

(c) He is hopeful that they all will survive.

(d) He is angry and bitter that so many died.

5. **Literary Analysis:** Read these lines from the poem. Then, complete the statements about the **repetition** in them.

> *Cannon to right of them,*
> *Cannon to left of them,*
> *Cannon in front of them*
>   *Volleyed and thundered.*

• The repetition in the lines includes the words	_____
• The repetition stresses the idea that the soldiers are	_____
• The repetition helps capture the sound of the	_____

6. **Reading Strategy:** Use the main **word part** in *stormed* to figure out what it means to be "*stormed* at with shot and shell." Write the meaning on the line below.

stormed: _____

Writing

Choose a battle you have learned about in school. Write a paragraph telling what happened.
- Do research using your social studies book or another source to get information.
- Indicate the war in which the battle took place.

_____

- Include the time and place of the battle.

_____

- Make clear the sides that were fighting.

_____

- Give some idea of the number of troops that fought and the number that died.

_____

- Indicate who won the battle or, if no one won, make that clear.

_____

- Write your completed paragraph on another piece of paper.

The Californian's Tale

Mark Twain

Summary

A man hunting for gold in California comes to the attractive, well-kept cabin of a miner named Henry. Henry invites the man in. He credits the loveliness of his home to his young wife who is away until Saturday night. He urges the visitor to stay until she returns. Henry's friends come over on Saturday and give Henry a drug that puts him to sleep. They explain that Henry's wife has been dead for 19 years. Every year, at the time of her death, they go through the act of pretending she's returning. They do this so that Henry doesn't go wild with anger and grief.

Visual Summary

Wednesday	Thursday	Friday	Saturday
• Narrator (story-teller) is hunting for gold. • He meets Henry outside a miner's cabin much nicer than others. • Henry explains that the pretty, comfortable home is the work of his wife, who is visiting relatives. • He insists that the narrator stay until Saturday, when his wife will return.	• Tom, a miner from three miles away, comes to visit that evening. • Henry reads him part of his wife's letter. • Tom promises to return to celebrate her homecoming on Saturday.	• Joe, another miner from nearby, comes to visit. • Henry reads him part of his wife's letter. • Joe too promises to return for the homecoming.	• The narrator checks his watch several times, eager for the wife's arrival. • Charley, Joe and Tom arrive. • Joe serves a drink to toast the wife before she arrives. • Henry is drugged by the drink and falls asleep. • Joe explains that Henry's wife has been dead for 19 years but that they pretend she is alive to keep Henry from going wild with grief.

LITERARY ANALYSIS
Local Color

Local color is the use of details specific to a region. Those details may include
- descriptions of places and things found in the region
- information about activities and customs in the region
- portraits of people typical of the region, including their way of speaking

"The Californian's Tale" takes place in the mining region of California in the years after the Gold Rush of 1849. In this passage, Mark Twain captures the emptiness of the landscape now that most of the Gold Rush miners have left.

> *It was a lonesome land! Not a sound in all those peaceful expanses of grass and woods but the drowsy hum of insects; no glimpse of man or beast; nothing to keep up your spirits and make you glad to be alive.*

As you read the story, look for other details that capture the local color of the California mining area.

READING STRATEGY
Summarizing

Summarizing means stating just the main points and important details of something you have read. You will often understand stories better if you pause after each paragraph or conversation to summarize what you have just read. For example, here is a paragraph from "The Californian's Tale":

> *A fiddle, a banjo, and a clarinet—these were the instruments. The trio took their places side by side, and began to play some rattling dance-music, and beat time with their big boots.*

You might summarize this paragraph with a single sentence:

> Three musicians played lively dance music.

As you read "The Californian's Tale," stop to summarize paragraphs and conversations. You can do the summaries in your head or write them down on a separate sheet of paper.

The Californian's Tale
Mark Twain

The narrator, or storyteller, recalls the time when he was hunting for gold in California some years after the Gold Rush of 1849.

◆ ◆ ◆

Thirty-five years ago I was out <u>prospecting</u> on the Stanislaus,[1] tramping all day long with pick and pan and horn,[2] and washing a hatful of dirt here and there, always expecting to make a rich <u>strike</u>, and never doing it.

◆ ◆ ◆

Since the Gold Rush is over, the narrator finds many of the mining towns empty.

◆ ◆ ◆

It was a lonesome land! Not a sound in all those peaceful <u>expanses</u> of grass and woods but the drowsy hum of insects; no glimpse of man or beast; nothing to keep up your spirits and make you glad to be alive.

◆ ◆ ◆

Every so often the narrator comes across a cabin where a miner from the Gold Rush days still lives. At night the narrator stays in these cabins, which are very bare and simple. Then, one afternoon he meets a man named Henry standing outside a cabin of a different sort.

◆ ◆ ◆

Vocabulary Development

prospecting (PRAH spek ting) *n.* searching for gold
strike (STRĪK) *n.* discovery of gold
expanses (ek SPAN sez) *n.* fairly large stretches of land

---

1. **Stanislaus** (STAN uh slawz) a river in California.
2. **pick and pan and horn** equipment used in hunting for gold.

It had the look of being lived in and petted and cared for and looked after; and so had its front yard. . . . I was invited in, of course, and required to make myself at home—it was the custom of the country.

◆ ◆ ◆

The narrator is delighted to be in such a place—a real home with wallpaper and pretty chairs and and all the little bits of decoration he associates with a woman's touch. The man notices the narrator's delight.

◆ ◆ ◆

"All her work," he said, caressingly;[3] "she did it all herself—every bit," and he took the room in with a glance which was full of affectionate worship.

◆ ◆ ◆

The narrator wants to wash his hands so the man takes him into the bedroom. The narrator describes another beautifully decorated room with:

◆ ◆ ◆

. . . white counterpane, white pillows, carpeted floor, papered walls, pictures, dressing-table, with mirror and pin-cushion and dainty toilet things; and in the corner a washstand.

◆ ◆ ◆

As Henry continues to praise his wife, the narrator looks around the pretty room. He sees a picture on the far wall and studies it more closely.

◆ ◆ ◆

◆ Literary Analysis

Local color includes the customs of an area. What custom is discussed here? Write your answer on the lines:

_____

_____

_____

_____

Now, circle the part of the paragraph that pointed to your answer.

◆ Stop to Reflect

Why do you think the narrator appreciates the home so much?

(a) He knows the wife from back East.

(b) He grew up there 35 years before.

(c) He misses his own home.

(d) He sells bedroom furnishings and recognizes quality when he sees it.

Vocabulary Development

counterpane (KOWNT uhr payn) *n.* bedspread; bed cover

---

3. **caressingly** (kuh RES ing lee) *adv.* lovingly.

It contained the sweetest girlish face, and the most beautiful, as it seemed to me, that I had ever seen. The man drank the admiration from my face, and was fully satisfied.

"Nineteen her last birthday," . . . ; "and that was the day we were married. When you see her—ah, just wait till you see her!"

◆ ◆ ◆

The narrator asks where the wife is. Henry explains that she went to see her family forty or fifty miles away. She has been gone for two weeks already.

◆ ◆ ◆

"She'll be back Saturday, in the evening—about nine o'clock, likely."

I felt a sharp sense of disappointment.

"I'm sorry, because I'll be gone by then," I said, regretfully.

"Gone? No—why should you go?

◆ ◆ ◆

Henry goes on to tell the narrator it would disappoint her not to meet him. He describes how much his wife likes to visit with people. He talks about the books she reads and what she knows. He suggests that the narrator would be just the kind of visitor his wife would like. Then he urges the narrator to stay until she returns.

The narrator feels a strange longing to meet Henry's wife. But he decides that he really ought to leave. But Henry brings his wife's picture over to his guest.

◆ ◆ ◆

"There, now, tell her to her face you could have stayed to see her, and you wouldn't."

◆ ◆ ◆

The narrator finds it impossible to say no, and agrees to stay until Saturday. He spends a pleasant, comfortable evening talking with Henry of many things, especially

◆ Reading Check

What is Henry's impression of the narrator? Circle the letter of your answer.

(a) educated and a good story-teller

(b) hard working and hungry for gold

(c) overly educated and snobby

(d) rough but kindhearted

◆ Read Fluently

Read the bracketed sentence aloud in the tone you think Henry might have used. Why do you think he is so eager for the narrator to stay until his wife gets home? Write your answer here:

_____

_____

_____

_____

Henry's wife. Then, on Thursday evening, a big miner named Tom, who lives three miles away, comes to visit Henry.

◆　◆　◆

"I only just dropped over to ask about the little madam, and when is she coming home. Any news from her?"

"Oh, yes, a letter. Would you like to hear it, Tom?"

◆　◆　◆

As he listens to parts of the letter, Tom's eyes get moist. Henry teases him, and Tom tries to explain his tears.

◆　◆　◆

"I am getting old, you know, and any little disappointment makes me want to cry. I thought she'd be here herself, and now you've got only a letter."

"Well, now, what put that in your head? I thought everybody knew she wasn't coming till Saturday."

◆　◆　◆

Tom is just one of several lonely miners still in the area from the Gold Rush. When he thinks about it, he says he did know she was due on Saturday. He has to leave, but says he'll be back for her arrival.

◆　◆　◆

Late Friday afternoon another gray <u>veteran</u> tramped over from his cabin a mile or so away, and said the boys wanted to have a little <u>gaiety</u> and a good time Saturday night, if Henry thought she wouldn't be too tired after her long journey to be kept up.

◆　◆　◆

Vocabulary Development

veteran (VET er uhn) *n.* someone with long experience in a particular job or activity

gaiety (GAY uh tee) *n.* joy; fun

What sort of person does the wife seem to be? Circle the letter of your answer.

(a) selfish

(b) thoughtful

(c) snobbish

(d) lazy

Now, circle the detail in this paragraph that pointed to your answer.

◆ **Read fluently**

Practice reading the bracketed quotation aloud. Which emotion or feeling do you think the speaker tries to convey?

_____

_____

_____

_____

◆ **Literary Analysis**

"Right down" used in this way is part of Henry's regional speech, or **dialect**. Twain includes dialect to add **local color** to his tale. Use the context or surroundings to figure out the meaning of "right down" as it is used here.

right down:

_____

_____

_____

_____

Henry says that, of course, she won't be tired. She'll want to see everyone of the boys.

The veteran, Joe, also asks to hear the letter and reacts as Tom did. He explains how much everyone misses Henry's wife. The narrator is just as eager to see her. Saturday afternoon, the narrator finds himself anxiously waiting for her. He's checking his watch a lot, and Henry notices.

◆ ◆ ◆

"You don't think she ought to be here so soon, do you?"

◆ ◆ ◆

Embarrassed, the narrator explains that he is simply in the habit of checking his watch whenever he expects anything. But Henry gets more and more nervous. The two men walk up the road and look for her four times.

◆ ◆ ◆

"I'm getting worried. I'm getting right down worried."

◆ ◆ ◆

Henry continues to worry out loud about his wife. He admits that she is not due home until later. But he still worries out loud. Then he asks the narrator whether he thinks something has happened.

The narrator tells Henry he is being foolish. Then, a miner named Charley shows up and does his best to get Henry to stop worrying. Soon Joe and Tom arrive. They all help decorate the house with flowers. Joe, Tom, and Charley take out musical instruments, a fiddle, a banjo, and a clarinet. They say they need to tune up before Henry's wife and the other guests arrive.

◆ ◆ ◆

The trio took their places side by side, and began to play some rattling dance-music, and beat time with their big boots.

♦ ♦ ♦

Joe brings out several glasses for a final toast before Henry's wife arrives. When the narrator is about to take one of the last two glasses, Joe orders him to take the other. Joe then serves Henry the first. Soon Henry grows pale and has to lie down on the sofa. Then he lifts his head.

♦ ♦ ♦

"Did I hear horses' feet? Have they come?"

One of the veterans answered, close to his ear: "It was Jimmy Parrish come to say the party got delayed but they're right up the road. . . . Her horse is lame, but she'll be here in half an hour."

♦ ♦ ♦

Henry falls fast asleep, and the three miners carry him to bed. As they prepare to leave, the narrator stops them.

♦ ♦ ♦

"Please don't go, gentlemen. She won't know me; I am a stranger."

They glanced at each other. Then Joe said:

"She? Poor thing, she's been dead nineteen years!"

"Dead?"

♦ ♦ ♦

Joe explains that Henry's wife went to see her folks half a year after she married. On the Saturday when she was returning, she was captured by Indians five miles away. She has never been heard of since.

♦ ♦ ♦

"And he lost his mind in consequence?"

♦ ♦ ♦

Circle five details in this paragraph that add to the **local color** of the story.

Local color also means showing the special way that local characters speak. Circle the phrase here that seems like a local expression.

Circle the letter of the best **summary** of this story.

(a) Henry lost his mind when he lost his wife, and he gets worse on the anniversary of that loss. His friends play along to try to help him get through it.

(b) Henry goes insane for a few days on the anniversary of his wife's death but then returns to normal afterward.

(c) Henry has friends who will come to his aid whenever he is in need. He is a lucky man in spite of his troubles.

(d) Henry's friends bring flowers into the house and get ready for a dance.

Why do you think Henry's friends help him in this way?

(a) They care about him.

(b) They cared about his wife.

(c) They are kindhearted and help neighbors out when they can.

(d) all of the above

Joe tells the narrator that Henry hasn't been sane since it happened. Around the time of year that it happened, Henry gets worse. To make him feel better, his friends come by three days before his wife is supposed to come home. They ask after her as if she'll really be coming home. Then on that Saturday they decorate the house and have a dance. They've been doing it for nineteen years. Joe explains that twenty-seven people came by the first year. Now there are only the three of them left.

◆　◆　◆

"We drug him to sleep, or he would go wild; then he's all right for another year—thinks she's with him till the last three or four days come round; then he begins to look for her, and gets out his poor old letter, and we come and ask him to read it to us. Lord, she was a darling!"

1. What makes Henry's house so special for the narrator? Circle the letter of the answer.

   (a) It is the only one with anyone inside.

   (b) It full of fancy foreign furnishings that cost a small fortune.

   (c) There is room for him to sleep there.

   (d) It is pretty and shows a woman's touch.

2. Write *T* in front of the true statements and *F* in front of the false ones.

   ____ Henry talks about his nineteen-year-old wife.

   ____ Henry lost his wife nineteen years ago.

   ____ Henry's wife was an orphan with no family of her own.

   ____ Henry's wife was well liked in the neighborhood.

   ____ Henry's wife was an educated woman who liked to read.

   ____ Henry's wife knew little about housekeeping.

3. Why do the miners pretend that Henry's wife is coming home? Write your answer on the lines.

   _____

   _____

4. What does the story show about life on the California frontier? Circle the letter of your answer.

   (a) It could be lonely but those who were there were often friendly.

   (b) It drove most people mad with grief and sorrow.

   (c) It was an easy life because so many found gold.

   (d) It was a hard life because no one ever offered a helping hand.

   (Continued)

5. **Literary Analysis:** What details add **local color** to the story? List at least one of each of these kinds of details.

Local character:	
Local way of speaking:	
Local place:	
Local activity:	

6. **Reading Strategy:** On the lines below, write a one-sentence **summary** of this paragraph from the story.

Thirty-five years ago I was out prospecting on the Stanislaus, tramping all day long with pick and pan and horn, and washing a hatful of dirt here and there, always expecting to make a rich strike, and never doing it.

_____

_____

_____

Writing or Listening and Speaking

In groups of five, act out the ending of "The Californian's Tale." Think of it as a short scene you might see in a play or on TV.

- Each person in your group, male or female, should take a different role—Henry, the narrator, Joe, Tom, and Charley.
- Follow any directions Twain gives about how words should be spoken or what body language you should use.
- Use the conversation that is there, and add more if necessary.

Four Skinny Trees
Sandra Cisneros

Summary

The speaker admires four skinny trees that grow outside the window of her city apartment. They possess a secret strength and keep surviving in spite of their surroundings. The trees inspire the speaker to keep going too.

Visual Summary

How Trees Are Similar to Speaker	How Speaker Is Similar to Trees
• Are only ones who understand speaker • Have skinny necks and pointy elbows • Do not belong in surroundings	• Is only one who understands the four trees • Has skinny neck and pointy elbows • Does not belong in her surroundings

Speaker will try to be like the four trees in other ways.

What Trees May Teach Speaker
• Have secret strength in hidden roots • Grab the earth with hairy toes • Bite sky with violent teeth • Stay angry and survive • How to survive • Grow despite concrete • Never forget to reach

LITERARY ANALYSIS

Levels of Meaning

Many works of literature contain different **levels of meaning**. On one level is the **literal meaning**—what the words are actually saying. Often there is also a deeper meaning of more importance. For example, on the literal level, "Four Skinny Trees" is about four trees that grow outside a young woman's window.

> Four skinny trees with skinny necks and pointy elbows like mine. Four who do not belong here but are here. Four raggedy excuses planted by the city. . . . They send ferocious roots beneath the ground.

The speaker compares the trees with herself. She speaks of the trees' struggle to survive in a place where they do not belong. Clearly she is talking about more than just four trees. On a deeper level, she is talking about the difficulties of growing up in a tough city neighborhood and about how all young people, wherever they live, struggle to make a place for themselves.

READING STRATEGY

Interpreting Figurative Language

Figurative language means something different than its literal, word-for-word meaning. For example, when the speaker says the four trees grew in spite of "concrete," she is not just talking about the concrete that blocked the soil and so made it hard for the trees to grow. She is talking about the many problems and obstacles that the four trees—and young people—faced in her neighborhood.

In order to understand the deeper level of "Four Skinny Trees," you need to understand its figurative language. As you read, you might fill out a chart like this one.

Author's Language	Literal Meaning	Meaning on a Deeper Level
"concrete"	hard building or paving material made from cement mixed with sand or small rocks and water	problems and obstacles

Four Skinny Trees
Sandra Cisneros

The speaker lives in a poor city neighborhood. It is not a place where gardens grow. Yet outside her window are four trees.

◆ ◆ ◆

They are the only ones who understand me. I am the only one who understands them. Four skinny trees with skinny necks and pointy elbows like mine. Four who do not belong here but are here. Four <u>raggedy</u> excuses planted by the city. From our room we can hear them, but Nenny[1] just sleeps and doesn't appreciate these things.

◆ ◆ ◆

The speaker admires the trees for being strong enough to keep, or survive, in unfriendly surroundings.

◆ ◆ ◆

Their strength is secret. They send <u>ferocious</u> roots beneath the ground. They grow up and they grow down and grab the earth between their hairy toes and bite the sky with violent teeth and never quit their anger. This is how they keep.

<u>Let one forget his reason for being, they'd all droop like tulips in a glass</u>, each with their arms around the other. Keep, keep, keep, trees say when I sleep. They teach.

◆ ◆ ◆

---

1. **Nenny** (NEN ee) the relative with whom the speaker shares a room.

◆ **Reading Check**

What are the trees like? Circle the letter of your answer.

(a) thin and scrawny

(b) large and lush

(c) young and beautiful

(d) old and diseased

Now, circle two words in the paragraph that are clues to the answer.

◆ **Literary Analysis**

The literal **meaning** of the underlined phrase might be "If one tree forgets why it exists, all the trees would wilt like cut flowers." Circle the letter of the sentence that gives a possible deeper meaning.

(a) If you forget who you are, you will not become a good teacher.

(b) If one person in a group loses his or her way, the whole group is affected.

(c) If one person is thirsty, everyone should drink.

(d) Do not cut the flowers.

Interpret the figurative language here. What do you think the speaker means by a "tiny thing against so many bricks"? Circle the letter of your answer.

(a) a superhuman being bursting through walls

(b) an atom

(c) alone in a difficult world

(d) an insect thrown against a wall

When the speaker feels weak or hopeless, the trees inspire her.

◆　◆　◆

When I am too sad and too skinny to keep keeping, when I am a tiny thing against so many bricks, then it is I look at trees. When there is nothing left to look at on this street. Four who grew <u>despite</u> concrete. Four who reach and do not forget to reach. Four whose only reason is to be and be.

Vocabulary Development

despite (di SPĪT) *prep.* in spite of

1. How are the speaker and the trees physically alike? Write your answer on the lines.

_____

_____

_____

2. In what sort of neighborhood do the trees and speaker grow up?

_____

3. Put a check in front of at least three values or attitudes that the trees teach the speaker.

____ strength   ____ sorrow   ____ greed

____ stubbornness   ____ hope   ____ pride

4. **Literary Analysis:** The sentences on the left illustrate the literal **level of meaning** in "Four Skinny Trees." Next to each, write a deeper meaning that you think the author communicates about a young person growing up or struggling to survive.

Literal Meaning	Deeper Meaning
The four trees do not belong here but are here.	_____ _____ _____
They send ferocious roots beneath the ground.	_____ _____ _____
They reach for the sky.	_____ _____ _____

5. **Reading Strategy: Interpret figurative meanings** by showing what each phrase from "Four Skinny Trees" literally means. Circle the letter of your answer

- "hairy toes" (p. 107) really means (a) roots (b) stems (c) tree toads (d) tulip bulbs

How do you know? _____

_____

- "violent teeth" (p. 107) really refers to (a) the trees' beauty (b) the trees' branches (c) woodpeckers (d) insects called termites eating the tree from the inside

How do you know? _____

_____

Listening and Speaking

What do you think the street with the four trees is like? What do you think it *sounds* like? Working in a small group, create a tape of background noises that would sound like that street.

- Discuss and list the sounds you hope to record. Consider those you will have to find, like the sounds of cars or of wind blowing in trees. Also consider those you can create yourself, like the sounds of car horns or of banging garbage cans. Write your ideas here.

_____

_____

_____

_____

_____

_____

- Record as many of the sounds as you can.
- Take notes as you record each sound so that you know what the sound is.
- Present the final tape to classmates, and be prepared to explain what the sounds are.

The Night the Bed Fell

James Thurber

Summary

James Thurber recalls the chain of events that led to confusion one night when he was a boy. His father went to sleep in the attic to do some thinking. His mother was afraid the wobbly attic bed would collapse. During the night, young James accidentally tipped over his cot. The noises caused his mother to scream. This woke his brother Herman, who yelled at the mother to calm herself. This woke Briggs, a visiting cousin, who spilled on himself because he thought he had stopped breathing. By this time James's other brother, Roy, and the dog Rex were also awake, with Rex barking and attacking Briggs. All the noise woke the father, who came down from the attic and asked what was going on.

Visual Summary

Mr. Thurber (Father)

Where he sleeps: attic

What he thinks: house is on fire

What he does: comes down and asks what's going on

Mrs. Thurber (Mother)

Where she sleeps: front room

What she thinks: Mr. Thurber's bed collapsed and he may have died

What she does: screams in fear, runs to attic door

Herman Thurber (Brother)

Where he sleeps: front room

What he thinks: mother is hysterical

What he does: yells to calm her, runs to attic door

Roy Thurber (Brother)

Where he sleeps: across hall from James and Briggs

What he does: shouts questions, stops Rex from attacking Briggs, pulls open attic door

What Really Happened

Young James's cot toppled over

Briggs Beall (Cousin)

Where he sleeps: next to front room, sharing with James

What he thinks: he is suffocating

What he does: pours smelly substance all over himself, breaks window, yells, joins others at attic door

Rex (Dog)

Where he sleeps: hall

What he thinks: Briggs is to blame for all trouble

What he does: barks, attacks Briggs

James Thurber (Author) When Young

Where he sleeps: next to front room, sharing with Briggs

What he thinks: he is in danger, trapped beneath his bed

What he does: yells for help, joins others at attic door

LITERARY ANALYSIS

Humorous Essay

A **humorous essay** is a short piece of nonfiction writing meant to be funny. In "The Night the Bed Fell," the humor comes from the characters' odd ideas and behavior and their mistakes and confusion on the night in question. Thurber also exaggerates, or stretches the truth, to add to the humor.

One character with odd ideas is Cousin Briggs. See the chart for a description of his behavior.

As you read, use this chart to keep track of the family's odd ideas, mistakes, and confusion.

Odd Ideas and Behavior	Mistakes and Confusion
• Briggs fears suffocating at night, keeps strong-smelling liquid camphor by his bed to sniff if he starts to choke	Briggs hears noise, thinks he is suffocating, pours awful-smelling liquid camphor all over himself
•	•
•	•

READING STRATEGY

Identifying Significant Events

Not all events are of equal importance. In a humorous essay, the author may include events just to be funny. But a **significant event**—a really important event—has to move the story forward. It does one or more of these things:
- causes one or more other events to happen
- adds a new complication
- changes the way a character thinks or acts
- settles a question or problem

As you read, look for significant events.

The Night the Bed Fell
James Thurber

James Thurber grew up about a hundred years ago in Columbus, Ohio. His noisy home included his mother, his father, brothers Herman and Roy, a dog named Rex, and other relatives.

◆   ◆   ◆

It happened . . . that my father had decided to sleep in the attic one night, . . . My mother <u>opposed</u> the <u>notion</u> strongly because, she said, the old wooden bed up there was unsafe: it was wobbly and the heavy headboard would crash down on father's head in case the bed fell, and kill him.

◆   ◆   ◆

In spite of the mother's worries, the father heads up to the attic bed.

◆   ◆   ◆

Grandfather, who usually slept in the attic bed, . . . had disappeared some days before. On these occasions he was usually gone eight days and returned growling and out of temper.

◆   ◆   ◆

A cousin of Thurber's is visiting and sharing his room. Briggs Beall is the nervous type. He thinks he needs to wake up every hour. Otherwise he might suffocate to death. To keep from choking, Briggs likes to set an alarm to ring throughout the night. James won't allow that. So Briggs instead puts liquid camphor on the table beside his bed. He figures he can sniff this strong-smelling

---

Vocabulary Development

opposed (ah POZD) *v.* was against
notion (NOH shun) *n.* idea

© Pearson Education, Inc.

substance to revive himself if his breathing stops.

◆ ◆ ◆

Briggs was not the only member of his family who had his crotchets.[1]

◆ ◆ ◆

Aunt Sarah Shoaf is afraid of burglars so she stacks cash and valuables outside her bedroom every night. She leaves a note telling the burglars it is all she has, asking them not to harm her. Another aunt, Gracie Shoaf, is sure burglars have been getting into her house every night for forty years. She has never found anything missing, but she says that's because she scares them off by throwing shoes. She prepares for the burglars each night by piling shoes close to her bed.

◆ ◆ ◆

Five minutes after she had turned off the light, she would sit up in bed and say "Hark!"[2] . . . Presently she would arise, tiptoe to the door, open it slightly, and heave a shoe down the hall.

◆ ◆ ◆

After describing various family members, Thurber returns to his tale of the night the bed fell. Everyone in the house was in bed by midnight.

◆ ◆ ◆

In the front room upstairs (just under father's attic bedroom) were my mother and my brother Herman, who sometimes sang in his sleep, . . . Briggs Beall and myself were in a

---

◆ **Reading Strategy**

Would you say the bracketed passage describes a **significant event**? Write *yes* or *no*, and explain your answer.

_____

_____

_____

_____

◆ **Reading Strategy**

Why do you think Thurber includes this event? Circle the letter of your answer.

(a) It is a **significant event**.

(b) It is funny.

(c) Both *a* and *b* are correct.

(d) Neither *a* nor *b* is correct.

◆ **Reading Check**

Show that you understand the layout by filling out who slept where on the floor plan below.

Top Floor Attic:

_____

_____

Next Room:	In Hall:	Across Hall:
_____	_____	_____
_____		_____
_____		_____

Floor Below Attic: Front Room:

_____

room adjoining this one. My brother Roy was in a room across the hall from ours. Our bull terrier, Rex, slept in the hall.

◆　◆　◆

Thurber sleeps on a metal cot that tips over easily. At two in the morning. Thurber rolls out of bed, and the cot rolls over on top of him.

◆　◆　◆

Always a deep sleeper, . . . I was at first unconscious of what had happened.

◆　◆　◆

Thurber still does not wake up completely. But the noise wakes his mother up. She thinks the bed has fallen on father. She starts yelling which wakes Herman, who yells "You're all right!" to try to calm her. Briggs wakes up and concludes that he is suffocating.

◆　◆　◆

With a low moan, he grasped the glass of camphor at the head of his bed and instead of sniffing it poured it over himself. The room <u>reeked</u> of camphor. "Ugf, ahfg," choked Briggs, like a drowning man.

◆　◆　◆

He rushes to the window and knocks out the glass to get some air. This fully awakens James, who now realizes he is under his bed.

◆　◆　◆

"Get me out of this!" I bawled. . . . "Gugh," gasped Briggs.

◆　◆　◆

◆ **Reading Strategy**

What do you think will happen when the mother hears James's bed tip over?

_____

_____

_____

_____

Do you think this is a **significant event?**

　　　yes　　　　　no

◆ **Stop to Reflect**

Why is it funny that the liquid camphor nearly causes Briggs to stop breathing? Write your answer on these lines.

_____

_____

_____

_____

◆ **Read Fluently**

Read aloud the two young men's remarks. What tone of voice do you think James should use? Circle the letter of your answer.

(a) happy　　　(c) angry

(b) frightened　(d) sleepy

Vocabulary Development

reeked (REEKT) *v.*　smelled really bad

While Thurber and Briggs are struggling, mother and Herman reach the attic door. They are frantic—and still yelling—because they think father's body is under the wreckage of the bed. The attic door is jammed. As they try to open the door, they make more noise. Roy is also awake and noisily trying to find out what is happening. Rex is barking. The noise finally wakes the father in the attic. He thinks the house is on fire and yells "I'm coming." But the mother thinks he is trapped under his bed.

◆ ◆ ◆

"He's dying!" she shouted.

"I'm all right!" Briggs yelled. . . . He still believed that it was his own closeness to death that was worrying mother. . . . The dog, who never did like Briggs, jumped for him—assuming he was the culprit.

◆ ◆ ◆

Roy rescues Briggs and manages to open the attic door. A sleepy father comes down and everyone finds out that he is safe and sound. He is, however, <u>irritable</u> about being waked. The mother starts to cry when she realizes he is okay. The dog responds by howling. Father demands to know what is going on.

◆ ◆ ◆

The situation was finally put together like a gigantic jigsaw puzzle. Father caught a cold from prowling around in his bare feet but there were no other bad results. "I'm glad," said mother, who always looked on the bright side of things, "that your grandfather wasn't here."

Vocabulary Development

irritable (IR i tuh buhl) *adj.*   cranky

1. Which description best fits most of Thurber's relatives? Circle the letter of your answer.

   (a) They have odd ideas.   (c) They are mean to each other.

   (b) They never worry.   (d) They are a quiet bunch.

2. Why does Cousin Briggs set an alarm clock and keep liquid camphor by his bed? Write your answer on the lines.

   _____

   _____

3. **Literary Analysis:** A lot of the humor in this **humorous essay** comes from the mistakes each character makes. What funny mistakes do these characters make? Fill in the chart.

Mother:	
Cousin Briggs:	
Rex the Dog:	

4. **Literary Analysis:** List three details that you think Thurber exaggerates to make his **humorous essay** funnier.

   • _____

   • _____

   • _____

5. **Reading Strategy:** Put a check in front of the **significant events**. Then, circle the event that you think causes all the confusion.

   ____ The father goes up to the attic to sleep.

   ____ Cousin Briggs sets an alarm clock.

   ____ Aunt Sarah piles her valuables by her door and leaves a note for the burglars.

The Night the Bed Fell **117**

____ Aunt Grace throws shoes at imaginary burglars.

____ Young James Thurber's cot collapses.

____ The mother fears the attic bed fell and hurt or killed the father.

____ Brother Herman yells to try to calm mother.

____ Cousin Briggs pours camphor all over himself.

____ Rex attacks Briggs.

____ The father thinks the house is on fire and comes downstairs.

Listening and Speaking

With other classmates, act out the confusing scene near the end. Each of you take on a different role—the mother, James, and so on.

- Use actual words from characters' conversations in the essay. Mark the words you will use.
- Add more conversation to the scene. Write three additions here.

_____

_____

_____

_____

- Use hand and body movements to show characters' feelings.
- Use sound effects—Rex the dog's barking, for example. Write one more sound effect to use.

_____

_____

All Summer in a Day
Ray Bradbury

Summary

On the planet Venus, seven years of rain is about to stop for a short while. The other students in Margot's class have forgotten what the sun is like. They look forward to seeing it. They tease Margot, who came from Earth and remembers what the sun is like. Margot is an outsider who does not join in most of their games. As a cruel joke, they lock her in a closet before going out to play in the only hour of sunshine they will see in seven years. When the rain starts up again, the children sadly return indoors. They realize they made Margot miss the sunshine. Knowing how cruel they have been, they slowly go to the closet to let her out.

Visual Summary

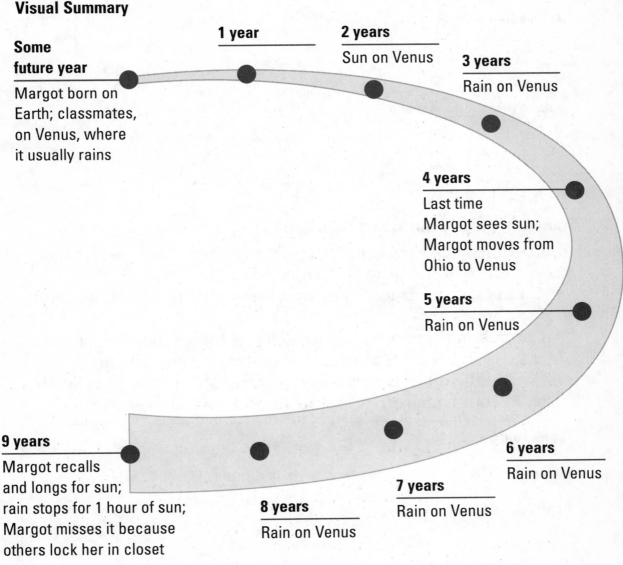

Some future year
Margot born on Earth; classmates, on Venus, where it usually rains

1 year

2 years
Sun on Venus

3 years
Rain on Venus

4 years
Last time Margot sees sun; Margot moves from Ohio to Venus

5 years
Rain on Venus

6 years
Rain on Venus

7 years
Rain on Venus

8 years
Rain on Venus

9 years
Margot recalls and longs for sun; rain stops for 1 hour of sun; Margot misses it because others lock her in closet

LITERARY ANALYSIS

Setting

The **setting** is the time and place of a story. "All Summer in a Day" is a science-fiction story. It takes place on the planet Venus in the future. The author provides many details to help us imagine what life there would be like. We learn, for example, that Venus is so rainy that children who were born there cannot remember ever seeing the sun.

As you read the story, use this chart to list details that help you understand the setting.

SETTING: Venus in the Future	
Details that indicate time	• Children all nine years old • Sun came out for one hour seven years ago •
Details that indicate place	• Rains almost all the time on Venus • •

READING STRATEGY

Comparing and Contrasting Characters

Sometimes you can understand story characters better if you compare and contrast them.

- **Comparing characters** means finding things that are similar about them.
- **Contrasting characters** means finding things that are different.

Margot is the main character in this story. Compare and contrast her to the other children in the story to understand what she is like. Fill out a chart to compare and contrast the characters.

Margot's Classmates	Margot
• nine years old	• nine years old
• born on Venus	• born on Earth
• play games	• stays apart

All Summer in a Day
Ray Bradbury

On the planet Venus some time in the future, Margot's[1] classmates are standing at the window.

◆　◆　◆

"Ready?"
"Ready."
"Now?"
"Soon."
"Do the scientists really know? Will it happen today, will it?"
"Look, look; see for yourself!"
The children pressed to each other like so many roses, so many weeds, intermixed, <u>peering</u> out for a look at the hidden sun.

◆　◆　◆

For seven years, Venus has known nothing but rain. Sometimes there were light showers; sometimes there were heavy storms; but always there was rain.

◆　◆　◆

A thousand forests had been crushed under the rain and grown up a thousand times to be crushed again. And this was the way life was forever on the planet Venus.

◆　◆　◆

Margot's classmates are used to it. They are the children of the rocket men and women who came to Venus from Earth to set up a space colony there. Margot isn't really part of the group of children.

◆ **Read Fluently**

Read these remarks aloud. In what tone of voice do you think the children speak? Circle the letter of your answer.

(a) excited　　(c) teasing
(b) bored　　　(d) very frightened

◆ **Literary Analysis**

Circle the words in the bracketed paragraphs that describe the **setting** of the story.

◆ **Reading Check**

Why do these children live on Venus?

_____

_____

_____

Vocabulary Development

peering (PEER ing) *n.*　looking out at

---

1. **Margot** (MAR goh)

◆ Reading Check

How old are the children? Circle the word that tells you. Then, on the line, write how old they were when they may have seen sun before:

_____

The children are nine years old. The only time the sun was out was when they were two. The sunshine only lasted an hour. They can't remember what it was like.

In class, they have been reading about the sun—how it looks and feels.

◆ ◆ ◆

And they had written small stories or essays or poems about it.

◆ ◆ ◆

The others cannot remember what the sun is like. But Margot can. She writes her poem from her memories. Then she quietly reads it aloud.

◆ ◆ ◆

I think the sun is a flower,
That blooms for just one hour. . . .
"Aw, you didn't write that!" <u>protested</u> one of the boys.
"I did," said Margot. "I did."
"William!" said the teacher.

◆ ◆ ◆

Today, as everyone waits for the sun, William shoves Margot. The others move away from her. She is a thin, lost-looking girl who often daydreams about the past. She behaves like an outsider, and her classmates treat her like one. She doesn't play games with the rest of the children in the echoing tunnels of their underground city. When the class sings, she only joins in when the songs are about the sun. She sings the songs and looks at the <u>drenched</u> windows.

◆ Reading Strategy

How is Margot different from William? On the lines below, put a check before the qualities each child has.

Margot   **William**

___ quiet   ___ quiet

___ shy   ___ shy

___ bold   ___ bold

___ mean   ___ mean

◆ Literary Analysis

Circle the detail in this sentence that tells you something about the **setting** on Venus.

◆ Stop to Reflect

Why do you think Margot sings the only songs about the sun? Write your answer on these lines.

_____

_____

_____

_____

Vocabulary Development

protested (proh TEST ed) *v.* complained
drenched (DRENCHT) *adj.* completely wet

For the rest of the class, Margot's biggest crime is having lived on Venus for only five years. Before that, she lived on Earth. She and her family lived in Ohio until she was four years old. Because of this, she remembers the sun. The rest of the children have lived all of their lives on Venus. Because they were only two when they saw the sun, they don't remember it. Out of the entire class, Margot is the only one who remembers the sun.

◆　◆　◆

"It's like a penny," she said once, eyes closed.

"No, it's not!" the children cried.

"It's like a fire," she said, "in the stove."

"You're lying, you don't remember!" cried the children.

◆　◆　◆

But Margot remembers. And because she does, she hates the rain. A month before, she refused to go into the school shower because she couldn't bear for any more water to touch her head. Since then, her classmates have realized that she is different from them. Margot's parents are thinking of moving back to Earth. She hopes very much that they do.

◆　◆　◆

And so, the children hated her for all these reasons. . . . They hated her pale snow face, her waiting silence, her thinness, and her possible future.

"Get away!" The boy gave her another push. "What're you waiting for?"

◆　◆　◆

© Pearson Education, Inc.

All Summer in a Day **123**

◆ **Reading Strategy**

Put circles around the **contrasts** between Margot and her classmates. Why do the others think Margot's past experience is a "crime"? Write your ideas here.

_____

_____

_____

_____

◆ **Reading Strategy**

What is Margot's possible future? Circle the detail in the bracketed paragraph that tells you. Why do you think this future makes the children hate her? Write your answer on these lines.

_____

_____

_____

_____

◆ **Reading Check**

When did Margot come to Venus?

_____

Where did she come from?

_____

_____

_____

_____

_____

◆ **Stop to Reflect**

What do you think will happen now that Margot is locked in the closet? Write your answer on these lines.

_____

_____

_____

_____

Thinking about the sun, Margot looks at William for the first time. He tells her that the sun really isn't going to come out, that it is all a joke. The other students back him up. They begin shoving Margot roughly.

◆ ◆ ◆

They <u>surged</u> about her, caught her up and <u>bore</u> her, protesting, and then pleading, and then crying, back into a tunnel, a room, a closet, where they slammed and locked the door.

◆ ◆ ◆

The children can tell that Margot is pounding on the inside of the closet door. They also can hear her <u>muffled</u> yells to let her out. They don't care. The are smiling as they head back through the tunnel. Just then their teacher arrives.

◆ ◆ ◆

"Ready, children?"

◆ ◆ ◆

Glancing at her watch, the teacher asks if everyone is there; the children say yes. She doesn't notice that Margot is missing. The group crowds into the doorway. Then the rain stops.

◆ ◆ ◆

The silence was so <u>immense</u> and unbelievable that you felt your ears had been stuffed or you had lost your hearing altogether.

◆ ◆ ◆

The door opens. The children can smell the world outside. It is waiting for them. Then they see the sun.

◆ ◆ ◆

Vocabulary Development

surged (SURJD) *v.* moved in a swelling motion, like a wave

bore (BOHR) *v.* carried

muffled (MUF uhld) *adj.* quieted; stifled

immense (IM mens) *adj.* huge; very large

It was the color of flaming bronze and it was very large. And the sky around it was a blazing blue tile color. And the jungle burned with sunlight as the children, released from their spell, rushed out, yelling, into the springtime.

◆ ◆ ◆

The teacher cautions them that they will only have two hours in the sun. The children play and run and jump. In the sunlight, they are joyful. They play games such as hide-and-seek and tag. They know only the warmth of sun lamps so the sun's warmth amazes them.

◆ ◆ ◆

Like animals escaped from their caves, they ran and ran in shouting circles. They ran for an hour and did not stop running.

And then—

◆ ◆ ◆

One of the girls wails, and all the children stop. They see a raindrop lying in the open palm of her hand. Looking at it, she starts to cry. The children glance quietly at the sky. They hear thunder and watch the lightning get closer and closer. The sky darkens. The children stand at the door until the rain is coming down hard again.

◆ ◆ ◆

[They] heard the gigantic sound of the rain falling in tons and avalanches,[2] everywhere and forever.

"Will it be seven more years?"

"Yes. Seven."

Then one of them gave a little cry.

"Margot!"

"What?"

"She's still in the closet where we locked her."

◆ ◆ ◆

---

2. **avalanches** (AV a LANCH iz) *n.* large amounts.

◆ **Literary Analysis**

Circle the words that help you picture the **setting**. Which of the terms below best describes Venus? Circle the letter of the answer.

(a) frozen icebergs

(b) thick rain forest

(c) dry and empty desert

(d) rocky mountains

◆ **Reading Checks**

Why does the girl cry?

_____

_____

_____

_____

◆ **Read Fluently**

Read the bracketed dialogue out loud with a partner. Each line is a different speaker.

How do you think Margot will
feel about what happened?
Write your answer on these
lines.

_____

_____

_____

_____

The children now feel terrible about
what they did to Margot. They can barely
look each other in the eye. They slowly walk
back to the room. The sounds and sights of
the rainstorm are with them as they go to
the closet door. They stand there.

◆ ◆ ◆

Behind the closet door was only silence.
They unlocked the door, even more slowly,
and let Margot out.

1. What is odd about the weather on Venus?

_____

_____

2. In the paragraph below, circle the choice in parentheses that best
   completes each sentence.

   Margot's classmates are jealous of her because (she is from Earth and
   remembers the sun, she is an outsider and stands apart). Because
   they are jealous, they (try to be nice to her, are mean to her). In the
   end they (regret, are happy about) their treatment of Margot.

3. What does the title of the story mean? Circle the letter of your answer.
   (a) Margot remembers good times in Ohio.

   (b) The sunny season lasts only a short time.

   (c) Children like to play in summer.

   (d) Margot will not see the sun today.

4. Put a check in front of each thing the story shows about the way
   people behave.

	Children are kinder than adults.
	Children can be mean to one another.
	Only children can really enjoy nature.
	Outsiders are often treated badly.
	People are mean when it rains.
	If you are mean, you may regret it later.

5. **Literary Analysis:** List three details in the story that help you picture
   the **setting**.

   _____

   _____

(Continued)

6. **Reading Strategy:** On the chart below, **compare and contrast** Margot with the rest of her classmates. List at least three similarities and three differences.

	Margot and Her Classmates
Similarities	1. _____ _____ 2. _____ _____ 3. _____ _____
Differences	1. _____ _____ 2. _____ _____ 3. _____ _____

Writing

In the story, Ray Bradbury describes the planet Venus as he imagines it to be. Write a paragraph in which you describe a setting. It can be a place and time you know or that you just imagine.
- Choose a time and place as your setting. Write what they are here.
  Time: _____ Place: _____
- Think of details about the way the setting looks, sounds, feels, and maybe even smells. Write them down here.

_____

_____

_____

_____

_____

- On a separate sheet of paper, write your paragraph using some or all of the details you listed.

The Highwayman
Alfred Noyes

Summary

A dashing highwayman, or thief of the road, rides to an inn to see his love, the innkeeper's beautiful daughter Bess. He promises to return by the next night. The stable worker Tim, in love with Bess himself, overhears the couple. The next day soldiers hunting for the highwayman arrive at the inn. They gag and tie up Bess, tying a gun to her body, and tell her to keep watch. She hears her love riding closer. With no other way to warn him, she pulls the trigger of the gun, killing herself. The highwayman hears the shot and flees. The next day, when he learns what happened, he returns and is shot and killed. The ghosts of the highwayman and Bess are said to haunt the inn.

Visual Summary

1	2	3	4	5
The story takes place on a winter night in England of the 1700s.	The highwayman rides to the inn to visit Bess, the innkeeper's daughter. He promises to return by the next night at the latest. Tim, a stable worker in love with Bess, overhears. The next day soldiers hunt down the highwayman. They tie and gag Bess with a gun tied to her body. Bess hears her love approaching.	As the highwayman nears, Bess warns him of danger by pulling the trigger and killing herself.	The highwayman flees when he hears the shot. The next day he learns what happened to Bess and returns, only to be shot and killed.	The ghosts of the highwayman and Bess haunt the inn.

LITERARY ANALYSIS

Suspense

Suspense is the tension or nervousness that you feel when you do not know what is going to happen. Writers use suspense to make things interesting. It keeps readers reading.

In "The Highwayman," suspense increases as the highwayman rides closer and closer to the inn. We know a trap has been set for him, but we don't know what will happen to him. Each new detail adds to the suspense.

Tlot-tlot; tlot-tlot! *Had they heard it? The horse hoofs ringing clear;*

Tlot-tlot, tlot-tlot, *in the distance? Were they deaf that they did not hear?*

Down the ribbon of moonlight, over the brow of the hill,
The highwayman came riding—

    Riding—riding—

As you read "The Highwayman," look for other details that create suspense.

READING STRATEGY

Identifying Causes and Effects

You will understand events better if you can identify both causes and effects.

- **Causes:** events that bring about other events
- **Effects:** events that result from other events

Sometimes the effect of one event can be the cause of another. As you read "The Highwayman," show the causes and effects on a diagram like this one.

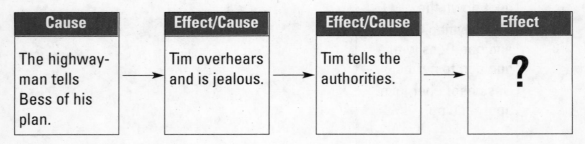

Cause	Effect/Cause	Effect/Cause	Effect
The highwayman tells Bess of his plan.	Tim overhears and is jealous.	Tim tells the authorities.	?

The Highwayman
Alfred Noyes

This poem takes place in England in the 1700s. People then still traveled on horseback or in horse-drawn coaches. The highways, or roads, had many inns where travelers stopped at night. Sometimes travelers were held up by robbers called highwaymen, like the one in this poem.

◆ ◆ ◆

The wind was a <u>torrent</u> of darkness among
   the <u>gusty</u> trees,
The moon was a ghostly galleon[1] tossed upon
   cloudy seas,
The road was a ribbon of moonlight over the
   purple moor,[2]
And the highwayman came riding—
   Riding—riding—
The highwayman came riding, up to the old
   inn door.

He'd a French cocked-hat on his forehead, a
   bunch of lace at his chin,
A coat of the claret[3] velvet, and breeches of
   brown doeskin.[4]
They fitted with never a wrinkle. His boots
   were up to the thigh.
And he rode with a jeweled twinkle,
   His pistol butts a-twinkle,
His rapier hilt[5] a-twinkle, under the jeweled
   sky.

Vocabulary Development

torrent (TOHR uhnt) *n.* flood
gusty (GUS tee) *adj.* windy

1. **galleon** (GAL yon) *n.* a Spanish sailing ship.
2. **moor** (MOOR) *n.* open, rolling land.
3. **claret** (KLAR et) *adj.* wine-colored.
4. **breeches** (BREECH es) **of brown doeskin** knee-length pants of brown deerskin.
5. **rapier** (RAY pee er) **hilt** large sword handle.

◆ **Reading Check**

At what time of day does the highwayman come riding? Write your answer on this line.

_____

Now, circle three words that told you the answer.

◆ **Stop to Reflect**

What do the details tell you about the highwayman? Circle the letter of your answer.

(a) He is handsome and well dressed.

(b) He is dull and ordinary.

(c) He is not capable of love.

(d) He is evil and wicked.

Now, circle five details that pointed to your answer.

Over the cobbles he clattered and clashed in
   the dark inn yard,
And he tapped with his whip on the <u>shutters</u>,
   but all was locked and barred;
He whistled a tune to the window, and who
   should be waiting there
But the landlord's[6] black-eyed daughter,
   Bess, the landlord's daughter,
Plaiting a dark red love knot[7] into her long
   black hair.

♦　♦　♦

      Tim takes care of horses in the inn's sta-
ble. An ugly man, he loves beautiful Bess.
Now he hears the highwayman and Bess
making plans.

♦　♦　♦

"One kiss, my bonnie[8] sweetheart, I'm after a
   prize tonight,
But I shall be back with the yellow gold before
   the morning light;
Yet, if they press me sharply, and harry[9] me
   through the day,
Then look for me by moonlight,
   Watch for me by moonlight,
I'll come to thee by moonlight, though hell
   should bar the way."

♦　♦　♦

      The highwayman cannot reach Bess's
lips, but he kisses her hair before riding off.

♦　♦　♦

He did not come in the dawning; he did not
   come at noon;
And out of the <u>tawny</u> sunset, before the rise o'
   the moon,

Vocabulary Development

shutters (SHUT erz) *n.* wooden window covers
tawny (TAW nee) *adj.* golden brown in color

---

6. **landlord's** (LAND lordz) *n.* owner of the inn's; innkeeper's.
7. **Plaiting** (PLAYT ing) **a dark red love knot** braiding a dark red ribbon.
8. **bonny** (BON ee) *adj.* beautiful.
9. **press . . . and harry** (HAR ee) close in on and attack.

When the road was a gypsy's ribbon, looping the purple moor,
A redcoat troop came marching—
Marching—marching—
King George's men came marching, up to the old inn door.

◆ ◆ ◆

The soldiers in red coats, or redcoat troop, serve England's King George. They are hunting for the highwayman. They gag Bess and tie her to her bed by the window. They tie a gun called a musket to her, with the barrel below her heart. "Now keep good watch!" they laugh. Looking out the window, she can see the road her love promised to come down that night.

◆ ◆ ◆

She twisted her hands behind her; but all the knots held good!
She <u>writhed</u> her hands till her fingers were wet with sweat or blood!
They stretched and strained in the darkness, and the hours crawled by like years,
Till, now, on the stroke of midnight,
Cold, on the stroke of midnight,
The tip of one finger touched it! The trigger at least was hers!

◆ ◆ ◆

Tied up and gagged, Bess desperately wants to warn her love of the danger that awaits him. Soon she hears a sound.

◆ ◆ ◆

Tlot-tlot; tlot-tlot! Had they heard it? The horse hoofs ringing clear;
Tlot-tlot, tlot-tlot, in the distance? Were they deaf that they did not hear?
Down the ribbon of moonlight, over the brow of the hill,

Vocabulary Development

writhed (RĪTHD) *v.* twisted

Moor, which means "open rolling land with swamps," is mainly a British word. You hear it in the U.S. mostly in stories and poems about Britain.

◆ **Literary Analysis**

Circle the words that add to the suspense of the story.

◆ **Read Fluently**

Read this stanza aloud. Make it as exciting as possible. What rhythm will you try to sound like in the third and fourth lines? Circle the letter of your answer.

(a) the rhythm of rain

(b) the rhythm of a train

(c) the rhythm of horses' hoofs

(d) the rhythm of Bess's breathing

The highwayman came riding—
  Riding—riding—
The redcoats looked to their priming![10] She
  stood up, straight and still!

Tlot-tlot, in the frosty silence! *Tlot-tlot*, in the
  echoing night!
Nearer he came and nearer! Her face was like a
  light!
Her eyes grew wide for a moment; she drew
  one last deep breath,
Then her finger moved in the moonlight,
  Her musket shattered the moonlight,
Shattered her breast in the moonlight and
  warned him—with her death.

        ◆   ◆   ◆

      The highwayman hears the warning
shot and rides away. The next morning he
learns what happened—how Bess died to
save him.

        ◆   ◆   ◆

Back, he spurred like a madman, shrieking a
  curse to the sky,
With white road smoking behind him, and his
  rapier <u>brandished</u> high!
Blood-red were his spurs in the golden noon,
  wine red was his velvet coat,
When they shot him down on the highway,
  Down like a dog on the highway,
And he lay in his blood on the highway, with a
  bunch of lace at his throat.

*And still of a winter's night, they say, when the
  wind is in the trees,
When the moon is a ghostly galleon tossed upon
  cloudy seas,*

Circle the words or phrases that add to the **suspense** here. What do you wonder about at this point in the poem? Write your answer on these lines.

_____

_____

_____

_____

◆ **Literary Analysis**

Why do you think the highwayman goes back? Write your answer on these lines.

_____

_____

_____

_____

Now, circle any words here that point to your answer.

◆ **Reading Check**

What did Bess do?

_____

_____

_____

Vocabulary Development

brandished (BRAN dishd) *v.* waved in a threatening way

---

10. **priming** (PRIM ing) *n.* explosive used to set the charge on a gun.

When the road is a ribbon of moonlight over the
   purple moor,
A highwayman comes riding—
   Riding — riding —
A highwayman comes riding, up to the old inn
   door.

Over the cobbles he clatters and clangs in the
   dark innyard;
And he taps with his whip on the shutters, but
   all is locked and barred;
He whistles a tune to the window, and who
   should be waiting there
But the landlord's black-eyed daughter,
   Bess, the landlord's daughter,
Plaiting a dark red love knot into her long black
   hair.

◆ **Reading Check**

What are the highwayman and
Bess in this part of the poem?
Circle the letter of your answer.

(a) travelers   (c) ghosts

(b) old people   (d) enemies

1. Why do you think the highwayman whistles to Bess, instead of going through the inn? Write your answer on the lines below.

_____

_____

2. Circle the words that tell what the highwayman, Bess, and Tim are like.

   Highwayman: dashing   cowardly   romantic   honest   loyal   mean

   Bess: beautiful   romantic   giggling   brave   loyal   jealous

   Tim: handsome   jealous   happy   brave   loving

3. What is the effect of the poem's rhythm? Circle the letter of the answer.

   (a) It captures the sound of the highwayman riding his horse.

   (b) It adds to the excitement of the story.

   (c) It makes the poem more musical.

   (d) all of the above

4. **Literary Analysis:** List three details that help build **suspense**.

_____

_____

_____

5. **Reading Strategy:** What do you think **causes** the soldiers to show up at the inn? Write your answer on the lines.

_____

_____

6. **Reading Strategy:** What **causes** Bess to pull the trigger? What are two **effects** of her pulling it? Write your answers on the lines.

Cause:

_____

_____

Two Effects:

1. _____

2. _____

Writing

Prepare a wanted poster that the soldiers might have written to help catch the highwayman.

- Review the poem for words describing the highwayman's appearance and activities. Write the words here.

_____

_____

- Use your imagination to add other details to put on the poster. For instance, you might list crimes the highwayman committed. You might mention a reward for his capture. Write these details here.

_____

_____

- Use some or all of the words you list in your final poster. Write the final words of your poster here.

_____

_____

_____

_____

Amigo Brothers
Piri Thomas

Summary

The "Amigo Brothers" are close friends of seventeen. They grew up in the same building in a poor neighborhood of New York City. They are very different in appearance, but they share a common passion: boxing. For years they have trained together, but now they must fight each other in the very important division finals. They train separately and worry about hurting each other. Yet, in the end, they throw their toughest punches. They realize that their friendship will endure no matter who wins. When the time comes to announce the winner of the match, the two friends have already embraced and left the ring.

Visual Summary

Setting	Place: poor neighborhood of New York City Time: July and August
Main Characters	Antonio Cruz and Felix Vargas, two 17-year-old boys
Background	Grew up in the same building. Are as close as brothers.
Goal	To be champion lightweight boxers
Problem	Must fight each other in important boxing match
Complications	• Don't want to hurt each other • Must do their best • Only one winner possible
Actions/Reactions	• Find it awkward to discuss upcoming fight • Agree to stop training together in last week • Fight with all they have, pulling no punches • Even have trouble stopping at final bell
	• Leave ring together before winner is announced • Realize friendship is more important than winning

LITERARY ANALYSIS

Third-Person Point of View

Point of view is the angle from which story events are told. In the **third-person point of view**, the storyteller sees the events from outside the story and is not a character in the story. The storyteller uses pronouns like *he* or *she* (not *I*) for all the characters. There are two types of third-person point of view:

- **third-person omniscient** (ahm NISH unt) The storyteller knows and tells the thoughts and feelings of all the characters. *Omniscient* means "all knowing."
- **third-person limited:** The storyteller tells the thoughts and feelings of only one character.

As you read "Amigo Brothers," pay attention to the thoughts and feelings of the characters. Decide if the story uses third-person omniscient or limited point of view.

READING STRATEGY

Drawing Inferences

An **inference** is a logical guess you make based on the information provided. For instance, in "Amigo Brothers," the author provides this information about Antonio and Felix:

Each youngster had a dream of someday becoming lightweight champion of the world. Every chance they had the boys worked out, sometimes at the Boys Club on 10th Street and Avenue A and sometimes at the . . . gym on 14th Street. Early morning sunrises would find them running along the East River Drive. . . .

From this information, you can **infer**, or conclude, that each boy worked hard to achieve his goal of becoming a boxing champion.

As you read, use the information in the story to make more inferences about Antonio and Felix.

Amigo[1] Brothers

Piri Thomas

◆ **Think Ahead**

What do Antonio and Felix both dream of becoming? Circle your answer. On the lines below, explain how their dream might affect their friendship.

_____

_____

_____

_____

Antonio Cruz and Felix Vargas were both 17. They grew up in the same building in a poor part of New York City. They were just close friends, or amigos, but thought of themselves as brothers. Yet they looked very different: Antonio was tall and fair; Felix was short and dark.

◆   ◆   ◆

Each youngster had a dream of someday becoming lightweight[2] champion of the world. Every chance they had the boys worked out, sometimes at the Boys Club on 10th Street and Avenue A and sometimes at the . . . gym on 14th Street. Early morning sunrises would find them running along the East River Drive. . . .

◆   ◆   ◆

◆ **Reading Check**

What event will be held in two weeks? Circle the information, and label it *What?* On what date will it be held? Circle the information, and label it *When?*

The two boys read about boxing and went to lots of matches. They boxed often and won many medals. They were both good but had different styles: Antonio moved better, but Felix's punches were stronger and more damaging.

◆   ◆   ◆

Now . . . they had been informed that they were to meet each other in the division finals that were scheduled for the seventh of August, two weeks away—the winner to represent the Boys Club in the Golden Gloves Championship Tournament.

◆ **Reading Strategy**

Based on the information presented, what do you think has caused this wall between the two friends? Write your **inference** on these lines.

_____

_____

_____

_____

The two boys continued to run together along the East River Drive. But even when joking with each other, they both sensed a <u>rising wall between</u> them.

◆   ◆   ◆

---

1. **amigo** (ah MEE goh) *adj.* Spanish for "friend."
2. **lightweight** (LĪT WAYT) referring to boxers weighing under 135 pounds.

Early one morning, a week before the big match, the two were running together as usual.

◆ ◆ ◆

After a mile or so, Felix puffed and said, "Let's stop a while, bro. I think we both got something to say to each other."

Antonio nodded. <u>It was not natural to be acting as though nothing unusual was happening</u>. . . . "It's about our fight, right?"

"Yeah, right." Felix's eyes squinted at the rising orange sun.

"I've been thinking about it too. . . . In fact, since we found out it was going to be me and you, I've been awake at night. . . ."

"Same here. It ain't natural not to think about the fight. I mean, we both . . . want to win. But only one of us can win. . . ."

Antonio nodded quietly. "Yeah. We both know that in the ring the better man wins. Friend or no friend, brother or no. . . ."

◆ ◆ ◆

Even though they didn't want to hurt each other, Felix knew they could not "pull their punches," or hold back when they fought.

◆ ◆ ◆

"When we get into the ring, it's gotta be like we never met. We gotta be like two . . . strangers that want the same thing and only one can have it. You understand, don'tcha?"

◆ ◆ ◆

The two agreed not to meet again before the fight. Felix went to stay with an aunt in another part of the city and trained at

◆ **Literary Analysis**

Who is thinking this thought? Circle the earlier words that tell you, and underline the character's name.

◆ **Reading Check**

Is it possible for the upcoming fight to end in a tie? Circle *yes* or *no*:

yes   no

Now, circle the words here that told you the answer.

◆ **Read Fluently**

Read this remark aloud. Circle two words with unusual spellings that show how Felix pronounces them. Write the proper English spellings for the words on the lines.

_____

_____

_____

_____

♦ ♦ ♦

When Felix finally left the theatre, he had figured out how to psyche himself[3] for tomorrow's fight. It was Felix the Champion vs.[4] Antonio the Challenger.

♦ ♦ ♦

Meanwhile, on the roof of their apartment house, Antonio was also thinking of the fight.

♦ ♦ ♦

How would the fight tomorrow affect his relationship with Felix? After all, fighting was like any other profession. Friendship had nothing to do with it. . . . Felix, his *amigo* brother, was not going to be Felix at all in the ring. Just an opponent with another face. Antonio went to sleep hearing the opening bell for the first round.

♦ ♦ ♦

The division finals drew such a large crowd that they were held outdoors in Tompkins Square Park.

♦ ♦ ♦

Antonio wore white trunks, black socks, and black shoes. Felix wore sky blue trunks, red socks, and white boxing shoes. Each had dressing gowns to match their fighting trunks with their names neatly stitched on the back.

♦ ♦ ♦

After about six other matches, it was time for Felix and Antonio to face each other.

♦ ♦ ♦

As the two climbed into the ring, the crowd exploded with a roar. . . . Antonio tried to be cool, but even as the roar was in its first birth,

---

3. **psyche** (SIK) **himself** slang for "put himself in the right frame of mind."
4. **vs.** short for versus (VER suhs) meaning "against; competing with."

◆ Literary Analysis

Circle any character's thoughts that appear in these paragraphs. Label them *Felix* or *Antonio*. Based on these details, is the narrator omniscient or limited?

_____

_____

◆ Reading Strategy

Felix is worried about how the fight will affect his friendship with Antonio. Do you think the friendship is important to him?

_____

How do you know?

_____

_____

_____

_____

◆ Stop to Reflect

What do you think the two boys are thinking here? Write your ideas on the lines below.

_____

_____

_____

_____

he turned slowly to meet Felix's eyes looking directly into his. Felix nodded his head and Antonio responded. And both as one, just as quickly, turned away to face his own corner.

◆ ◆ ◆

An announcer spoke in English and Spanish.

◆ ◆ ◆

"Ladies and Gentlemen. *Señores y Señoras.*"[5] . . . In this corner, weighing 134 pounds, Felix Vargas. And in this corner, weighing 133 pounds, Antonio Cruz. The winner will represent the Boys Club in the tournament of champions, the Golden Gloves. . . . May the best man win."

◆ ◆ ◆

The crowd cheered while the referee told the two boxers the rules for keeping it a fair fight. The two touched gloves and went to their corners. Then the bell rang and the fight began.

◆ ◆ ◆

BONG! BONG! ROUND ONE. Felix and Antonio turned and faced each other squarely in a fighting pose. Felix wasted no time. He came out with a straight left. He missed a right cross as Antonio slipped the punch and <u>countered</u> with one-two-three lefts that snapped Felix's head back. . . . If Felix had any small doubt about their friendship affecting their fight, it was being neatly <u>dispelled</u>.

Antonio danced, a joy to behold. His left hand was like a piston[6] pumping jabs one right

---

◆ Read Fluently

Read the announcer's speech aloud. Read it with expression, as if you were the announcer trying to excite the crowd.

◆ Reading Strategy

How are the two boxers different? Circle the letter of the best answer below. Also circle details in the paragraph that helped you make your **inference**.

(a) Antonio is more experienced.

(b) Felix is more graceful.

(c) Antonio can stand more punches than Felix can.

(d) Felix is shorter.

Vocabulary Development

countered (KOWN terd) *v.* came back with

dispelled (di SPELD) *v.* driven away; made to disappear

---

5. **Señores** (sen YO res) **y Señoras** (se NYO ras) Spanish for "Ladies and Gentlemen."
6. **piston** (PIS tuhn) *n.* engine part that moves quickly back and forth.

after another with seeming ease. Felix . . . never stopped <u>boring</u> in. He knew that at long range he was at a disadvantage. Antonio had too much reach on him. Only by coming in close could Felix hope to achieve the dreamed-of knockout.

◆ ◆ ◆

Finally the bell signaled the end of round one. Both fighters returned to their corners. All too soon, the bell rang again. The two resumed fighting with all their strength. Then Antonio hit Felix right on the chin.

◆ ◆ ◆

Felix's legs momentarily <u>buckled</u>. He fought off a series of rights and lefts and came back with a strong right that taught Antonio respect. . . .

Rights to the body. Lefts to the head. Neither fighter was giving an inch. Suddenly a short right caught Antonio squarely on the chin. His long legs turned to jelly. . . . Fighting off the growing haze, Antonio struggled to his feet, got up, ducked, and threw a smashing right that dropped Felix flat on his back.

Felix got up as fast as he could. . . . In a fog, he heard the roaring of the crowd, who seemed to have gone insane. His head cleared to hear the bell sound at the end of the round. He was very glad.

◆ ◆ ◆

The bell again rang for round three, the last round. Antonio came in fighting hard and drove Felix to the ropes. Then Felix went on the attack.

◆ ◆ ◆

Vocabulary Development

boring (BOHR ing) *n.* forcing your way in
buckled (BUK ld) *v.* bent and gave way

Both pounded away. Neither gave an inch and neither fell to the canvas.[7] Felix's left eye was tightly closed. . . . Blood poured from Antonio's nose. They fought toe-to-toe.

The sounds of their blows were loud in contrast to the silence of a crowd gone completely <u>mute</u>. The referee was stunned by their <u>savagery</u>.

Bong! Bong! Bong! The bell sounded over and over again. Felix and Antonio were past hearing. Their blows continued to pound on each other like hailstones.

◆ ◆ ◆

Finally, the referee broke up the fight by pouring cold water on the boys. Because neither had knocked the other to the canvas, officials would have to decide the winner. But the boxers suddenly rushed toward each other.

◆ ◆ ◆

A cry of alarm surged through Tompkins Square Park. Was this a fight to the death instead of a boxing match?

The fear soon gave way to wave upon wave of cheering as the two amigos embraced.

No matter what the decision, they knew they would always be champions to each other.

◆ ◆ ◆

The announcer began to declare the winner.

◆ ◆ ◆

"Ladies and Gentlemen. *Señores y Señoras.* The winner and representative to the Golden Gloves Tournament of Champions is . . ."

Vocabulary Development

mute (MYOOT) *adj.* silent
savagery (SAV ij ree) *n.* wildness; violence

---

7. **canvas** (CAN vuhs) *n.* the floor of the boxing ring.

◆ **Reading Check**

Who is winning the fight?

_____

_____

◆ **Stop to Reflect**

Why do you think the boys keep fighting after the bell has rung? Write your ideas on these lines.

_____

_____

_____

_____

◆ **Reading Strategy**

What do the boys realize here? Circle the letter of the best answer. Also circle the words that helped you make your **inferences**.

(a) They fought their best.

(b) They are still friends.

(c) Their friendship matters more than winning.

(d) all of the above

The announcer turned to point to the winner and found himself alone. Arm in arm the champions had already left the ring.

1. Circle the letter of the statement that best describes Antonio and Felix.

   (a) They are brothers.

   (b) They are close friends and neighbors who feel like brothers.

   (c) They were friends until one moved out of the neighborhood.

   (d) They were once friends but are now jealous of each other.

2. On the lines, explain how boxing brings the two boys together but also drives them apart.

   How it brings them together: _____

   _____

   _____

   _____

   How it drives them apart: _____

   _____

   _____

   _____

3. In front of each detail, write *A* if the detail describes Antonio. Write *F* if it describes Felix.

   ____ tall   ____ boxes better when he comes in close

   ____ short   ____ boxes more gracefully

   ____ dark   ____ has better moves as a boxer

   ____ fair   ____ keeps boring down on his opponent

4. Complete this sentence to show what the two boys learn in the story.

   _____ is more important than _____.

5. **Literary Analysis:** Prove that this story uses third-person omniscient point of view by listing different characters' thoughts and impressions.

Felix (list 2 thoughts):

1. _____

2. _____

Referee (list 1 thought): _____

Crowd (list 1 thought): _____

6. **Reading Strategy:** Put a check in front of each **inference** you can draw from the information provided in the story.

_____ Antonio and Felix are Irish American.

_____ Antonio and Felix work very hard to fulfill their dreams about boxing.

_____ The two boys often face each other in important boxing matches.

_____ The Golden Gloves is an important tournament in the world of boxing.

_____ Felix is the clear winner of the boxing match.

Listening and Speaking

Imagine that you are raising money for neighborhood sports. Give a **persuasive talk** to convince a group of community business people to donate money. Before you give your talk, be sure you have your facts and details straight.

- List three neighborhood sports that the business people might support. For each sport, list the equipment and other things that need to be paid for.

_____

- List at least three reasons for supporting neighborhood sports.

_____

- Organize your information into your talk. Then, practice delivering it. When you are ready, present your talk to a small group or to your class.

Our Finest Hour

Charles Osgood

Summary

TV reporter Charles Osgood describes a series of mistakes on the night he was the substitute anchor on the *CBS Evening News*. First the lead story he introduced did not appear on the monitor—a different story ran instead. Then the next report didn't appear either. Then there was no commercial when there was supposed to be. Later a peculiar news story that no one had checked in advance showed up on the monitor and had to be cut in the middle. Then the executive producer's angry scream in the studio was picked up by a microphone and broadcast on the air. To top it all off, journalists from China were visiting the studio that night to observe the news.

Visual Summary

B A D

1 ⟶ Osgood introduces lead story. Monitor shows a different story.

2 ⟶ Second story doesn't show on monitor.

3 ⟶ Commercial doesn't come on when cued.

4 ⟶ Osgood introduces Washington story but monitor shows series of French people pretending to be dead. Since report was never previewed, it is pulled in middle.

5 ⟶ Executive producer's scream is picked up by the microphone.

6 ⟶ Visitors from China viewing news broadcast see all the errors.

! ! ! W O R S E ! ! !

LITERARY ANALYSIS

Humor

Humor is writing or speech that tries to make people laugh. Describing real-life bloopers, or mistakes, is often a good way to create humor. One person's embarrassing moments often seem funny to others. In fact, over time, even the embarrassed person often finds the experience funny.

In "Our Finest Hour," the news show that Charles Osgood anchors becomes a series of bloopers. As you read, list the mistakes that take place on a chart like this one.

Supposed to Happen	Actually Happened
Osgood announces first story and first story appears on monitor.	Osgood announces first story and second story appears on monitor.

READING STRATEGY

Recognizing Author's Purpose

Authors usually write with a goal or **purpose** in mind. You can often tell the author's purpose from the kinds of details he or she provides. Study this chart of four common purposes. The second column shows the kinds of details that signal each purpose.

Purpose	Details Provided
• to persuade or convince	emotional language, one side of issue, call to action
• to entertain	humor, mystery, suspense
• to give information	facts and details
• to reflect on an experience	details of writer's life, comments by writer

As you read "Our Finest Hour," look for the kinds of details in the selection. Use them to help you determine the author's purpose.

Our Finest Hour
Charles Osgood

In this essay, Charles Osgood recalls events that took place soon after he began working for CBS News. In those days, he worked mainly as a TV reporter and radio announcer.

◆ ◆ ◆

Only occasionally do most reporters or correspondents get to "anchor" a news broadcast. Anchoring, you understand, means sitting there in the studio and telling some stories into the camera and introducing the reports and pieces that other reporters do.

It looks easy enough. It is easy enough, most of the time. . . .

◆ ◆ ◆

But the first time Osgood did it, it turned out not to be so easy.

◆ ◆ ◆

It was a Saturday night and I was filling in for Roger Mudd[1] on the *CBS Evening News.* Roger was on vacation. The regular executive producer[2] of the broadcast, Paul Greenberg, was on vacation, too.

◆ ◆ ◆

Also on vacation were the cameraman, editor, and director who usually worked on the show. The show was live, as the TV news usually is.

◆ ◆ ◆

Vocabulary Development

correspondents (car reh SPAHN duhntz) *n.* person hired by a news organization to report news from a distant place

broadcast (BRAWD kast) *n.* an airing of a TV show

---

1. **Roger Mudd:** CBS news reporter who usually anchored the news on weekends.
2. **executive producer:** main person in charge of a TV show.

Circle the sentence you think is funniest in the bracketed paragraph. What does the big buildup to this sentence show about the **author's purpose**? Circle the letter of your answer below.

(a) He wants to present all the facts about being a news anchor.

(b) He wants to persuade us to avoid mistakes like this one.

(c) He wants to entertain us with humor.

(d) He wants to examine his past thoughtfully. He wants to come to a conclusion about its meaning.

On the lines below, explain what is funny about the incident in the bracketed passage.

_____

_____

_____

_____

Circle the reason Osgood gives for the decision to stop the story in the middle. What about the story might worry CBS News? Write your ideas on the lines below.

_____

_____

_____

I said "Good evening" and introduced the first report and turned to the <u>monitor</u> to watch it. What I saw was myself looking at the monitor. Many seconds passed. Finally there was something on the screen. A reporter was beginning a story. It was not the story I had introduced.

◆ ◆ ◆

Osgood realized the reporter was doing what should have been the second story. So he found his notes for that story. When the report was done, Osgood explained it. He then reintroduced the first story, which he figured would now come second. Only it didn't. Finally, the director signaled him to move on to the third story.

◆ ◆ ◆

So I introduced the next report. It didn't come up either, so I said we'd continue in just a moment. Obvious <u>cue</u> for a commercial, I thought, but it took a while. . . .

◆ ◆ ◆

Finally the commercial came on. Everyone rushed to fix the problems. They didn't. After the commercial, Osgood introduced a political story from Washington, DC. But what came up on the monitor were pictures of people in a small town in France. The people were pretending to be dead to show the dangers of smoking. People in the news studio were frantic. They were trying to fix the problems with the broadcast.

◆ ◆ ◆

It was a nice story well told, but since nobody in authority at CBS News, New York, had seen it or knew what was coming next, they decided to dump out of it and come back to me. I, of course, was sitting there looking at

---

Vocabulary Development

monitor (MON i ter) *n.* TV screen
cue (KYEW) *n.* signal

the piece with <u>bewilderment</u> written all over my face, when suddenly, in the midst of all these French people pretending to be dead, I saw myself, bewilderment and all.

◆ ◆ ◆

Finally, Osgood introduced the last story, which was supposed to be about rafting. Nothing happened on the monitor, however.

◆ ◆ ◆

"What is going on?" screamed the fill-in executive producer. I could hear him perfectly clearly, and so could half of America. The microphone on my tie-clip was open. Standing in the control room watching this with what I'm sure must have been great interest, was a <u>delegation</u> of visiting <u>journalists</u> from the People's Republic of China. They must have had a really great <u>impression</u> of American electronic journalism.

◆ ◆ ◆

On Monday, the head of CBS News came to see Osgood. "What *was* going on?" he asked.

◆ **Literary Analysis**

Circle the words that tell what two things Osgood saw on the monitor. Which one is funny?

_____

_____

Why? _____

_____

_____

◆ **Read Fluently**

Read the bracketed passage aloud. What feeling should you try to show? Circle the letter of your answer.

(a) jolly; giggling

(b) sarcastic; meaning the opposite of what you say

(c) frightened; nervous

(d) very formal and serious

Vocabulary Development

bewilderment (bee WIL duhr muhnt) *n.* puzzlement; confusion

journalists (JUR nal istz) *n.* reporters

delegation (DEL e GAY shun) *n.* group sent by others

impression (im PRESH un) *n.* idea or image that stays in the mind

1. What is probably the reason so many things go wrong on the night of Osgood's broadcast? Circle the letter of the best answer.

   (a) Osgood has little experience as a news anchor and does a bad job.

   (b) New equipment at CBS is not working properly.

   (c) The news people are very nervous about the foreign visitors.

   (d) Many people who usually work on the news are on vacation.

2. How would you describe Osgood's behavior during the broadcast? Circle *two* words.

   calm   panicked   angry   professional   joking

3. At the end of the essay, do you think the head of CBS News was mad at Osgood? Write *yes* or *no* on these lines, and then tell why.

   _____

   _____

   _____

4. **Literary Analysis:** What bloopers, or mistakes, help create the **humor**? On the chart below, explain what was supposed to happen and what actually happened in at least three of the bloopers.

Supposed to Happen	Actually Happened

5. **Reading Strategy:** List three details that show that the author's purpose is mainly to entertain.

- _____
  _____

- _____
  _____

- _____
  _____

Writing

A **summary** of a work gives just its main ideas or events. Write a one-paragraph summary of "Our Finest Hour." Follow these steps.

- Complete this sentence and use it to open your summary.

In "Our Finest Hour," _____ tells of the series of

humorous _____ that occurred on the night he

_____

_____

_____

- List at least five main events to include in your summary.

_____

_____

_____

_____

_____

- Now, create your one-paragraph summary on a separate sheet of paper. Use the opening sentence and main events you listed above.

Cat on the Go

James Herriot

Summary

Animal doctor James Herriot and his assistant Tristan save the life of a badly injured stray cat brought to their office. Herriot's wife Helen then cares for the cat in their home and names it Oscar. The cat is unusually friendly. After he recovers, he disappears one evening and shows up at a church meeting. Another night, he sits in on a darts championship. After the third such incident, the Herriots realize that Oscar enjoys large gatherings of people. One day the cat's previous owners, who live some distance away, show up after a long search to claim him. The Herriots sadly give him up. Then they decide to visit him. Oscar is out when they arrive but greets them warmly when he returns—from sitting in on a local yoga class.

Visual Summary

Oscar the Stray	Oscar the Herriot Pet	Oscar Back with His Owners
• Found by Marjorie Simpson, postman's teenaged daughter	• Becomes one of the family	• Was pet of a Gibbons family, who finally locate and claim him
• Is badly injured and near death	• Visited often by Tristan	• Leaves the Herriots, who miss him a lot
• Brought to animal doctor James Herriot and his assistant Tristan	• Vanishes one night and is brought back from a church meeting	• Is not home at first when the Herriots pay a visit
• Saved by unusual surgery	• Disappears again and is brought back from a darts championship	• Recognizes them and seems happy to see them
• Nursed to health by Helen Herriot, who calls him Oscar	• Goes off again, this time to a Women's Institute meeting	• Had been sitting in on a local yoga class when they arrived
	• Continues to appear at neighborhood gatherings	

LITERARY ANALYSIS
Character Traits

The qualities displayed by a human or animal character are called **character traits**. They are the details that tell you what a character is like. They show a character's personality.

Sometimes authors tell you these traits directly. Sometimes you have to figure them out from a character's words or behavior. For example, in "Cat on the Go," Oscar the cat often sits in on people's meetings and other group activities. We can tell from his behavior that he is a friendly cat.

As you read "Cat on the Go," keep track of character traits by completing this diagram.

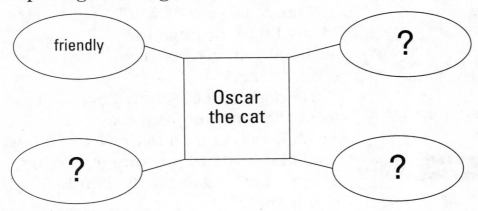

READING STRATEGY
Interpreting Idioms

An **idiom** is an expression with a meaning different from what the words actually say. For example, "on the go" is an idiom. If you think of the words separately, they don't make much sense. The expression, however, has a meaning different from its separate words. It means "to be active" or "to be out and busy."

As you read, list the idioms in "Cat on the Go" on a chart like the one below. Use the words nearby to help you figure out the meanings of unfamiliar idioms.

Idiom	Meaning
on the go	to be active; to be out and busy

Cat on the Go
James Herriot

James Herriot writes of his experiences as a veterinarian, or animal doctor, in the farm communities of northern England. Herriot and his assistant Tristan treat all kinds of animals, including household pets. One day the postman's daughter brings in a cat so badly injured that his guts are spilling from his body.

◆ ◆ ◆

"I saw this cat sittin' in the dark. . . . Then I saw 'e was badly hurt and I went home for a blanket and brought 'im round to you."

"That was <u>kind</u> of you," I said. "Have you any idea who he belongs to?"

The girl shook her head. "No, he looks like a stray to me."

"He does indeed." I dragged my eyes away from the terrible wound. . . .

"Well, I reckon I'd better leave 'im with you. You'll be going to <u>put him out of his misery</u>. There's nothing anybody can do about . . . about that?"

I shrugged and shook my head. The girl's eyes filled with tears, she stretched out a hand and touched the <u>emaciated</u> animal then turned and walked quickly to the door.

◆ ◆ ◆

The doctors see that the cat is badly hurt. They are both very sad about having to end the poor cat's life. When Tristan gently strokes his cheek, the cat purrs.

◆ ◆ ◆

Vocabulary Development

emaciated (e MAY shee AYT ed) *adj.* extremely thin; starving

"My God, do you hear that?"

"Yes . . . amazing in that condition. He's a good-natured cat."

Tristan, head bowed, continued his stroking. . . . At last he looked up at me and gulped. "I don't fancy[1] this much, Jim. Can't we do something?" . . .

"But the <u>bowels</u> are damaged—they're like a <u>sieve</u> in parts."

"We could stitch them, couldn't we?"

I lifted the blanket and looked again. . . . "Come on, then," I said. "We'll <u>have a go</u>."

◆ ◆ ◆

Herriot and Tristan carefully clean and stitch the cat's insides, trying to put everything back in place. Herriot still believes the cat will die. But his wife Helen brings the cat home to try to nurse it back to health. For the next few days she carefully spoons milk, broth, and expensive baby foods down his throat. She names him Oscar. The cat does better than Herriot ever expected.

◆ ◆ ◆

It was as though Oscar's animal <u>instinct</u> told him he had to move as little as possible because he lay absolutely still day after day and looked up at us—and purred.

His purr became part of our lives and when he eventually left his bed . . . it was a moment of <u>triumph</u>. . . . From then on it was sheer joy to watch the furry scarecrow fill out and grow

---

Vocabulary Development

bowels (BOW uhlz) *n.* intestines; guts
sieve (SIV) *n.* a metal strainer with many holes
instinct (IN stinkt) *n.* inborn understanding
triumph (TRY umf) *n.* victory

---

1. **fancy** (FAN see) *v.* feel in the mood for; want; wish.

◆ **Think Ahead**

What do you think will happen to the cat? Write your prediction on the lines below.

_____

_____

_____

_____

◆ **Reading Strategy**

Use the words nearby to help you figure out the meaning of the British **idiom** "have a go." Circle the letter of the correct meaning below.

(a) try   (c) leave

(b) cry   (d) busy

◆ **Stop to Reflect**

Why is it important for the cat to remain still? Write your ideas on the lines below.

_____

_____

_____

_____

◆ **Reading Check**

What change takes place in Oscar? Circle the letter of your answer below. Also circle the story details that point to your answer.

(a) He becomes fat and lazy.

(b) He fills out and becomes a nice-looking cat.

(c) After he gains weight, he looks like a furry scarecrow.

(d) He is no longer good-natured.

_____

_____

_____

_____

strong, and as he ate and ate and the flesh spread over his bones the true beauty of his coat showed. . . .

◆ ◆ ◆

Tristan visits, teasing Oscar playfully. Oscar also gets along well with the Herriots' dog. But one night, James comes home to find his wife very upset. Helen has hunted everywhere, and Oscar is missing! Then the doorbell rings.

◆ ◆ ◆

I could see Mrs. Heslington, the vicar's[2] wife, through the glass. I threw open the door. She was holding Oscar in her arms.

"I believe this is your cat, Mr. Herriot," she said.

"It is indeed, Mrs. Heslington. Where did you find him?"

She smiled. "Well it was rather odd. We were having a meeting of the Mothers' Union at the church house and we noticed the cat sitting there in the room . . . as though he were listening to what we were saying and enjoying it all. It was unusual. When the meeting ended I thought I'd better bring him along to you."

◆ ◆ ◆

Not long afterward, Oscar disappears again. The man who brings him back explains that he showed up at a local darts tournament, sat with the players, and seemed to enjoy himself. Three nights later, Oscar appears at the local Women's Institute. A woman from the meeting reports that he enjoyed the slides and was very interested in the cakes. After she leaves, James shares his thoughts with his wife.

◆ ◆ ◆

---

2. **vicar** (VIK er) *n.* local priest in the Church of England, where priests can marry.

"I know about Oscar now," I said.

"Know what?"

"Why he goes on these nightly outings. He's not running away—he's visiting."

"Visiting?"

"Yes," I said. "Don't you see? He likes getting around, he loves people, especially in groups, and he's interested in what they do. He's a natural mixer."

Helen looked down at the attractive mound of fur curled on her lap. "Of course . . . that's it . . . he's a . . . cat-about-town!"

◆ ◆ ◆

One evening a farm worker named Sep Gibbons visits James Herriot's office with his two little boys. They live a few towns away and have been hunting for their lost cat for months. Sep describes a cat that looks like Oscar and always goes to gatherings. James thinks they must be looking for Oscar. Deeply upset, James takes them home and explains the situation to Helen.

◆ ◆ ◆

She stood very still for a moment and then smiled faintly. "Do sit down. Oscar's in the kitchen. I'll bring him through."

She went out and reappeared with the cat in her arms. She hadn't got through the door before the little boys gave tongue.

"Tiger!" they cried. "Oh, Tiger, Tiger!"

The man's face seemed lit from within. He walked quickly across the floor and ran his big work-roughened hand along the fur. . . .

As the two little boys rolled on the floor our Oscar rolled with them, pawing playfully, purring with delight. . . .

Helen said it for me. "Well, Mr. Gibbons." Her tone had an unnatural brightness. "You'd better take him."

◆ **Read Fluently**

Read aloud this conversation between James and Helen Herriot. Which words might you say with a little laugh in your voice? Circle those words.

◆ **Stop to Reflect**

Why do you think the Gibbons family called the cat Tiger? Write your guess on the lines below.

_____

_____

_____

_____

◆ **Literary Analysis**

Helen is upset to lose Oscar, but she welcomes Sep into her home. List two **character traits** that you think Helen shows in this section.

1. _____

2. _____

_____

_____

_____

_____

◆ Literary Analysis

What does Helen feel when Oscar recognizes her? Circle the word that tells you. Then, circle the letter of the choice below that best describes Helen's **character traits**.

(a) She is warm and caring.

(b) She is distant and cold.

(c) She is shy and hates attention.

(d) She is selfish and mean about sharing her possessions.

The man <u>hesitated</u>, "Now then, are ye sure, Missis Herriot?"

"Yes . . . yes, I'm sure. He was your cat first."

◆ ◆ ◆

The Herriots miss Oscar a lot. One night after seeing a movie near the Gibbons's home, they drop by to visit. Sep and his wife make them welcome, but there is no sign of Oscar.

◆ ◆ ◆

"How—" I asked. . . . "How is—er—Tiger?"

"Oh, he's grand," the little woman replied briskly. She glanced up at the clock on the mantelpiece.[3] "He should be back any time now, then you'll be able to see 'im."

As she spoke, Sep raised a finger. "Ah think ah can hear 'im now."

He walked over and opened the door and our Oscar strode in with all his old grace and majesty. He took one look at Helen and leaped onto her lap. With a cry of delight she put down her cup and stroked the beautiful fur. . .

"He knows me," she murmured. "He knows me."

. . . I went over and tickled Oscar's chin, then I turned to Mrs. Gibbons. "By the way, it's after nine o'clock. Where has he been till now?" . . .

"Let's see, now," she said. "It's Thursday, isn't it? Ah yes, it's 'is night for the Yoga class."

Vocabulary Development

hesitated (HEZ i TAYT ed) *v.* waited or paused because of feeling uncertain

---

3. **mantelpiece** (MAN tuhl pees) *n.* the shelf over a fireplace.

1. Why does Oscar survive? Circle the letter of the best answer.

   (a) He is not as seriously injured as he seems.

   (b) He is a very active cat and refuses to be still for a moment.

   (c) He is a good patient and gets lots of loving care.

   (d) all of the above

2. List two ways in which Oscar surprises James Herriot.

   • _____

   • _____

3. How do the Herriots feel about returning Oscar to the Gibbons family? Answer the question by completing this sentence.

   The Herriots are very _____ about returning

   Oscar, but they also realize that _____

   _____

   _____.

4. What does the story show about pets? Circle the letter of your answer.

   (a) Pets can cause danger to people.

   (b) Pets can be like members of the family.

   (c) Pets can make people do things they regret.

   (d) all of the above

   Explain how the story shows this idea. _____

   _____

   (Continued)

5. **Literary Analysis:** Put a check in front of the words or phrases that name or describe the **character traits** of each character below.

Oscar the Cat	James Herriot	Helen Herriot
____ friendly	____ skilled as a doctor	____ caring
____ bad tempered	____ good storyteller	____ selfish
____ affectionate	____ no sense of humor	____ shy

6. **Reading Strategy:** On the line, explain the meaning of the **idiom** in italics. Use the story context as a clue.

Oscar was always *on the go*: Oscar was always _____.

Let's *have a go* p. 159: Let's _____.

The two boys *gave tongue* p. 161: The two boys _____.

Writing

Write a paragraph describing a character in the story. Show what the character is like by focusing on his or her character traits.
- Choose the character you want to describe. Write the character's name in the chart below.
- List the character's three main personality traits. For each, give an example from the story.

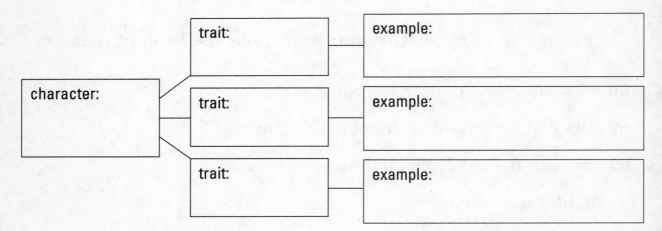

- Write your paragraph on a separate sheet of paper. Discuss the three traits. Support each trait with the examples you have listed.

The Luckiest Time of All
Lucille Clifton

Summary

Elzie tells her great-granddaughter Tee the story of how she and her friend Ovella ran off to see the Silas Greene show, a kind of traveling circus, when they were young. On the show grounds, a cute dancing dog amused the crowd. Seeing people toss coins at the dog, Elzie threw her "lucky stone." But the stone hit the dog on the nose, and he began chasing Elzie. She was then rescued by a boy named Amos Pickens. Meeting Amos changed her life, since he would later become her husband. So the stone proved very lucky indeed!

Visual Summary

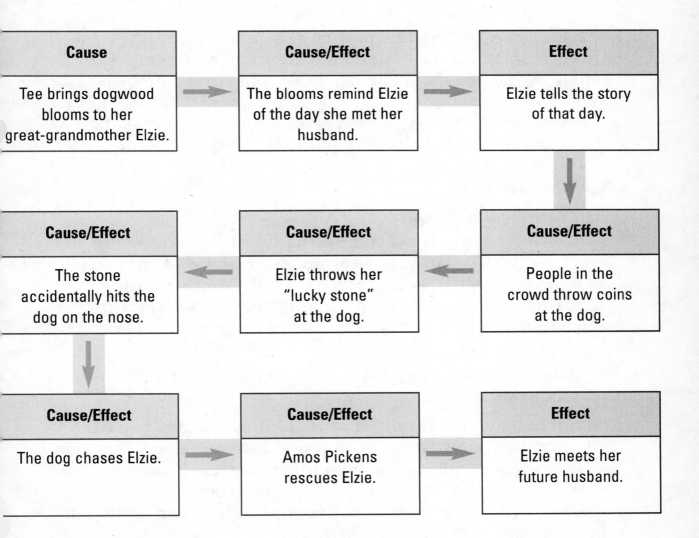

Cause	Cause/Effect	Effect
Tee brings dogwood blooms to her great-grandmother Elzie.	The blooms remind Elzie of the day she met her husband.	Elzie tells the story of that day.

Cause/Effect	Cause/Effect	Cause/Effect
The stone accidentally hits the dog on the nose.	Elzie throws her "lucky stone" at the dog.	People in the crowd throw coins at the dog.

Cause/Effect	Cause/Effect	Effect
The dog chases Elzie.	Amos Pickens rescues Elzie.	Elzie meets her future husband.

LITERARY ANALYSIS

Hyperbole

Hyperbole (hī PUHR boh lee) is exaggeration done for effect. People use hyperbole all the time to make a story funny or to make a point.

If you say "I'm hungry enough to eat a horse," that is hyperbole. You don't really mean that you would eat a whole horse. You are exaggerating to stress the idea that you are hungry.

In "The Luckiest Time of All," Elzie uses hyperbole to describe Amos Pickens on the day she met him. Look at this example:

> Right behind me was the dancin dog and right behind him was _the finest fast runnin hero in . . . Virginia_.

Amos may be fast, and he may even be a hero, but he probably isn't "the finest fast-running hero" in all of Virginia. Elzie simply exaggerates to make her point. She thinks Amos is wonderful.

As you read the story, look for more examples of hyperbole. You may find that hyperbole makes this story funny.

READING STRATEGY

Clarifying Word Meanings

When you read, you will come across words with meanings you aren't sure of. To **clarify**, or clear up, the meaning of an unfamiliar term, you need to look at its context, the words near it.

In "The Luckiest Time of All," Elzie Pickens uses certain terms that you may not be sure of. For example, read this passage where Elzie describes a dog's behavior.

> Well, . . . he _lit out_ after me and I flew! Round and round the Silas Greene we run. . . .

Even though you may not know what _lit out_ means, you can tell from the context what the dog and Elzie are doing. The dog is chasing Elzie, and they are both running. So _lit out_ must mean "started running or chasing" or "took off."

As you read the story, use the context to help you figure out the meanings of other unfamiliar terms.

The Luckiest Time of All
Lucille Clifton

Elzie F. Pickens is rocking in a chair on her porch when her great-granddaughter Tee visits. Tee brings her blooms from a dogwood tree that remind Elzie of the day she met Amos Pickens, her husband and Tee's great-grandfather.

◆　◆　◆

"It was just this time, spring of the year, and me and my best friend Ovella Wilson, who is now gone, was goin to join <u>the Silas Greene</u>. Usta be a kinda show went all through the South, called it the Silas Greene show. Somethin like the circus. Me and Ovella wanted to join that thing and see the world. Nothin wrong at home or nothin, we just wanted to travel and see new things. . . ."

◆　◆　◆

So the two girls got all dressed up. They headed for the show. They decided to explore the grounds before signing up to join.

◆　◆　◆

"While we was viewin it all we come up on this dancin dog. Cutest one thing in the world next to you, Sweet Tee, dippin and movin and head bowin to that music. Had a little ruffly skirt on itself and up on two back legs twistin and movin to the music. Dancin dancin dancin till people started throwin pennies out of they pockets."

◆　◆　◆

Ovella and Elzie joined the others who were throwing money for the dog. Ovella tossed the dog a tiny pin she had won in Sunday school. Elzie threw her lucky stone. But the stone hit the dog in the nose!

◆　◆　◆

◆ Reading Strategy

What is the Silas Greene? Circle the words nearby that help you **clarify the meaning**.

◆ Reading Check

Why do Elzie and Ovella want to join the Silas Greene? Circle the words that tell you.

◆ Literary Analysis

Elzie uses hyperbole to describe the dog. Circle the example of **hyperbole** in this paragraph. On the lines below, explain why the remark is an exaggeration.

_____

_____

_____

_____

"Well, . . . he lit out after me and I flew! Round and round the Silas Greene we run, through every place me and Ovella had walked before, but now that dancin dog was a runnin dog and all the people was laughin at the new show, which was us!

"I felt myself slowin down after a while and I thought I would turn around a little bit to see how much gain that cute little dog was makin on me. When I did I got such a surprise! Right behind me was the dancin dog and right behind him was the finest fast runnin hero in . . . Virginia."

◆　◆　◆

The hero was Amos Pickens, who would later be Elzie's husband. Amos twirled some twine around in his hand, like a cowboy in the Silas Greene show. He then looped the twine over the back leg of the dancin dog, bringing it down.

◆　◆　◆

"I stopped then and walked slow and shy to where he had picked up that poor dog to see if he was hurt, cradlin him and talking to him soft and sweet. That showed me how kind and gentle he was, and when we walked back to the dancin dog's place in the show he let the dog loose and helped me to find my stone. . . . We searched and searched and at last he spied it!"

◆　◆　◆

By this time, Ovella and Elzie had changed their minds about joining the Silas Greene show. Instead, they decided it was time to leave the show. They began walking home.

◆　◆　◆

"And a good little way, the one who was gonna be your Great-granddaddy was walkin on behind. Seein us safe. Yes," Mrs. Pickens' voice trailed off softly and Tee noticed she had a little smile on her face.

"Grandmama, that stone almost got you bit by a dog that time. It wasn't so lucky that time, was it?"

Tee's Great-grandmother shook her head and laughed out loud.

"That was the luckiest time of all, Tee Baby. It got me acquainted with Mr. Amos Pickens, and if that ain't luck, what could it be! Yes, it was luckier for me than for anybody, I think. Least mostly I think it."

Practice reading aloud Elzie's remarks here. What is funny about the last sentence? Write your ideas on the lines below.

_____

_____

_____

_____

1. What words below describe Elzie and Ovella as girls? Circle at least two of the words.

    adventurous   stingy   fun-loving   cruel   shy

    On the lines below, write one circled word. Then, explain how you know the word describes the girls.

    _____

    _____

2. Circle all the words that seem to describe Elzie's opinion of Amos.

    heroic   thoughtful   mean   protective   bossy   nice

3. In what way was Elzie's stone unlucky? In what way was it lucky? Answer these questions on the lines below.

    It was unlucky because _____

    _____.

    It was lucky because _____

    _____.

4. **Literary Analysis:** On the lines below, list two examples of **hyperbole** in the story.

    - _____

    _____

    - _____

    _____

5. **Literary Analysis:** Elzie tells the story of an adventure she had many years ago. How might the time that has passed help Elzie remember events and use hyperbole?

    _____

    _____

    _____

6. **Reading Strategy:** Use the words in the rest of each sentence to help you clarify the meaning of the word in italics. Then, circle the meaning from the choices given.

We searched and searched and at last he *spied* it!

spied: (a) lied   (b) snooped   (c) spotted   (d) crawled

. . . where he had picked up that poor dog to see if he was hurt, *cradlin* him and talking to him soft and sweet.

cradlin: (a) throwing   (b) holding gently   (c) biting hard
            (d) whistling loudly

Listening and Speaking

With a partner, act out a short conversation that might have taken place between two characters in the story. It could be between Tee and Elzie, Elzie and Ovella, or Elzie and Amos.

• Name the characters you have chosen.

_____ and _____

• List a few words to describe each character

FIRST CHARACTER   **SECOND CHARACTER**

_____   _____

_____   _____

_____   _____

• Reread all or part of the story for ideas about what the characters might say.

_____

_____

• In the space below, list some ideas about what these characters might say to each other.

_____

_____

• Act out the conversation using appropriate tones, movements, and body language.
• Practice until you feel comfortable with your work and then share it with a group of classmates.

How the Snake Got Poison

Zora Neale Hurston

Summary

The snake went up to God and explained how dangerous it was crawling around on his belly in the dust. So God gave him poison to protect himself. But then he bit and killed so many small animals that they complained to God. So God sent for the snake and asked why he was biting everything instead of using the poison only to protect himself. The snake explained that he could not tell who was friend and who was foe and had to bite everything to protect himself. So God gave the snake a kind of bell to tie on his tail. That way, those who weren't out to harm the snake would avoid him when they heard the warning sound. And that is how the snake got his poison and his rattles.

Visual Summary

Problem	Solution
• Snake complains that, because he crawls on his belly in the dust, everyone stamps on and kills him.	• God gives him poison for protection.
• Snake still does not know who is friend and who is foe.	• Snake bites and kills everything with his poison.
• Small animals complain snake is killing them off.	• God gives snake bells, or rattles, to warn away those not trying to harm him. Snake will then bite only those who come near.

LITERARY ANALYSIS
Character's Perspective

A **character's perspective** is the way a character sees events in a story. A character's perspective will depend on the character's background. It may also depend on the character's experiences. For example, a character who is a student may have an entirely different point of view than a character who is a teacher—just as a student and teacher might in real life.

In "How the Snake Got Poison," the snake sees events very differently than the other small animals do.

Snake	sees getting poison as a means of protection
Other Animals	see the snake's getting poison as a deadly danger

As you read Hurston's tale, look for other ways in which the characters' perspectives differ.

READING STRATEGY
Evaluating an Author's Message

The **author's message** is a main idea that a writer wants you to understand through a piece of writing. For example, one idea that Hurston wants to show in "How the Snake Got Poison" is that animals have special traits or abilities that help them survive.

To **evaluate** an author's message, first figure out the idea the author is presenting. Then, decide whether it is true. Ask yourself these questions:

- What message is the author trying to convey?
- What details or examples does the author give to support the message? How good is the author's support?
- Does the message seem reasonable based on my own knowledge and experiences? Why, or why not?

How the Snake Got Poison

Zora Neale Hurston

Zora Neale Hurston retells an old African American folktale that was first told orally. To show the sound of the spoken story, she uses a non-standard form of English with many unusual spellings. The folktale tries to explain how snakes came to have poison.

◆ ◆ ◆

Well, when God made de snake he put him in de bushes to <u>ornament</u> de ground. But things didn't suit de snake so one day he got on de ladder and went up to see God.

"Good mawnin', God."

"How do you do, Snake?"

"Ah ain't so many,[1] God, you put me down here on my belly in de dust and everything trods upon me and kills off my <u>generations</u>. Ah ain't got no kind of protection at all."

God looked off towards <u>immensity</u> and thought about de subject for awhile, then he said, "Ah didn't mean for nothin' to be stompin' you snakes lak dat. You got to have some kind of a protection. Here, take dis poison and put in yo' mouf and when they tromps on you, protect yo'self."

◆ ◆ ◆

The snake took the poison and went away. But after a time a group of small animals such as mice and rats went up to speak with God.

◆ ◆ ◆

◆ Reading Check

What did the snake climb to visit God? Circle the word that answers this question. Then, on the line below, explain where you think the ladder is supposed to lead.

_____

◆ Read Fluently

The writer uses a southern **dialect** in this story. Dialect shows how the words actually sound. It also shows the words and accent of a specific region or group of people. Read the snake's remarks out loud. What words does he use for *I* and *the*? Circle both words, and mark them *I* and *the*.

Vocabulary Development

ornament (OR nuh ment) *v.* decorate
generations (JEN er AY shuns) *n.* children, grandchildren, and so on
immensity (i MEN si tee) *n.* endless space

---

1. **ain't so many:** I am not doing so well.

"Good evenin', God."

"How you making it,[2] varmints?"

"God, please do something' 'bout dat snake. He' layin' in de bushes there wid poison in his mouf and he's strikin' everything dat shakes de bushes. He's killin' up our generations. Wese skeered to walk de earth."

◆ ◆ ◆

So God sent for the snake. He told the snake that He had given him poison for protection. He did not expect the snake to kill every single creature that came near him.

◆ ◆ ◆

De snake say, "Lawd, you know Ah'm down here in de dust. Ah ain't got no claws to fight wid, and Ah ain't got no feets to git me out de way. All Ah kind see is feets comin' to tromple me. Ah can't tell who my enemy is and who is my friend. You gimme dis protection in my mouf and Ah uses it."

◆ ◆ ◆

God thought about the situation for a time. Finally he spoke again:

◆ ◆ ◆

"Well, snake, I don't want yo' generations all stomped out and I don't want you killin' everything else dat moves. Here take dis bell and tie it to yo' tail. When you hear feets comin' you ring yo' bell and if it's yo' friend, he'll be keerful. If it's yo' enemy, it's you and him."

So dat's how de snake got his poison and dat's how come he got rattles.

2. **How you making it, varmints:** How are you getting by, creatures? How are things going, creatures?

◆ **Literary Analysis**

How does these **characters' perspective** differ from the snake's perspective? Answer by completing the sentence below.

The snake feels he needs

_____

but the small animals feel they need _____

_____.

◆ **Reading Strategy**

Based on God's remarks, what seems to be the **author's message** about the animal world?

(a) In nature, only the strongest and fittest animals survive.

(b) All types of animals are part of creation and should not be allowed to be hurt.

(c) Only animals useful to human beings are worth protecting.

(d) Animals are kind and generous.

On the lines below, explain why you agree or disagree with the message.

_____

_____

_____

_____

◆ **Stop to Reflect**

Why would the rattles warn friends but not enemies? Write your answer on the lines below.

_____

_____

_____

1. According to the story, why does God give the snake poison? Write your answer on the lines below.

   _____

   _____

   _____

2. According to the story, how are the snake's rattles supposed to work? Circle the letter of the correct answer.

   (a) by attracting enemies   (c) by warning friends

   (b) by frightening enemies   (d) by attracting friends

3. The snake's problems could have been solved if God gave him legs or claws. Why do you think the story couldn't end that way? Answer on these lines.

   _____

   _____

   _____

   _____

   _____

4. **Literary Analysis:** Complete these sentences to show the different characters' perspectives.

   The small animals complain that the snake's poison is

   _____

   _____

   The snake explains that he has to _____

   because _____ .

5. **Reading Strategy:** Put a check in front of the statements that you think show the **author's messages**.

_____ A snake's rattles protect the snake from large animals.

_____ A snake's rattles protect small animals from the snake.

_____ All types of animals created by God deserve to remain on earth.

_____ Animals have special traits or abilities to help them survive.

_____ Only the strongest and fittest animals should survive.

Then, **evaluate** those messages. Circle the ones that you think are true.

Listening and Speaking

With a partner, find three unusual facts about an animal. Then include those facts in an oral story about the animal.
- Do research to find your three unusual facts. List them here.

1. _____

2. _____

3. _____
- Working with your partner, decide what problem the animal in your story will face. Write the problem on these lines.

_____

_____

Next, outline a very short story that includes the three unusual facts. Write your plan on these lines.

_____

_____

- Practice your story aloud. You and your partner should each present a different part of the story. Work until you feel comfortable telling the story. Then present the story to classmates.

Rikki-tikki-tavi

Rudyard Kipling

Summary

In this story set in India, Rikki-tikki-tavi is a mongoose, a small furry animal that eats snakes. When a flood washes him from his underground home, he is adopted by the family of a young boy named Teddy. Exploring the garden, he meets Nag and Nagaina, two deadly cobras. Later he rescues Teddy by killing a smaller poisonous snake. That night he overhears the cobras' plot to enter the house and kill Teddy's family. Rikki attacks Nag in the bathroom, fighting until Teddy's father shoots the cobra. The next day Rikki finds Nagaina's eggs and begins crushing them. When she threatens to kill Teddy, Rikki draws her away by threatening to destroy her last egg. Rikki then chases her into her hole and kills her. Teddy's family and the garden animals hail Rikki as a hero.

Visual Summary

Who?	Rikki-tikki-tavi, a small furry animal called a mongoose
Where?	house and grounds of a British family in India
When?	late 1800s, when India was a British colony
What?	saves the lives of Teddy and the rest of the family
How?	fights with and kills several poisonous snakes
Why?	likes the family who adopted him; is natural enemy of snakes

LITERARY ANALYSIS

Plot

The **plot** is the arrangement of events in a story. It usually has the following parts or sections:

- The **exposition** is the background that sets up the situation.
- In the **rising action**, a problem gets worse.
- The **climax** is the high point of tension.
- In the **falling action**, events after the climax lead to the ending.
- The **resolution** is the final outcome, in which all loose ends are tied up.

This diagram shows how the five parts are organized into a plot. As you read, identify the five parts of this story's plot.

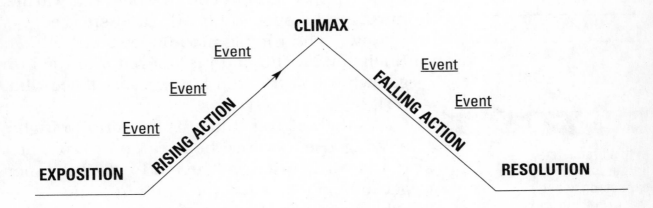

READING STRATEGY

Predicting

When you read a good story, you wonder what will happen next. Often you will **predict**, or make an educated guess, about what is coming next. The details you know can help you predict what you don't know.

As you read the story, try to predict what will happen. Use the details you know as clues. Look at this example.

Clues
- Rikki is the natural enemy of snakes
- Rikki likes Teddy and his family
- Nag is sneaking into the house to kill the family

Prediction
Rikki will try to stop Nag from killing the family

Rikki-tikki-tavi
Rudyard Kipling

This story takes place when India was a British colony. Rikki-tikki-tavi is a mongoose, a small furry animal that kills snakes. One day, a flood washes him from his underground home. It carries him to the grounds of a large bungalow, or one-story house, where a British family lives.

◆　◆　◆

When he <u>revived</u>, . . . a small boy was saying: "Here's a dead mongoose. Let's have a funeral." . . .

They took him into the house, and a big man picked him up between his finger and thumb, and said he was not dead but half choked; so they wrapped him in cotton wool, and warmed him, and he opened his eyes and sneezed.

"Now," said the big man (he was an Englishman who had just moved into the bungalow); "don't frighten him, and we'll see what he'll do."

It is the hardest thing in the world to frighten a mongoose, because he is eaten up from nose to tail with curiosity. The motto of all the mongoose family is "Run and find out"; and Rikki-tikki was a true mongoose. He looked at the cotton wool, decided that it was not good to eat, ran all around the table, sat up and put his fur in order, scratched himself, and jumped on the small boy's shoulder.

"Don't be frightened, Teddy," said his father. "That's his way of making friends."

◆　◆　◆

Vocabulary Development

revived (ree VĪVD) *v.* became conscious again

Rikki eats and dries himself on the verandah, or porch. Then he explores his new home. At night he sleeps in Teddy's room. Teddy's mother worries he might bite Teddy, but the father says he will protect Teddy from snakes. The next day Rikki explores the gardens. There he meets Darzee the bird and his wife, who are crying.

◆　◆　◆

"We are very miserable," said Darzee.

"One of our babies fell out of the nest yesterday, and Nag[1] ate him."

"H'm!" said Rikki-tikki, "that is very sad—but I am a stranger here. Who is Nag?"

. . . From the thick grass at the foot of the bush there came a low hiss—a horrid cold sound that made Rikki-tikki jump back two clear feet. Then inch by inch out of the grass rose up the head and spread hood of Nag, the big black cobra, and he was five feet long from tongue to tail. . . . "Who is Nag?" said he. "I am Nag."

◆　◆　◆

Nag recognizes Rikki as a natural enemy. He talks with Rikki while his wife Nagaina[2] sneaks up from behind. But Darzee sees her and warns Rikki. After the snakes slink off, Teddy comes to pet Rikki. Then a new danger threatens: Karait,[3] a tiny but deadly brown snake.

◆　◆　◆

Karait struck out. Rikki jumped sideways and tried to run in, but the wicked little dusty gray head lashed within a fraction of his shoulder, and he had to jump over the body, and the head followed his heels close.

---

1. **Nag** (NAG)
2. **Nagaina** (na GAYn uh)
3. **Karait** (kuh RAYT)

◆ **Reading Check**

Circle the words that tell you why Darzee and his wife are crying.

◆ **Reading Strategy**

What do you **predict** may happen between Rikki and Nag later in the story? Circle the letter below.

(a) They will become friends.

(b) They will fight.

(c) They will ignore each other.

(d) They will work together for the common good of all the animals.

List at least one earlier detail that helped you make your prediction.

_____

_____

_____

◆ **Literary Analysis**

In this passage, the problem with snakes gets worse. Which part of the **plot** is this event? Circle the letter of your answer.

(a) exposition

(b) rising action

(c) climax

(d) falling action

Rikki decides not to eat Karait. He is afraid such a big meal will slow him down. What future event does he think he needs to be fast for? Answer on these lines.

_____

_____

_____

Teddy shouted to the house: "Oh, look here! Our mongoose is killing a snake"; and Rikki-tikki heard a scream from Teddy's mother. His father ran out with a stick, but by the time he came up, Karait had <u>lunged</u> out once too far, and Rikki-tikki had sprung, jumped on the snake's back, dropped his head far between his <u>fore</u>legs, bitten as high up the back as he could get hold, and rolled away. That bite <u>paralyzed</u> Karait, and Rikki-tikki was just going to eat him up from the tail, after the custom of his family at dinner, when he remembered that a full meal makes a slow mongoose. . . .

◆   ◆   ◆

Teddy's parents hug Rikki and praise him for saving Teddy. That night Rikki patrols the house. He hears Nag enter on the bathroom drainpipe and hears Nagaina whispering. She reminds Nag their eggs may hatch the next day. She tells him to kill the family and return to hunt Rikki with her. Nag curls up by the water jar to wait for the man. Rikki waits too—until Nag falls asleep.

◆   ◆   ◆

◆ **Reading Check**

Circle the words that tell you what Rikki hopes to do on the first bite. Do you think he will do it?

_____

Why or why not? Answer on these lines.

_____

_____

_____

Rikki-tikki looked at his big back, wondering which would be the best place for a good hold. "If I don't break his back at the first jump," said Rikki, "he can still fight; and if he fights— O Rikki!" He looked at the thickness of the neck below the hood. . . . "It must be the head," he said at last; "the head above the hood; and when I am once there, I must not let go."

Vocabulary Development

lunged (LUNJD) *v.* jumped
fore (FOHR) *adj.* front
paralyzed (pa ruh LĪZD) *v.* prevented from moving

Then he jumped. The head was lying a little clear of the water jar, under the curve of it; and, as his teeth met, Rikki braced his back. . . . He was <u>battered</u> to and fro as a rat is shaken by a dog—to and fro on the floor, up and down, and round in great circles. . . . He was dizzy, aching, and felt shaken to pieces when something went off like a thunderclap just behind him; a hot wind knocked him senseless, and red fire <u>singed</u> his fur. The big man had been wakened by the noise, and had fired both barrels of a shotgun into Nag just behind the hood.

Rikki-tikki held on with his eyes shut, . . . and the big man picked him up and said: "It's the mongoose again, Alice; the little chap[1] has saved our lives now."

Rikki feels stiff from the fight but better in the morning. Skipping breakfast, he goes to the garden. Everyone there knows Nag is dead, for his body was thrown on the garbage heap.

"Nag is dead—is dead—is dead!" sang Darzee. "The <u>valiant</u> Rikki-tikki caught him by the head and held fast. The big man brought the bang-stick, and Nag fell in two pieces! He will never eat my babies again."

◆ ◆ ◆

Rikki learns that Nagaina's eggs are in the melon bed. He gets there just in time— the baby cobras are due to hatch the next day. He has smashed all but one egg when Darzee's wife screams that Nagaina is heading for the house. Rikki races to the family, who are at breakfast.

◆ ◆ ◆

Vocabulary Development

battered (BAT erd) v. knocked
singed (SINJD) v. burned the edges
valiant (VAL yuhnt) adj. acting with courage; brave

---

4. **chap** (chap) n. fellow.

◆ **Literary Analysis**

In this passage, the problem between Rikki and Nag is very strong. What do you think will happen?

_____

_____

_____

◆ **Reading Strategy**

What do you **predict** Rikki will do soon? Circle the letter of the answer. Then, on the lines, explain why you think he will do that.

(a) try to kill Nagaina

(b) try to kill Darzee

(c) become like a father to Nag's fatherless children

(d) hide in the house

_____

_____

_____

_____

Put a check in front of the statements that seem to apply to Nagaina.

___ She is a concerned mother.

___ She is glad Nag is gone as she now has the garden to herself.

___ She is angry that Nag was killed and wants revenge.

___ She is less dangerous than Nag.

___ She is kind and thoughtful.

Read these bracketed remarks aloud in a tone Rikki may have used. Why do you think he teases Nagaina here? Circle the letter of your answer.

(a) He wants to take her attention away from the family.

(b) He wants to comfort Teddy.

(c) He likes to bully those weaker than he is.

(d) He is jealous of Nagaina.

They sat stone-still, and their faces were white. Nagaina was coiled up on the matting by Teddy's chair, within easy striking distance of Teddy's bare leg. . . .

Rikki-tikki came up and cried: "Turn round Nagaina; turn and fight!"

"All in good time," she said, without moving her eyes. . . . "Look at your friends, Rikki-tikki. . . . They dare not move, and if you come a step nearer I strike."

"Look at your eggs," said Rikki-tikki, "in the melon bed near the wall. Go and look, Nagaina."

The big snake turned half round, and saw the egg on the verandah. "Ah-h! Give it to me," she said.

Rikki-tikki put his paws one on each side of the egg, and his eyes were blood-red. "What price for a snake's egg? For a young cobra? For a young king cobra? For the last—the very last of the brood?[5] . . ."

Nagaina spun clear round, forgetting everything for the sake of the one egg; and Rikki-tikki saw Teddy's father shoot out a big hand, catch Teddy by the shoulder, and drag him across the little table with the teacups, safe and out of reach of Nagaina.

♦ ♦ ♦

Nagaina throws herself at Rikki over and over, backing him away. Then she grabs the egg and runs. Darzee's wife flaps her wings near her head but fails to slow her. Rikki chases Nagaina down the rat hole where she lives.

♦ ♦ ♦

Darzee said: "It is all over with Rikki-tikki! We must sing his death song. Valiant Rikki-tikki is dead! For Nagaina will surely kill him underground."

---

5. **brood** (brood) *n.* all the eggs laid or cared for at one time.

So he sang a very <u>mournful</u> song that he made up on the spur of the minute, and just as he got to the most touching part the grass <u>quivered</u> again, and Rikki-tikki, covered with dirt, dragged himself out of the hole leg by leg, licking his whiskers. Darzee stopped with a little shout. Rikki-tikki shook some of the dust out of his fur and sneezed. "It is all over," he said. "The widow will never come out again."

Rikki-tikki curled himself up in the grass and slept where he was, . . . for he had done a hard day's work.

◆ ◆ ◆

The Coppersmith, a bird who spreads the news, sings of Rikki's triumph. The frogs join the song. Meanwhile, Rikki returns to the house.

◆ ◆ ◆

That night he ate all that was given him till he could eat no more, and went to bed on Teddy's shoulder, where Teddy's mother saw him when she came to look late at night.

"He saved our lives and Teddy's life," she said. . . .

Rikki-tikki had a right to be proud of himself; but he did not grow too proud, and he kept that garden as a mongoose should keep it, with tooth and jump and spring and bite, till never a cobra dared show its head inside the walls.

◆ **Literary Analysis**

What happens to Nagaina? Write your answer on these lines.

_____

_____

_____

How does this event help fix the problem?

_____

_____

_____

◆ **Literary Analysis**

The **resolution** is the final outcome of the story. How has Rikki's life changed? Write your answer on the lines.

_____

_____

_____

Mark the Text

Vocabulary Development

mournful (MOHRN ful) *adj.* showing grief over a death; very sad

quivered (KWI verd) *v.* shook

---

1. Circle all the words that you think describe Rikki-tikki-tavi.

      brave   nosey   snobby   sloppy   shy

2. Why do Rikki and cobras fight? Write two reasons on these lines.

   1. _____

   _____

   2. _____

   _____

3. Why does Rikki destroy the eggs? Circle the letter of the best answer.

   (a) He is hungry.

   (b) He wants revenge for Nag's attack the night before.

   (c) He is mean and wants to torture Nagaina.

   (d) He wants to clear the garden of deadly cobras.

4. **Literary Analysis:** The problem in this story is the danger of the snakes. List three events that make up the **rising action**. These events show how dangerous the snakes are.

   1. _____

   _____

   2. _____

   _____

5. **Literary Analysis:** What is the **climax** of the story (When the trouble or problem is greatest)?
Climax:

   _____

   _____

6. **Reading Strategy:** List a clue that helped you **predict** each event.

Event: Rikki will fight Nag one day.

Clue: _____

Event: Rikki will try to destroy the cobra eggs.

Clue: _____

Event: Rikki will fight Nagaina one day.

Clue: _____

Writing

Do research to learn more about an unfamiliar animal, like a cobra or a mongoose. Then write a paragraph about the animal you research.

- Use reliable Internet or library sources. List two sources here.

_____

_____

- List key facts you learn about the animal. Focus on these questions:

What does it look like? _____

_____

_____

Where is it found? _____

_____

_____

How does it behave?_____

_____

_____

- Use your facts in a paragraph that you write on another sheet.

After Twenty Years

O. Henry

Summary

One night a police officer walks the nearly empty streets of a New York business area. In a dark store doorway is a man named Bob waiting to meet his friend Jimmy Wells. Bob explains that he hasn't seen Jimmy since leaving New York twenty years ago to make his fortune out west. The two promised to meet in twenty years at Big Joe Brady's restaurant, now this store. Bob is sure Jimmy will show up. After the officer leaves, another man arrives and greets Bob by name. Bob soon realizes this man is not Jimmy. In fact he is a plainclothes officer who arrests "Silky Bob" for crimes in Chicago. He hands Bob a note from Jimmy, who actually was the first officer. Jimmy came to meet his old friend but recognized Bob as a wanted man. He didn't have the heart to arrest Bob himself, so he sent a fellow officer.

Visual Summary

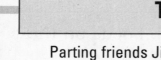

Twenty Years Ago

Parting friends Jimmy Wells and Bob agree to meet again
at Big Joe Brady's New York restaurant in twenty years

What Happens to Jimmy Wells	What Happens to Bob
• remains in New York City	• leaves New York to seek his fortune out west
• unknown to Bob and reader, becomes a New York City police officer	• unknown to Jimmy and reader, becomes "Silky Bob," gangster wanted in Chicago
• unknown to Bob and reader, keeps appointment outside closed store that was once Big Joe's	• keeps appointment outside closed store that was once Big Joe's
• recognizes Bob as a wanted man	• fails to recognize Jimmy in uniform
• doesn't have the heart to arrest his old friend	• is sure loyal friend Jimmy will keep appointment
• sends another officer to arrest Bob	• recognizes second arrival is not Jimmy
• sends note with second officer, explaining situation to Bob (and reader)	• learns the truth (as reader does) when he is arrested and reads Jimmy's note

LITERARY ANALYSIS
Surprise Ending

The events in most stories usually build to a climax, or high point. Then, they wind down to the ending. In some stories, however, there is a **surprise ending** that is different from what most readers expect. A good surprise ending comes as a surprise but it still makes sense to the reader. In some cases, earlier details may hint at the surprise. In other cases, earlier details make more sense once the surprise is revealed.

O. Henry is famous for his surprise endings. As you read his story, ask yourself these questions:

- How do you think the story will end?
- Which details seem to hint at the ending?

Once you finish the story, ask yourself these questions:

- Does the surprise ending seem believable? Why or why not?
- What earlier details gave hints about the ending?

READING STRATEGY
Breaking Down Sentences

Sometimes it is hard to understand the meaning of long, complex sentences. If you **break down sentences** into smaller groups of words, you can often understand them better. Underline the heart of the sentence—the main subject and action. Then break the sentence into logical chunks. Think about how those chunks relate to the main part.

In the sentence below, the main part is underlined. *A tall man* is the subject—the person or thing the sentence is about; *hurried across* is the main action he performs. The rest of the sentence is divided into logical chunks that tell you more about the man and from where he hurried.

A tall man | *in a long overcoat,* | *with collar turned up to his ears,* | *hurried across* | *from the opposite side of the street.*

After Twenty Years

It is ten o'clock on a rainy, windy night. A police officer in New York City walks his beat with his usual style, even though almost no one is there to see him. The neighborhood is a business area, and most of the stores and office buildings are closed for the night.

◆　◆　◆

About midway of a certain block the policeman suddenly slowed his walk. In the doorway of a darkened hardware store a man leaned, with an unlighted cigar in his mouth. As the policeman walked up to him the man spoke up quickly.

"It's all right, officer," he said, reassuringly. "I'm just waiting for a friend. It's an appointment made twenty years ago. . . . About that long ago there used to be a restaurant where this store stands—'Big Joe' Brady's restaurant."

"Until five years ago," said the policeman. "It was torn down then."

The man in the doorway struck a match and lit his cigar. The light showed a pale, square-jawed face with keen eyes, and a little white scar near his right eyebrow. His scarfpin was a large diamond, oddly set.

"Twenty years ago tonight," said the man, "I dined here at 'Big Joe' Brady's with Jimmy Wells, my best chum, and the finest chap[1] in the world. He and I were raised here in New York, just like two brothers, together. I was eighteen and Jimmy was twenty. The next

Vocabulary Development

reassuringly (ree uh SHOOR ing lee) *adv.* in a way that eases concern; confidently

keen (KEEN) *adj.* sharp

chum (CHUM) *n.* friend; pal

---

1. **chap** (chap) *n.* slang for fellow; guy.

morning I was to start for the West to make my fortune. You couldn't have dragged Jimmy out of New York; he thought it was the only place on earth. Well, we agreed that night that we would meet here again exactly twenty years from that date and time, no matter what our condition might be or from what distance we might have to come. We figured that in twenty years each of us ought to have our <u>destiny</u> worked out and our fortunes made, whatever they were going to be."

◆ ◆ ◆

The man explains that it was exactly ten o'clock when he and Jimmy parted twenty years before and that they are supposed to meet at the same time now. The policeman seems interested in the story. He asks if the man and Jimmy have been in touch. The man says they lost touch years before.

◆ ◆ ◆

"Did pretty well out West, didn't you?" asked the policeman.

"You bet! I hope Jimmy has done half as well. He was a kind of <u>plodder</u>, though, good fellow as he was. I've had to compete with some of the sharpest wits going to get my pile. . . ."

◆ ◆ ◆

The policemen continues on his beat. The man in the doorway feels a little silly to have come a thousand miles to keep an appointment made twenty years ago. Still, he smokes his cigar and continues to wait.

◆ ◆ ◆

Vocabulary Development

destiny (DES tin ee) *n.* future; fate

plodder (plod er) *n.* someone who moves slowly and carefully; a slowpoke

---

Circle the detail that suggests that the man is hiding his appearance. What sort of **surprise ending** might this detail hint at? Write your guess on the lines.

_____

_____

_____

_____

A tall man in a long overcoat, with collar turned up to his ears, hurried across from the opposite side of the street. He went directly to the waiting man.

"Is that you, Bob?" he asked, doubtfully.

"Is that you, Jimmy Wells?" cried the man in the door.

"Bless my heart!" exclaimed the new arrival, grasping both the other's hands with his own. "It's Bob, sure as fate. I was certain I'd find you here if you were still in existence."

◆ ◆ ◆

The two men continue with warm greetings. They walk up the street arm in arm. The man from the West outlines his successful career; the other listens with interest. Then the two move into the glare of brightly lit drugstore window.

◆ ◆ ◆

The man from the West stopped suddenly and released his arm.

"You're not Jimmy Wells," he snapped. "Twenty years is a long time, but not long enough to change a man's nose from a Roman to a pug."[2]

"It sometimes changes a good man into a bad one," said the tall man. "You've been under arrest for ten minutes, 'Silky' Bob."

◆ ◆ ◆

What do you think the criminal nickname "Silky" Bob might mean?

(a) Bob is known as a stylish dresser who likes to wear silk shirts.

(b) Bob is a slick or smooth operator—smooth as silk.

(c) Both *a* and *b* seem likely.

(d) Neither *a* nor *b* seems likely.

The tall man turns out to be a plainclothes police officer. He explains that the Chicago police contacted New York to say that "Silky" Bob was heading that way. The Chicago police want to question Bob and asked that he be taken into custody. When the officer sees that Bob is going quietly with him, he pauses.

◆ ◆ ◆

---

2. **change a man's nose from a Roman to a pug:** A Roman nose has a high, bony bridge; a pug nose is short, thick, and turned up at the end.

"Now, before we go to the station, here's a note I was asked to hand to you. You may read it here at the window. It's from Patrolman Wells."

The man from the West unfolded the little piece of paper handed him. His hand was steady when he began to read, but it trembled a little by the time he had finished. The note was rather short.

Bob: I was at the appointed place on time. When you struck the match to light your cigar, I saw it was the face of the man wanted in Chicago. Somehow I couldn't do it myself, so I went around and a got a plain clothes man to do the job. Jimmy.

◆ Literary Analysis

Were you surprised by the ending?

_____

Did you think it made sense? On the lines below, explain your answer.

_____
_____
_____
_____
_____

1. On the lines below, sum up the agreement that Bob and Jimmy made twenty years ago.

_____

_____

2. Which statement best describes the relationship between Bob and Jimmy? Circle the letter of the best answer.

   (a) They were close in childhood and are just as close now.

   (b) They were close in childhood but have taken different paths in life.

   (c) They are much closer today than they were in childhood.

3. Why do you think Bob keeps the appointment, even though he is a criminal? Check at least two possible reasons.

   ____ He wants to keep a promise to an old friend.

   ____ He wants to show off his success.

   ____ He is a hunted man and wants to escape capture.

   ____ Deep down he feels guilty and wants to be arrested.

   ____ He is curious to see his old friend.

4. Why is Jimmy unable to arrest Bob himself? Explain on these lines.

_____

_____

5. **Literary Analysis:** On the lines below, explain what happens in the **surprise ending**.

_____

_____

6. List two earlier details that point to the surprise, even though you may not have known that earlier.

    1. _____

    2. _____

7. **Reading Strategy:** Draw lines to **break down this sentence** into logical parts. Circle the main subject and action. Then answer the two questions about the sentence.

    In the doorway of a darkened hardware store a man leaned, with an unlighted cigar in his mouth.

Where did the man lean? _____

What was in his mouth? _____

Listening and Speaking

Imagine that you are a radio announcer reading a news bulletin about the arrest of "Silky" Bob. On the lines, list information to include in your bulletin. Include details from the story and details you make up.

• What does "Silky" Bob look like? _____

_____

_____

• What was Bob wearing? _____

_____

• Where is Bob wanted by the police? _____

_____

• Where was Bob captured? _____

_____

• What crimes is Bob suspected of committing? _____

_____

Now use the details in a news bulletin that you announce. Speak clearly, and raise and lower your voice for effect.

Papa's Parrot

Cynthia Rylant

Summary

A boy named Harry Tillian once enjoyed visiting his father's candy store. As he grows older, however, he goes there less often. Meanwhile his father gets a talking parrot that he keeps in the store. Because his father talks so much to the parrot, Harry is embarrassed and goes to the store even less often. Then one day, Harry's father falls ills and has to go to the hospital. Harry goes to the store to help out. He is amazed when the parrot keeps saying, "Where's Harry? Miss him." Harry realizes the bird is echoing his father's words. After a long cry, Harry goes to visit his father at the hospital.

Visual Summary

Before Harry Starts Junior High	After Harry Starts Junior High	After Harry's Father Gets Ill
• Harry visits his father's candy and nut shop often.	• Harry stops going to his father's shop.	• Harry goes to his father's shop to take care of things.
• Harry's friends often stop by.	• His father gets a parrot that he names Rocky.	• The parrot keeps saying "Where's Harry?" and "Miss him."
	• Harry is embarrassed to see his father talking with the parrot.	• Harry realizes the parrot is echoing his father's words.
	• Harry's father gets ill and must go to the hospital.	• Harry weeps.
		• Harry goes to visit his father in the hospital.

LITERARY ANALYSIS

Characterization

Characterization is the way in which a writer tells readers about characters. There are two basic methods.

- In **direct characterization**, the author *tells* you a character's personality or attitudes.
- In **indirect characterization**, the author *shows* you what the character is like. From the character's actions and speech, you figure out his or her personality and attitudes.

As you read "Papa's Parrot," pay attention to the characterization of Harry and his father. You might fill in a characterization chart like this one.

Direct Characterization	"Harry Tillian liked his papa."
Indirect Characterization	"For years, after school, Harry had always stopped in to see his father at work."
What it shows	Harry Tillian liked his father.

READING STRATEGY

Identifying with a Character

You can understand a story better if you identify with the characters. To **identify with a character**, put yourself in his or her place. Think how you might react to the same situations.

As you read "Papa's Parrot," identify with either Harry or his father. For each main event, create an organizer like the one below. Identify the event, write the character's reaction, and write what you would have done or said in the same situation.

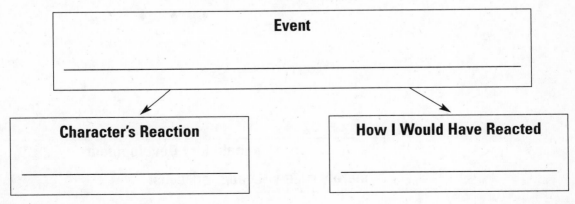

Event

Character's Reaction

How I Would Have Reacted

Papa's Parrot

Cynthia Rylant

The main characters in this story are a boy named Harry Tillian and his father. There is also a bird named Rocky, a large parrot that can imitate the words spoken by human beings.

◆ ◆ ◆

Though his father was fat and <u>merely</u> owned a candy and nut shop, Harry Tillian liked his papa. . . . For years, after school, Harry had always stopped in to see his father at work. Many of Harry's friends stopped there too, to spend a few cents. . . . Mr. Tillian looked forward to seeing his son and his son's friends every day. He liked the company.

◆ ◆ ◆

When Harry and his friends start junior high school, they stop coming to the shop. They have other things to do like play video games and hang out at the burger place.

That same year, Harry's father bought a parrot at the pet store. Mr. Tillian named the parrot Rocky. He kept it at the candy store. Harry thought it was a strange thing for his father to do. But Mr. Tillian ignored his son's opinion. He found Rocky to be good company. When business was slow, he and the bird would sit and watch TV.

◆ ◆ ◆

Vocabulary Development

merely (MEER lee) *adj.*   only; just

The more Mr. Tillian grew to like his parrot, and the more he talked to it instead of to people, the more embarrassed Harry became. Harry would <u>stroll</u> past the shop, on his way somewhere else, and he'd take a quick look inside to see what his dad was doing.

♦ ♦ ♦

Whenever Harry looks in the shop, he sees his father talking to the bird. Harry is embarrassed so he keeps walking.

Then, Mr. Tillian has a heart attack one day while he is opening the boxes of caramels. A customer comes into the shop and finds that Mr. Tillian has fallen. An ambulance is called, and Mr. Tillian goes to the hospital.

Harry visits his father in the hospital. Mr. Tillian asks him to take care of the store and to feed Rocky. So the next day after school, Harry goes to the store. He picks up the spilled caramels and puts them back in the box. Then he begins opening the other boxes of candy that his father never got to. Suddenly Rocky starts to talk.

♦ ♦ ♦

"Hello, Rocky!"
Harry stared at the parrot. . . . "Hello," Harry said.
"Hello, Rocky!" answered the parrot. . . .
"Is that all you can say, you dumb bird?" Harry mumbled. . . .
"Where's Harry?"

♦ ♦ ♦

◆ Literary Analysis

Circle the words that show Harry's attitude toward his father. Also circle the actions that show his attitude. Label each circle *D* for **direct characterization** or *I* for **indirect characterization**.

◆ Reading Check

Circle the words spoken out loud in this section. Then label each remark R if it is spoken by Rocky or H if it is spoken by Harry.

Vocabulary Development

stroll (STROHL) *v.* walk slowly

In what tone of voice would you say Harry's underlined words? Circle the letter of the best answer.

(a) annoyed   (c) silly

(b) joyous   (d) excited

Now say the Harry's words aloud, trying to use the tone you circled.

Who does Harry realize has been saying "Where's Harry?" and "Miss him"? Write your answer on the line.

_____

Harry looks at the bird as it keeps repeating the same question. He wonders what it means.

◆ ◆ ◆

Harry swallowed and said, "I'm here. I'm here, you stupid bird."

"You stupid bird!" said the parrot.

◆ ◆ ◆

Harry thinks the bird has one thing right—it's stupid. But the parrot goes back to saying "Where's Harry?" and adds "Miss him."

Harry gets more upset as the bird keeps repeating "Where's Harry?" and "Miss him." He throws some peppermints at the bird. Then, he leans on a glass counter and begins to cry.

◆ ◆ ◆

"Papa." . . . Harry sighed and wiped his face on his sleeve.

◆ ◆ ◆

Harry has figured out that the bird is repeating what his father has been saying. As he thinks about how his father must have missed him, Harry finishes up his work in the shop.

◆ ◆ ◆

He checked the furnace so the bird wouldn't get cold. Then he left to go visit his papa.

Vocabulary Development

furnace (FUR nis) *n.* equipment like a boiler, used to heat a building

1. Why does Harry almost never visit his father's candy and nut store any more? Put a check in front of all the reasons.

   _____ He has outgrown the store and no longer finds it as interesting.

   _____ He does not want to get fat like his father.

   _____ He and his friends now have more money and go to more places.

   _____ He does not like his father.

   _____ He is jealous of his father's parrot.

   _____ He is embarrassed that his father talks so much to a parrot.

2. Why does Harry's father buy a parrot to keep in his shop? Circle the letter of the best answer.

   (a) He needs something to make noise at night and scare off robbers.

   (b) He wants to insult some customers and uses the bird to do it.

   (c) He wants to attract young children to his shop.

   (d) He is lonely and misses his son's visits.

3. What does Harry learn from the bird's remarks? Write your answer on the lines below.

   _____

   _____

4. **Literary Analysis:** List one statement of **direct characterization** that tells us something about each of these characters.

   Harry: _____

   _____

   Mr. Tillian: _____

   _____

   (Continued)

5. For each of Harry's qualities or attitudes below, write an example of **indirect characterization** that shows us the quality or attitude.

He is embarrassed by his father: _____

_____

He loves his father: _____

_____

6. **Reading Strategy:** Can you **identify** with the embarrassment Harry feels in parts of the story? Why or why not? Explain on these lines.

_____

_____

_____

Writing

A summary is a short version of a story that tells only the main points and details. Write your own summary of "Papa's Parrot."

• Complete this story outline.

Story Outline
Setting: _____
Characters: _____
_____
Events: _____
_____
_____
Outcome: _____
_____

• Use the information in your outline in a summary that you write on a separate sheet of paper.

Ribbons

Laurence Yep

Summary

Stacy's grandmother comes from Hong Kong to live with the family. It is difficult for the family and especially Stacy, who must give her grandmother her room. Grandmother knows some English, but she seems to favor Stacy's brother Ian, who has learned some Chinese. Then the grandmother gets upset with Stacy's ribboned ballet shoes and demands the ribbons be destroyed. Stacy is very upset until she learns that her grandmother, as a child in China, was forced to bind her feet with ribbons. This painful old practice supposedly made Chinese women more beautiful. But it has left the grandmother's feet all twisted and aching. She objected to the ribboned ballet shoes because she thought the custom was similar. But Stacy explains it is not and dances for her. The two finally bond.

Visual Summary

Grandmother	Grandfather
• feet bound in ribbons in China to be "beautiful" • removed ribbons created great pain • now comes to U.S. and stays in Stacy's room • reacts badly to Stacy's ballet-shoe ribbons • finally accepts Stacy's ballet dancing	• died in China

Stacy's Mother	Stacy's Father
• saved as baby by mother in China • tries to make mother comfortable in U.S. • takes Stacy's ballet-shoe ribbon at mother's request • has promised not to speak of mother's bad feet	• unpacks car for Grandmother • cannot afford Stacy's ballet and settling Grandmother • is not of Chinese background

Stacy	Ian
• gives up room and ballet lessons for Grandmother • thinks Grandmother likes Ian because he looks Chinese • doesn't understand Grandmother's reaction to her ballet-shoe ribbons • sees Grandmother's damaged feet and learns why Grandmother hated her shoe ribbons • shows the ballet she loves to Grandmother • bonds with Grandmother and realizes shared love	• younger than Stacy • bow of greeting pleases Grandmother • learns more Chinese to talk with Grandmother • looks more like Chinese mother than Stacy does

LITERARY ANALYSIS

Theme

The **theme** of a work is its central message. The story's details point to the theme, which is a general message about life or human behavior. For example, suppose a story is about a grandmother from China and granddaughter in America who come to understand each other. The theme might be "Love can span age and cultural differences." It might also be "The more time you spend with people, the more you will understand them."

Sometimes a theme is stated in a story. More often, it is not stated, and you must decide what theme the details suggest. Many stories have more than one theme.

As you read "Ribbons," think about its theme or themes. Consider what the details show about life or human behavior.

READING STRATEGY

Asking Questions

One way to understand a story and its themes is by **asking questions** as you read. For example, you might ask questions like these:

- Why is the author telling me this?
- Why does the character do, say, or think that?
- How does this event fit into what happened so far?

As you read "Ribbons," jot down questions and answers on a chart like this one.

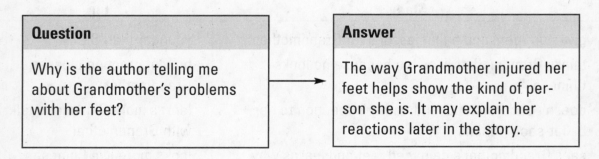

Question	Answer
Why is the author telling me about Grandmother's problems with her feet?	The way Grandmother injured her feet helps show the kind of person she is. It may explain her reactions later in the story.

Ribbons

Laurence Yep

Stacy and her younger brother Ian (EE uhn) are waiting for their Chinese grandmother. The grandmother fled communist China years ago, after she lost her husband. Strapping Stacy's mother—then a baby—to her back, she walked all the way to the British colony of Hong Kong. Now, many years later, she is coming to live with her daughter's family in San Francisco.

◆ ◆ ◆

A car stopped outside, and Ian rushed to the window. "She's here! She's here!" he shouted excitedly. "Paw-paw's here!" *Paw-paw* is Chinese for grandmother—for "mother's mother." . . .

Grandmother was a small woman in a padded silk jacket and black slacks. Her hair was pulled back into a bun behind her head. On her small feet she wore a pair of quilted cotton slippers shaped like boots, with furred tops that hid her ankles.

"What's wrong with her feet?" I whispered to Mom.

"They've always been that way. And don't mention it," she said. "She's <u>sensitive</u> about them."

◆ ◆ ◆

Stacy greets Grandmother with a big hug and kiss. But Grandmother seems to prefer Ian's Chinese-style bow. Walking with two canes, she goes up to the room where she'll be staying—Stacy's room. As Stacy's father goes back and forth unloading

---

Vocabulary Development

sensitive (SEN suh tiv) *adj.* easily hurt or annoyed; touchy

© Pearson Education, Inc.

♦ ♦ ♦

"Now that Grandmother's here, can I begin
my ballet lessons again?" I asked.

Dad turned toward the house. "We'll see, hon."

Disappointment made me <u>protest</u>. "But you
said I had to give up the lessons so we could
bring her from Hong Kong," I said. "Well, she's
here." . . .

"Try to understand, hon. We've got to set
your grandmother up in her own apartment.
That's going to take even more money. Don't
you want your room back?"

♦ ♦ ♦

Stacy is very disappointed in the next
few weeks. She has lost both her room and
her ballet lessons. And Grandmother seems
to prefer Ian. She had taught him to speak
some Chinese. She even gives Ian an ice
cream bar that Stacy bought for herself.

♦ ♦ ♦

When I complained to Mom about how
Grandmother was spoiling him, she only
sighed. "He's a boy, Stacy. Back in China,
boys are everything."

♦ ♦ ♦

Stacy decides that the reason
Grandmother likes Ian better is because he
looks more Chinese. Ian looks a lot like their
mother. Stacy looks more like their father,
whose background is not Chinese. Stacy is
upset to think that her own grandmother
views her as an outsider.

♦ ♦ ♦

◆ Reading Check

Circle the two things in
this bracketed passage
Stacy has given up
because of her grand-
mother's arrival.

◆ Stop to Reflect

What do *you* think is the main
reason Grandmother spends
more time with Ian than with
Stacy? Circle the letter of your
opinion. Then explain it on the
lines below.

(a) because he is a boy

(b) because he learned Chinese

(c) because he looks Chinese

(d) because he is younger

(e) because he is nice to her

_____

_____

_____

Vocabulary Development

protest (PROH test) *v.* complain

Even so, I kept telling myself: Grandmother is a hero. She saved my mother. She'll like me just as much as she likes Ian once she gets to know me. And, I thought in a flash, the best way to know a person is to know what she loves. For me, that was the ballet.

◆ ◆ ◆

Stacy takes out her ballet shoes to show Grandmother. When the satin ribbons on the shoes come off, Stacy decides to ask her grandmother for help. But instead of helping, Grandmother is horrified by the ribbons. She won't believe Stacy that they are for dancing shoes. The two argue until Stacy's mother runs into the room.

◆ ◆ ◆

"Stop yelling at your grandmother!" she said.
By this point I was in tears. "She's taken everything else. Now she wants my toe-shoe ribbons."
Grandmother panted as she learned on Mom. "How could you do that to your own daughter?"
"It's not like you think," Mom tried to explain. However, Grandmother was too upset to listen. . . . "Take them away. Burn then. Bury them."
Mom sighed. "Yes, Mother."

◆ ◆ ◆

Stacy can't understand. Her mother explains that to Grandmother, ribbons mean something awful, but she won't say what. Grandmother made her promise never to tell. The next day, Stacy is angry and won't talk to Grandmother. Later she goes into the bathroom and finds Grandmother sitting on edge of the bathtub, soaking her feet.

◆ ◆ ◆

"Don't you know how to knock?" she snapped, and dropped a towel over her feet.

© Pearson Education, Inc.

◆ **Literary Analysis**

Circle the words here that might state one of the story's **themes**.

◆ **Reading Strategy**

What **questions** do you have when you read this? Write one question on the lines below.

_____

_____

_____

_____

_____

What do you think Stacy is going to find out here in the bathroom? Write your ideas on the lines below.

_____

_____

_____

◆ **Reading Strategy**

Circle one question you might ask here. Then, on the lines below, write one more question you might ask when you read these details.

_____

_____

_____

◆ **Literary Analysis**

To what **theme** might the mother's words point? Circle the letter of the best choice below.

(a) People try to spare their loved ones from pain.

(b) Uncomfortable shoes make people behave in odd ways.

(c) Grandparents want their grandchildren to be as much like them as possible.

(d) Pain in life cannot be avoided.

However, she wasn't quick enough, because I saw her bare feet for the first time. Her feet were like <u>taffy</u> that some had stretched out and twisted. Each foot bent downward in a way that feet were not meant to, and her toes stuck out at odd angles, more like lumps than toes. I didn't think she had all ten of them, either.

"What happened to your feet?" I whispered in shock.

◆ ◆ ◆

Grandmother won't answer Stacy's question. She orders her out of the bathroom. Later, Stacy's mother explains that Grandmother is too embarrassed to let anyone see her feet. The terrible damage was caused by the old Chinese custom of binding a girl's feet to give them a shape and small size considered beautiful.

◆ ◆ ◆

I shook my head. "There nothing lovely about those feet."

"I know. But they were usually bound up in silk ribbons.". . .

Finally the truth dawned on me. "And she mistook my toe-shoe ribbons for her old ones."

Mom . . . nodded <u>solemnly</u>. "And she didn't want you to go through the same pain she had."

◆ ◆ ◆

Later that night, Grandmother listens as Stacy reads Ian the story of the little mermaid. When Stacy comes to the part about the mermaid walking on land even though each step hurts, she looks up at Grandmother. At the end of the story, the mermaid turns to sea foam.

◆ ◆ ◆

Vocabulary Development

taffy (TAF ee) *n.*   a type of candy that stretches
solemnly (SAHL um lee) *adv.*   seriously

"I would rather have gone on swimming," he insisted.

"But maybe she wanted to see new places and people by going on the land," Grandmother said softly. "If she had kept her tail, the land people would have thought she was odd. They might even have made fun of her."

◆ ◆ ◆

Stacy realizes that Grandmother is talking about herself. Then Stacy tries to explain that her ribbons aren't like the silk ones Grandmother wore. To show they don't hurt, she puts her ballet shoes on and begins dancing.

◆ ◆ ◆

"See? I can move fine."

She took my hand and patted it clumsily. I think it was the first time she had showed me any sign of affection. "When I saw those ribbons, I didn't want you feeling pain like I do."

I covered her hands with mine. "I just wanted to show you what I love best—dancing."

"And I love my children," she said. I could hear the ache in her voice. "And my grandchildren. I don't want anything bad to happen to you."

Suddenly I felt as if there were an <u>invisible</u> ribbon binding us, tougher than silk and satin, stronger even than steel; and it joined her to Mom and Mom to me.

◆ **Literary Analysis**

The story about the mermaid helps show a message. Put a check on the line in front of all the themes that you think the fairy tale helps express.

____ People will undergo hardship to experience more of life.

____ No one swims when they can walk.

____ People will do painful things to be more accepted.

____ Everyone likes to be different.

◆ **Stop to Reflect**

What is the invisible ribbon? Write your ideas on the lines below.

_____

_____

_____

Vocabulary Development

invisible (in VIZ uh buhl) *adj.* unseen

1. Put a check in front of each true statement about Grandmother.

____ Grandmother is a brave woman who escaped communist China with her daughter.

____ Grandmother was too scared to go against the communists.

____ Grandmother hurt her feet escaping the communists.

____ Grandmother was a ballet dancer in China.

____ Grandmother values freedom and independence.

2. Why do you think Grandmother gives more attention to Ian than to Stacy? Circle the letter of the best answer.

(a) She dislikes Stacy because Stacy is a girl.

(b) She dislikes Stacy because Stacy doesn't look Chinese.

(c) She dislikes Stacy because of the ribbons on Stacy's ballet shoes.

(d) She can talk more with Ian, who has learned more Chinese.

3. What mistake does Grandmother make about the ribbons on Stacy's ballet shoes? Write your answer on the lines provided.

_____

_____

_____

4. What is the "invisible ribbon" at the end of the story? Circle the letter of your answer.

(a) the memory of Grandmother's silk ribbons in China

(b) the satin ribbon on Stacy's ballet shoe

(c) Grandmother's Chinese heritage, which pulls her away from Stacy

(d) the loving family ties between Stacy, her mother, and Grandmother

5. **Literary Analysis:** Put a check in front of the statements that you think are **themes** in the selection.

_____ Love and understanding can bring family members closer together.

_____ Good health is very important.

_____ People do unusual things to try to be different.

_____ We don't want those we love to experience pain and suffering.

_____ The best way to know a person is to know what he or she loves.

6. **Reading Strategy:** In the left column, list three **questions** you asked as you read the story. In the right column, write the answers.

Question	Answer
•	
•	
•	

Writing

Write a paragraph in which you state a theme of the story and show that it *is* one of the story's themes.

In the space below, list an important theme of the story.

_____

List at least three details from the story that point to the theme.

• _____

_____

• _____

_____

• _____

_____

Write your paragraph on a separate sheet of paper. State the theme, and then support it with the details you listed.

The Treasure of Lemon Brown
Walter Dean Myers

Summary

One night, Greg leaves home so he doesn't have to listen to his father's complaints about how badly Greg is doing in school. In an abandoned building near his home, Greg meets Lemon Brown, a homeless man who was once a noted blues musician. Brown proudly shows Greg old newspaper reviews of his performances—reviews that Brown's son was carrying when he died in the war. Greg returns home with a new respect for his own father.

Visual Summary

Greg's Attitude in the Beginning	Events That Change Greg's Attitude	Greg's Attitude in the End
• angry with father for lecturing him about schoolwork and not letting him play basketball • not interested in father's proud talk of passing test for postal service and years of hard work • tries to avoid father and ducks into empty building when rain starts	• meets Lemon Brown, who talks of his "treasure" • helps Brown frighten off troublemakers coming after Brown's treasure • looks at Brown's "treasure"—Brown's old harmonica and clippings about his successful blues career; Brown gave these to his son when his son went off to war. They were returned when his son died	• is happy to go home, even if only to his father's lecture • sees his father's hopes for him as a kind of treasure

LITERARY ANALYSIS
Theme

The **theme** of a story is its central message about life or human behavior. The story's details point to the theme. In some cases, the theme may be directly stated within the work. In other cases, it is suggested by the details. For example, suppose a character who used to be a blues musician places great value on his old harmonica. The theme might be one of these messages:

- Our past achievements are important
- The worth of something is not determined by money value alone.

Stories sometimes have more than one theme. As you read "The Treasure of Lemon Brown," identify the theme or themes. To do this, ask yourself what the details show about life or human behavior.

READING STRATEGY
Asking Questions

You can often understand a story and its themes better if you **ask questions** as you read. For example, you might ask questions like these:

- Why is the author telling me this?
- Why does the character do, say, or think that?
- How does this event fit into what happened so far?

As you read "The Treasure of Lemon Brown," write down your questions and answers on a chart like the one below.

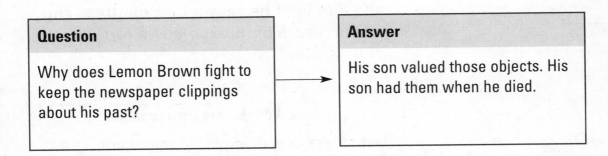

Question	Answer
Why does Lemon Brown fight to keep the newspaper clippings about his past?	His son valued those objects. His son had them when he died.

The Treasure of Lemon Brown
Walter Dean Myers

Fourteen-year-old Greg Ridley has been invited to play basketball with a very good local team. But his father won't give him permission to join the team unless Greg does better in school. The principal just sent his father a letter warning that Greg is failing math.

♦ ♦ ♦

The dark sky, filled with angry, swirling clouds, reflected Greg Ridley's mood as he sat on the stoop[1] of his building. His father's voice came to him again. . . .

"I had to leave school when I was thirteen," his father had said. . . . "If I'd had half the chances that you have, I'd . . . ."

Greg had sat in the small, pale green kitchen listening, knowing the <u>lecture</u> would end with his father saying he couldn't play ball with the Scorpions.

♦ ♦ ♦

Greg's father has told him he can't play basketball. He tells him to go to his room and "hit those books."

That was two nights ago. Now Greg cannot bring himself to go inside to hear more of the same. Instead he heads down the street and escapes the rain by entering an empty old apartment building there. In the dim light he sees a torn mattress and some pieces of broken-down furniture.

♦ ♦ ♦

---

1. **stoop** (STOOP) *n.* outdoor steps and small porch area in front of the door of a building.

He went to the couch. The side that wasn't broken was comfortable enough, though a little creaky. From the spot he could see the blinking neon sign over the bodega[2] on the corner. He sat awhile, watching the sign blink first green then red.

◆ ◆ ◆

Greg thought about the Scorpions. Then he started thinking about his father. He'd heard his father's story way too many times. But he knew his father had worked hard to pass the test for the post office. He was proud to be a postal worker.

◆ ◆ ◆

For a moment Greg thought he heard something that sounded like a scraping against the wall. He listened carefully, but it was gone. . . . Still, he thought, as soon as the rain let up he would leave. . . .

"Don't try nothin' 'cause I got a razor here sharp enough to cut a week into nine days!"

◆ ◆ ◆

Greg is scared until he realizes the voice belongs to an old man from the neighborhood. Greg has seen the man, dressed in rags, picking through trash cans.

◆ ◆ ◆

"Who are you?" Greg hardly recognized his own voice.

"I'm Lemon Brown," came the answer. "Who're you?"

"Greg Ridley."

"What you doing here?" The figure <u>shuffled</u> forward again, and Greg took a small step backward.

Vocabulary Development

shuffled (SHUF uld) *v.* walked slowly

---

2. **neon sign over the bodega:** Brightly lit outdoor sign over the Latino grocery store.

The Treasure of Lemon Brown **215**

◆ **Stop to Reflect**

Why do you think Greg's father often tells Greg how hard he worked to pass the test? Write your ideas on the lines below.

_____

_____

_____

_____

_____

◆ **Read Fluently**

Say the bracketed words aloud. What do they tell you about the man who speaks them? Circle the letter of the best answer.

(a) He fears being attacked.

(b) He is cruel and violent himself.

(c) He has no valuable possessions.

(d) He used to sing the blues.

◆ **Reading Strategy**

What **question** do you have about the figure? Write it here.

_____

_____

_____

_____

_____

_____

_____

◆ Literary Analysis

Circle the words that might be a **theme** of the story.

**Mark
The Text**

◆ Stop to Reflect

Do you think the person speaking is telling the truth in the underlined statement? Circle *yes* or *no*:

     yes   no

Then circle other remarks near the statement that point to your answer.

**Mark
The Text**

"It's raining," Greg said. . . .

"Ain't you got no home?"

"I got a home," Greg answered.

"You ain't one of them bad boys looking for my treasure, is you?" Lemon Brown <u>cocked</u> his head to one side and squinted one eye. "Because I told you I got me a razor."

"I'm not looking for your treasure," Greg answered, smiling. "*If* you have one."

"What you mean, *if* I have one," Lemon Brown said. "Every man got a treasure. You don't know that, you must be a fool!"

◆ ◆ ◆

The old man explains that he was once a blues singer nicknamed Sweet Lemon Brown because he sang so sweetly. He even had a boy just like Greg. While he and Greg continue talking, they hear noise. Three neighborhood troublemakers are breaking into the building. They are armed with pieces of pipe, and one of them carries a flashlight.

◆ ◆ ◆

"Hey! Rag man!" A voice called. "We know you in here. What you got up under them rags? You got any money? . . . We heard you talking about your treasure." The voice was slurred. "We just want to see it, that's all.". . .

There was a footstep on the stairs, and the beam from the flashlight danced crazily along the peeling wallpaper. . . .

Lemon Brown stood at the top of the stairs, both arms raised high above his head.

"There he is!" A voice cried from below.

"Throw down your money, old man, so I won't have to bash your head in!"

Vocabulary Development

cocked (KOKT) *v.* tilted

Lemon Brown didn't move. . . . He was an eerie sight, a bundle of rags standing at the top of the stairs, his shadow on the wall looming over him. Maybe, the thought came to Greg, the scene could be even eerier.

◆ ◆ ◆

So Greg begins howling while Lemon Brown throws himself directly at the trouble-makers. Between the two of them, they scare the three men off. Brown even winds up with their flashlight. Afterward, Greg asks about the treasure, and Brown offers to show it to Greg. He unties the rags on one leg and removes a piece of plastic that contains yellowed newspaper clippings and a bent harmonica. All the clippings are reviews from over fifty years ago. The reviews praise Sweet Lemon Brown, a blues singer and harmonica player.

Brown tells Greg how he used to travel around and perform his music to earn a living. He earned enough to take good care of his wife and son, Jesse. When Brown's wife died, Jesse went to live with his aunt. After he was grown, Jesse was a soldier in the war. By then, Brown's musical career wasn't what it had been. He didn't have anything to give to his son except his "treasure." Those things told his son who his father was and where he came from. Brown felt like his son would be able to do something since he knew his father had.

◆ ◆ ◆

Vocabulary Development

eerie (EER ee) *adj.* spooky; weird
looming (LOOM ing) adj. taking shape in a large or threatening way

---

◆ Think Ahead

Greg thinks the scene "could be even eerier." What do you think Greg will do to make the scene even eerier? Write your guess on the lines below.

_____

_____

_____

◆ Read Fluently

Read the bracketed passage aloud as you think about how Lemon Brown might have told these things to Greg. What tone would he probably have used to say he took good care of his family? Circle the letter of your answer.

(a) sad   (c) proud

(b) angry   (d) snobby

◆ Literary Analysis

Circle the sentence here that might state a **theme** of the story. What earlier behavior does this remark help explain?

Circle the letter of the best answer.

(a) Greg's father not letting him join the basketball team

(b) Greg's anger at not being able to join the basketball team

(c) Greg's father telling how he studied hard to pass the postal test

(d) the troublemakers' attack on Lemon Brown

Look at the details in the first paragraph on this page. They point toward a theme or message. Circle the letter of the **theme** that the details might match.

(a) It is important to do your best.

(b) We often work harder for those we love.

(c) War is a terrible evil.

(d) Music can soothe your sorrow.

◆ Stop to Reflect

What effect do you think the experiences that Lemon Brown shares may have on Greg's relationship with his own father?

Write your ideas on these lines.

_____

_____

_____

_____

_____

"Anyway, he went off to war, and I went off still playing and singing. 'Course by then I wasn't as much as I used to be, not without somebody to make it worth the while. You know what I mean?"

"Yeah," Greg nodded, not quite really knowing.

"I traveled around, and one time I come home, and there was this letter saying Jesse got killed in the war. Broke my heart, it truly did.

"They sent me back what he had with him over there, and what it was is this old mouth fiddle[3] and these clippings. Him carrying it around with him like that told me it meant something to him. That was my treasure, and when I give it to him he treated it just like that, a treasure. . . ."

"You really think that treasure of yours was worth fighting for?" Greg asked. "Against a pipe?"

"What else a man got 'cepting what he can pass on to his son, or his daughter, if she be his oldest?" Lemon Brown said, "For a big-headed boy you sure do ask the foolishest questions."

◆ ◆ ◆

Greg knows it is well past time to go home but does not like leaving Lemon Brown alone. Brown tells him not to worry— the troublemakers are too scared to come back that night, and he will be heading west in the morning. The rain has stopped as Greg makes his way home. Greg knows it's late and his father will have something to say about what time he is coming home. He thinks about whether he should tell his father about Lemon Brown. By the time he gets home, he has decided not to say anything

_____

3. **mouth fiddle:** A slang term for a harmonica.

about Lemon Brown. The old man will be just fine with his memories and treasure.

◆ ◆ ◆

Greg pushed the button over the bell marked Ridley, thought of the lecture he knew his father would give him, and smiled.

◆ **Stop to Reflect**

Why do you think Greg smiles?

_____

_____

_____

_____

_____

1. Why doesn't Greg go home when it starts to rain? Circle the letter of the best answer.

   (a) He does not want his father to know that he is failing math.

   (b) He is angry that his father won't let him play basketball.

   (c) He is worried about Lemon Brown and wants to visit with him.

   (d) He is blocks from home, and the rain is very heavy.

2. Why do the troublemakers break in to Lemon Brown's house? Circle the letter of the correct answer.

   (a) They want to get out of the rain.

   (b) They are friends of Greg's and follow him there.

   (c) They have heard that Brown has a treasure and want to steal it.

   (d) They don't like Greg and want to frighten him.

3. Next to each description, list one or two details from the story to show how the description applies to Lemon Brown.

Description	Detail
poor	_____
	_____
talented	_____
	_____
loved family	_____
	_____
proud	_____
	_____
sad	_____
	_____

4. What is the treasure of Lemon Brown? Describe it on these lines.

_____

_____

5. **Literary Analysis:** Put a check in front of the statements that you think are **themes** in the selection.

_____ A real treasure is worth a lot of money.

_____ A person's achievements are a treasure that can be passed down.

_____ It is impossible to live up to a parent's achievements.

_____ Basketball is less useful than math.

_____ Just about everyone has a treasure of some kind.

6. **Reading Strategy:** In the left column, list three **questions** you asked as you read the story. In the right column, write the answers.

Question	Answer
•	
•	
•	

Listening and Speaking

With a group of other students, prepare an oral presentation about the blues. Include information you research. If possible, play music for classmates. For your research, use reliable Internet or library sources and information provided with CD recordings. Try to answer the following questions on a separate sheet of paper. Then include the information in your presentation.

- What is the blues?
- When did the blues develop?
- Who are some of the important early blues artists?
- How has the blues changed over the years?
- How does the blues continue to influence music today?

I Am a Native of North America
Chief Dan George

Summary

The author of "I Am a Native of North America" remembers the culture in which he grew up. He reflects on the love that Native American people showed one another. He thinks about their great love of the earth and its precious gifts. he compares his culture with white society. He thinks that people in white society have to learn to appreciate one another. They have to learn to appreciate and respect nature. He thinks white society lacks love. In the end, he says, we all need love. He hopes that white society will take the gift of love from Native American culture.

Visual Summary

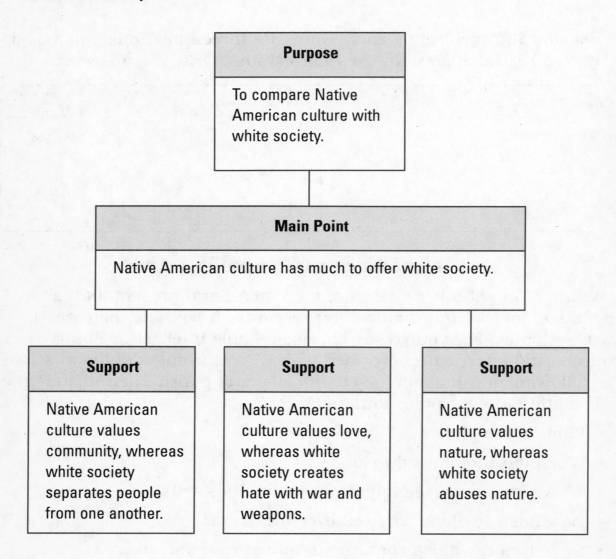

Purpose

To compare Native American culture with white society.

Main Point

Native American culture has much to offer white society.

Support

Native American culture values community, whereas white society separates people from one another.

Support

Native American culture values love, whereas white society creates hate with war and weapons.

Support

Native American culture values nature, whereas white society abuses nature.

LITERARY ANALYSIS

Essay

An **essay** is a short piece of writing in which an author gives an opinion on a topic or experience. Chief Dan George's essay is a **reflective essay**. He presents his ideas about two different cultures. He explains how his own experiences shaped his point of view.

The chart below shows some of the author's ideas about each culture. As you read the essay, add other ideas to the chart.

Native American Culture	White Society
People learn to respect the rights of their neighbors through communal living.	People live near one another but do not know or care about their neighbors.
People love and respect nature.	People abuse nature.

READING STRATEGY

Evaluate Support

When authors make a statement, they should back it up with support or evidence. Readers should **evaluate the support** to decide whether they agree with the author. In "I am a Native of North American," the author makes many statements about the Native American culture and white society. For example, he tells us that white society abuses nature. He backs up this statement with the following support:

- They strip the land.
- They poison the water.
- They poison the air.

To evaluate this and other statements, ask yourself these questions: Is the supporting information logical? Is it true? Do I agree with what the author is saying?

I Am a Native of North America
Chief Dan George

In the course of my lifetime I have lived in two distinct[1] cultures. I was born into a culture that lived in <u>communal</u> houses. My grandfather's house was eighty feet long. . . . It stood down by the beach along the inlet.[2] All my grandfather's sons and their families lived in this large dwelling.

◆　◆　◆

The communal house had one fire in the middle. That open fire was used for all of their cooking. The areas where they slept had blankets hanging between them. The people of the tribe learned to live together well. They learned how to help each other and respect one another's rights. Children and adults shared the space. The children shared in the adult responsibilities. They weren't threatened by adults.

The author's culture also loved and respected nature. He says nature was considered a gift from the great spirit. The way to thank the great spirit was to treat nature well. As a child, the author fished with his father and saw him raise his arms to give thanks. Once the author went fishing just for fun. For this, his father scolded him. He told him that the fish were his brothers. They fed him when he was hungry and should be respected.

Vocabulary Development

communal (kah MYOO nuhl) *adj.* shared by all

1. **distinct** (di STINKT) *adj.* separate and different.
2. **inlet** (IN let) *n.* narrow strip of water jutting into a body of land from a river, a lake, or an ocean.

When the author grew older, he learned about a different culture, white culture. He says he did not understand how people could live near one another other but not know or care for one another. He could not understand all the hate among people. Wars and weapons did not make sense. He was saddened to see people abuse nature. They stripped the land and poisoned the water and air.

◆ Reading Strategy

What details **support** the idea that white society does not respect nature? Circle the details in the text.

◆ ◆ ◆

My white brother does many things well for he is more clever than my people but I wonder if he knows how to love well.

◆ ◆ ◆

The author wonders whether the people of the white culture ever learned to love. He thinks that they may love the things they own. But this isn't love. Man must love the things that are beyond him. Chief Dan thinks that people must love all creation in order to love any of it.

◆ ◆ ◆

Man must love fully or he will become the lowest of the animals. It is the power of love that makes him the greatest of them all . . . for he alone of all animals is capable of love.

◆ ◆ ◆

◆ Stop to Reflect

What is the meaning of the underlined statement?

_____

_____

Do you agree with this state-ment? Circle one: Yes   No

Why or why not?

_____

_____

_____

The author explains the importance of love in everyone's life. He says that love is necessary for the spirit. Without love, people lose strength, self-esteem suffers, and courage fails. People that do not have love in their lives turn away from the world. When they turn inward, they eventually destroy themselves.

◆ ◆ ◆

◆ Literary Analysis

In the author's opinion, what happens without love?

_____

_____

_____

Do you agree with the idea that all things belong to nature and should be shared? Circle your answer.

      yes   no

Why or why not?

_____

_____

◆ Reading Strategy

How does the author **support** his statement that Native American culture will soon be forgotten? Underline the supporting information in the text.

◆ Reading Check

What is it that Native American culture must forgive?

_____

_____

You and I need the strength and joy that comes from knowing that we are loved.

◆ ◆ ◆

The author explains that Native American culture valued friendship and companionship. It did not value privacy because privacy divides people. He says that divided people do not trust one another. People from the author's culture did not collect material possessions. They believed that all things belonged to nature and should be shared. He says people should take only what they need.

The author wishes that white society would take some of these values from his Native American culture. Soon Native American culture will be forgotten. Many young people have forgotten the old ways. They have been made to feel ashamed of their Indian ways.

◆ ◆ ◆

The only thing that can truly help us is genuine love. You must truly love us, be patient with us and share with us. And we must love you—with a genuine love that forgives and forgets . . . a love that forgives the terrible sufferings your culture brought ours . . . with a love that forgets and lifts up its head and sees in your eyes an answering love of trust and acceptance.

This is brotherhood . . . anything less is not worthy of the name.

I have spoken.

1. What two cultures does the essay compare?

_____

_____

2. How does Native American culture view nature?

_____

_____

3. Write a sentence that explains the author's idea of *brotherhood.*

_____

_____

4. **Literary Analysis:** In the chart below, give two ideas the author expresses about Native American culture and two ideas the author expresses about white society.

Native American Culture	White Society
1. _____	1. _____
_____	_____
_____	_____
2. _____	2. _____
_____	_____
_____	_____

5. **Reading Strategy:** Did the author provide convincing support for his main idea that Native American culture has something important to offer white society? Write a few sentences to explain your answer.

_____

_____

_____

(Continued)

Writing

Summary of an Essay

Write a summary of the first page of the essay. Answer the questions below to help you. Write your final draft on a separate sheet of paper.

Main points:	How has the author lived over the course of his lifetime?	
Author's message in your own words	How does he describe the communal houses of his culture?	
Restate the main points in your own words.	What did people learn by living this way?	

Explain the author's message in your own words.

_____

_____

_____

All Together Now
Barbara Jordan

Summary

In "All Together Now," Barbara Jordan appeals to Americans to be tolerant of other races. She encourages us to make friends with people of different background. She asks us to be open to the feelings and beliefs or other cultures. She asks parents to teach tolerance to their children. She believes that by working together—at home, at school, and at work—we can make the world a more loving and peaceful place.

Visual Summary

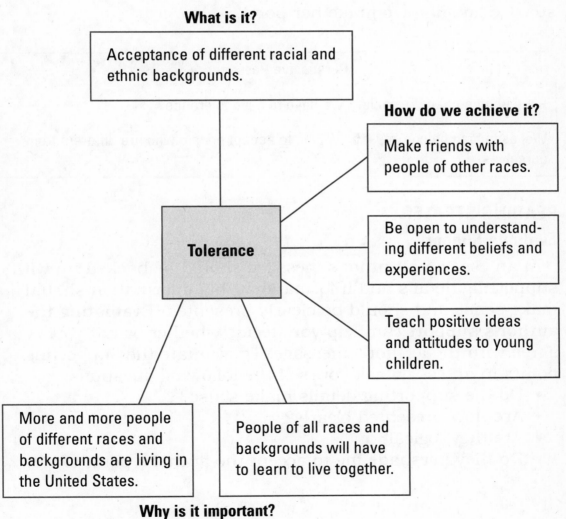

What is it?

Acceptance of different racial and ethnic backgrounds.

Tolerance

How do we achieve it?

Make friends with people of other races.

Be open to understanding different beliefs and experiences.

Teach positive ideas and attitudes to young children.

More and more people of different races and backgrounds are living in the United States.

People of all races and backgrounds will have to learn to live together.

Why is it important?

LITERARY ANALYSIS
Persuasive Essay

In an **essay**, a writer presents a topic from his or her point of view. Essays are written for different reasons, such as to entertain, to persuade, or to inform. "All Together Now" is written to inspire readers and **persuade** them that civil rights are very important. The writer wants readers to do something in response to her essay.

The chart below shows passages in which Barbara Jordan tries to persuade readers to accept her point of view. As you read the essay, notice other passages where Jordan uses persuasive language to make her point.

Persuasive Passages
If we want a peaceful society, we have to have tolerance.
We, as human beings, must be willing to accept people who are different from ourselves.

READING STRATEGY
Evaluate Support

In an essay, an author's message should be backed up with supporting details and information. This information should make sense and should be clearly presented. **Evaluating the author's support** can help you decide whether or not you agree with the author's message. To evaluate the supporting points in an essay, ask yourself the following questions:
- Do the supporting details make sense?
- Are they presented clearly?
- Are they logical?
- Do they persuade me to accept the author's point of view?

All Together Now
Barbara Jordan

The author begins by saying that the relationships between different races in America has improved. Laws have changed to be fairer to everyone. But the real race problem is not government. It is people. She says that individual people need to be more tolerant. And parents are very important in making a <u>tolerant</u> society.

Jordan explains that in the 1960s Dr. Martin Luther King, Jr. led marches and protests against segregation.[1] In 1964, President Lyndon B. Johnson helped pass the Civil Rights Act of 1964. The Voting Rights Act was passed in 1965 to make sure everyone could vote. The laws supported equal rights for all. But laws cannot create tolerance between groups of people. In order for that to happen, people's attitudes have to change.

She explains that Civil Rights issues are just as important today as they were in the past. More and more people of different races and backgrounds are living in America. If we want a peaceful society, we have to have tolerance.

◆　◆　◆

If we are concerned about community, if it is important to us that people not feel <u>excluded</u>, then we have to do something. Each of us can decide to have one friend of a different race or background in our mix of friends. If we do this, we'll be working together to push things forward.

Vocabulary Development

tolerant (TAHL er ent) *adj.* free from bigotry or prejudice
excluded (eks CLEWD id) *adv.* left out

---

1. **segregation** (SEG ruh GAY shun) *n.* the practice of separating racial groups.

yes   no

Why or why not?

_____

_____

_____

◆ **Stop to Reflect**

Why is it best to start small when making big changes?

_____

_____

_____

_____

_____

_____

◆ **Literary Analysis**

In the final paragraph, circle a phrase that shows how Jordan hopes to inspire readers by her own example.

One thing is clear to me: We, as human beings, must be willing to accept people who are different from ourselves. I must be willing to accept people who don't look as I do and don't talk as I do. It is crucial that I am open to their feelings, their inner reality.

What can parents do? We can put our faith in young people as a positive force. I have yet to find a racist baby. Babies come into the world as blank as slates and, with their beautiful innocence, see others not as different but as enjoyable companions. Children learn ideas and attitudes from the adults who <u>nurture</u> them. I absolutely believe that children do not adopt <u>prejudices</u> unless they absorb them from their parents or teachers.

The best way to get this country faithful to the American dream of tolerance and equality is to start small. Parents can actively encourage their children to be in the company of people who are of other racial and ethnic backgrounds.

◆ ◆ ◆

The author concludes by saying that the rest of her life will be spent bringing people together. She loves other people because they are humans. And she hopes that her love will help others to love. Everyone can work toward racial peace—at home, school, and work.

Vocabulary Development

nurture (NUR chur) *v.* care for

prejudices (PREJ oo disis) *n.* unfair opinions based on someone's race

1. Complete this sentence: The real problem in race relations is

   _____

2. Name two laws that support equal rights for all.

   1._____

   2._____

   Did these laws bring about racial tolerance? Why or why not?

   _____

   _____

3. What does the author mean when she says "Babies come into the world as blank as slates . . ."?

   _____

   _____

4. **Literary Analysis:** Why did Barbara Jordan write "All Together Now"?

   _____

   _____

   What does she want people to do?

   _____

   _____

5. **Reading Strategy:** Name two questions you used to evaluate Jordan's supporting information.

   1._____

   _____

   2._____

   _____

Was the support strong enough to convince you to do as she says? Why or why not?

_____

_____

Writing

Summary of an Essay

Follow the steps below to write a summary of the following paragraph from "All Together Now."

What can parents do? We can put our faith in young people as a positive force. I have yet to find a racist baby. Babies come into the world as blank as slates and, with their beautiful innocence, see others not as different but as enjoyable companions. Children learn ideas and attitudes from the adults who nurture them. I absolutely believe that children do not adopt prejudices unless they absorb them from their parents or teachers.

Write one sentence to explain each part of the paragraph.

Beginning	
Middle	
End	

Now combine your sentences to write one summary of the whole paragraph.

_____

_____

_____

_____

_____

How to Enjoy Poetry

James Dickey

Summary

The author of this essay loves poetry. He wants to help others enjoy it, too. He talks about the connections that words have with our hearts. He explains how rhyme and rhythm leave lasting impressions. He suggests ways that readers can think about poetry. He even encourages them to try writing it. Reading poetry, he says, can change your life.

Visual Summary

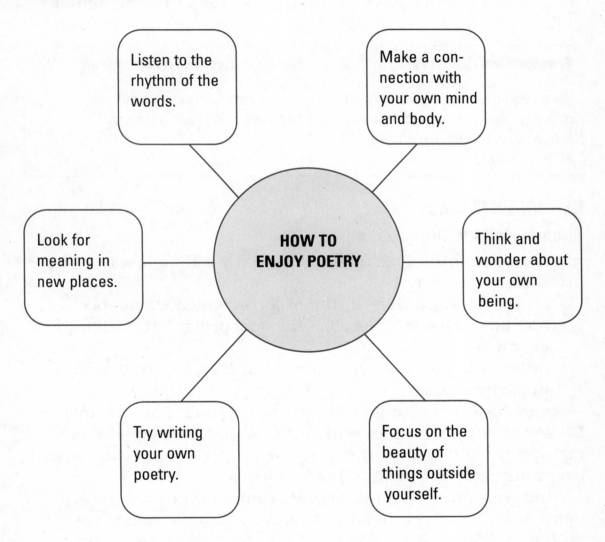

Listen to the rhythm of the words.

Make a connection with your own mind and body.

Look for meaning in new places.

HOW TO ENJOY POETRY

Think and wonder about your own being.

Try writing your own poetry.

Focus on the beauty of things outside yourself.

LITERARY ANALYSIS
Expository Essay

An essay is a short piece of writing about a topic. One type of essay is the expository essay. In an **expository essay**, the writer explains something or gives information about it. For example, "How to Enjoy Poetry" explains what readers can do to help themselves enjoy poetry.

The writer also includes his own feelings and opinions about his explanations. The chart below shows one example. As you read, look for other passages that show the author's opinion.

Passage from the essay	How it shows the writer's feelings
When you really feel it, a new part of you happens, or an old part is renewed, with surprise and delight at being what it is.	The writer describes his surprise and delight in reading poetry.

READING STRATEGY
Recognizing the Organization

Writers organize their material in many different ways. These are some of the ways:
- chronological order—in the order in which events occur
- spatial order—in a specific physical order, left to right, for example
- order of importance—in a way that leads up to the most important point

Sometimes they use more than one method. For example, Dickey organizes his essay in sections that offer tips for enjoying poetry. At the same time, he uses order of importance by beginning with his most important ideas.

When you **recognize the organization** of an essay, you can more easily follow its main points. As you read, notice the section headings. They will give you clues about the main point of each section.

How to Enjoy Poetry
James Dickey

What is poetry? And why has it been around so long? Many have suspected that it was invented as a school subject, because you have to take exams on it. But that is not what poetry is or why it is still around. That's not what it feels like, either. When you really feel it, a new part of you happens, or an old part is renewed, with surprise and delight at being what it is.

◆ ◆ ◆

Where Poetry Is Coming From

From the beginning, people have known that words and things, words and actions, words and feelings, go together, and that they can go together in thousands of different ways, according to who is using them. Some ways go shallow, and some go deep.

◆ ◆ ◆

Your Connection With Other Imaginations

The first thing to understand about poetry is that it comes to you from outside you, in books or in words, but that for it to live, something from within you must come to it and meet it and complete it. Your response with your own mind and body and memory and emotions gives the poem its ability to work its magic; if you give to it, it will give to you, and give plenty.

When you read, don't let the poet write down to you; read up to him. Reach for him from your <u>gut</u> out, and the heart and muscles will come into it, too.

◆ ◆ ◆

Vocabulary Development

gut (guht) *n.* innermost self

Sidebar

◆ **Literary Analysis**

Underline the sentence that shows how the writer feels about poetry.

◆ **Reading Check**

What three things go together with words?

_____

_____

_____

◆ **Reading Check**

What is the "first thing" Dickey wants you to understand about poetry?

_____

_____

_____

_____

Which Sun? Whose Stars?

People living thousands of years ago saw the same sun and stars that you see now. Poetry can describe the sun and stars in different ways and from different perspectives. So poetry can make the sun and stars personal for each of us.

The poet Aldous Huxley[1] wrote about Orion,[2] a constellation of stars in the winter sky. His poem shows the personal emotion he felt when seeing it.

◆ ◆ ◆

Up from among the emblems of the
   wind into its heart of power,
The Huntsman climbs, and all his
   living stars
Are bright, and all are mine.

◆ ◆ ◆

Where to Start

To begin enjoying poetry, you should start with yourself. You should think and wonder about your own being. Then, you might think about something outside of yourself. For example, you might focus on the beauty of a rock or a leaf. Or, you might focus on the sun, the source of all living things.

"Start with the sun," D. H. Lawrence[3] said, "and everything will slowly, slowly happen."

◆ ◆ ◆

The Poem's Way of Going

Part of the spell of poetry is in the rhythm of language, used by poets who understand how

---

◆ **Reading Strategy**

Underline the main point of the bracketed section "Which Sun? Whose Stars?"

Mark the Text

◆ **Literary Analysis**

In the section "Where to Start," what does Dickey explain?

_____
_____
_____
_____

◆ **Reading Strategy**

Circle the heading of the bracketed section. How does the heading relate to the main point of the section? Explain your choice.

Mark the Text

(a) It refers to the mysterious path a poem travels before it is done.

(b) It hints at the way a poem flows, or sounds, when you read it.

(c) It suggests that poetry can go too far if you let it.

Vocabulary Development
spell (spel) *n.* magic
rhythm (RI thum) *n.* sound and beat

---

1. **Aldous Huxley:** English poet, essayist, and novelist (1894–1963).
2. **Orion** (oh RI un)
3. **D. H. Lawrence:** English poet and novelist (1885–1930).

powerful a factor rhythm can be, how <u>compelling</u> and unforgettable. Almost anything put into rhythm and rhyme is more memorable than the same thing said in <u>prose</u>. Why this is, no one knows completely, though the answer is surely rooted . . . in the circulation of the blood that goes forth from the heart and comes back, and in the repetition of breathing.

◆ ◆ ◆

Some Things You'll Find Out

You might like to try writing poetry. <u>Limericks</u> are fun to write. And you can write about any topic. The rhymes in limericks make the poem complete and memorable.

◆ ◆ ◆

How It Goes With You

Reading poetry helps you to look at your own life differently. You will see that your own life is full of words, images, and rhythms. You will look for meaning and you will help others look for meaning. You will make connections between things that you never made before.

◆ **Literary Analysis**

Mark the Text

Why does the author think poetry is more memorable than prose? Underline the sentence that shows his opinion.

◆ **Stop to Reflect**

Do you think that writing poetry has the same effect as reading poetry? Circle one:

Yes   No

Explain your answer.

_____

_____

_____

Vocabulary Development

compelling (kuhm PEL ling) *adj.* attractive; appealing
prose (prohz) *n.* Nonpoetic language
limericks (LIM er iks) *n.* type of funny poem that has five
   rhyming lines

1. What does Dickey say is "the first thing to understand about poetry"? Circle the letter of the correct answer.

   a) poetry is fun to read

   b) poetry is difficult to understand

   c) poetry comes to you from outside you and something from within you must meet it

2. Reread "Your Connection With Other Imaginations." Explain what it means to "give" to poetry?

   _____

   _____

   _____

   _____

3. Why are rhythm and rhyme important to poetry?

   _____

   _____

   _____

4. **Literary Analysis:** Write two things that Dickey explains to readers in the opening paragraphs of the essay.

   1._____

   2._____

5. **Reading Strategy:** List three main points that Dickey makes in the essay. List them in the order in which Dickey states them.

   1._____

   _____

2._____

_____

3._____

_____

Writing

Write a paragraph explaining an activity that you enjoy. Your goal is to make the reader want to try the activity. To begin, complete the chart below. Then, use the information in the chart to write your paragraph on a separate sheet of paper.

Name three activities that you enjoy. Circle the one you want to write about.

Jot down three reasons why you enjoy the activity that you circled.

Turn each reason into a complete sentence.

Activity:	Activity:	Activity:
Reason 1:	Reason 2:	Reason 3:

1. _____

_____

2. _____

_____

3. _____

_____

"The Chase"
from An American Childhood
Annie Dillard

Summary

In "The Chase," the author describes an experience from her childhood. She tells us about a winter morning, shortly after Christmas, when she and some neighborhood friends were throwing snowballs at passing cars. The driver of one car surprised the children by stopping. He got out and chased them on foot for ten blocks before finally catching up with them. Dillard is impressed that the driver chases them over such a long distance. The experience strengthens her belief that people should throw themselves into an activity with all their energy if they want to win. She wishes the excitement of the chase could last forever.

Visual Summary

The Chase

Dillard and her friends throw snowballs at cars. They are chased by an angry and determined driver.

Main Event	Values	Ideas
The children lead the driver on a ten-block chase. They run across yards, through bushes, and up hills. Finally, he catches them.	The author values the thrill of the chase. She enjoys activities that require concentration, courage, and strength.	You have to throw yourself into an activity with all your energy if you want to win. You should never give up.

LITERARY ANALYSIS
Autobiography

An **autobiography** is a person's life story written by that person. Autobiographies often show main events in the author's life. They also show the author's values, ideas, and struggles. For example, in "The Chase," the author shows that she values a good challenge when she tells us how much she enjoys the chase. As you read, fill in the word web with other things that Dillard values.

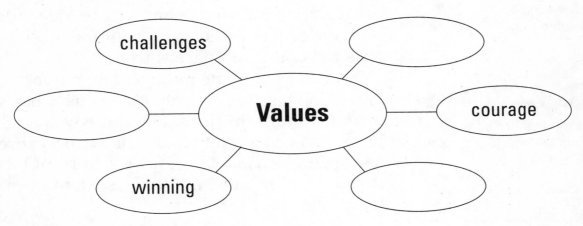

READING STRATEGY
Understanding the Author's Purpose

An **author's purpose** is his or her reason for writing. Authors who write autobiographies might write to entertain, teach a lesson, or explain themselves or their values. As the chart below shows, Annie Dillard has all three of these purposes for writing "The Chase." As you read, look for passages that show each purpose.

Purpose	Example
To Entertain	Dillard amuses readers with an exciting and suspenseful account of the ten block chase.
To Teach	She shares a lesson about putting all of your energy into an activity in order to win.
To Explain	She explains something about herself by letting us know what qualities she values in herself and other people.

"The Chase" from An American Childhood
Annie Dillard

Some boys taught me to play football. This was fine sport. You thought up a new strategy for every play and whispered it to the others.

◆　◆　◆

Dillard also likes going out for a pass. Her favorite part of the game is tackling. She goes all out when she plays football.

◆　◆　◆

Your fate, and your team's score, depended on your concentration and courage. Nothing girls did could compare with it.

Boys welcomed me at baseball, too, for I had . . . what was weirdly known as a boy's arm. In winter, in the snow, there was neither baseball nor football, so the boys and I threw snowballs at passing cars. I got in trouble throwing snowballs, and have seldom been happier since.

◆　◆　◆

One winter morning when Dillard was seven, there was six inches of new snow. She and the boys waited for cars and pelted them with snowballs. Then, a black Buick came towards them. They spread out, aimed at the Buick, and threw.

◆　◆　◆

A soft snowball hit the driver's windshield right before the driver's face. It made a smashed star with a hump in the middle.

◆　◆　◆

Dillard and the others expected to hit the target—that's usually what happened when they threw snowballs. This time, it's different. The man stops the car and gets out. He leaves the car running, and he also leaves the door open.

◆　◆　◆

He ran after us, and we ran away from him, up the snowy Reynolds sidewalk. At the corner, I looked back; incredibly, he was still after us. He was in city clothes: a suit and tie, street shoes. Any normal adult would have quit, having sprung us into flight and made his point. This man was gaining on us. He was a thin man, all action. All of a sudden, we were running for our lives.

♦ ♦ ♦

◆ **Reading Strategy**

Circle the words in the bracketed paragraph that describe how the driver is dressed. What is Dillard's **purpose** in including this information?

_____
_____
_____
_____

The group splits up. They are on their turf so they figure they can use what they know about the neighborhood to get away. Dillard sees Mikey Fahey heading around the corner of a house. She follows him. The man from the car picks the two of them to follow. He doesn't seem to have anywhere he has to be as he chases them.

The man chased Dillard and Mikey all over the neighborhood. They ran across yards, over driveways, up hills, through bushes, between houses, and across streets. Whenever Dillard looked back, the man was always there. She expected that he would eventually give up, but he didn't. Then she realized that the man knew the same thing she did: You have to throw yourself into an activity with all your energy if you want to win.

◆ **Literary Analysis**

In the bracketed paragraph, underline a passage that shows an idea the author strongly believes in.

Dillard and Mikey kept running. Dillard felt cold and happy and scared all at the same time. After ten blocks, the man finally caught them by their jackets, and they all stopped.

♦ ♦ ♦

◆ **Stop to Reflect**

Do you think the driver does the right thing by chasing the children? Circle your answer.

yes   no

Why or why not?

_____
_____
_____
_____

Vocabulary Development

turf (terf) *n.* an area considered to be under one's control

---

What does Dillard's view of the driver as a "hero" and her "excitement" tell you about her?

_____

_____

_____

_____

Why does the author include details about the man's clothing after the chase?

_____

_____

_____

_____

We three stood there staggering, half blinded, coughing, in an <u>obscure</u> hilltop backyard: a man in his twenties, a boy, a girl. He had released our jackets, our pursuer, our captor, our hero: he knew we weren't going anywhere. We all played by the rules.

◆　◆　◆

There were tracks in the snow around them. Dillard and Mikey had been breaking new snow throughout their chase. They both unzipped their jackets. No one looked at anyone else. Dillard was <u>cherishing</u> her feeling of excitement at that point. The man's clothing and shoes showed signs of plowing through the snow—wet pants legs, cuffs full of snow, and his shoes and socks covered with snow. The three stand there with no one else around. They are the only players.

It's a long time before anyone can speak. Dillard, at first, can't even remember what has brought them here. Her lips, eyes, and lungs are feeling the effects of the chase.

◆　◆　◆

"You stupid kids," he began <u>perfunctorily</u>. We listened perfunctorily indeed, if we listened at all, for the chewing out was <u>redundant</u>, a mere formality, and beside the point. The point was that he chased us passionately without giving up, and so he had caught us. Now he came down to earth. I wanted the glory to last forever.

◆　◆　◆

Vocabulary Development

obscure (ahb SKYOOR) *adj.* difficult to see; isolated
cherishing (CHER ish ing) *v.* enjoying; valuing
perfunctorily (per FUNK tah rah lee) *adv.* without enthusiasm; routinely
redundant (ri DUN dent) *adj.* more than enough; not needed

But Dillard knew the glory couldn't last. Even if the man had chased them all over North America, the chase would have ended sometime. And he still would have called them stupid kids. She reflects that if the driver of the black Buick had cut off their heads, she would have died happy. That's because the chase in the snow required more of her than anything else ever has.

◆ **Reading Check**

What does Dillard feel was the most satisfying thing about her experience?

_____

_____

_____

_____

1. Why does Dillard enjoy playing football?

_____

_____

2. Write two sentences to describe Dillard's personality.

1._____

_____

2._____

_____

3. **Literary Analysis:** How does the author feel about the man who catches them? Explain your answer.

_____

_____

_____

_____

4. **Reading Strategy;** Complete the chart by giving one passage that shows each purpose.

Passage that explains something about the author:	
Passage that entertains:	
Passage that teaches a lesson:	

Writing

Comparison-and-Contrast Paragraph

Follow the steps below to write a paragraph comparing and contrasting Annie Dillard with the man who chases her in "The Chase."

1. Complete the Venn diagram to show the similarities and differences between Annie Dillard and the man.

Annie Dillard   **The Man**

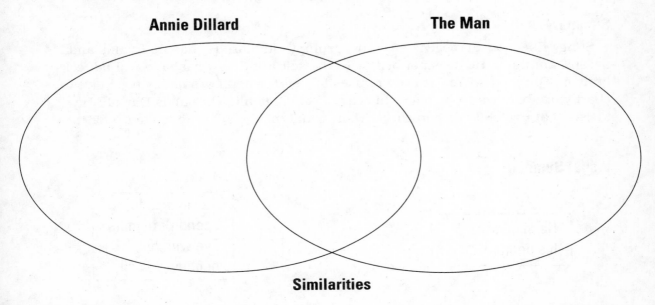

Similarities

2. Use the information in the chart to write two sentences describing how they are similar.

_____

_____

_____

3. Use the information in the chart to write two sentences describing how they are different.

_____

_____

_____

4. Write your final draft on a separate sheet of paper.

        "The Chase" from *An American Childhood* **249**

A Christmas Carol: Scrooge and Marley, Act 1, Scenes 1 and 2

Israel Horovitz

adapted from *A Christmas Carol* by Charles Dickens

Summary

Stingy Ebenezer Scrooge is a greedy, grumpy old man. He has no friends and doesn't want any. He does not believe in the spirit of Christmas, and will not celebrate on Christmas Eve. He even refuses to visit his nephew's family or to give to charity. He barely agrees to give his clerk, Bob Cratchit, Christmas Day off! He insists that Cratchit come in earlier than usual the day after, to make up for it.

Visual Summary

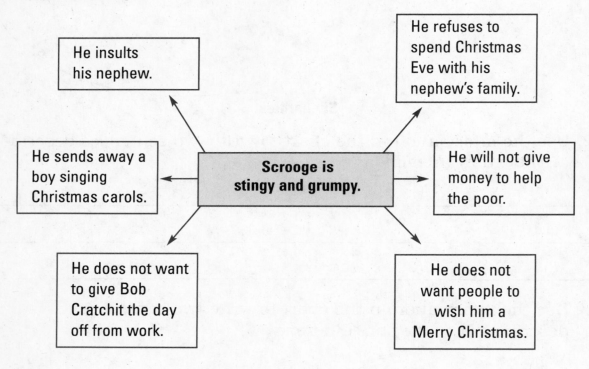

He insults his nephew.

He refuses to spend Christmas Eve with his nephew's family.

He sends away a boy singing Christmas carols.

Scrooge is stingy and grumpy.

He will not give money to help the poor.

He does not want to give Bob Cratchit the day off from work.

He does not want people to wish him a Merry Christmas.

LITERARY ANALYSIS

Elements of Drama

In drama, characters reveal information about themselves through their actions and words. **Stage directions**, in square brackets, describe the setting. They also describe how the characters look, move, and speak. For example, the stage directions in the passage below show that Scrooge's nephew moves and speaks in a cheerful manner.

Example 1:

NEPHEW. [*Cheerfully; surprising SCROOGE*] A merry
Christmas to you, Uncle! God save you!

READING STRATEGY

Picturing the Action

When you read drama, use descriptive details to create pictures in your mind. You will read those details in the stage directions and in the dialogue. Imagine the sights, sounds, and actions in each scene. When you **picture the action**, you increase your understanding of the play. You also make your reading experience more enjoyable and entertaining. To help yourself picture the action, draw a sketch of the stage in each scene. You can also jot down details that help you "see" each character. To do this, use this chart. Complete the chart as you read "A Christmas Carol."

Details About . . .	
MARLEY	
SCROOGE	
NEPHEW	cheerful, full of Christmas spirit, sneaks up on uncle
CRATCHIT	

A Christmas Carol: Scrooge and Marley, Act 1, Scenes 1 & 2

Israel Horovitz

adapted from *A Christmas Carol* by Charles Dickens

THE PEOPLE OF THE PLAY

Jacob Marley, a <u>specter</u>
Ebenezer Scrooge, not yot dead, which is to say still alive
Bob Cratchit, Scrooge's clerk
Fred, Scrooge's nephew
Thin Do-Gooder
Portly Do-Gooder
Specters (Various), carrying money-boxes
The Ghost of Christmas Past
Four <u>Jocund</u> Travelers
A Band of Singers
A Band of Dancers
Little Boy Scrooge
Young Man Scrooge
Fan, Scrooge's little sister
The Schoolmaster
Schoolmates
Fezziwig, a fine and fair employer
Dick, young Scrooge's co-worker
Young Scrooge
A Fiddler
More Dancers
Scrooge's Lost Love
Scrooge's Lost Love's Daughter
Scrooge's Lost Love's Husband
The Ghost of Christmas Present
Some Bakers
Mrs. Cratchit, Bob Cratchit's wife
Belinda Cratchit, a daughter
Martha Cratchit, another daughter
Peter Cratchit, a son
Tiny Tim Cratchit, another son
Scrooge's Niece, Fred's wife
The Ghost of Christmas Future, a mute Phantom

Three Men of Business
Drunks, Scoundrels, Women of the Streets
A Charwoman
Mrs. Dilber
Joe, an old second-hand goods dealer
A Corpse, very like Scrooge
An Indebted Family
Adam, a young boy
A Poulterer
A Gentlewoman
Some More Men of Business

The action in these scenes takes place on Christmas Eve, 1843, in Ebenezer Scrooge's offices in London.

Scene 1

[Ghostly music in auditorium. A single spot light on JACOB MARLEY, D. C. He is ancient; awful, dead-eyed. He speaks straight out to auditorium.]

◆　◆　◆

MARLEY. [*Cackle-voiced*] My name is Jacob Marley and I am dead. [*He laughs.*] Oh, no, there's no doubt that I am dead. The register of my burial was signed by the clergyman, the clerk, the undertaker . . . and by my chief mourner . . . Ebenezer Scrooge . . . [*Pause; remembers*] I am dead as a doornail.

◆　◆　◆

Jacob Marley introduces Ebenezer Scrooge and says that Scrooge is a greedy old man. The audience sees Scrooge sitting in his office counting money. Scrooge cannot see Marley.

Marley tells the audience that he and Scrooge were business partners for many years. When Marley died, Scrooge was too stingy to remove Marley's name from the sign on their office. Scrooge has no friends. But he likes it that way.

◆ **Vocabulary and Pronunciation**

Poultry are animals raised for meat, such as chickens, turkeys, ducks, and geese. What do you think a *poulterer* does?

_____

_____

◆ **Reading Check**

On what night does the story take place?

_____

◆ **Read Fluently**

Read Marley's first speech aloud. Then, read it again paying attention to the stage directions. Do what the stage directions say as you read.

Marley tells the audience that it must watch to see what will happen to Scrooge. It is Christmas Eve and Scrooge is in his counting house. It's a bitterly cold night. Then Marley disappears.

Scene 2

This scene opens to the sound of Christmas music. Scrooge is sitting at his desk. His clerk, Bob Cratchit, is working in a cold and dark corner. He tries to warm himself. Scrooge's nephew enters, unseen.

◆ ◆ ◆

SCROOGE. What are you doing, Cratchit? Acting cold, are you? Next, you'll be asking to <u>replenish</u> your coal from my coal-box, won't you? Well, save your breath, Cratchit! Unless you're prepared to find <u>employ</u> elsewhere!

NEPHEW. [*Cheerfully; surprising SCROOGE*] A merry Christmas to you, Uncle! God save you!

SCROOGE. Bah! Humbug![1]

NEPHEW. Christmas a "humbug," Uncle? I'm sure you don't mean that.

SCROOGE. I do! Merry Christmas? What right do you have to be merry? What reason have you to be merry? You're poor enough!

NEPHEW. Come, then. What right have you to be dismal? What reason have you to be <u>morose</u>? You're rich enough.

SCROOGE. Bah! Humbug!

NEPHEW. Don't be cross, Uncle.

Vocabulary Development

replenish (ri PLEN ish) *v.* to fill again
employ (em PLOY) *n.* work; a job
morose (muh ROHS) *adj.* gloomy; ill-tempered

---

1. **Humbug** (HUM BUG) *interj.* Nonsense!

SCROOGE. What else can I be? Eh? When I live in a world of fools such as this? Merry Christmas? What's Christmastime to you but a time of paying bills without any money; a time for finding yourself a year older, but not an hour richer. If I could work my will, every idiot who goes about with "Merry Christmas" on his lips, should be boiled with his own pudding, and buried with a stake of holly through his heart. He should!

NEPHEW. Uncle!

SCROOGE. Nephew! You keep Christmas in your own way and let me keep it in mine.

NEPHEW. Keep it! But you don't keep it, Uncle.

SCROOGE. Let me leave it alone, then. Much good it has ever done you!

◆   ◆   ◆

Scrooge's nephew says that Christmas is the time when people open their hearts to each other. He invites Scrooge to eat with his family on Christmas. But Scrooge rudely refuses. He criticizes his nephew and Cratchit for having wives and children to support. After arguing, the nephew leaves.

Two kind men enter the office. They have come to ask Scrooge to give a donation for the poor and needy. Instead Scrooge tells the men that the prisons and workhouses are for the poor and needy. Both men are shocked at Scrooge's cold heart. Scrooge asks them to leave him alone and rudely returns to his desk. Bob Cratchit walks the men to the door and gives them a small amount of money as a donation.

After the men leave, the clock strikes six and Cratchit prepares to go home.

◆   ◆   ◆

◆ **Stop to Reflect**

What does Scrooge think is the most important thing? Circle the letter of the correct answer.

(a) spending money

(b) celebrating Christmas

(c) making money

(d) spending time with family

◆ **Reading Check**

How does Scrooge respond when his nephew invites him to dinner? Underline the answer in the text.

Mark the Text

◆ **Reading Strategy**

Picture the action in the scene with Scrooge and the two men. Draw a diagram to show how the people could move around on the stage.

SCROOGE. Hmmm. Oh, you'll be wanting the whole day tomorrow, I suppose?

CRATCHIT. If quite convenient, sir.

SCROOGE. It's not convenient, and it's not fair. If I was to stop half-a-crown for it, you'd think yourself ill-used, I'll be bound?[2]

[*CRATCHIT smiles faintly.*]

CRATCHIT. I don't know, sir . . .

SCROOGE. And yet, you don't think me ill-used when I pay a day's wages for no work . . .

CRATCHIT. It's only but once a year . . .

SCROOGE. A poor excuse for picking a man's pocket every 25th of December! But I suppose you must have the whole day. Be here all the earlier the next morning!

CRATCHIT. Oh, I will, sir, I will. I promise you. And, sir . . .

SCROOGE. Don't say it, Cratchit.

CRATCHIT. But let me wish you a . . .

SCROOGE. Don't say it, Cratchit. I warn you . . .

◆ ◆ ◆

Cratchit leaves, saying "Merry Christmas" as he goes. A boy outside sings "Away in a Manger." Scrooge sends the boy away. Then he grumbles and turns off the lights.

[SCROOGE will walk alone to his rooms from his offices. As he makes a long slow cross of the stage, the scenery should change. Christmas music will be heard, various people will cross by SCROOGE, often smiling happily.

---

2. **If I was to stop half-a-crown for it, you'd think yourself ill-used, I'll be bound?:** If I reduced your pay by half-a-crown for missing work, you'd think I had treated you poorly, wouldn't you?

There will be occasional pleasant greetings tossed at him.

SCROOGE, in contrast to all, will grump and mumble. He will snap at passing boys, as might a horrid old hound . . . This statement of SCROOGE'S character, by contrast to all other characters, should seem comical to the audience. . . .]

Use the stage directions to write a sentence comparing Scrooge to the other people in London.

_____

_____

_____

1. Who is Jacob Marley?

_____

2. Where do Scenes 1 and 2 take place?

_____

3. Why doesn't Scrooge want to give Bob Cratchit the whole day off on Christmas?

_____

_____

4. **Literary Analysis:** Give two examples of things Scrooge says and two examples of things he does that reveal his attitude towards Christmas.

Things Scrooge Says:

1. _____

_____

2. _____

_____

Things Scrooge Does:

1. _____

_____

2. _____

_____

5. **Reading Stategy:** In your own words, describe how you picture Scrooge as he walks from his offices to his rooms. How does he move? What are his facial expressions?
  - How he moves:

  _____

  _____

  _____

  - His facial expressions:

  _____

  _____

  _____

Listening and Speaking

In small groups, assign parts and then prepare and perform readings of scenes from *A Christmas Carol*.

- When you are assigned your role, read through your lines silently. Circle any words that you have trouble pronouncing. Ask your teacher to help you pronounce the words.

- Make sure that you understand the meaning of the lines you are to speak.

- Practice reading your lines aloud to yourself until you can read them smoothly. Then, read them and use the stage direcitons that are given for emotion and movement.

- Perform your scene for the rest of the class.

A Christmas Carol: Scrooge and Marley, Act 1, Scenes 3, 4, and 5

Israel Horovitz

adapted from *A Christmas Carol* by Charles Dickens

Summary

At home on Christmas Eve, Scrooge is visited by the ghost of his dead business partner, Jacob Marley. The ghost warns Scrooge that he must be better to other people or he will end up a miserable, chain-dragging ghost like him. He tells Scrooge that three spirits will visit him during the next three nights. Then he disappears. Later, the Ghost of Christmas Past takes Scrooge back in time. Scrooge sees himself as a young schoolboy, an older schoolboy, and a young worker. Finally, he sees himself as a young man whose sweetheart leaves him because he thinks only about money. Scrooge becomes upset. He begins to regret the choices he has made in life. The ghost disappears, and Scrooge goes to sleep.

Visual Summary

Ideas	Evidence
Scrooge was not always a stingy, greedy, cold-hearted man.	As a young boy, he loved Christmas music even though he was lonely.
	As a 12-year-old, he loved his sister.
	As a young worker, he was happy with his friends and his boss.
	As a young man, he loved a young woman and planned to marry her.
Scrooge begins to regret the choices he has made in his life.	He wishes he had given something to the boy singing Christmas carols.
	He wishes he had treated Cratchit more kindly.
	He regrets that his greed caused the woman he loved to end their engagement.

LITERARY ANALYSIS

Elements of Drama

In drama, writers use action and dialogue to develop characters. They also use **stage directions** to describe each character's actions and appearance. Stage directions are not meant to be spoken. They give instructions about what is happening on the stage.

As you read Act I, Scenes 3–5 of *A Christmas Carol*, look for new information about Scrooge. Analyze his actions, his words, and the information in the stage directions. Use this information to complete the chart below.

New Information About Scrooge:
• Scrooge tries to ignore things he doesn't understand.
• He is afraid of ghosts.
• As a young boy, he was lonely

READING STRATEGY

Picturing the Action

Reading drama is like watching a movie in your head. As you read, **picture the action** so that it becomes real to you. Use the stage directions to help you see what is happening. For example, in the passage below, the Ghost of Christmas Past commands Scrooge to fly:

PAST. [*Motioning to* SCROOGE *and taking his arm*] Rise! Fly with me! [*He leads* SCROOGE *to the window.*]

SCROOGE. [*Panicked*] Fly, but I am a mortal and cannot fly!

The stage directions tell you that Scrooge panics. Bring this event to life by picturing *how* he panics. Does he stop walking? jerk his arm away? What are his facial expressions? Does his voice squeak when he talks?

A Christmas Carol: Scrooge and Marley, Act 1, Scenes 3–5

Israel Horovitz

adapted from *A Christmas Carol* by Charles Dickens

Scene 3

◆ **Reading Check**

What does Scrooge see that startles him?

_____

_____

_____

◆ **Reading Strategy**

Circle all the details that help you picture Marley's Ghost.

◆ **Reading Check**

List four things that are attached to Marley's chain.

_____

_____

_____

Why do you think these things are on this chain?

_____

_____

_____

Scrooge arrives home. As he unlocks his door, the door knocker changes into Marley's face. Scrooge is startled. Then, the face disappears. When Scrooge gets inside, he goes through the house looking to see if anyone is there. The pictures on the walls show Marley's face. Then, all the bells in the house begin to ring. Scrooge hears a loud chain dragging across his basement floor and up the stairs. He hears doors fly open. He refuses to believe these things are happening.

[MARLEY'S GHOST enters the room. He is horrible to look at: pigtail, vest, suit as usual, but he drags an enormous chain now, to which is fastened cash-boxes, keys, padlocks, ledgers, deeds, and heavy purses fashioned of steel. He is transparent. MARLEY stands opposite the stricken SCROOGE.]

◆ ◆ ◆

SCROOGE. Who are you?

MARLEY. Ask me who I *was*.

SCROOGE. Who *were* you then?

MARLEY. In life, I was your business partner: Jacob Marley.

SCROOGE. I see . . . can you sit down?

MARLEY. I can.

SCROOGE. Do it then.

MARLEY. I shall. [MARLEY *sits opposite* SCROOGE, *in the chair across the table, at the front of the fireplace.*] You don't believe in me.

SCROOGE. I don't.

◆ ◆ ◆

Marley screams a ghostly scream and removes his head from his shoulders. This convinces Scrooge that he is real. Marley says that he continues to walk the earth as a ghost because he did not care for other people during his life. He is forced to carry the chain because he cared too much for business and money.

Scrooge is frightened that a chain will appear around his body, but Marley cannot comfort him. However, he warns Scrooge that he has a chance to save himself. He tells him he will be haunted by Three Spirits. They are Scrooge's only hope. If he does not listen to the spirits, he will end up like Marley.

After Marley's Ghost leaves, Scrooge wonders if he imagined the whole thing.

Scene 4

Marley's Ghost appears to the audience. It tells them that they are going to witness a change in Scrooge.

A bell rings and Scrooge is awakened from his sleep. He sees a hand drawing back the curtains. A figure stands in front of Scrooge. It looks like both a child and an old man. It is the Spirit called PAST.

◆ ◆ ◆

SCROOGE. Who, and what are you?

PAST. I am the Ghost of Christmas Past.

SCROOGE. Long past?

PAST. Your past.

SCROOGE. May I ask, please, sir, what business you have here with me?

◆ **Literary Analysis**

Draw a sketch of the scene with Scrooge and Marley sitting in front of the fireplace.

◆ **Reading Check**

How does Marley convince Scrooge that he is real?

_____

_____

_____

◆ **Stop to Reflect**

How was Marley similar to Scrooge when he was alive?

_____

_____

_____

◆ **Reading Strategy**

Reread the bracketed passage. How do you picture a figure that looks like a child and like an old man at the same time. Describe your picture.

_____

_____

_____

_____

PAST. Your welfare.

SCROOGE. Not to sound ungrateful, sir, and really, please do understand that I am plenty obliged for your concern, but, really, kind spirit, it would have done all the better for my welfare to have been left alone altogether, to have slept peacefully through this night.

PAST. Your <u>reclamation</u>, then. Take <u>heed</u>!

SCROOGE. My what?

PAST. [*Motioning to* SCROOGE *and taking his arm*] Rise! Fly with me! [*He leads* SCROOGE *to the window.*]

SCROOGE. [*Panicked*] Fly, but I am a <u>mortal</u> and cannot fly!

PAST. [*Pointing to his heart*] Bear but a touch of my hand here and you shall be upheld in more than this!

◆ ◆ ◆

[SCROOGE touches the spirit's heart and the lights dissolve into sparkly flickers. Lovely crystals of music are heard. The scene dissolves into another. Christmas music again.]

Scene 5

[SCROOGE and the GHOST OF CHRISTMAS PAST walk together across an open stage. In the background, we see a field that is open; covered by a soft, downy snow: a country road.]

Vocabulary Development

reclamation (REK luh MAY shun) *n.* reclaiming; rescuing or bringing something back

heed (HEED) *n.* attention or warning

mortal (MOR tul) *n.* a human being

SCROOGE. Good Heaven! I was bred in this place. I was a boy here!

◆ ◆ ◆

The Ghost of Christmas Past notices that Scrooge is crying. Four men pass by singing a Christmas carol. Scrooge remembers the beauty of the song. The Ghost is surprised that Scrooge has happy memories of Christmas.

Then they see a boy weeping in a schoolhouse. It is the young Scrooge, all alone. The real Scrooge sobs and says the little boy was very lonely. He thinks of the young caroler whom he shooed away from his office earlier that night. He says he wishes he had given him something. The Ghost smiles and takes Scrooge to another past Christmas.

This time, Scrooge is twelve. He is at the school where he lives with a harsh teacher. His six-year old sister Fan comes to take him home for Christmas. The real Scrooge says he loved his little sister very much. In real life, she is dead. But she had one child, Scrooge's nephew.

Next, the Ghost and Scrooge go to a warehouse where Scrooge worked as a young man. He sees his former boss and coworkers. They are dancing and playing music on Christmas Eve. The young Scrooge and his friends talk fondly of their boss. The real Scrooge regrets that he hasn't been kinder to his own employee, Bob Cratchit.

◆ ◆ ◆

[In a flash of light, EBENEZER is gone, and in his place stands an OLDER SCROOGE, this one a man in the prime of his life. Beside him stands a young woman in a mourning dress. She is crying. She speaks to the man, with hostility.]

◆ Reading Check

In the paragraph that begins "Then they see a boy . . . ," what does Scrooge say that shows he might be changing? Underline the answer in the text.

◆ Reading Check

Who does Scrooge think about when he sees himself with his former boss and coworkers?

_____

What does he wish?

_____

_____

◆ Reading Strategy

How do the stage directions that begin "In a flash of light . . . ," help you picture what is happening in the play?

_____

_____

_____

_____

_____

_____

◆ Reading Check

Restate the underlined passage by completing the following sentences:

The world is hard on people who

_____

_____

_____ .

It punishes people who

_____

_____

_____ .

◆ Stop to Reflect

Why do you think Scrooge is yelling "No!" here?

_____

_____

_____

WOMAN. It matters little . . . to you, very little. Another idol has displaced me.

MAN. What idol has displaced you?

WOMAN. A golden one.

MAN. <u>This is an even-handed dealing of the world. There is nothing on which it is so hard as poverty; and there is nothing it professes to condemn with such severity as the pursuit of wealth!</u>

WOMAN. You fear the world too much. Have I not seen your nobler <u>aspirations</u> fall off one by one, until the master-passion, Gain, engrosses you? Have I not?

SCROOGE. No!

MAN. What then? Even if I have grown so much wiser, what then? Have I changed towards you?

WOMAN. No . . .

MAN. Am I?

WOMAN. Our contract is an old one. It was made when we were both poor and content to be so. You _are_ changed. When it was made, you were another man.

MAN. I was not another man: I was a boy.

WOMAN. Your own feeling tells you that you were not what you are. I am. That which promised happiness when we were one in heart is fraught with misery now that we are two . . .

SCROOGE. No!

Vocabulary Development

aspirations (AS puh RAY shuns) _n._ goals

WOMAN. How often and how keenly have I thought of this, I will not say. It is enough that I *have* thought of it, and can release you . . .

SCROOGE. [*Quietly*] Don't release me, madam . . .

MAN. Have I ever sought release?

WOMAN. In words. No. Never.

MAN. In what then?

WOMAN. In a changed nature; in an altered spirit. In everything that made my love of any worth or value in your sight. If this has never been between us, tell me, would you seek me out and try to win me now? Ah, no!

◆　◆　◆

The woman leaves the man, telling him to be happy in the life he has chosen. The real Scrooge cries out as she leaves. He begs the Spirit to take him away. In a flash of light, the Spirit is gone and Scrooge is back in his bedroom. Marley's Ghost appears again to tell the audience that Scrooge must sleep. He still has to meet Christmas Present and Christmas Future.

◆ **Reading Check**

What is the woman releasing the young Scrooge from?

_____

_____

_____

◆ **Stop to Reflect**

What scenes from your own life would you enjoy seeing again?

_____

_____

_____

◆ **Reading Check**

Complete this timeline of the major events in Scenes 3–5

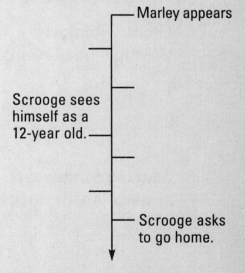

Marley appears

Scrooge sees himself as a 12-year old.

Scrooge asks to go home.

1. Why must Marley's ghost carry a chain full of cash-boxes, keys, padlocks, ledgers, deeds, and heavy purses?

   _____

   _____

2. Who visits Scrooge after Marley leaves?

   _____

3. Complete the chart by describing how Scrooge responds to each of the past Christmases he visits.

Past Christmases	
Scrooge as a young boy:	
Scrooge as a twelve-year-old boy:	
Scrooge with his coworkers:	
Scrooge with his fiancée:	

4. **Literary Analysis:** List two new things you learned about Scrooge through his actions and dialogue.

   1. _____

   2. _____

5. **Reading Strategy:** In your own words, describe how Scrooge responds when the Ghost of Christmas Past tells him to fly.

   _____

   _____

Writing

Pretend that you are a drama critic for a newspaper. You have just seen a production of *A Christmas Carol*. Write a review of Act 1 of *A Christmas Carol*.

Answer the following questions to help you with your review.

- Write three things that you liked about the play.

_____

_____

_____

- Write three things that you disliked about the play.

_____

_____

_____

- Who is your favorite character? Explain why.

_____

_____

- Which character did you like the least? Explain why.

_____

_____

Now write a paragraph summarizing the answers to the questions. Conclude your paragraph by telling your readers whether you think they should see the play or not. Then, explain why you do or do not recommend the play.

_____

_____

_____

The Cremation of Sam McGee

Robert Service

Summary

"The Cremation of Sam McGee" is the story of a Tennessee miner who hated the cold. Still, he joined the gold rush in northern Canada, where it is extremely cold. He knew he couldn't survive the cold, so he asked the narrator to cremate him when he died. When Sam dies from the cold, the narrator travels across the frozen landscape with Sam's corpse to find a place to cremate him. On a frozen lake, he finds an abandoned ship. He attempts to cremate Sam's body in the ship's furnace, but when the corpse is warmed by the fire, Sam comes back to life!

Visual Summary

Sequence of Events					
1. →	2. →	3. →	4. →	5. →	6.
Sam McGee and miners are working in northern Canada.	McGee asks narrator to cremate him when he dies.	McGee dies.	Narrator carries the body on the sleigh to find a place to cremate him.	Narrator attempts to cremate the body.	When narrator checks on the cremation, Sam McGee is alive in the fire.

LITERARY ANALYSIS

Types of Poetry

Poetry comes in different forms. "The Cremation of Sam McGee" is a **narrative poem**. Narrative poems tell stories. Like other poems, they also use rhythm, rhyme, and repetition.

- Narrative poems tell a story using characters, setting, and plot events.

Characters:	Sam McGee, the narrator who tells the story
Setting:	the Arctic
Plot events:	1. Sam McGee and the narrator search for gold in the Arctic. 2. Sam dies of the cold. 3. The narrator searches for a place to burn Sam's dead body. 4. He burns it in an old ship's furnace. 5. When he checks the furnace, he discovers that the heat has revived Sam.

- Narrative poems may use rhythm. In this line, notice the strong beat:

  > Well he seemed so low that I couldn't say no

- Narrative poems may also use repetition. Repetition is the repeated use of words or lines.

READING STRATEGY

Interpreting Figures of Speech

A **figure of speech** is a creative way of expressing an idea. Usually a figure of speech makes a comparison between two things that are not alike. This chart shows common figures of speech.

Figure of speech	Explanation	Example
Simile (SIM uh lee)	A comparison using *like* or *as*	"the cold stabbed *like* a driven nail"
Hyperbole (hī PER buh lee)	exaggeration	"a smile you could see a mile"
Personification (per SAHN uh fi CAY shun)	giving something human qualities	"the stars . . . were dancing heel and toe"

The Cremation of Sam McGee
Robert Service

The narrator begins by saying that gold miners in the Arctic have many strange stories to tell. But the strangest thing the miners ever saw was the <u>cremation</u> of Sam McGee.

Sam McGee was from Tennessee, where the weather was warm. But he wanted to get rich, so he traveled to the North Pole to find gold. One Christmas Day, the miners walked through cold so bitter their eyelashes froze.

◆ ◆ ◆

Talk of your cold! through the parka's fold
    it stabbed like a driven nail.
15 If our eyes we'd close, then the lashes froze
    Til sometimes we couldn't see;
It wasn't much fun, but the only one
    to <u>whimper</u> was Sam McGee.

◆ ◆ ◆

Sam McGee was miserable. That night he told the narrator he was going to die. But he had one final request.

◆ ◆ ◆

Well, he seemed so low that I couldn't say no;
    Then he says with a sort of moan:
"It's the cursed cold, and it's got right hold
    till I'm chilled clean through to the bone.
Yet 'tain't being dead—it's my awful dread
    of the icy grave that pains;
So I want you to swear that, foul or fair,
    you'll cremate my <u>last remains</u>."

Vocabulary Development

cremation (cree MAY shun) *n.* the burning of a dead body into ashes

whimper (HWIM per) *v.* make low, crying sounds; complain

© Pearson Education, Inc.

25 A pal's last need is a thing to heed,
      so I swore I would not fail;
And we started on at the streak of dawn;
      but God! he looked <u>ghastly</u> pale.
He crouched on the sleigh, and he raved
   all day
      of his home in Tennessee;
And before nightfall a corpse was all
      that was left of Sam McGee.

◆　◆　◆

   The frightened narrator carried McGee's body on the sleigh. He had promised to cremate the body, and he was going to keep his promise. The next days were hard as he carried the body over the freezing land.
   Finally the narrator came to the edge of a lake. He saw an old ship there. He took boards from the ship and lit a fire in the furnace. When it was hot, he pushed Sam McGee's body inside. Then he took a walk to get away from the sound of the burning body.

◆　◆　◆

I do not know how long in the snow
      I wrestled with <u>grisly</u> fear;
But the stars came out and they danced
   about
      ere again I ventured near;
55 I was sick with dread, but I bravely said:
      "I'll just take a peep inside.
I guess he's cooked, and it's time I looked"; . . .
      then the door I opened wide.

◆ **Literary Analysis**

In this part of the narrative poem, what happens to Sam McGee?

_____

_____

_____

◆ **Stop to Reflect**

What do you think will happen in the rest of the poem?

_____

_____

_____

_____

_____

◆ **Literary Analysis**

Circle *snow*. Then, circle the word that rhymes with *snow*. Draw a box around *fear*. Then, draw a box around the word that rhymes with *fear*. Find and mark *out*, *dread*, *cooked*, and *wide*. For each, draw an arrow to the rhyming word.

Mark the Text

Vocabulary Development

ghastly (GAST lee) *adj.* ghostlike, frightful
grisly (GRIZ lee) *adj.* horrible

Check which of the following elements of a narrative poem are shown in the bracketed lines:

_____ Character

_____ Setting

_____ Plot

Explain your answer.

_____

_____

_____

_____

_____

And there sat Sam, looking cool and calm,
    in the heart of the furnace roar:
And he wore a smile you could see a mile,
    and he said, "Please close that door.
It's fine in here, but I greatly fear
    you'll let in the cold and storm—
60 Since I left Plumtree, down in Tennessee,
    it's the first time I've been warm."

      ◆   ◆   ◆

    At the end of the poem, the narrator repeats the ideas from the beginning of the poem. He says the gold miners in the Arctic have many strange stories to tell. The narrator ends by saying that no story is stranger than the story of Sam McGee.

REVIEW AND ASSESS

1. Complete this sentence: Sam McGee thinks the weather in the Arctic is _____.

2. Why doesn't Sam go home?

   _____

   _____

   _____

3. What does the narrator promise Sam McGee?

   _____

   _____

4. Why is the narrator determined to keep his promise?

   _____

   _____

5. What did the narrator find when he opened the door to the furnace?

   _____

   _____

   _____

6. **Literary Analysis:** Give examples from the poem of the following features of a narrative poem:

   • **a setting** (the time and place the events of a story occurs)

   _____

   • **characters** (the people in a story) _____

   _____

   • **rhythm** (a strong beat) _____

   _____

   (Continued)

7. **Reading Strategy:** Look at the following examples of figures of speech. For each, explain what the comparison means.

Figure of speech	Example	What it means
simile	the cold stabbed like a driven nail	
hyperbole	he wore a smile you could see a mile	
personification	I wrestled with fear	

Writing

Write a paragraph to introduce "The Cremation of Sam McGee" to a friend. In your writing, point out two or three things you liked and that you think make the poem effective. You could mention the story, the rhythm, the rhyme, or the language.

- Use the chart below to list your ideas

What I like	Why it makes the poem effective

- Then write your final paragraph on another piece of paper

Annabel Lee

Edgar Allan Poe

Summary

The poem "Annabel Lee" tells of the deep love between the young man who tells the poem and Annabel Lee. Annabel Lee is a young woman who lives by the sea. When Annabel Lee dies from a chill, her lover grieves over her death. Still, he believes that their love is so deep that their souls are never truly separated.

Visual Summary

Setting	What Happens
• "kingdom by the sea" • "tomb by the sea"	• "The angels... / Went envying her and me" • "...the wind came out of a cloud, chilling / And killing my Annabel Lee" • "... the moon [brings] me dreams / Of the beautiful Annabel Lee" • "... I lie down by the side / Of my darling, my darling, my life and my bride... / In her tomb by the side of the sea."

LITERARY ANALYSIS

Rhythm and Rhyme

Rhythm in a poem is its beat: the pattern of stressed and unstressed sounds. Read the following lines aloud. To hear the rhythm, stress the words or syllables in dark type.

> For the **moon** never **beams** without **bring**ing me **dreams**
> Of the **beau**tiful **Ann**abel **Lee**;

Rhyme is the repetition of end sounds in words. The words *me, sea,* and *Lee* rhyme. Poets often use rhyme at the end of lines. Sometimes they use rhyme within lines, as well. For example, in the line above, the words *beams* and *dreams* rhyme.

Use this chart to record the rhyming words at the end of lines in "Annabel Lee."

Stanza 1	
Stanza 2	
Stanza 3	

READING STRATEGY

Paraphrasing

Paraphrasing means restating an idea in your own words. You can do this to understand lines that may be confusing. Look at the example in the chart below. You can use this chart to paraphrase lines from the poem as you read.

Lines from poem	Paraphrase
"For the moon never beams without bringing me dreams Of the beautiful Annabel Lee"	The moon always reminds me of Annabel Lee.

Annabel Lee

Edgar Allan Poe

The narrator tells about his love for the young woman Annabel Lee. They lived by the sea when they were very young. They loved each other so much that the angels in heaven were jealous of them. But one night a cold wind chilled Annabel Lee, and she died.

◆ ◆ ◆

The angels, not half so happy in Heaven,
    Went envying her and me:—
Yes! that was the reason (as all men know,
    In this kingdom by the sea)
That the wind came out of a cloud, chilling
    And killing my Annabel Lee.

But our love it was stronger by far than the love
    Of those who were older than we—
    Of many far wiser than we—
And neither the angels in Heaven above
    Nor the demons down under the sea,
Can ever <u>dissever</u> my soul from the soul
    Of the beautiful Annabel Lee:—

For the <u>moon</u> never <u>beams</u> without <u>bringing</u>
    me <u>dreams</u>
Of the <u>beautiful</u> <u>Annabel</u> <u>Lee</u>;
And the <u>stars</u> never <u>rise</u> but I <u>see</u> the bright
    <u>eyes</u>
    Of the <u>beautiful</u> <u>Annabel</u> <u>Lee</u>;

Vocabulary Development

dissever (di SEV er) *v.* separate

Write three words to describe what the narrator's life was like after the death of Annabel Lee.

1. _____

2. _____

3. _____

20 And so, all the <u>nighttide</u>, I lie down by the side
Of my darling, my darling, my life and my bride,
    In her <u>sepulcher</u> there by the sea—
    In her tomb by the side of the sea.

Vocabulary Development

nighttide (NĪT TĪD) *n.* nighttime
sepulcher (SEP uhl ker) *n.* vault for burial; grave; tomb

---

1. Whom does the narrator blame for Annabel Lee's death?

_____

Explain your answer.

_____

_____

_____

2. Why does the narrator talk about the sea?

_____

_____

_____

3. **Literary Analysis:** Underline the words to stress to create the rhythm in these lines:

But our love it was stronger by far than the love
    Of those who were older than we—
    Of many far wiser than we—

4. **Literary Analysis:** Record four sets of rhyming words in the final stanza.

Set #1	Set #2	Set #3	Set #4

5. **Reading Strategy:** Paraphrase the final stanza of the poem.

_____

_____

_____

_____

Writing

Different readers respond to a poem in different ways. Write a paragraph about your response to "Annabel Lee." To begin, fill in the following chart. In it, write two things that you noticed about rhyme, rhythm, and meaning.

Rhyme	Rhythm	Meaning
1.	1.	1.
2.	2.	2.

Draft your paragraph on the lines below. On your own paper, write your final paragraph.

_____

_____

_____

_____

_____

_____

_____

_____

Maestro

Pat Mora

Summary

In "Maestro," a great musician plays the violin in concert. As he bows before an audience, he recalls the sound of his mother's voice and his father's guitar. When the audience applauds, he hears the music he and his parents played together at home.

Visual Summary

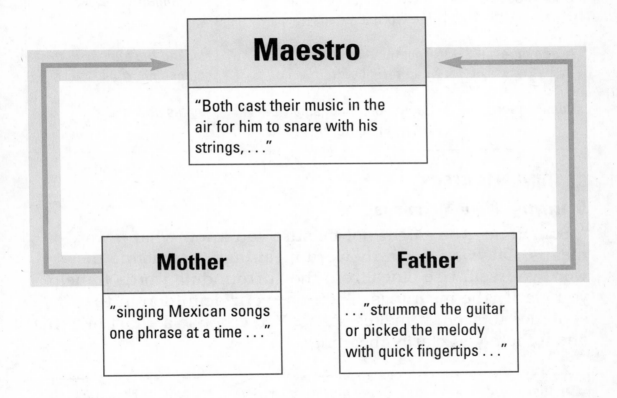

Maestro

"Both cast their music in the air for him to snare with his strings, . . ."

Mother

"singing Mexican songs one phrase at a time . . ."

Father

. . ."strummed the guitar or picked the melody with quick fingertips . . ."

LITERARY ANALYSIS

Sound Devices

Poetry uses **sound devices** that make the words pleasant to hear. Rhyme is one sound device. Words that rhyme have the same ending. For example *hat* and *bat* rhyme. The following chart shows other sound devices.

Sound Device	Explanation	Example
Onomatopoeia	A word that sounds like the word it means	*strummed*
Assonance	Repetition of vowel sounds in different words	*picked the melody with quick fingertips*
Consonance	Repetition of consonant sounds in different words	*as his bow slid*

READING STRATEGY

Clarifying Word Meanings

Sometimes you might not be sure you know what a word means. One way to **clarify word meanings** is to define the word yourself. Use clues from the surrounding words to help you clarify the meanings. Then use your definition in the sentence to see if it makes sense. You can use a chart like this one to help you clarify meanings.

Unclear Word	Clues that Help Clarify	Clarified Meaning
strummed	"his father strummed the guitar" "with quick fingertips"	Strumming is a way to move your fingers over guitar strings.

Maestro
Pat Mora

In this poem a grown man remembers his childhood. An audience claps for his violin-playing. He is reminded of the Mexican music in his home when he was young. The music of his youth was his inspiration.

◆ ◆ ◆

He hears her
when he bows.
Rows of hands clap
again and again he bows
to stage lights and <u>upturned</u> faces
but he hears only his mother's voice

years ago in their small home
singing Mexican songs
one phrase at a time
while his father strummed the guitar
or picked the melody with quick fingertips.
Both cast their music in the air
For him to <u>snare</u> with his strings,
songs of *lunas*[1] and *amor*[2]
learned bit by bit.
She'd nod, smile, as his bow slid
note to note, then the trio
    voz,[3] *guitarra,*[4] *violín*[5]
would blend again and again
to the last pure note
sweet on the tongue.

Vocabulary Development

maestro (MĪS troh) *n.* great musician
snare (SNAYR) *v.* catch or trap

1. **lunas** (LOO nas) *n.* Spanish for "moon."
2. **amor** (ah MOHR) *n.* Spanish for "love."
3. **voz** (VOHS) *n.* Spanish for "voice."
4. **guitarra** (gee TAHR uh) *n.* Spanish for "guitar."
5. **violín** (vee oh LEEN) *n.* Spanish for "violin."

◆ **Reading Strategy**

Clarify the meaning of *upturned*. Draw a line between the two parts. Then switch the order of the parts, and write them here.

_____

◆ **Reading Check**

Who does he hear when the audience claps?

_____

_____

_____

◆ **Stop to Reflect**

How can a musical note be sweet on the tongue? Explain.

_____

_____

_____

_____

1. What is the trio that the poet describes?

_____

_____

2. Write three words to describe the maestro's feelings about his childhood.

1. _____

2. _____

3. _____

3. **Literary Analysis:** Circle the word in this quotation that sounds like the thing it describes:

"while his father strummed the guitar."

4. **Reading Strategy:** Clarify the meaning of *cast* as it is used in these lines in the poem:

Both cast their music in the air

For him to snare with his strings, . . .

Unclear Word	Clues that Help Clarify	Clarified Meaning
cast		

Writing

Write a paragraph about the Maestro's childhood. Go back to the poem and reread the lines beginning "years ago . . ."

1. In your own words, describe what happened during those years.

_____

_____

_____

- What did he learn from his mother? You can answer using words from the poem.

_____

_____

- What did he learn from his father? You can answer using words from the poem.

_____

_____

2. How did those years influence his adult life?

_____

_____

_____

On another piece of paper, put all your ideas together in one paragraph.

The Village Blacksmith
Henry Wadsworth Longfellow

Summary

"The Village Blacksmith," a strong, muscular man, works at his forge under a chestnut tree. He is a hard and honest worker. The children pass by on their way home from school. They like to look in at the fire. On Sundays, the blacksmith goes to church with his children. He thinks of his children's mother, who has died, and he sheds a tear. His life is a lesson to all: Life should be forged by working hard and setting good examples.

Visual Summary

The Blacksmith's Life		
He works hard at his forge every day.	Children like to look in at the fire as they pass by.	He goes to church on Sundays. He feels sad that his children's mother has died.
Lesson		
Live life well, and shape your fortune by your deeds and thoughts.		

LITERARY ANALYSIS
Figurative Language

Poets use **figurative language** to describe things in lively ways. Figurative language compares one object, person, or idea to another. Two types of figurative language are simile and metaphor.

Figure of speech	Example	Explanation
simile: a comparison using *like* or *as*	*His brawny arms/ Are strong as iron bands*	Arms are as strong as iron bands.
metaphor a comparison that does not use *like* or *as*	*At the flaming forge of life/ Our fortunes must be wrought*	Life is a burning oven Fortunes are iron that must be bent and worked.

READING STRATEGY
Using Your Senses

Poetic language often appeals to the **senses**: taste, sight, touch, smell, and sound. Words and details that appeal to the senses are called **sensory language**. You can use your senses to experience a poem more fully. As you read the poem, look for the sensory language. You can write the phrases in this chart.

Sight	• Spreading chestnut tree (broad, shady)
	•
	•
Touch	• Strong as iron hands (heavy, smooth)
	•
Sound	• He hears the parson pray and preach (loud, passionate)
	•
	•

_____

_____

_____

_____

Circle the words in the bracketed lines that help you to **hear** the action.

Why does the blacksmith cry?

_____

_____

_____

_____

_____

The Village Blacksmith
Henry Wadsworth Longfellow

Under a spreading chestnut tree
    The village smithy[1] stands;
The smith, a mighty man is he,
    With large and sinewy[2] hands;
5 And the muscles of his <u>brawny</u> arms
    Are strong as iron bands.

◆ ◆ ◆

    The blacksmith is an honest man. He earns his living working hard every day. The village children like to look into his shop and see the hammer and the fire. His work is a steady pattern in their lives.

◆ ◆ ◆

25 He goes on Sunday to the church,
    And sits among his boys;
He hears the parson pray and preach,
    He hears his daughter's voice,
Singing in the village choir,
30   And it makes his heart rejoice.
It sounds to him like her mother's voice,
    Singing in Paradise!
He needs must think of her once more,
    How in the grave she lies;
35 And with his hard, rough hand he wipes
    A tear out of his eyes.

◆ ◆ ◆

    The blacksmith's life is full work, joy, and sadness. But he carries on every day.

◆ ◆ ◆

---

1. **smithy** (SMITH ee) _n._ the workshop of a blacksmith.
2. **sinewy** (SIN yoo ee) _adj._ tough and strong.

Thanks, thanks to thee, my worthy friend,
    For the lesson thou hast taught!
Thus at the flaming <u>forge</u> of life
    Our fortunes must be <u>wrought</u>;
Thus on its sounding <u>anvil</u> shaped
    Each burning deed and thought.

◆ Stop to Reflect

How are human lives like the work of the blacksmith?

_____

_____

_____

_____

_____

Vocabulary Development

forge (FOHRJ) *n.* furnace where metal is shaped
wrought (WRAHT) *v.* shaped through hammering
anvil (AN vil) *n.* a heavy block on which a blacksmith
    shapes metal with a hammer

1. Was the blacksmith's life difficult or easy?

_____

Explain your answer.

_____

_____

2. Write three words to describe the blacksmith's appearance.

   1. _____

   2. _____

   3. _____

3. What sound reminds the blacksmith of his dead wife?

_____

_____

4. **Literary Analysis:** Complete the sentence. In the final stanza, a **metaphor** compares life to

_____

_____

5. **Reading Strategy:** In the following chart, list examples of sensory language from the poem. In the first column, write the sense. In the second column, write the words and phrases that appeal to that sense.

Sense	Sensory Language

Writing

In "The Village Blacksmith" the poet compares life to a blacksmith's work. Write your own metaphor comparing life to something else.

1. Make a list of possible metaphors.

Life is _____

Life is _____

Life is _____

Life is _____

Life is _____

2. Circle the one you like the best.

3. Write three ways that life is like the thing you chose.

    1. _____ _____

    2. _____ _____

    3. _____ _____

4. Write a topic sentence that introduces your metaphor.

_____

_____

Write the final paragraph on your own paper.

Popocatepetl and Ixtlaccihuatl

Juliet Piggott

Summary

"Popocatepetl and Ixtlaccihuatl" is a legend that explains the origin of two volcanoes near present-day Mexico City. A powerful emperor in the Aztec capital of Tenochtitlan forbids his daughter, the beautiful princess Ixtla, to marry Popo, the brave warrior she loves. Eventually, the aging emperor offers his daughter's hand to the warrior who will defeat his enemies. After a lengthy war, the emperor's men prevail. Most soldiers agree that Popo has fought hard and is responsible for the victory. But a few jealous warriors hurry back to the city and report that Popo has been killed. This news causes Ixtla to fall ill and die. Popo returns and responds by killing the guilty soldiers and refusing to become emperor. He then has two stone pyramids built outside the city. He buries Ixtla near the peak of one and then takes his place atop the taller of the two. He holds a lighted torch and watches over Ixtla's body for the rest of his days. The two volcanoes stand as reminders of the two lovers who dreamed of always being together.

Visual Summary

Elements of Legend

Larger-than-life characters	Exaggerated details
Popo, brandishing his club and shield, leads the warriors to victory.	Popo stands on top of stone pyramid for the rest of his life, holding the torch in memory of Ixtla.

POPO AND IXTLA

Reveals values of culture	Fantastic details
Legend reflects Aztec belief in loyalty and bravery.	Two stone pyramids built by Popo turn into two volcanoes.

LITERARY ANALYSIS

Legend

Legends are part of the oral tradition. They were passed down by word of mouth from generation to generation. Some people, places, or events in a legend may be based on real people, places, or events of the past.

For example, the following details from the legend of "Popocatepetl and Ixtlaccihuatl" are connected to real people, places, or events:

Detail from the Legend	Real Places or Events
• Tenochtitlan	• Once the Aztec capital, now Mexico City
• Two stone pyramids built by Popo became two snow-capped volcanoes	• Two volcanoes near Mexico city: Popocatepetl and Ixtlaccihuatl
• Popo and the other warriors fought bravely for their emperor	• Aztec warriors conquered other Mexican tribes

Details in legends become exaggerated over time. In this story, you will read about the following exaggerated details:

- smoke in the memory of the princess
- pyramids that change to volcanoes
- Popo's decision to stand on top of the pyramid forever

The qualities of the characters in legends often reveal the values and attitudes of the cultures from which they come. For example, Popo's bravery and loyalty suggest that these qualities were admired by the Aztecs.

READING STRATEGY

Rereading and Reading Ahead

Rereading and **reading ahead** can help you to understand the authors' words and ideas.

If you do not understand a certain passage, reread it. Look for connections among the words and sentences. It might also help to read ahead because a word or idea may be clarified further on.

Popocatepetl and Ixtlaccihuatl
Juliet Piggott

Have you ever looked at a mountain and wondered how it got there? People who lived long ago answered such questions by inventing legends. "Popocatepetl and Ixtlaccihuatl" is a legend that explains the origin of two volcanoes near present-day Mexico City.

The story begins with a description of Tenochtitlan and the two nearby volcanoes:

◆　◆　◆

Before the Spaniards came to Mexico and marched on the Aztec capital of Tenochtitlan (te NOCH tee TLAN)[1] there were two volcanoes to the southeast of that city. The Spaniards destroyed much of Tenochtitlan and built another city in its place and called it Mexico City. It is known by that name still, and the pass through which the Spaniards came to the ancient Tenochtitlan is still there, as are the volcanoes on each side of that pass. Their names have not been changed. The one to the north is Ixtlaccihuatl (EES tlah SEE WAT uhl) and the one on the south of the pass is Popocatepetl (po po kah TEE PET uhl). Both are snowcapped and beautiful, Popocatepetl being the taller of the two. That name means Smoking Mountain. In Aztec days it gushed forth smoke and, on occasion, it does so still. It erupted too in Aztec days and has done so again since the Spaniards came. Ixtlaccihuatl means The White Woman, for its peak was, and still is, white.

◆　◆　◆

---
1. **Tenochtitlan:** The Spanish conquered the Aztec capital in 1521.

The legend of "Popocatepetl and Ixtlaccihuatl" comes from the Aztec Indians of Mexico. They were great builders and engineers—their capital city of Tenochtitlan, built on a lake, had a complex system of canals for transportation and floating gardens for crops. The influence of Aztec culture continues in Mexico's art, language, and food.

◆ Reading Check

What was the name of the Aztec Capital?

_____

_____

_____

According to an Aztec legend, there was once a very powerful Emperor in Tenochtitlan. Some thought he was wise, while others doubted his wisdom. The Emperor had a beautiful daughter. Her name was Ixtlaccihuatl, but people called her Ixtla. When the princess grew up, she became a serious young woman. She knew that the Emperor expected her to rule in his place someday.

◆ ◆ ◆

Another reason for her being so serious was that she was in love. This in itself was a joyous thing, but the Emperor forbade her to marry. He wanted her to reign and rule alone when he died, for he trusted no one, not even his wife, to rule as he did except his much loved only child, Ixtla.

◆ ◆ ◆

This is why some doubted the wisdom of the Emperor. Not allowing his daughter to marry was selfish and not truly wise. And if an emperor was not truly wise, he could not be truly great or truly powerful either.

The man with whom Ixtla was in love was a young warrior named Popocatepetl. Ixtla and his friends called him Popo. Ixtla and Popo loved each other very much, and they would have been very happy had they been allowed to marry.

In time, the Emperor became very old and ill. His enemies, the tribes that lived in the mountains, realized this. Before long, the city of Tenochtitlan was <u>besieged</u>. The Emperor knew that unless his enemies were driven off, Tenochtitlan would be destroyed.

Vocabulary Development

besieged (bi SEEJD) *n.* surrounded

_____

_____

_____

What reward does the Emperor promise for lifting the siege?

_____

_____

_____

What does the account of the battle suggest about the Aztecs' attitudes about war?

_____

_____

_____

Why do the warriors report false news?

_____

_____

_____

He also knew that he was too old and too ill to lead his warriors into battle.

◆　◆　◆

Instead of appointing one of his warriors to lead the rest into battle on his behalf, he offered a <u>bribe</u> to all of them. Perhaps it was that his wisdom, if wisdom he had, had forsaken him, or perhaps he acted from fear. Or perhaps he simply changed his mind. But the bribe he offered to whichever warrior succeeded in lifting the siege of Tenochtitlan and defeating his enemies in and around the Valley of Mexico was both the hand of his daughter and the equal right to reign and rule, with her, in Tenochtitlan.

◆　◆　◆

And so the warriors went to war. Although each fought hard, showing great skill and courage, the war was long and fierce. Battle followed battle, and the final outcome was uncertain. As time went by, Popo emerged as the leader. <u>Brandishing</u> his club and shield, he led a great charge of warriors across the valley. The enemies fled before them for the safety of the jungles beyond the mountains. The warriors regarded Popo as the man most responsible for the victory. When they returned to Tenochtitlan, Popo would claim Ixtla as his wife at last.

But a few warriors were jealous of Popo. They slipped away from the others at night and raced back to Tenochtitlan. They reported to the Emperor that the enemies had been defeated and that Popo had been killed. The Emperor then told Ixtla the news.

Vocabulary Development

bribe (BRĪB) _n._ money or a reward offered to someone to get him to do something for the giver

brandishing (BRAN dish ing) _adj._ waving in a menacing way

He added that he did not yet know who her husband would be. Ixtla was overcome with grief. She went to her room and lay down. If Popo was dead, she did not wish to live. So she became very ill and died.

The very next day, Popo returned to Tenochtitlan. When he heard how Ixtla had died, he spoke not a word. He and the other warriors found the men who had given the false news. Popo killed each one of them in single combat. Then Popo returned to the palace. He went to Ixtla's room, lifted her body, and carried it out of the palace and out of the city. The warriors followed him.

◆ ◆ ◆

When he had walked some miles he gestured to them again and they built a huge pile of stones in the shape of a pyramid. They all worked together and they worked fast while Popo stood and watched, holding the body of the princess in his arms. By sunset the mighty <u>edifice</u> was finished. Popo climbed it alone, carrying Ixtla's corpse with him. There, at the very top, under a heap of stones, he buried the young woman he had loved so well and for so long, and who had died for the love of him.

That night Popo slept alone at the top of the pyramid by Ixtla's grave. In the morning he came down and spoke for the first time since the Emperor had told him the princess was dead. He told the warriors to build another pyramid, a little to the southeast of the one which held Ixtla's body and to build it higher than the other.

He told them too to tell the Emperor on his behalf that he, Popocatepetl, would never reign and rule in Tenochtitlan. He would keep watch

---

Vocabulary Development

edifice (ED uh fis) *n.* large structure

Put a checkmark in front of each detail that helps explain where the mountains came from.

_____ Popo had two pyramids built.

_____ Popo stood next to Ixtla's pyramid holding a torch for the rest of his days.

_____ The emperor was not very wise.

_____ Tenochtitlan was the capital.

◆ Stop to Reflect

Do you believe this explanation of the origin of the mountains?

_____

Why do you think it was told?

_____

_____

_____

over the grave of the Princess Ixtlaccihuatl for the rest of his life.

The messages to the Emperor were the last words Popo ever spoke. Well before the evening the second mighty pile of stones was built. Popo climbed it and stood at the top, taking a torch of <u>resinous</u> pine wood with him.

And when he reached the top he lit the torch and the warriors below saw the white smoke rise against the blue sky, and they watched as the sun began to set and the smoke turned pink and then a deep red, the color of blood.

So Popocatepetl stood there, holding the torch in memory of Ixtlaccihuatl, for the rest of his days.

The snows came and, as the years went by, the pyramids of stone became high white-capped mountains. Even now the one called Popocatepetl emits smoke in memory of the princess whose body lies in the mountain which bears her name.

Vocabulary Development

resinous (REZ in us) *adj.* full of resin, a sticky gum that oozes from pines

1. Why are Ixtla and Popo unable to marry?

_____

_____

_____

2. How do the Emperor's actions show his selfishness?

_____

_____

_____

3. What effect does the Emperor's selfishness have on the safety of his kingdom? Circle the letter of the correct answer.

   (a) The kingdom ends up with no ruler.
   (b) The kingdom rests safely in Ixtla's hands.
   (c) Popo and Ixtla rule the kingdom together.
   (d) The kingdom is overthrown by enemies.

4. What leads to Ixtla's death at the end of the war?

_____

_____

_____

5. **Reading Strategy:** Why is it sometimes a good idea to **read ahead**?

_____

_____

_____

(Continued)

6. **Literary Analysis:** List three things from this story that show that it is a **legend**.

1. _____

_____

2. _____

_____

3. _____

_____

Writing

Research Summary

Read one or two articles on how volcanoes are formed. While you read, write down the main steps in the process. Then, make a list of the steps in the correct time order. Choose only the steps that cause or lead to another part of the process. For example, your list might look something like this:

- **Temperatures deep under the surface of the Earth are close to 1200 degrees C, hot enough to melt rock.**

- **As rock melts and becomes magma, it produces gas.**

- **Gas expands and needs more space, which puts pressure on the rock above it.**

- **The ground rises and expands, creating a volcano.**

Now use the steps you have listed from your research to write a summary of how a volcano is formed. How is your explanation different from the explanation in the legend of "Popocatepetl and Ixtlaccihuatl"?

_____

_____

_____

The People Could Fly
Virginia Hamilton

Summary

In "The People Could Fly," the story is told that long ago in Africa people knew how to fly. When they were captured and sent away in slave ships, it was too crowded and the people who knew how to fly lost their wings. As the enslaved African Americans labored in the fields, they had to work very hard and were often mistreated. An old man, Toby, helps the people to fly away from their misery by whispering magic words that help them remember how to fly. He finally flies himself, leaving those who cannot fly to tell the tale to others.

Visual Summary

Details of Cultural Context

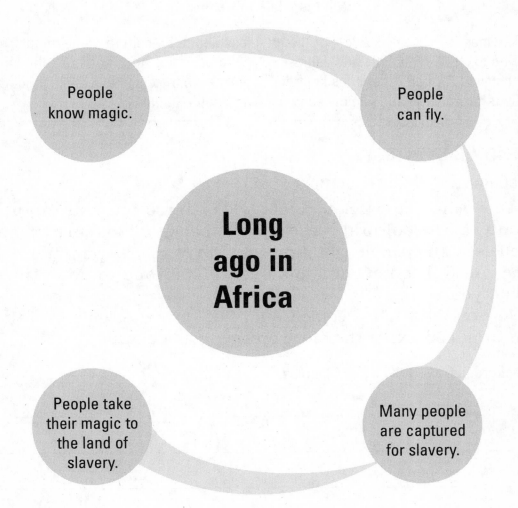

People know magic.

People can fly.

Long ago in Africa

People take their magic to the land of slavery.

Many people are captured for slavery.

LITERARY ANALYSIS

Folk Tales

Many cultures have **folk tales**. Folk tales are stories that are passed from person to person by word of mouth. Folk tales communicate the ideas and values that are important to people in a culture. The following are important questions to consider:

Where do folk tales come from?
No one knows who first created folk tales. Modern writers sometimes retell folk tales. They try to capture the feeling and spirit of the stories as they have been told for hundreds of years.

What is a folk tale's message?
The message of a folk tale—or theme—tells about the culture of the people who tell it. Their beliefs and values are reflected in the story. For example, enslaved African Americans kept their hopes alive by telling folk tales about the fight for freedom and justice, such as "The People Could Fly."

READING STRATEGY

Recognizing Cultural Context

One way to appreciate a folk tale is to recognize its **cultural context**. The cultural context is the background, customs, and beliefs of the people who first told the story. Keeping track of the cultural context of a folk tale will help you to understand what you read.

As you read "The People Could Fly," jot down details of the cultural context of the story on the lines below:

Background   **Customs**   **Beliefs**

_____   _____   _____

_____   _____   _____

_____   _____   _____

The People Could Fly
Virginia Hamilton

Have things ever seemed so bad that
you wished you could just fly away and
leave all your troubles behind? In the African
American folk tale "The People Could Fly,"
an old man, Toby, helps the enslaved
Africans fly away from their misery. He whispers magic words that help them remember
how to fly.

As the story begins, the author tells how
people in Africa a long time ago were able to
fly. But they lost that ability once they were
enslaved.

◆ ◆ ◆

They say the people could fly. . . .
Then, many of the people were captured for
Slavery. The ones that could fly shed their
wings.

◆ ◆ ◆

Many of the enslaved people got sea-
sick on the slave ships. Missing Africa and
feeling sick, the people were full of misery.
They didn't think about flying then.

Even though the people who could fly
didn't take their wings, they kept their power.
Despite being enslaved, the magic of flying
stayed with the people—but they kept it
secret. Because they looked the same as the
other dark-skinned people who had been
coming over from Africa, it wasn't possible
to know which people could fly.

◆ ◆ ◆

© Pearson Education, Inc.

◆ **Reading Strategy**

Underline details in the
bracketed passage that
describe the **culture**.

◆ **Reading Check**

Why are the people full of misery?

_____

_____

_____

_____

◆ **Reading Check**

What special gift do some of the
people have?

_____

_____

_____

◆ Literary Analysis

Circle the words in this bracketed paragraph that tell you this story has been passed on orally?

◆ Reading Check

Why can't Sarah stop working to take care of her baby?

_____

_____

_____

_____

_____

◆ Reading Strategy

List two negative things that you have learned about the culture depicted in this story?

1. _____

_____

2. _____

_____

_____

One such who could was an old man, call him Toby. And standin tall, yet afraid, was a young woman who once had wings. . . . Now Sarah carried a babe. . . .

◆　◆　◆

The slaves work hard in the fields from sunup to sundown. The owner of the slaves is a hard, cruel man who calls himself their Master. His Overseer[1] on horseback points out slaves who are slowing down. A man called Driver[2] whips those slaves to make them work faster. The Driver's whip cuts into the slaves, hurting them badly. So they work fast to avoid the whip.

Sarah hoes and chops the row, but she carries her baby on her back. While Sarah works, the baby sleeps. When the baby grows hungry, it begins to cry. Sarah can't stop working to feed it or soothe it.

◆　◆　◆

"Keep that thing quiet," called the Overseer. . . . The woman scrunched low. The Driver cracked his whip across the babe anyhow. The babe hollered like any hurt child, and the woman fell to the earth.

◆　◆　◆

The old man, Toby, helps Sarah to her feet. She tells Toby that she must go soon. He tells her it will be soon. Sarah is so weak she can no longer stand up. She sits down in the row. The Overseer shouts at her to get up. The Driver whips her. Her dress is torn and her legs are bleeding, but she can't get up.

◆　◆　◆

---

1. **overseer** (OH ver SEE er) _n._ someone who watches over and directs the work of others.
2. **driver** _n._ someone who forced (drove) the slaves to work harder.

"Now, before it's too late," panted Sarah. "Now, Father!"

"Yes, Daughter, the time is come," Toby answered. "Go, as you know how to go!"

He raised his arms. . . . *"Kum . . . yali, kum buba tambe,"* and more magic words, said so quickly, they sounded like whispers and sighs.

◆　◆　◆

◆ **Literary Analysis**

In the bracketed paragraph, underline two details that show how the author writes in the style of a story being told.

> First, Sarah lifts one foot. Then she lifts the other. She isn't graceful. She's holding the baby. Then the magic that she knew in Africa returns. She begins to fly like a bird.

> As Sarah flies away, the Overseer rides after her. Nothing can stop her. She flies until no one can see her anymore. No one talks about Sarah flying away. They aren't sure whether to believe it happened. But those who were there knew that it happened.

> The next day Toby helps several more slaves fly away. The Overseer cries out to the Driver to seize the old man. The Driver gets his whip ready. The one calling himself Master comes running. He pulls out his gun, meaning to kill Toby. But Toby just laughs and sighs the ancient words to the other slaves.

◆　◆　◆

". . . buba yali . . . buba tambe. . . ."

There was a great outcryin. . . . Old and young who were called slaves and could fly joined hands. Say like they would ring-sing.[3] But they didn't <u>shuffle</u> in a circle. They didn't sing. They rose on the air.

◆　◆　◆

◆ **Reading Check**

Why do you think the Master wants to kill Toby?

_____

_____

_____

_____

◆ **Reading Check**

What are the magic words that Toby says? Write them here.

_____

_____

Vocabulary Development

shuffle (SHUF uhl) *v.* walk with dragging feet

---

3. **ring-sing** joining hands in a circle to sing and dance.

What do you think the message of this story was to enslaved African Americans? Circle the letter of the best answer.

(a) If you try hard enough, you can fly.
(b) Keep hoping. Someday you will be free.
(c) All overseers are bad.
(d) If you can't fly, you will die.

◆ Stop to Reflect

Do you think this folktale inspires hope?

_____

Explain why or why not?

_____

_____

_____

_____

The people flew in a flock. They left the plantation and their slavery. The flew to freedom.

Toby flies too. He takes care of the people. He isn't "cryin or laughin." He is the seer.[4] As he is flying, he sees the slaves who cannot fly. They are waiting. But Toby can't help those who can't fly. There is no time to teach them. They will have to wait for a chance to run. He calls out "goodie-bye" and flies away.

◆ ◆ ◆

So they say. The Overseer told it. The one called Master said it was a lie, a trick of the light. The Driver kept his mouth shut.

The slaves who could not fly told about the people who could fly to their children.

◆ ◆ ◆

And so the story of the people who could fly passes from generation to generation.

_____

1. **seer** (SEE uhr) *n.* one who has supposed power to see the future; prophet.

1. How did the people lose their wings?

_____

_____

_____

2. Why does Sarah tell Toby that she must leave soon?

_____

_____

_____

3. How does Toby help Sarah?

_____

_____

_____

4. **Literary Analysis:** List three examples of words or phrases from the story that tell you that this story was spoken aloud.

1. _____

2. _____

3. _____

(Continued)

5. Reading Strategy: What was life like for the enslaved Africans?

_____

_____

_____

Speaking and Listening

Retelling

Folk tales are stories told by ordinary people. The stories are passed along from person to person orally.

Imagine that you are going to help carry on the folk tale tradition by telling "The People Could Fly" aloud to your class. You are going to retell the story in your own words, as if you were passing it along to a younger generation Do the following:

- Review the story to remember the most important events.
- Practice reading it aloud.
- Add details of your own.
- Remember that part of the oral tradition involves adding your own personality to your retelling.
- Now practice telling the story in your own words.
- When you are ready, tell the story to the class.

Demeter and Persephone

Anne Terry White

Summary

"Demeter and Persephone" explains the Earth's seasons. When Pluto, king of the underworld, appears on Earth, Eros causes him to fall in love with Persephone. Pluto kidnaps Persephone and carries her away. When she is unable to find her daughter, Demeter, goddess of the harvest, becomes angry and makes the Earth infertile. Because humankind is threatened with starvation, Zeus asks for Persephone's release—upon the condition that she has not tasted food in the underworld. Pluto reluctantly agrees. Unfortunately, Persephone has tasted four pomegranate seeds, so she must return to Pluto for four months of every year while her mother grieves. These months are known as winter. During the months she is home, the soil is fertile and productive.

Visual Summary

Prediction Chart

CLUE	PREDICTION
• Eros shoots an arrow into Pluto's heart.	• Pluto will fall in love with Persephone.
• Pluto kidnaps Persephone.	• Demeter will be angry.
• Demeter blames the land for Persephone's disappearance.	• Demeter will not let anything grow on earth.
• Zeus knows where Persephone is.	• Zeus will send Hermes to bring Persephone back home.

LITERARY ANALYSIS

Myth

Since time began, people have tried to understand the world around them. Ancient peoples created **myths**, or stories to explain natural occurrences. For example, the ancient Greeks created myths to explain

- **the sun's daily travel across the sky.**
- **the changing seasons.**

Myths also expressed beliefs about right and wrong. Even though we can explain many things today in scientific terms, myths still make sense to us because they explain the world in human terms.

For example, Demeter [duh MEE ter] is angry because her daughter Persephone [pur SE fu nee] has been kidnapped. So she doesn't let anything grow on earth. Later, Persephone has to return to Pluto in the underword four months out of each year. Demeter causes winter during those four months. This was how the Greeks explained winter.

READING STRATEGY

Making Predictions

A **prediction** is an educated guess about what will happen. The guess is based on hints or clues in the story. In some myths, characters get into trouble because they happen to be in the wrong place at the wrong time. For example, in "Demeter and Persephone," Persephone gets kidnapped by Pluto because Eros shoots an arrow into Pluto's heart. Often, characters' troubles are the result of their own actions.

As you read, predict when a character's actions may lead to trouble. Then, read on to see if your predictions were correct.

Demeter and Persephone
Anne Terry White

Do you know what causes the changing seasons? Today, scientists explain that as the Earth revolves around the sun during the course of a year, it tilts. Part of its surface gets more sunlight, and the other part gets less. In regions getting more direct sunlight, it is summer. In areas tilting away from the sun's rays, it is winter. Thousands of years ago, the ancient Greeks explained the changing seasons with the myth of "Demeter and Persephone."

As the story begins, Pluto, the king of the underworld, becomes alarmed at the shaking of the earth.

◆ ◆ ◆

Deep under Mt. Aetna [ET nuh], the gods had buried alive a number of fearful, fire-breathing giants. The monsters heaved and struggled to get free. And so mightily did they shake the earth that Pluto, the king of the underworld, was alarmed.

"They may tear the rocks <u>asunder</u> and leave the realm of the dead open to the light of day," he thought. And mounting his golden chariot, he went up to see what damage had been done.

Now the goddess of love and beauty, fair Aphrodite [AF roh DĪT ee], was sitting on a mountainside playing with her son, Eros [ER os].[1] She saw Pluto as he drove around with his coal-black horses and she said:

◆ **Literary Analysis**

What natural event might these sentences describe?

_____

_____

_____

_____

_____

◆ **Reading Strategy**

Eros, the god of love, shoots gold-tipped arrows that cause people to fall in love. **Predict** what will happen in the story.

_____

_____

_____

_____

_____

Vocabulary Development

asunder (ah SUN der) *adv.*   apart

---

1. **Eros** in Greek mythology, the god of love. Identified by the Romans as Cupid.

"My son, there is one who defies your power and mine. Quick! Take up your darts! Send an arrow into the breast of that dark <u>monarch</u>. Let him, too, feel the pangs of love. Why should he alone escape them?"

◆   ◆   ◆

Eros shoots an arrow straight into Pluto's heart. The grim Pluto has seen many fair maids. But never has his heart been touched. Now he is filled with a warm feeling. Before him is a young woman gathering flowers. She is Persephone [per SEF uh nee], daughter of Demeter [duh MEET er] goddess of the harvest. Pluto looks at Persephone and falls in love with her.

Pluto sweeps Persephone onto his chariot and speeds away. As she struggles, her girdle[2] falls to the ground, but Pluto holds her tight. Soon they reach the River Cyane.[3] Pluto strikes the bank with his trident.[4] The earth opens and darkness swallows them all—horses, chariot, Pluto, and weeping Persephone.

Demeter searches all over the earth, but no one can tell her where Persephone is. Worn out and filled with despair, Demeter returns to Sicily. There, near the River Cyane, where Pluto has gone down to the underword, a river nymph[5] brings her Persephone's girdle.

◆   ◆   ◆

The goddess knew then that her daughter was gone indeed, but she did not suspect Pluto of carrying her off. She laid the blame on the innocent land.

Vocabulary Development

monarch (MAHN ark) _n._   king or queen

---

2. **girdle** (GER dul) _n._ belt or sash for the waist.
3. **River Cyane** (SĪ an) a river in Sicily, an island just south of Italy.
4. **trident** (TRĪD ent) _n._ spear with three points.
5. **river nymph** (NIMF) _n._ goddess living in a river.

"Ungrateful soil!" she said. "I made you fertile. I clothed you in grass and nourishing grain, and this is how you reward me. No more shall you enjoy my favors!"

That year was the most cruel mankind had ever known. Nothing prospered, nothing grew. The cattle died, the seed would not come up, men and oxen toiled in vain. There was too much sun. There was too much rain. Thistles[6] and weeds were the only things that grew. It seemed that all mankind would die of hunger.

"This cannot go on," said mighty Zeus. "I see that I must <u>intervene</u>." And one by one he sent the gods and goddesses to plead with Demeter.

But she had the same answer for all: "Not till I see my daughter shall the earth bear fruit again."

◆ ◆ ◆

Zeus, of course, knows where Persephone is. He is sorry to take from his brother the one thing that brings joy to his life. But he must if mankind is to be saved. So he calls Hermes [HUR meez][7] to him and says:

◆ ◆ ◆

"Descend to the underworld, my son. Bid Pluto release his bride. Provided she has not tasted food in the realm of the dead, she may return to her mother forever."

Down sped Hermes on his winged feet, and there in the dim palace of the king, he found Persephone by Pluto's side. She was pale and joyless. Not all the glittering treasures of the underworld could bring a smile to her lips.

Vocabulary Development

intervene (IN ter VEEN) v.   interfere

---

6. **thistles** (THIS uhlz) n. stubborn, weedy plants with sharp leaves and usually purplish flowers.
7. **Hermes:** God who served as a messenger.

◆ Reading Strategy

From Demeter's reaction, what can you **predict** she will do?

_____

_____

_____

_____

_____

◆ Literary Analysis

How did the ancient Greeks explain natural disasters?

_____

_____

_____

_____

_____

◆ Reading Strategy

Zeus knows where Persephone is. What do you think might happen next?

_____

_____

_____

_____

_____

◆ Reading Check

Complete this sentence. Persephone may return to her mother forever, if she has not

_____

_____.

_____

_____

_____

_____

◆ **Reading Strategy**

Persephone cannot leave the underworld forever. What do you think will happen to her?

_____

_____

_____

_____

◆ **Literary Analysis**

According to the **myth**, why do we have winter?

_____

_____

_____

_____

"You have no flowers here," she would say to her husband when he pressed gems upon her. "Jewels have no <u>fragrance</u>. I do not want them."

◆   ◆   ◆

When Persephone sees Hermes and hears his message, she is filled with joy. She gets ready to leave at once. But one thing troubles her—she cannot leave the underworld forever. For she has accepted a pomegranate[8] from Pluto and has sucked the sweet pulp from four of the seeds.

Pluto helps Persephone into his chariot and Hermes takes the reins. "Dear wife," says Pluto, "think kindly of me, for I love you truly. It will be lonely here these eight months you are away. So fare you well—and get your fill of flowers!"

Hermes drives the chariot straight to the temple of Demeter. Persephone flys to her mother's arms. The sad tale of each turns into joy in the telling.

◆   ◆   ◆

So it is to this day. One third of the year Persephone spends in the gloomy <u>abode</u> of Pluto—one month for each seed that she tasted. Then Nature dies, the leaves fall, the earth stops bringing forth. In spring Persephone returns, and with her come the flowers, followed by summer's fruitfulness and the rich harvest of fall.

Vocabulary Development

fragrance (FRAY grentz) *n.*   sweet odor; perfume
abode (uh BOHD) *n.*   home

---

8. **pomegranate** (PAHM uh GRAN it) *n.* round fruit with a red leathery rind and many seeds.

1. Why does Pluto take Persephone to his kingdom?

_____

_____

_____

2. What does Demeter do when she discovers her daughter is lost? Circle the letter of the correct answer.

   (a) She goes to the underworld to get her.
   (b) She calls on Zeus to help her.
   (c) She blames the land and punishes it.
   (d) She cries a river.

3. How does Zeus solve the problem?

_____

_____

_____

4. How do the seasons change as Persephone moves between the earth and the underworld?

_____

_____

_____

5. **Literary Analysis:** Ancient peoples often created **myths** to explain events in nature. Complete this sentence: The myth of "Demeter and Persephone explains _____

_____

_____.

(Continued)

6. **Reading Strategy:** Write a **prediction** you made about the following. Then tell what happened in the story.

	Prediction	Actual Outcome
• Persephone	_____	_____
	_____	_____
	_____	_____
• Demeter	_____	_____
	_____	_____
	_____	_____

Writing

Myth

Choose a natural event such as an earthquake or volcanic eruption. Imagine that you have never heard of any scientific explanation of the causes of the event. Write a myth that offers an explanation. Remember that you are not going to use science in your explanation. Think in terms of the gods or heroes and their actions that might have caused the event. For example, an earthquake might be caused by a god stamping his foot. Do the following:
- Begin by identifying the natural event. _____
- Describe people's reactions to the event. _____
- Think of possible ways a god might have caused the event.

_____

- On a sheet of paper, prepare an outline to help you organize details and events in your myth.
- Write the myth in clear time order.

Icarus and Daedalus

Josephine Preston Peabody

Summary

In the myth of "Icarus and Daedalus," a boy's impulsive nature brings about a terrible punishment. Daedalus, once the master architect for King Minos of Crete, finds himself imprisoned on that island along with his son, Icarus. In order to escape, Daedalus puts his inventive mind to work and creates wings from feathers, thread, and wax. As he attaches the wings to Icarus' back, he warns his son not to fly too close to the sun. However, all Icarus can think about is the wonder and excitement of being able to fly. He barely hears his father's warning. Predictably, he soars too close to the sun, melts his wings, and crashes into the sea.

Visual Summary

Prediction Chart

CLUE	PREDICTION
• Daedalus is looking for a way to escape from Crete. He observes the flight of sea-gulls.	• Daedalus will make wings with which he and Icarus can fly to freedom.
• Daedalus warns Icarus not to fly too high or too low, but Icarus doesn't pay attention.	• Icarus is going to have trouble when he attempts to fly.
• Icarus flies too close to the sun.	• Icarus' wings will melt and he will fall into the sea and drown.

LITERARY ANALYSIS

Myth

People of many cultures have created **myths**, to explain natural occurrences or to express beliefs about right and wrong. The ancient Greeks believed that a person would be punished for being overly proud or arrogant. Greek mythology suggests that the gods punish humans for daring too much or for reaching too high.

For example, Daedalus may have taken too much pride in his own cleverness. He may have dared too much by thinking he could fly like a god. As a result, he is punished by the gods, who take the life of Icarus, Daedalus' young son. Icarus reaches too high when he forgets Daedalus' warning and flies toward the sun. One of the lessons in this myth is that reckless behavior can be very dangerous.

READING STRATEGY

Making Predictions

A **prediction** is an educated guess about what will happen. Use this chart to predict what will happen in the story. Then, fill in what really happens.

Prediction	What Happens

Icarus and Daedalus

Josephine Preston Peabody

Have you ever imagined what it would be like to fly through the air like a bird? Thousands of years ago, the ancient Greeks created the myth of "Icarus and Daedalus," in which a clever man figures out a way to fly by watching the sea-gulls. As the story begins, Daedalus looks for a way to escape from Crete.

◆ ◆ ◆

Among all those mortals who grew so wise that they learned the secrets of the gods, none was more cunning[1] than Daedalus. [DED uhl es]

He once built, for King Minos of Crete,[2] a wonderful Labyrinth[3] of winding ways so cunningly tangled up and twisted around that, once inside, you could never find your way out again without a magic clue. But the king's favor veered[4] with the wind, and one day he had his master architect imprisoned in a tower. Daedalus managed to escape from his cell; but it seemed impossible to leave the island, since every ship that came or went was well guarded by order of the king.

At length, watching the sea-gulls in the air— the only creatures that were sure of liberty—he thought of a plan for himself and his young son Icarus, who was captive with him.

◆ ◆ ◆

Daedalus gathers a whole bunch of feathers. He fastens them together with thread, molds them in with wax, and makes two great wings like those of a bird. He fits

◆ **Reading Check**

In the bracketed sentence, circle the thing that Daedalus built for King Minos.

◆ **Reading Check**

Why did it seem impossible to leave the island?

_____

_____

_____

_____

_____

◆ **Reading Strategy**

What do you **predict** Daedalus will do?

_____

_____

_____

_____

_____

---

1. **cunning** (KUN ing) *adj.* skillful; clever.
2. **King Minos** (MĪ nohs) **of Crete** (KREET) King Minos was a son of the god Zeus. Crete is a Greek island in the eastern Mediterranean Sea, southeast of Greece.
3. **Labyrinth** (LAB uh RINTH) *n.* maze.
4. **veered** (VEERD) *v.* changed directions.

◆ ◆ ◆

Without delay, he fell to work on a pair of wings for the boy Icarus [IK uh rus], and taught him carefully how to use them, bidding him beware of <u>rash</u> adventures among the stars. "Remember," said the father, "never to fly very low or very high, for the fogs about the earth would weigh you down, but the blaze of the sun will surely melt your feathers apart if you go too near."

For Icarus, these cautions went in at one ear and out by the other. Who could remember to be careful when he was to fly for the first time? Are birds careful? Not they! And not an idea remained in the boy's head but the one joy of escape.

◆ ◆ ◆

◆ Reading Strategy

Predict what will happen if Icarus' does not remember his father's instructions.

_____

_____

_____

_____

The day comes when the wind is right. Up they fly. They leave Crete far beneath them.

At first Daedalus and Icarus are afraid. When they look down, they feel dizzy. Icarus forgets all the instruction and soars as high as he can. His father is way below him.

◆ ◆ ◆

◆ Reading Strategy

Predict what will happen if Icarus flies too high in the sky.

_____

_____

_____

_____

Vocabulary Development

rash *adj.* reckless; hasty

Alas for him! Warmer and warmer grew the air. Those arms, that had seemed to uphold him, relaxed. His wings wavered, drooped. He fluttered his young hands vainly—he was falling—and in that terror he remembered. The heat of the sun had melted the wax from his wings; the feathers were falling, one by one, like snowflakes; and there was none to help.

He fell like a leaf tossed down the wind, down, down, with one cry that overtook Daedalus far away. When he returned, and sought high and low for his poor boy, he saw nothing but the birdlike feathers afloat on the water, and he knew that Icarus was drowned.

The nearest island he named Icaria, in memory of the child; but he, in heavy grief, went to the temple of Apollo in Sicily, and there hung up his wings as an offering. Never again did he attempt to fly.

◆ **Reading Check**

In the bracketed sentence, underline what happens to Icarus' wings.

◆ **Stop to Reflect**

Icarus lost his life because he ignored his father's warning. In the same situation, would you have done what Icarus did? Why or why not?

_____

_____

_____

_____

1. Where is Daedalus when the story begins?

_____

_____

2. How does Daedalus plan to escape?

_____

_____

3. What warning does Daedalus give to Icarus?

_____

_____

4. What happens to Icarus at the end of the myth?

_____

_____

_____

5. **Literary Analysis:** What lesson does this **myth** teach?

_____

_____

_____

6. **Reading Strategy:** What clues might lead you to **make a prediction** that Icarus will fall from the sky? List them below.

   • _____

_____

- _____

_____

- _____

_____

Writing

Myth

Greek mythology suggests that the gods punish humans for daring too much or for reaching too high. For example, Daedalus might have dared too much by thinking that people should be able to fly. The gods punish him by taking Icarus' life. Icarus reaches too high by heading toward the sun and is punished by drowning in the sea.

Write a myth about a situation today in which people might be daring too much. Use your imagination. Think about things that might seem impossible for people to do, for example:

- daring to swim across the ocean
- daring to explore the inside of a volcano
- daring to travel to Mars

Create your myth by doing the following:
- Begin by choosing a topic. _____

_____

- Invent a character who dares to do the impossible. Write your character's name: _____
- Prepare a brief story outline to help you organize details and events in your myth.

_____

_____

_____

_____

_____

- On another piece of paper, write the myth in clear time order.

Part 2

Selection Summaries With Alternative Reading Strategies

Part 2 contains summaries of all selections in *Prentice Hall Literature: Timeless Voices, Timeless Themes*. An alternative reading strategy follows each summary.

- Use the summaries in Part 2 to preview or review the selections.
- Use the alternative reading strategies in Part 2 to guide your reading or to check your understanding of the selection.

"The Cat Who Thought She Was a Dog and the Dog Who Thought He Was a Cat"
by Isaac Bashevis Singer

Summary Jan Skiba, a poor peasant, lives a simple life with his wife, his daughters, a cat, and a dog in a small hut. The family does not own a mirror, and they have rarely seen their images. Because the dog and cat have never seen other dogs and cats, the dog thinks he is a cat and the cat thinks she is a dog. One day the family buys a mirror from a peddler. The mirror causes a stir. Each girl is upset about her looks and fears she'll never make a good marriage. The dog and cat, disturbed by their images, fight. Skiba decides that having a mirror is troublesome and that the family would be better off admiring the world around them than themselves. He exchanges the mirror for other goods. Life returns to normal for the family and its pets.

Use Context Clues While you are reading, you may come across a word whose meaning you don't know. The context, or the words before and after the unfamiliar word, can provide clues to help you understand the meaning of the word. Context clues may be in the same sentence in which the unfamiliar word appears or in sentences before or after the word. Notice the word *gulden* in the following sentence from the story.

They asked the peddler his price and he said a half gulden, which was a lot of money.

You probably don't know the meaning of the word *gulden*, but you do know that the peddler was giving a price. The sentence also includes the word money. From these context clues, you can figure out that a gulden is probably an amount of money.

DIRECTIONS: Read the sentences below from the selection. Use context clues to determine the meaning of each underlined word. Find the meaning of the word in the following list. Write its letter in the blank.

a. one of several payments
b. very interested
c. proposal
d. faults or flaws

_____ 1. After a while, Jan Skiba's wife, Marianna, made a <u>proposition</u> to the peddler. She would pay him five groshen a month for the mirror.

_____ 2. Now they could see themselves clearly and they began to find <u>defects</u> in their faces, defects they had never noticed before. Marianna was pretty but she had a tooth missing in front and she felt that this made her ugly.

_____ 3. That day the women became so <u>absorbed</u> in the mirror they didn't cook supper, didn't make up the bed, and neglected all the other household tasks.

_____ 4. When the peddler came for his monthly <u>installment</u>, Jan Skiba gave him back the mirror and, in its stead, bought kerchiefs and slippers for the women.

"Two Kinds" by Amy Tan

Summary A Chinese immigrant who has started life over in the United States wants her American-born daughter to be a famous prodigy. To that end, she pushes the reluctant girl first to be an actress like Shirley Temple, then a musician like a young pianist she saw performing on TV. Despite the girl's fiasco at a talent show, her mother expects her to continue piano lessons and eventually become a famous musician. The girl balks. She asserts in a forceful and hurtful way that she's not the obedient daughter her mother wants. In conflict with her mother's expectations, the daughter says that she can only be herself. Years later, she realizes that she is two kinds of daughter—one who follows her own mind and one who is obedient.

Apply Word Identification Strategies "Two Kinds" includes a number of compound words, or words that are made up of two or more words put together. Here are two examples from the story.

> hair + cut = haircut   bath + room = bathroom

A compound word may seem long and completely unfamiliar. However, if you break it into the words that make it up, you will often find that you know the meaning of one or more of the shorter words. For example, in the selection, Jing-mei finds some *handwritten* scales. Suppose you do not know the word *handwritten*. You probably recognize the word *hand*, and the word *written*. You can figure out that *handwritten* means "written by hand." Some compound words, such as *speed-reading*, have a hyphen between the words that make them up.

DIRECTIONS: Examine each of the following compound words from "Two Kinds." Beside each word, write the two words that make it up. If you do not know the meaning of the compound word, try to figure it out from the two smaller words. If necessary, use a dictionary for help. Write the meaning of the compound word on the line provided

1. tiptoes   _____   _____

   meaning: _____

2. housecleaning   _____   _____

   meaning: _____

3. high-pitched   _____   _____

   meaning: _____

4. earsplitting   _____   _____

   meaning; _____

5. daydreamed   _____   _____

   meaning: _____

6. showpiece   _____   _____

   meaning: _____

from "Song of Myself" by Walt Whitman
"I'm Nobody" by Emily Dickinson
"Me" by Walter de la Mare

Summary These three poems discuss the idea of identity—who we are, what makes each of us different, and how we are viewed by others. The speakers in these poems accept and like themselves just as they are. In "Song of Myself," the speaker celebrates himself and all selves as equally important. In "I'm Nobody," the speaker is proud of being a "Nobody" because, she says, a "Somebody" needs the praise of other people to feel worthwhile. In "Me," the speaker compares himself to trees and flowers. Like the things in nature, he says, he will always be who he is and no other.

Read Poetry According to Punctuation Reading poetry aloud helps you hear the speaker's voice, and helps you understand the meaning of the poem.

DIRECTIONS: Listen to the audiocassette recordings of the poems as you follow along in your textbook. Listen carefully for the places where the reader pauses and stops. Then, with a partner, take turns reading the poems aloud. Practice pausing briefly at commas, ellipsis points (three dots), and dashes and longer at end marks. Don't stop at the ends of lines if there is no punctuation. You may use the following chart to note the various places in the poems where you should pause.

Poems	Pausing Points
from "Song of Myself"	
"I'm Nobody"	
"Me"	

"My Furthest-Back Person" by Alex Haley

Summary In this essay, Alex Haley describes how he traced his ancestors. Remembering family names he had heard from his grandmother, he began his search by examining old census reports. He recalled stories about the family's "furthest-back person"—an African kidnapped from his native land and sold into slavery in the United States. He thought the strange "k" sounds his grandmother had muttered over the years might be words from an African language. He discovered that one of the sounds, Kin-tay (Kinte) is the name of an old African clan. He flew to Gambia and, after traveling on foot and by boat deep into the back country, he finally found his distant relatives. An old man told him the clan's history, confirming that Haley's "furthest-back person" was a Kinte, kidnapped in Africa and sold into slavery in Annapolis, Maryland, in 1767.

Break Down Long Sentences Many of the sentences in this story are three lines long—or even longer. To help understand the long sentences, break them down into parts. Use the punctuation marks (commas, dots, dashes, colons, and semicolons) to find appropriate places to break. You may need to add a word or two to have the part make sense. Study the following example.

Sentence: I was beginning to tire, when in utter astonishment I looked upon the names of Grandma's parents: Tom Murray, Irene Murray … older sisters of Grandma's as well—every one of them a name that I'd heard countless times on her front porch.

Sentence broken into parts: I was beginning to tire. In utter astonishment I looked upon the names of Grandma's parents. [Their names were] Tom Murray, Irene Murray. [The names included] older sisters of Grandma's as well. Every one of them [was] a name that I'd heard countless times on her front porch.

DIRECTIONS: Find at least four more sentences in the essay that are three or more lines long. Break them into parts. Compare your sentences with those of your classmates.

_____

_____

_____

_____

_____

_____

_____

_____

_____

_____

_____

_____

_____

_____

"The Third Level" by Jack Finney

Summary Grand Central Station is supposed to have two levels. Yet Charlie finds a tunnel that takes him down to a third level, where he finds himself in the year 1894. Charlie wants to buy himself and his wife train tickets for a small town called Galesburg as it was in 1894. However, the ticket clerk will not take his modern money. Charlie later buys old-style money and tries without success to find the third level. His psychiatrist friend, Sam, says that Charlie must have imagined the third level to escape from pressures of the present. Sam later disappears. Charlie finds a letter in his grandfather's stamp collection. It is dated 1894 and addressed to Charlie. It is from Sam, who says he found the third level and has a hay and feed business in Galesburg.

Use Context to Determine Meaning When you come across a name, word, or phrase you don't know, use its context—the words, phrases, and sentences around it—to figure out its meaning. To help you identify context clues, look for words and phrases that define, compare, contrast, describe, provide examples, or offer information about the unfamiliar word or phrase.

DIRECTIONS: Practice identifying context clues. On the lines provided, write the context clues for each underlined word or phrase.

1. That made my wife kind of mad, but he explained that he meant the modern world is full of <u>insecurity</u>, fear, war, worry and all the rest of it, and that I just want to escape.

   insecurity _____

2. I am just an <u>ordinary</u> guy named Charley, thirty-one years old…; I passed a dozen men who looked just like me.

   ordinary_____

3. Sometimes I think Grand Central is <u>growing like a tree</u>, pushing out new corridors and staircases like roots.

   growing like a tree: _____

4. It's a wonderful town still, with big old frame houses, huge lawns and tremendous trees whose branches meet overhead and <u>roof the streets</u>.

   roof the streets _____

"A Day's Wait" by Ernest Hemingway

Summary When Schatz has the flu, his father calls the doctor. The doctor says Schatz's temperature is 102 degrees. A few hours later, Schatz asks about his temperature. He is very quiet and worried, and his father cannot understand why. Finally, Schatz asks when he is going to die. His father says he is not that ill, and will not die. Schatz says boys at school in France told him a person could not live with a temperature of 44 degrees. His father then realizes Schatz has been waiting to die all day. He explains to Schatz that the French use a different kind of thermometer. On that thermometer, a normal temperature is 37 degrees. On Schatz's thermometer, normal is 98. Schatz is relieved by the explanation and becomes visibly relaxed.

Reread When you read a story, you may be puzzled at first by the way a character behaves. By the end of the story, your questions may be answered. If they are not, you can read part or all of the story again. The second time, look for specific details that will answer your questions about the character's behavior.

DIRECTIONS: Use a Character Behavior Chart like the following to describe Schatz's actions. As you read the story the first time, list details that tell how Schatz behaves. If you understand why he behaves that way, check the box under "Read." If you don't understand, read the story a second time to find the answer. Then check the box under "Reread." The first action is listed for you.

BEHAVIOR	READ	REREAD
Schatz enters his father's room and closes the window.		

Name _____ Date _____

"Was Tarzan a Three-Bandage Man?" by Bill Cosby
"Oranges" by Gary Soto

Summary These selections deal with childhood memories. "Was Tarzan a Three-Bandage Man?" recalls a time when the author and his friends tried to act cool by imitating their heroes. Bill's mother scolds him for walking funny to imitate a famous baseball player and putting bandages on his face like a prizefighter. In the end, Bill realizes it might have been better to admire the injurer rather than the injured. In "Oranges," a boy of twelve walks with a girl for the first time. He has two oranges and a nickel in his pocket. When he asks what she wants from a store, the girl chooses a ten-cent chocolate. He puts his nickel and an orange on the counter. Silently, the clerk accepts them.

Context Clues This article may contain some words that you don't know. You could look up each word in a dictionary. But you also may be able to figure out the meaning by using **context clues**. Look at the words and phrases that are near the word you don't know. The familiar words and phrases can help you guess the meaning of the unfamiliar word.

DIRECTIONS: In each sentence below, read the word in **boldface print**. Then find another word or phrase in the sentence that can help you guess the word's meaning. Underline your clues. Write what you think the word means. You may check a dictionary if necessary. The first one has been done for you.

1. We **imitated** their walk. When they walked bowlegged, <u>we did it too</u>.
   Meaning: did the same thing as someone else _____

2. People with **acne** walked that way too, but it wasn't their bad skin that we admired.
   Meaning: _____

3. Tough guys wore bandages over their eye, but really tough guys wore **tourniquets** around their necks.
   Meaning: _____

4. Trying to be like the injured was ridiculous, since we should have been **emulating** those who caused the injuries.
   Meaning: _____

5. (Supply your own sentence from the selection here.)

   _____

   _____

   Meaning: _____

from *In Search of Our Mothers' Gardens* by Alice Walker

Summary In this moving and solemn tribute, the author praises her mother and other black women like her for their hard work, dedication, and inspiration. Walker views her mother as an artist whose creative spirit inspired her own life as a writer. Her mother shared herself as an artist through the stories she told and through the beautiful flower gardens she grew, despite the family's poverty. Walker admires how black women of her mother's generation managed to "hold on," despite the exhausting labors placed upon them. As a result, Walker inherited a respect for strength as well as a love of beauty in life.

Ask Questions A good way to better understand the selection is to ask yourself questions as you read. As you read, think of what you already know about the subject, and then think of what questions you would like answered.

DIRECTIONS: Think about people you know who work tirelessly. Remembering how you feel about them will help you develop a deeper understanding of the woman Alice Walker describes in *In Search of Our Mothers' Gardens*. Discuss your ideas with a small group. Then begin a KWL chart like the one shown to record interesting ideas and details you know and questions you have.

- Start the chart by filling in what you know about people who work hard.
- Add questions about what you want to know.
- As you read the excerpt from *In Search of Our Mothers' Gardens*, continue the KWL chart with what you Learn, and add new questions that come up.

What I **K**now	What I **W**ant to Know	What I've **L**earned

Name _____ Date _____

"Seventh Grade" by Gary Soto
"Melting Pot" by Anna Quindlen

Summary These two selections examine, in different ways, how people relate to each other. In "Seventh Grade," Victor goes through the first day of school trying to impress Teresa, who he hopes will be his girlfriend. Though Victor embarrasses himself in class by pretending to speak French, Teresa is fooled and impressed, much to Victor's surprise and pleasure. In "Melting Pot," the author describes how her New York neighborhood is a mixture of different ethnic groups. She sees the concept of the American melting pot existing where she lives, but only on a person-to-person basis. As groups, the neighbors may not get along, but as individuals, they often are friends.

Relate to Your Own Experience One way to get more enjoyment out of what you read is to relate the characters' experiences to your own. To help you link your experience with a character's, form a mental picture of the scenes described by the author. As you read "Seventh Grade," pause from time to time. Picture each scene in your mind. Use this page to jot down notes to describe what you imagine. Then work with a partner to draw sketches of what Gary Soto describes in each of the following scenes. If you prefer, choose some scenes from "Melting Pot" and write notes about them. Then draw sketches of the scenes you imagined.

Victor and Michael exchanging greetings on the first day of school

Victor practicing his scowling as a girl looks at him

Victor lingering in homeroom after the bell rang, hoping to bump into Teresa as she leaves

Victor sitting at a table outside, near where Teresa is sitting under a plum tree

Victor pretending to know how to speak French

Mr. Bueller shuffling papers in the classroom as Victor and Teresa talk about French

"Fable" by Ralph Waldo Emerson
"If—" by Rudyard Kipling
"Thumbprint" by Eve Merriam

Summary These three poems focus on the ideas of individuality and wholeness. In "Fable," a squirrel resents that a mountain has called it a "little prig." The squirrel responds by saying that although a mountain is big, it is not as lively as a squirrel and it cannot crack a nut. In other words, individuals possess their own special talents that make them no better or worse than other individuals. In "If—," the speaker details the positive qualities that a person must possess to be considered a successful and complete individual. In "Thumbprint," the speaker celebrates her singularity through the special design of curved lines that make up her unique thumbprint.

Paraphrase Sometimes the language of poetry is different from familiar, everyday language. The words themselves might be unfamiliar, or the order of the words might be unusual. As you read these poems, identify and list examples of poetic language. Then write more familiar words or word order for the phrases you list. Create a chart like the one below. A few phrases from Rudyard Kipling's poem have been modeled for you. Choose more from his poem, and choose some from Ralph Waldo Emerson's and Eve Merriam's poems as well.

Poetic Language	More Familiar Language
If you can keep your head when all about you / Are losing theirs and blaming it on you	If you can stay calm when others cannot
If you can force your heart and nerve and sinew / To serve your turn long after they are gone	If you can keep on going when you feel worn out

Name _____ Date _____

"Mother to Son" by Langston Hughes
"The Courage That My Mother Had" by Edna St. Vincent Millay
"The Hummingbird That Lived Through Winter" by William Saroyan

Summary These three selections focus on the themes of courage and persistence. In "Mother to Son," the speaker talks of the hardships she has endured. She uses her own experiences to warn her son not to give up when he faces similar obstacles. In "The Courage That My Mother Had," the poet praises the courage her deceased mother showed when she was living. Though her mother left her a golden brooch, the poet would prefer the treasure of her mother's courage for herself because she needs it now. "The Hummingbird That Lived Through Winter" tells about an elderly, sight-impaired man lovingly nursing an ailing hummingbird back to life, exhibiting a love for all living creatures.

Question: After reading a selection, you need to determine what you understand and don't understand about it. You can write down questions that you may have, and then seek help from your teacher or a classmate.

Directions: Use the chart below to record what you do and do not understand about each selection. Then discuss your questions with another person.

Selection	What I Understand	What I Do Not Understand

"The Third Wish" by Joan Aiken

Summary Mr. Peters discovers a swan tangled in thorns. He frees the swan, which turns into a little man—the King of the Forest. Mr. Peters requests three wishes as a reward. The King obliges, giving him three leaves to wish upon, but warns that wishes often leave people worse off than before. Mr. Peters wishes for a beautiful wife and receives Leita, a former swan. Over time, Leita grows unhappy because she misses her sister, who is still a swan. Mr. Peters uses his second wish to turn Leita back into a swan. He and the two swans remain close. One morning, old Mr. Peters is found dead in bed, smiling, with a leaf and feather in his hands—he never used his last wish.

Clarify Sometimes when you read, the meaning of a passage may not be clear. To help you understand it better, you can write down questions that you have about the passage. Then try reading the section again. As you read, look for details that will answer your questions. Also, use a dictionary to look up words you do not understand.

Use a chart like the one below to help clarify the meaning of passages in "The Third Wish." First record your questions about each passage. Then reread the passage and tell what you now understand that you did not understand before.

Questions (What I Don't Understand)	Answers (What I Now Understand)

"A Boy and a Man" by James Ramsey Ullman
from *Into Thin Air* by Jon Krakauer

Summary Both selections deal with the drama of mountain climbing. In "A Boy and a Man," Rudi Matt risks his life to save a man who has fallen in an icy crevasse, or deep crack, in the Alps. The man, renowned mountaineer Captain John Winter, is surprised to discover that Rudi is only sixteen. He seeks Rudi's advice on climbing the Citadel, a peak upon which Rudi's father died while climbing. Rudi makes Winter promise not to tell his mother that he was mountain climbing. In the second selection, Jon Krakauer describes his dangerous trek up the Icefall on Mt. Everest, detailing how the ice made the climb an uncertainty. Krakauer's experience leaves him awestruck at the task of reaching Everest's peak.

Predict As you read a story, you can be an active reader by trying to **predict**, or guess, what will happen next. Your predictions should not be wild guesses, however. Good story predictions are always based on details and hints that the author gives you along the way.

Use the chart below to predict events from "A Boy and a Man" and from *Into Thin Air*. After each prediction, record the details and hints that led you to make that prediction.

My Prediction	Details and Hints
"A Boy and a Man"	
from *Into Thin Air*	

"The Charge of the Light Brigade" by Alfred, Lord Tennyson
from *Henry V,* "St. Crispian's Day Speech" by William Shakespeare
"The Enemy" by Alice Walker

Summary All of these poems deal with war. In "The Charge of the Light Brigade," a brigade of six hundred cavalry soldiers charges into an enemy position heavily fortified with cannon. Many of the soldiers are killed, but their bravery will be honored always. In the excerpt from *Henry V,* King Henry speaks of the glory that will come to soldiers who fight in a battle to be fought on St. Crispian's Day. Those who survive the battle and live to old age will proudly tell battle stories to their sons. In "The Enemy," the tiny fist of a dead child holds the "crumpled heads / of pink and yellow flowers." This is a harsh reminder that when a country goes to war, the children suffer.

Reading Poetic Contractions A contraction is a shortened form of a word or words. For example, the contraction *aren't* is short for the words *are not.* Notice that an apostrophe (') takes the place of the missing *o* in the contraction. Often in poetry, you find special contractions, called **poetic contractions,** that you do not find in ordinary writing. For example, in "The Charge of the Light Brigade," the author uses the contraction *sab'ring*, a shortened form of the word *sabering.* When you come across such a contraction, look at it closely to figure out what letter or letters are missing. Then read the word as if all the letters were there.

Use the chart below to record the word or words that are shortened in each poetic contraction. The first one is done for you.

Contraction	Missing Letter or Letters	Full Word or Words
sab'ring	e	sabering
call'd		
rememb'red		
ne'er		
accurs'd		

"The Californian's Tale" by Mark Twain
"Valediction" by Seamus Heaney

Summary Both selections deal with the effect a woman's absence has on a home. In "The Californian's Tale," a California gold prospector comes to the well-kept home of Henry, who invites the traveler in. Henry credits the niceness of his home to his young wife, who is away until Saturday night. He urges his guest to stay until she returns. Henry's friends come over on Saturday and give Henry a drink with a drug that puts him to sleep. They explain that Henry's wife has been dead for nineteen years. They go through the annual act of pretending she's returning, so that Henry won't go wild. In "Valediction," the speaker mourns the absence of the lady who once brightened his home but for whom he now grieves.

Summarize When you read a story, you can check your understanding along the way by summarizing different sections as you complete them. To summarize, first jot down all the important events and details that appear in a section of the story you are reading. Then, write a brief summary based on your notes.

Use the chart below to summarize sections of "The Californian's Tale." Record the main events and details in each section. Then use them to summarize the section. The beginning of the story has been done for you.

Main Events and Details	Summary
Thirty-five years ago Twain prospected on the Stanislaus. Once heavily populated, the area was now empty.	Mark Twain prospected on the Stanislaus, an area once heavily populated. Now the region has few people.

"Stopping by Woods on a Snowy Evening" by Robert Frost
"Four Skinny Trees" by Sandra Cisneros
"Miracles" by Walt Whitman

Summary These three selections celebrate the wonders of nature, each in a different way. In "Stopping by Woods on a Snowy Evening," a traveler pauses to watch snow fall in woods that belong to someone else. The traveler cannot stay, however, because of promises to keep and miles yet to be traveled. In "Four Skinny Trees," the narrator admires the determination of four scrawny trees outside her window that possess the secret strength to keep growing and going on. The trees inspire the narrator to continue going on, too. In "Miracles," the speaker celebrates all aspects of nature—both indoors and outdoors—which some people might consider ordinary, but which he sees as miracles.

Respond to Levels of Meaning Often when you read a piece of literature, you can find several meanings in it. You may find one meaning that other readers find as well. But you may also find a personal meaning that other readers don't necessarily experience.

Work with a partner. First, read the three selections together. Then, discuss what each selection means to each of you personally. How do you both feel about the work? Use the chart to record your individual feelings, and then see how similar or different they are.

Selection	What It Means to Me	What It Means to My Partner
"Stopping by Woods ..."		
"Four Skinny Trees"		
"Miracles"		

"The Night the Bed Fell" by James Thurber

Summary In this hilarious story, James Thurber recalls the chain of events that led to chaos one night when he was a youth. His father had gone to the attic to sleep, despite his mother's protests that the wobbly bed might collapse. During the night, young James accidentally tipped over his own cot. The noise caused his mother to scream, which woke up a visiting cousin, Briggs, who immediately poured camphor—a strong-smelling medicine—on himself, thinking he had stopped breathing. The camphor made the room smell so foul that Briggs broke a window to get air. James's mother, still thinking her husband had fallen, went to the attic. The father was puzzled by all the commotion. Eventually the confusion was sorted out.

Identify Causes and Effects In many stories, there is a pattern of causes and effects. A **cause** is the reason something happens. An **effect** is what happens as a result of the cause. For example, in Thurber's story, Father wants to be away where he can think. Therefore, he goes to the attic to sleep. His desire to be alone is the cause; sleeping in the attic is the effect.

Think about the things that happen in "The Night the Bed Fell." Record each important cause and the effect that it leads to.

Cause		Effect
_____	>	_____
_____	>	_____
_____	>	_____
_____	>	_____
_____	>	_____
_____	>	_____
_____	>	_____
_____	>	_____
_____	>	_____
_____	>	_____
_____	>	_____
_____	>	_____
_____	>	_____
_____	>	_____
_____	>	_____

Name _____ Date _____

"All Summer in a Day" by Ray Bradbury

Summary A class of nine-year-old children, living on the planet Venus, looks forward to seeing the sun for the very first time. A seemingly endless seven-year rainfall is predicted to stop for a short time. The children taunt a frail classmate, Margot, who came from Earth and had seen the sun from there. They don't believe her reports about what the sun is like. As a cruel joke, the children lock Margot in a closet before going out to play in the sun for the only hour of sunshine after seven years. When the rain resumes, and the children sadly return indoors, they realize that Margot has missed the sunshine. Knowing how cruel they have been, they slowly go to the closet to let Margot out.

Envision Setting and Actions When you **picture a setting and actions,** you picture what is happening and where it is happening. As you read, pay close attention to story details that describe the setting. If you were standing in that setting, what would you see? Hear? Touch? Smell? Taste? Also pay attention to details that describe the action. Picture everything that is happening around you.

Record details about "All Summer in a Day" in the chart below.

"All Summer in a Day"

What I see _____

_____

What I hear _____

_____

What I feel _____

_____

What I smell _____

_____

"The Highwayman" by Alfred Noyes
"The Real Story of a Cowboy's Life" by Geoffrey C. Ward

Summary In "The Highwayman," a dashing highwayman tells Bess, his beloved, that he'll return to her after a short while. Tim, the horse keeper, overhears the conversation and informs authorities who then tie Bess with a musket aimed at her heart. When the highwayman returns, Bess pulls the trigger, to warn him of danger, and is killed. The highwayman comes back to avenge her death, but is shot and killed. "The Real Story of a Cowboy's Life" describes the dirty and dangerous work of a cattle drive. Among numerous difficulties are settlers angered over cattle crossing their land and nighttime stampedes that sometimes cause cowboys' deaths. However, a cowboy's life is also full of small pleasures like the beauty of the animals crossing the plains and the songs of the other cowboys.

Identify Cause and Effect In many stories, there is a pattern of causes and effects. A **cause** is the reason something happens. An **effect** is what happens as a result of the cause. Think about the things that happen in each of the three selections. Record each important cause and the effect that follows.

"The Highwayman"

Cause		Effect
_____	>	_____
_____	>	_____
_____	>	_____

"The Real Story of a Cowboy's Life"

Cause		Effect
_____	>	_____
_____	>	_____
_____	>	_____

Name _____ Date _____

"Amigo Brothers" by Piri Thomas
"The Walk" by Thomas Hardy
"Justin Lebo" by Phillip Hoose
"The Rider" by Naomi Shihab Nye

Summary Finding a way around a problem is a central theme of these selections. The "Amigo Brothers" are best friends who must fight against each other for a championship. They train separately and they worry about hurting each other. In the ring, they throw their toughest punches, learning that their friendship will endure no matter who wins. The speaker in "The Walk" finds a way to appreciate a walk to a hilltop even without the company of a special companion. Justin Lebo overcomes difficulties while making bikes to give to less fortunate boys. He learns to collaborate with his parents and others who can help him with money, know-how, and bike parts. He tolerates publicity because it helps him meet his goal, giving joy to others. The speaker in "The Rider" learns to leave loneliness behind while riding around the neighborhood on a bicycle.

Make Inferences When you **make an inference,** you take a guess about something not stated directly in the story. For example, in "The Rider," the speaker never says that she feels lonely. However, you could make that inference for two reasons: She wonders if riding a bicycle can rid a person of loneliness, and she is riding a bicycle. From those two clues you infer that she may feel loneliness herself.

Make an inference about a character or event in each selection. Give the reasons that lead you to make each inference.

"Amigo Brothers"

Inference . . . . .Reasons

_____   _____

_____   _____

"The Walk"

Inference . . . . .Reasons

_____   _____

_____   _____

"Justin Lebo"

Inference . . . . .Reasons

_____   _____

_____   _____

"The Rider"

Inference . . . . .Reasons

_____   _____

_____   _____

"Our Finest Hour" by Charles Osgood

Summary In this humorous essay, journalist Charles Osgood describes the series of mistakes that occurred the night he was a substitute anchor on the *CBS Evening News* telecast. First, the lead story that Osgood introduced did not appear on the monitor; a different story ran instead. The next report didn't appear on the monitor, either. Then, a cue for a commercial brought no commercial. Later, a news story that no one had pre-screened was abruptly cut during its broadcast. After another mishap, a worker's outrage was picked up by a microphone. To top off Osgood's embarrassment, that night journalists from China visited the studio to observe the broadcast.

Distinguish Fact From Opinion As you read, it is important to recognize when writers are stating facts and when they are stating opinions. A **fact** is a statement that can be proven true. An **opinion** is a statement that expresses someone's personal feelings or taste, and cannot be proven true or false.

Read each statement from "Our Finest Hour." Tell whether it is a fact or an opinion. If it is a fact, tell how you could prove it. If it is an opinion, tell what word or words in the statement express a personal feeling.

1. Anchoring is easy enough, most of the time.
   Fact or opinion? Why?

   _____

   _____

2. A reporter was beginning a story.
   Fact or opinion? Why?

   _____

   _____

3. When the commercial was over, I introduced a piece from Washington.
   Fact or opinion? Why?

   _____

   _____

4. All in all, it was not the finest broadcast CBS News had ever done.
   Fact or opinion? Why?

   _____

   _____

5. They must have had a really great impression of American electronic journalism.
   Fact or opinion? Why?

   _____

   _____

"Cat on the Go" by James Herriot

Summary Veterinarian James Herriot relates his experiences with an unusual cat. Herriot and his assistant perform surgery to save the stray cat after it is brought near death to his office. Herriot and his wife Helen then nurture the cat in their home. One evening the cat disappears, and is found later at a church meeting. Another night, the cat is found at a darts championship. After a third incident, the Herriots realize that the cat enjoys visiting places at night before returning home. They are devastated, however, when the cat's real owners unexpectedly show up one day to reclaim it. After giving up the pet, the Herriots visit it about a month later, and are thrilled that it recognizes them.

Understand Bias In their writings, writers show bias—the knowledge and interest that they have in their subject. You can see bias in the details they use, such as descriptions of characters and their actions. For example, when James Herriot says of the cat Oscar, "He was a warm and cherished part of our home life," you can tell the writer really loves and enjoys animals.

Explain what you can tell about writer James Herriot from each of his statements below from "Cat on the Go."

1. I had no more desire to pour ether onto that comradely purring than he had.
   What it tells about Herriot:

   _____

   _____

2. I am fond of cats but we already had a dog in our cramped quarters and I could see difficulties.
   What it tells about Herriot:

   _____

   _____

3. This time Helen and I scoured the marketplace and side alleys in vain and when we returned at half past nine we were both despondent.
   What it tells about Herriot:

   _____

   _____

4. Ever since our cat had started his excursions there had been the gnawing fear that we would lose him, and now we felt secure.
   What it tells about Herriot:

   _____

   _____

5. Feeling helpless and inadequate, I could only sit close to her and stroke the back of her head.
   What it tells about Herriot:

   _____

   _____

"The Luckiest Time of All" by Lucille Clifton
"in Just-" by E. E. Cummings
"The Microscope" by Maxine Kumin
"Sarah Cynthia Sylvia Stout Would Not Take the Garbage Out" by Shel Silverstein
"Father William" by Lewis Carroll

Summary These selections celebrate unusual personalities. In "The Luckiest Time of All," a woman tells how she met her husband by running off to see the circus when she was young. She was chased by a dog and rescued by her future husband. "in Just-" describes different individuals who are out enjoying a spring day. "The Microscope" describes how Anton Leeuwenhoek invented the microscope, despite people's sneers at him and his odd pursuit. In "Sarah Cynthia...," the title character refuses to take out the garbage and, as a result, winds up with a pile of garbage from coast to coast. In "Father William," an elderly yet lively father offers humorous answers to his son's questions about how he has managed to stay fit all these years.

Recognize Author's Purpose Authors usually write with a specific purpose in mind. Sometimes they want to *amuse* or *entertain* you. Sometimes they wish to *inform* or *educate* you about a topic. Sometimes they want to *reflect* or *reminisce* about an experience. Sometimes they wish to *persuade* you to accept their opinion or to *take action* on an issue.

The author's purpose in all of the selections in this grouping is to amuse and entertain readers.

Below each selection title, write a passage that demonstrates the purpose of amusing and entertaining readers. The first one has been done for you.

1. "The Luckiest Time of All"
   But the stone was gone from my hand and Lord, it hit that dancin dog right on his nose! _____

2. "in Just-"
   _____
   _____
   _____

3. "The Microscope"
   _____
   _____
   _____

4. "Sarah Cynthia Sylvia Stout Would Not Take the Garbage Out"
   _____
   _____

5. "Father William"
   _____
   _____
   _____

Name _____ Date _____

Summary These three selections look humorously at the world through the eyes of animals. In "Zoo," a professor comes to Earth bringing a spaceship full of animals from other planets. Humans pay to see the creatures. Ironically, the animals believe that they are visiting a zoo of odd creatures on Earth, and pay the professor as well! In "The Hippopotamus," the speaker suggests that though a hippo looks strange to us, we probably look equally strange to the hippo. "How the Snake Got Poison" explains how snakes were given poison as a means of protection against other creatures. But the snake starts using the poison too often, so he is given a rattle to warn creatures that the snake is there.

Evaluate an Author's Message Most authors have a message that they convey in their writing. As a responsible reader, you must decide what that message is. What is the author trying to teach you about people, or about life in general, through the characters and events in the writing?

Read each passage below. Identify the author's message. The first one has been done for you.

"Zoo"
1. "There are bars to protect us from them .... Next time you must come with us. It is well worth the nineteen commocs it costs .... It was the very best Zoo ever ...."

   Author's message: <u>Feelings of superiority are often the result of an individual's perspective, or</u>
   <u>how one views others.</u>

"Zoo"
2. "And the crowd slowly filed by, at once horrified and fascinated by these strange creatures that looked like horses but ran up the walls of their cages like spiders. 'This is certainly worth a dollar,' one man remarked, hurrying away."

"The Hippopotamus"
3. We laugh at how he looks to us / And yet in moments dank and grim / I wonder how we look to him.

   Author's message: _____

   _____

"How the Snake Got Poison"
4. "When you hear feets comin' you ring yo' bell and if it's yo' friend, he'll be keerful. If it's yo' enemy, it's you and him."

   Author's message: _____

   _____

"After Twenty Years" by O. Henry

Summary A New York police officer walking his beat one night comes upon a man, Bob, who says he's waiting to meet a friend, Jimmy Wells, whom he hasn't seen in twenty years. Bob, who left New York twenty years ago to make a fortune out West, is confident that loyal, honest Jimmy will honor their appointment. Once the officer leaves, another man arrives and greets Bob. After talking briefly, Bob realizes that the other man is not Jimmy. He is a plainclothes officer, who arrests Bob for suspicion of a crime commited in Chicago. He hands Bob a letter from Jimmy, the first officer, who explains that he didn't have the heart to arrest Bob himself.

What Happens Next? We all like to predict what will happen next, whether it is in a movie, in real life, or in stories that we read.

DIRECTIONS: As you read "After Twenty Years," pause from time to time to ask yourself what will happen next. Keep track of your predictions in this chart. When you find out what actually does happen, record that information on the chart, too. A sample entry has been given.

Event	My Prediction	What Actually Happens
The policeman walks his beat.	He will see someone.	He sees a man in a darkened doorway.

"Rikki-tikki-tavi" by Rudyard Kipling

Summary In India, a mongoose named Rikki-tikki-tavi is washed from his burrow by a flood. He is adopted by the family of a young boy named Teddy. Exploring the garden of his new home, Rikki meets Nag and Nagaina, two deadly cobras. Rikki instinctively recognizes the snakes as enemies who are meant to be killed. Later that day, Rikki rescues Teddy by killing a small poisonous snake. That night, Rikki overhears the cobras' plot to enter the house and kill Teddy's family. Rikki attacks Nag in the bathroom, fighting until Teddy's father shoots the cobra dead. The next day, Rikki finds Nagaina's eggs and begins crushing them. When the cobra threatens to kill Teddy, Rikki chases her into the rat hole in which she lives and kills her. Teddy's family and the garden animals hail Rikki as a hero.

Predict Trying to figure out what will happen next is one way to stay interested in a story. You can use prior knowledge, or what you already know before you start reading, to help yourself make predictions. For example, if you find out that a cobra is one of the characters in a story, you can use what you already know about cobras to predict what will happen. You can also use clues from the story to help predict the outcome.

DIRECTIONS: As you read "Rikki-tikki-tavi," stop occasionally and think about what might happen next. Record your predictions and your reasons for making them in this chart. In the last column, keep track of whether you were right. A sample entry has been made.

What I Predict	Why I Predict It	Was I Right?
The mongoose will survive the flood that washed him from his burrow.	The opening paragraph says that "Rikki-tikki did the real fighting," so he must have survived.	Yes.

"Papa's Parrot" by Cynthia Rylant

Summary This touching story examines the relationship between a father and his son. A boy named Harry once enjoyed visiting and helping at his father's candy store, but as he grows older, he goes there less often. In Harry's absence, the father keeps a parrot in the shop, talking to the parrot instead of his son. Harry is embarrassed by his father's behavior, and continues to stay away from the shop. When his father falls ill, Harry goes to the store to help out. To his astonishment, he hears the parrot repeatedly say, "Where's Harry? Miss him." Harry realizes the bird is echoing his father's words. Understanding that his father misses their time together in the shop, Harry goes to visit him in the hospital.

Identify with a Character The characters you read about in stories are not much different from characters you meet in real life. In fact, as you read a story, you might even recognize some attitudes, feelings, or qualities of your own in the characters of the story.

DIRECTIONS: Choose one of the characters in "Papa's Parrot." Then choose one of the story events. Put yourself in that character's place as the event took place. Think about how you would have felt if you had been there. Write a diary entry based on the event, from the point of view of the character. Use the lines provided to make notes and to write your diary entry.

Character: _____

Story Event: _____

How You Feel: _____

_____

_____

_____

Dear Diary,

_____

_____

_____

_____

_____

_____

_____

_____

_____

_____

_____

"Suzy and Leah" by Jane Yolen

Summary This story is told through a series of diary entries written by two girls during World War II. Leah, a German-Jewish refugee of World War II, has been sent to America with her brother. The rest of her family has been killed in Germany. Suzy, an American girl, visits the refugee shelter and brings treats and clothing to the refugees. But she does not try to understand what the refugees have suffered. She is puzzled and offended by Leah's shyness and distrust of others. When Leah goes to the hospital with appendicitis, Suzy visits her. After secretly reading Leah's diary, Suzy understands her better, and offers her own diary for her new friend to read.

Make Inferences It wouldn't be much fun to read a story in which the author told you everything straight out. It's more fun to put the clues together and figure out what the author is telling you about the characters or the setting. For example, if an author says, "Bob was very poor," that doesn't give you much to figure out. However, the author might say, "Bob's shoes were so full of holes that Bob had to stuff newspaper inside them so his feet wouldn't touch the ground." This gives you the chance to infer that Bob was poor.

DIRECTIONS: Choose two paragraphs from "Suzy and Leah." List three details from each paragraph. For each detail, tell what it suggests about the character or the setting.

Paragraph 1

Paragraph beginning with the words _____

Detail #1: _____

What it suggests: _____

Detail #2: _____

What it suggests: _____

Detail #3: _____

What it suggests: _____

Paragraph 2

Paragraph beginning with the words _____

Detail #1: _____

What it suggests: _____

Detail #2: _____

What it suggests: _____

Detail #3: _____

What it suggests: _____

"Ribbons" by Laurence Yep
"The Treasure of Lemon Brown" by Walter Dean Myers

Summary In "Ribbons," Stacy, a Chinese-American girl, is offended when her grandmother, a recent immigrant from Hong Kong, disapproves of her ribboned ballet shoes. Later Stacy learns that, as a child, her grandmother had been forced to bind her feet with ribbons, a Chinese tradition believed to enhance a woman's beauty. Stacy explains to her grandmother the purpose of ballet shoes, dances for her, and bonds with her. In "The Treasure of Lemon Brown," Greg, a teenager, leaves home one night to avoid his father's lecture on the importance of school. In an abandoned building, Greg meets Lemon Brown, a homeless man who was once a noted musician. Brown proudly shows Greg old newspaper reviews of his performances, which his son had been carrying when he died in the war. Greg returns home with a new respect for his father.

Ask Questions Sometimes it is difficult to understand what you are reading. One way to make it easier is to ask yourself questions as you read. When you come across a difficult passage, ask yourself why the author is including it. Does it tell you more about the setting, the characters, or the theme? Does it give a hint about what might happen next? How does this part relate to what has happened before?

DIRECTIONS: As you read "Ribbons" and "The Treasure of Lemon Brown," practice this reading strategy by writing questions and answers in the ovals below. One sample has been given.

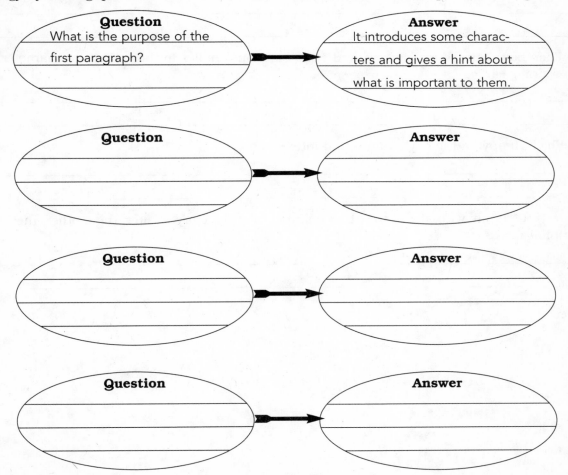

Question
What is the purpose of the first paragraph?

→ **Answer**
It introduces some characters and gives a hint about what is important to them.

Question

→ **Answer**

Question

→ **Answer**

Question

→ **Answer**

"Stolen Day" by Sherwood Anderson

Summary This story looks at the relationship of a parent and child, particularly a son's need to feel his mother's love. The boy is fascinated and frightened by a neighbor's disease of inflammatory rheumatism. Imagining he also has it, the boy is scared and leaves school to go home. Once home, however, his mother does not treat him as if he has a serious disease. The boy is sure that he will die and is bothered by his mother's busyness and seeming lack of pity. He recalls how she had once show great compassion for a drowned child, and aches for the same show of compassion for himself.

Identify with the Characters: Identifying with characters can help you appreciate their stories and the themes or ideas the story conveys. When you identify with a character, you put yourself in the character's place, and think about how you would act.

Think about the boy from the story "Stolen Day." Try to identify with him by answering these questions on the lines provided.

1. How is the boy's situation in life similar to your own?

   _____

   _____

2. In what ways, if any, are his problems similar to any that you have faced in your life?

   _____

   _____

3. When have you felt joy, sorrow, and other emotions similar to those that the character experiences?

   _____

   _____

4. Which, if any, of the boy's values and interests do you share?

   _____

   _____

5. Do you identify with any of the other characters in the story (Walter, the mother, the siblings)?

   _____

   _____

"How to Enjoy Poetry" by James Dickey

Summary In this expository essay, the writer explores what poetry is, what it can do, and his own feelings about poetry. James Dickey loves poetry. He wants to help others enjoy it, too. To start enjoying poetry, Dickey suggests to readers that they skip their experiences with poetry in classrooms, textbooks, tests, and libraries; instead, he thinks the way to start is by going straight to personal experiences. He talks about the connections that words have with our hearts. He explains how rhyme and rhythm leave lasting impressions on people. He suggests ways that readers can think about poetry. He even encourages writing poetry. Reading poetry, he says, can change your life—the deeper a person's encounters with poetry, the deeper his or her experiences with life.

Recognize the Organization One way to read and understand nonfiction more effectively is by noting how the information is organized. In "How to Enjoy Poetry," author James Dickey chooses to list his advice for reading poetry in chronological order. That is, he tells you what you should do first, next, and so on. Notice how, early in his essay, he writes, "The first thing to understand about poetry is. . . ." That phrase is a clue that Dickey is presenting his suggestions in chronological order.

Copy the chart below. As you read Dickey's essay, jot down in chronological order his tips for enjoying poetry. Start with the advice that he offers first.

"How to Enjoy Poetry"
Tip #1:
Tip #2:
Tip #3:
Tip #4:
Tip #5:
Tip #6:
Tip #7:
Tip #8:
Tip #9:
Tip #10:

"No Gumption" by Russell Baker
"The Chase" from *An American Childhood* by Anne Dillard

Summary In these autobiographical pieces, the authors recall memorable childhood experiences. In "No Gumption," Baker describes how, in 1932 during the Depression, his mother was concerned with his laziness. She encouraged him, at age eight, to sell magazines in town, first on the streets, and then door to door. Unable to sell any, Russell was then shown up by his younger sister, whose determination enabled her to sell all Russell's magazines. Later, an A grade on a school composition inspired Russell to choose a writing career, which he saw as requiring no gumption. In "The Chase," the author describes how she and friends, as children, threw a snowball at a passing car. The driver chased the children on foot for ten blocks until finally catching up with them. While Dillard was unimpressed by the driver's scolding words, she was astonished that he had chased them over such a long distance.

Understand the Author's Purpose Authors write for different purposes, or reasons. Some wish to *inform*, some wish to *entertain*, and others wish to *persuade*. Sometimes a writer has more than one purpose in mind when writing. Russell Baker and Anne Dillard each manage to inform, entertain, and persuade at various points in their essays.

Answer these questions about the two essays.

1. Where does Baker *entertain* you with a humorous description of himself?

_____

_____

2. Where does he *inform* you about the kind of town he lived in as a boy?

_____

_____

3. Where does he try to *persuade* you that he had no gumption?

_____

_____

4. Where does Dillard *entertain* you with a humorous description of the chase?

_____

_____

5. Where does she *inform* you about the children in her neighborhood?

_____

_____

6. Where does she try to *persuade* you that she is as tough as the boys?

_____

_____

"Nolan Ryan" by William W. Lace

Summary This selection looks at the habits and balanced lifestyle of major-league baseball pitcher Nolan Ryan. Ryan continues the good habits he learned in early life: eating only wholesome, low-fat foods and working out daily even in the off-season. Ryan takes care of his mental health, as well, by keeping up his interests in other things. His family and his commitment to the community are a big part of his life. He raises cattle on several different ranches and participates in charity work whenever he can. He has a generosity of spirit until he's on the mound and his drive to win takes over, making him a fierce competitor. Ryan's character makes him an exciting person to watch, on or off the baseball field.

Set a Purpose for Reading Before you read a selection, it is helpful to know why you are reading it. You can decide that for yourself by **setting a purpose for reading.** First, learn the topic of the selection. Next, think of specific questions you would like answered by reading the selection. Then, as you read, look for details that will help you answer your questions.

For the selection, list four questions you have about the topic. Then, as you read the selection, see if you can answer each question.

Question 1:

_____

Question 2:

_____

Question 3:

_____

Question 4:

_____

Answer 1:

_____

Answer 2:

_____

Answer 3:

_____

Answer 4:

_____

from *Barrio Boy* by Ernesto Galarza
"I Am a Native of North America" by Chief Dan George
"Rattlesnake Hunt" by Marjorie Kinnan Rawlings
"All Together Now" by Barbara Jordan

Summary In the excerpt from *Barrio Boy*, the author tells of his entrance into first grade as a fearful Mexican boy trying to learn English. Thanks to a dedicated teacher, he ultimately triumphs. In "I Am a Native of North America," the author recalls his father's great love of the earth and its precious gifts, contrasting his culture with that of white society, which he sees as lacking love. In "Rattlesnake Hunt," the author describes how she overcame her fear of snakes by joining a snake expert on a rattlesnake hunt. In "All Together Now," Barbara Jordan appeals to American parents to teach their children to tolerate racial and ethnic differences in order to cultivate a love for all humanity.

Identify the Author's Main Points In an essay, an author usually makes several main points. A main point is a general and important idea. It is supported by specific details such as facts, statistics, stories, and examples.

For each selection below, list one main point that the author makes. Then cite at least two details that help support the main point.

from *Barrio Boy*

(a) Main Point _____

(b) Supporting Details _____

"I Am a Native of North America"

(a) Main Point _____

(b) Supporting Details _____

"Rattlesnake Hunt"

(a) Main Point _____

(b) Supporting Details _____

"All Together Now"

(a) Main Point _____

(b) Supporting Details _____

Name _____ Date _____

"A Christmas Carol: Scrooge and Marley" Act I by Charles Dickens
dramatized by Israel Horovitz

Summary On Christmas Eve, stingy Ebenezer Scrooge rejects all holiday celebration. He refuses to visit his nephew's family or to give to charity. He even chases away a caroler, and only reluctantly agrees to give his clerk, Bob Cratchit, the next day off. That night at home, Scrooge is visited by the ghost of his dead business partner, Jacob Marley. The ghost warns Scrooge to open his heart to humanity or suffer serious consequences. After telling Scrooge that three spirits will visit him on successive nights, Marley disappears. Later, the first spirit, the Ghost of Christmas Past, comes and takes Scrooge back in time. Scrooge is upset to see himself first as a lonely schoolboy, and then as a young man whose fiancee leaves him because of his obsession with money. The ghost then disappears, and Scrooge goes to sleep.

Picture As you read a play, it helps if you picture the production in your mind. You can do that with the help of stage directions, which appear in italic type enclosed in brackets. Always read stage directions carefully. Use details about the setting to imagine what the stage looks like in each scene. Use details about the characters to imagine how the actors move and speak on stage.

Use the chart below to record important stage directions in Act I. Tell how each direction helps you envision the play. The first one has been done for you.

Stage Direction	How It Helps Me Picture the Play
Ghostly music in the auditorium. A single spotlight on JACOB MARLEY, D.C. He is ancient; awful, dead-eyed ….	The scene is eerie, and Jacob Marley is frightening.

Adapted Reader's Companion **363**

"A Christmas Carol: Scrooge and Marley" Act II by Charles Dickens
dramatized by Israel Horovitz

Summary In Act I, Ebenezer Scrooge revisited the Christmases of his past, where he recalled a lonely childhood and a young adulthood in which he benefited from the kindness of a generous supervisor. In Act II, he visits first his Christmas Present—and sees how poorly he is regarded by his nephew and his wife and by the family of his clerk, Bob Cratchit. He moves on to the Christmas of his future. There, he looks in on three vagrants who have made off with the trappings of his deathbed, including even the shirt on his back. Determined to change both present and future, Scrooge awakens on Christmas day and sets off to provide richly for family, friends, and strangers alike.

Question As you read a play, you may have questions about the characters or their actions. You might wonder what a character meant by a particular comment. You might not understand why a character behaved as he or she did. When you have questions, it is best to write them down. Then, as you read on, see if you can find the answers.

Use the left column of the chart below to record questions about things you don't understand as you read Act II. Then, as you find answers, record them in the right column.

What I Don't Understand	What I Now Understand

"The Monsters Are Due on Maple Street" by Rod Serling

Summary It is an ordinary day in an ordinary town. Suddenly, a flash of light appears overhead and all electrical devices in town stop working or go on and off haphazardly. The townspeople, in their panic, look for someone to blame. They accuse one another of being the alien behind the strange happenings. One particularly disturbed man even shoots another. The blaming and confusion continue and increase. No one is safe from the mob that is seeking answers. While all this happens on Maple Street, two aliens watch from their spacecraft, which is sitting atop a nearby hill. They discuss how the most dangerous enemy humans confront is themselves.

Predict As you read a play, it can be fun to predict, or guess, what will happen next. The most reliable predictions are those based on story details you've already read. Before you make a prediction, ask yourself: What has each character done so far? What type of person is each character? If I were a character in the story, what might I do next?

Use the chart below to record your predictions in the story. For each prediction, explain why you think it will happen.

What I Predict Will Happen	Why I Think It Will Happen

"The Cremation of Sam McGee" by Robert Service
"Washed in Silver" by James Stephens
"Winter" by Nikki Giovanni

Summary These three poems demonstrate the impact that nature has on our lives. "The Cremation of Sam McGee," is the story of the Tennessee miner who died of the cold during the Gold Rush in the Yukon. The narrator tells the tale of the final trip across the frozen landscape with Sam's corpse. But when the corpse is warmed by the fire, Sam comes back to life! In "Washed in Silver," poet James Stephens describes the transforming power of the moonlight that shines on the landscape, and how he himself blends into the silvery light. The poem "Winter" describes how creatures large and small, including humans, have the natural instinct to prepare for the cold months.

Identify the Speaker The **speaker** in a narrative poem is the person telling the story. Sometimes the speaker is a character who takes part in the story's action. At other times he or she may be an observer who merely reports the action. Either way, you can learn about the speaker from the way he or she tells the story. The things the speaker says, and the way the speaker says them, are important clues to the speaker's personality and to the meaning of the poem.

Read each statement below made by the speaker in "The Cremation of Sam McGee." Then explain what the comment seems to indicate about the speaker's personality. The first one has been done for you.

1. Why he left his home in the South to roam 'round the Pole, God only knows.

   What it indicates about the speaker: He doesn't think that traveling to the Pole is an
   activity meant for everyone.

2. Well, he seemed so low that I couldn't say no.

   What it indicates about the speaker: _____
   _____

3. A pal's last need is a thing to heed, so I swore I would not fail.

   What it indicates about the speaker: _____
   _____

4. In the days to come, though my lips were dumb, in my heart how I cursed that load.

   What it indicates about the speaker: _____
   _____

5. The trail was bad, and I felt half mad, but I swore I would not give in.

   What it indicates about the speaker: _____
   _____

6. Then I made a hike, for I didn't like to hear him sizzle so.

   What it indicates about the speaker: _____

"Seal" by William Jay Smith
"The Pasture" by Robert Frost
"Three Haiku" by Matsuo Bashō, translated by Daniel C. Buchanan

Summary These descriptive poems paint pictures with words. "Seal"—a poem whose words are arranged in the shape of a seal—describes the actions of a seal. The animal dives with a zoom and swims "Quicksilver-quick," past sting ray and shark. Soon, the seal resurfaces and "...plops at your side / With a mouthful of fish!" In "The Pasture," the poet states in a conversational tone that he is going to the pasture. He's going "to rake the leaves away" or to fetch a calf that's young and still totters on its legs when the mother licks it. He invites the reader also to come to the pasture. The poems that make up the selection "Three Haiku" describe the beauty of nature. One of the poems describes sunrise. Another depicts spring, and the third one reflects upon an evening graced by the fragrance of blossoms.

Read According to Punctuation Punctuation marks are like traffic lights. They tell you when to stop and go. In poetry, it is not always obvious from the structure of the lines where you should pause and stop as you read. You should not necessarily stop at the end of a line. To help you read, pay close attention to the **punctuation**. Stop at a period, even if it's in the middle of a line. Pause at a comma or a dash. Read with emphasis at an exclamation point.

Read each of the three poems. Find places where punctuation helps you understand how to read the passage. Record each example in its proper place in the chart. One example has been done for you.

Punctuation Signals and Passages
Stop at a Period
_____
_____
_____
_____
Pause at a Comma or Hyphen
_____
_____
_____
_____
Read with Emphasis at an Exclamation Point
See how he dives from the rocks with a zoom!
_____
_____
_____

"Martin Luther King" by Raymond Richard Patterson
"Annabel Lee" by Edgar Allan Poe

Summary These poems use words designed to call up intense, often vivid feelings, about someone who has died. In his poem about the late civil rights leader Martin Luther King, Jr., Patterson's choice of words shows how the passion of King's beliefs made him admirable and keeps him memorable, even after his death. "He showed what Man can be/Before death sets him free." The poem "Annabel Lee" tells of the deep love between the young woman Annabel Lee, who lived by the sea, and a young man. When Annabel Lee dies from a chill, her lover grieves her death. But he believes that their love is so profound that their souls are never truly separated.

Paraphrase When you **paraphrase** the lines of a poem, you restate the ideas in your own words. Paraphrasing can help you discover how well you understand the passage. When you paraphrase, you change the poetic language into language you might use in prose writing or conversation. A paraphrase does not have to rhyme, even if the original lines of the poem do. Above all, remember not to change the meaning of the lines when you paraphrase them.

Read each passage below from the three poems. Restate the same idea in your own words. The first one has been done for you.

Original Passage	Paraphrase
1. His love so deep, so wide, / He could not turn aside.	He had too much love in him to ignore the problems of others.
2. His passion, so profound, / He would not turn around.	
3. He taught this suffering Earth, / The measure of Man's worth.	
4. So that her highborn kinsmen came / And bore her away from me.	
5. With a love that the winged seraphs of Heaven / Coveted her and me.	
6. ... The stars never rise but I see the bright eyes / Of the beautiful Annabel Lee.	

"Full Fathom Five" by William Shakespeare
"Onomatopoeia" by Eve Merriam
"Maestro" by Pat Mora

Summary The focus in these poems is on different types of music, real or imagined. In "Full Fathom Five," a son is told that his father lies dead beneath the sea. However, the father is transformed into the beautiful pearls and coral of the depths; and sea nymphs, or goddesses, ring bells in his honor. "Onomatopoeia" is about the sounds water makes when it flows from a rusty spigot. There is a stream of noise that becomes its own symphony. In the poem by Pat Mora, the maestro plays the violin in concert. As he bows before an audience he recalls the lyrical sound of his mother's voice. Each time the audience applauds, instead of hearing the clapping he hears in his mind the music that he and his parents played together at home.

Listen as You Read Poetry Poems are meant to be read, but even more so, they are meant to be heard. When you read a poem, read it out loud in order to **listen** to the musical language. Listen for rhyme, rhythm, and repetition of sounds and words. Don't just silently read a passage such as, "Full fathom five thy father lies." Say the line aloud, and hear the effective repetition of the *f* sound four times.

Read each passage below aloud. Describe the special or unusual sounds you hear. The first one has been done for you.

Passage	What I Hear
1. Full fathom five thy father lies.	the repetition of the *f* sound four times
2. "Hark! Now I hear them—ding-dong, bell."	
3. slash, / splatters, / scatters, / spurts, / finally stops sputtering / and plash!	
4. gushes rushes splashes / clear water dashes.	
5. while his father strummed the guitar / or picked the melody with quick fingertips.	
6. *voz, guitarra, violin* / would blend again and again	

"Fog" by Carl Sandburg
"Life" by Naomi Long Madgett
"Loo-Wit" by Wendy Rose
"The Village Blacksmith" by Henry Wadsworth Longfellow

Summary Each of these poems makes a comparison. In "Fog," Carl Sandburg compares fog to a cat, giving fog the cat's quiet, stealth-like qualities. In "Life," Naomi Madgett shows how a watch is like a life. She demonstrates the passage of time by characterizing the watch as a lively toy used to amuse an infant. As time goes by and the end of life draws near, the watch runs down, unwinding. In "Loo-Wit," a volcano takes on the characteristics of an old woman. The land surrounding the volcano's crater, or the woman's throat, is described as patches of her skin. "The Village Blacksmith" compares life to the blacksmith's forge, where everything we do works to shape us into who we are.

Respond to Poetry When poets speak to you in their work, they do not want you merely to read or listen. They also want you to **respond**. When you respond to a poem, you consider how its ideas relate to your own life and experiences. You think about whether or not you agree with the poet's ideas. You allow the poem to inspire you to ask questions, and then you try to answer those questions.

Complete the outline below with your responses to each poem.

I. "Fog"

How I feel about the poet's ideas:

_____

II. "Life"

How I feel about the poet's ideas:

_____

III. "Loo-Wit"

How I feel about the poet's ideas:

_____

IV. "The Village Blacksmith"

How I feel about the poet's ideas:

_____

"Popocatepetl and Ixtlaccihuatl" by Juliet Piggott

Summary This Mexican legend explains the origin of the volcanoes Popocatepetl and Ixtlaccihuatl. An aging Aztec emperor plans for his daughter, Ixtla, to succeed him as ruler. She loves the warrior Popo, but her father forbids her to marry anyone. However, when his empire is threatened by enemy tribes, he changes his mind. He decrees that Ixtla will marry the warrior who can defeat his enemies. All the warriors wish to marry the princess, but Popo is the one who defeats the enemy. After the battle, some jealous warriors run ahead to tell the emperor that Popo is dead. Hearing the news, Ixtla dies. A mournful Popo has a giant pyramid of stones built and buries Ixtla at the top. Then, from atop a second pyramid, he watches over her grave for the rest of his life.

Predict As you read a legend, you may be able to guess, or **predict**, things that will happen in the story. To make a good prediction, pay close attention to story details. Think about everything that has happened so far in the legend. Think what you have learned about the characters so far. By doing so, you will be better able to predict what characters may do next or what may happen to them.

As you read "Popocatepetl and Ixtlaccihuatl," make predictions about future events. Tell why you think each event will occur. Then, once you finish the story, record what actually happens.

My Prediction:

_____

Why It May Happen:

_____

What Actually Happens:

_____

My Prediction:

_____

Why It May Happen:

_____

What Actually Happens:

_____

My Prediction:

_____

Why It May Happen:

_____

What Actually Happens:

_____

"The People Could Fly" by Virginia Hamilton
"All Stories Are Anansi's" by Harold Courlander
"The Lion and the Statue" by Aesop
"The Fox and the Crow" by Aesop

Summary Folk tales and fables demonstrate how stories are used to explain ideas and teach lessons. In "The People Could Fly," African slaves escape plantations by floating into air and flying to freedom. "All Stories are Anansi's" tells how a clever spider gained ownership of all stories by capturing the hornets, the great python, and the leopard for the Sky God. "The Lion and the Statue" shows a lion and man arguing their strength. Readers learn that people often see things only as they want them to be. In "The Fox and the Crow," a hungry fox plays upon a crow's vanity by flattering the crow into singing. The crow opens its mouth to sing, and drops a piece of cheese right to the fox!

Recognize Storyteller's Purpose When you **recognize a storyteller's purpose,** you understand why the story was written. Some tales are told in order to entertain or amuse the audience. Others are told to inform or educate listeners. Still others are told to persuade the audience to accept an opinion, or to teach listeners a lesson about life.

For each of the selections below, identify the storyteller's purpose and tell what you learned from the story.

1. **"The People Could Fly"**
   Storyteller's purpose:

   _____

   What I learned:

   _____

2. **"All Stories are Anansi's"**
   Storyteller's purpose:

   _____

   What I learned:

   _____

3. **"The Lion and the Statue"**
   Storyteller's purpose:

   _____

   What I learned:

   _____

4. **"The Fox and the Crow"**
   Storyteller's purpose:

   _____

   What I learned:

   _____

"Phaëthon, Son of Apollo" by Olivia Coolidge
"Demeter and Persephone" by Anne Terry White
"Icarus and Daedalus" by Josephine Preston Peabody

Summary These three selections relate Greek myths. In "Phaëthon, Son of Apollo," the sun god Apollo grants Phaëthon's request to drive his chariot across the sky so that the boy can prove he is Apollo's son. Phaëthon loses control, and is killed after Zeus destroys the carriage to save the earth. In "Demeter and Persephone," Persephone, daughter of the harvest goddess Demeter, is rescued from the underworld. Because she has eaten food there, Persephone can stay on earth for only eight months a year. The myth explains why nothing grows there just before spring. In "Icarus and Daedalus," Daedalus builds wings for himself and his son to escape the king. When Icarus flies too close to the sun, he dies.

Predict As you read a myth, you may be able to guess, or **predict**, things that will happen in the story. To make a good prediction, pay close attention to story details. Think about everything that has happened so far in the myth. By doing so, you will be better able to predict what will happen next.

As you read the three myths, make predictions about future events. Tell why you think each event will occur.

1. "Phaëthon, Son of Apollo"

My Prediction: _____

Why It May Happen: _____

_____

2. "Demeter and Persephone"

My Prediction: _____

Why It May Happen: _____

_____

3. "Icarus and Daedalus"

My Prediction: _____

Why It May Happen: _____

_____

(Acknowledgments continued from page ii)

Helmut Hirnschall
"I Am a Native of North America" by Chief Dan George, from *My Heart Soars.* Copyright © 1974 by Clarke Irwin.

International Paper Company
"How to Enjoy Poetry" by James Dickey from *The Power of the Printed Word Program.*

Alfred A. Knopf Children's Books, a division of Random House, Inc.
"People Could Fly" from *The People Could Fly: American Black Folktales* by Virginia Hamilton, copyright © 1985 by Virginia Hamilton.

Charles Neider
Excerpt from "The Californian's Tale" by Mark Twain, from *The Complete Short Stories of Mark Twain.* Copyright © 1957 by Charles Neider.

Hugh Noyes, on behalf of the Trustees of Alfred Noyes
"The Highwayman" from *Collected Poems* by Alfred Noyes (J.B. Lippincott).

Random House, Inc.
"Melting Pot" from *Living Out Loud* by Anna Quindlen, copyright © 1987 by Anna Quindlen.

William Saroyan Foundation for the Trustees of Leland Stanford Junior University
"The Hummingbird That Lived Through Winter" by William Saroyan, from *Dear Baby.* Copyright © 1935, 1936, 1939, 1941, 1942, 1943, 1944 by William Saroyan.

St. Martin's Press, Inc., and Harold Ober Associates, Inc.
"Cat on the Go" from *All Things Wise and Wonderful* by James Herriot. Copyright © 1976, 1977 by James Herriot.

Scribner, a division of Simon & Schuster Inc.
"A Day's Wait" from *Winner Take Nothing* by Ernest Hemingway. Copyright © 1933 Charles Scribner's Sons. Copyright renewed © 1961 by Mary Hemingway.

Simon & Schuster Books for Young Readers, an imprint of Simon & Schuster Children's Publishing Division
"Papa's Parrot" by Cynthia Rylant from *Every Living Thing* by Cynthia Rylant. Copyright © 1985 Cynthia Rylant.

Piri Thomas
"Amigo Brothers" by Piri Thomas from *El Barrio.* Copyright © 1978 by Piri Thomas.

Rosemary A. Thurber and The Barbara Hogensen Agency
"The Night The Bed Fell" by James Thurber. Copyright © 1933, 1961, James Thurber, from *My Life and Hard Times,* published by Harper & Row.

Viking Penguin, a division of Penguin Putnam
"Was Tarzan a Three-Bandage Man?" from *Childhood* by Bill Cosby. Copyright © 1991 by William H. Cosby. Reprinted by permission of Viking Penguin, a divison of Penguin Putnam Inc.

Note: Every effort has been made to locate the copyright owner of material reprinted in this book. Omissions brought to our attention will be corrected in subsequent editions.

The Cat Who Thought She Was a Dog and the Dog Who Thought He Was a Cat

p. 6 Reading Strategy Students should circle *poor farmer.*

p. 6 Stop to Reflect They may be poor but they still are generous.

p. 6 Reading Strategy Students should circle *traveled from door to door, buying and selling things.*

peddler: someone who travels door to door, buying and selling things

p. 7 Reading Check Students should circle *they saw problems they had never noticed before.*

p. 7 Stop to Reflect Most students are likely to find the characters' behavior believable, since people are often dissatisfied with their appearance. Students may also mention people's common habit of staring in a mirror or complaining about something they don't like in their face.

p. 7 Reading Check Students should write numbers near *first, the second,* and *third.* The first daughter pinched her nose; the second daughter pushed her chin; and the third daughter scrutinized her freckles.

p. 8 Read Fluently After reading the sentence aloud, students should circle *deeply felt its poverty and envied the rich.*

p. 8 Literary Analysis Possible response: The beauties of nature are more important than your own appearance; the world is more important than you.

p. 8 Literary Analysis Possible response: A person's actions toward others are more important than his or her appearance; being kind and generous is more important than how you look.

Review and Assess

1. Possible response: poor, happy, loving
2. Marianna Skiba—missing tooth; first daughter—nose too snub and broad; second daughter—chin too narrow and long; third daughter—freckles; Kot—realizes she is not a dog.
3. Jan gives back the mirror because it has disrupted the house, and he realizes it is not good to spend so much time looking at one's self.
4. The following words help readers understand the meaning of the word *trinket:* jewelry and kerchiefs.
5. *glimpse:* a quick look
6. Students should check the first, fourth, and fifth sentences.

Two Kinds

p. 13 Reading Check Students should circle *anything you wanted to be, rich,* and *instantly famous.*

p. 13 Reading Strategy Students should circle *super, talent,* and *ed.* Possible completed sentence: A *supertalented* child is a child with more than normal talent.

p. 14 Stop to Reflect Both are young girls of Chinese background.

p. 14 Reading Check Students should circle *I felt as though I had been sent to hell. I whined and then kicked my foot a little when I couldn't stand it anymore.*

p. 14 Literary Analysis Students should circle *Only ask you be your best. For your sake.*

p. 14 Read Fluently Students should circle *He was deaf.*

p. 15 Reading Strategy Students should circle *un* and *able.*

un-: not ; *-able:* able

p. 15 Reading Check Students should circle *some nonsense that sounded like a cat running up and down on top of garbage cans.* Mr. Chong praises her because he is deaf.

p. 15 Stop to Reflect No, Auntie Lindo does not think Jing-mei's mother is lucky. Auntie Lindo is really indirectly bragging that her daughter Waverly is more talented than Jing-mei.

p. 15 Literary Analysis The correct answer is *C*; students should circle *bragged*

p. 16 Stop to Reflect Students should predict that Jing-mei will play badly, since she has been taught by someone who does not hear her mistakes and praises playing that does not really sound good.

p. 16 Literary Analysis Students should circle *jealousy*

p. 17 Stop to Reflect Possible responses: yes; she has been prevented from being her true self and forced to do what she has no natural inclination or talent for; no, she is exaggerating her feelings because she is angry and ashamed and no longer wants to study the piano and resents being forced to do so.

p. 17 Reading Check Students should circle and number (1) *those who are obedient* and (2) *those who follow their own mind.*

p. 17 Literary Analysis Students should circle *I wanted to see it spill over.* They should also circle *anger.*

p. 18 Reading Check Students should number four things that Jing-mei does that disappoint her mother: (1) She does not get straight A's or (2) become class president. (3) She does not get accepted to Stanford University. (4) She even drops out of college.

p. 18 Reading Strategy Students should put a line between *forgive* and *ness.* Possible meaning: the act or state of forgiving

p. 18 Reading Check The correct answer is *B.* Students should circle all or part of *I realized they were two halves of the same song.*

Review and Assess

1. Students should circle *famous* and *herself.*
2. Kind 1: those who are obedient
   Kind 2: those who follow their own mind
3. She is both an obedient daughter who wants love and approval and an independent daughter who has gone her own way.
4. *unlike:* not similar to
   childish: like a young person
   childhood: state or condition of acting like a young person

5. Possible motives for pushing Jing-mei to be famous: hope, pride, love
   Possible motives for arranging the talent show: pride, competitive spirit
   Possible motives for offering the piano: love, forgiveness
   Possible motives for agreeing to take piano lessons: desire for attention, respect for mother, need to please mother, need to gain approval
   Possible motives for refusing to take more lessons: shame, fear, need for independence
   Possible motives for saying hurtful words: anger, shame, desire to win the battle and end the piano lessons

My Furthest-Back Person (The Inspiration for *Roots*)

p. 23 Reading Check Students should circle *slave forbears.*

p. 23 Reading Strategy Students might put a line after the first comma, the second comma, *astonishment*, the colon, the second *Murray, well,* and *heard.* Accept reasonable variations: for example, some students may not put a line after *heard.* Students should circle C, Haley's great-grandparents

p. 24 Literary Analysis Students should circle *wasn't, hadn't,* and *didn't.* Accept reasonable alternatives.

The use of italics adds to the conversational style by showing that *didn't* should be stressed, as it might be in a conversation. Also, it may call attention to the fact that Haley is knowingly breaking a grammatical rule by introducing a double negative.

p. 24 Reading Strategy Students might put a line after *bent, herself,* and *overjoyed.* Accept reasonable variations; for example, some students may also put a line after *wrinkled.* Students should circle *she was so overjoyed.*

p. 24 Stop to Reflect *ko*; She says *ko* means *banjo.* Students should circle *true.*

p. 25 Read Fluently Students should say *Kamby* with the same /a/ sound that they use for the first /a/ in *Gambia.* Most students will circle *yes.*

p. 25 Stop to Reflect The correct answer is D; he said he has to get to the Gambia River, and the paragraph before said the Gambia River flows near the old kingdom of Mali in Africa.

p. 25 Reading Strategy Students might put a line after *something, fantasized* (or after the dash), *country*, the first comma, and the second comma. Accept reasonable variations.

Students should circle *very old men* and *who could tell centuries of the histories of certain very old family clans*. Accept reasonable variations.

A *griot* is a very old African man who can tell centuries of the histories of certain very old African family clans.

p. 26 Reading Check the correct answer is B. Students might circle three or more of the following: *upriver, bank, ashore, (on) foot.*

p. 26 Reading Check Students should circle *years*; Kunta Kinte was about 16 years old.

p. 26 Literary Analysis In the text, students might circle *sob, bawling,* and *weeping.*
In the margin, students should circle *joy.* Haley is proud to have made this journey and made a critical connection to his own history.

p. 27 Stop to Reflect Students should write *Annapolis.*

p. 28 Stop to Reflect 42 out of 140; It shows that conditions were *foul,* as Haley says, and that the slaves were treated terribly.

p. 28 Literary Analysis Students should circle *cargo, choice,* and *healthy.* Also accept *Gambia, Africa,* and/or *slaves* if students can explain these answers adequately.

Review and Assess

1. Kunta Kinte was an African who was the first person in Alex Haley's family to come to America.

2. He was kidnapped near the Gambia River, shipped to Annapolis, Maryland, and sold into slavery.

3. Students should include at least five details of information.
   details of grandmother's story (African said his name was *Kin-tay,* banjo was *ko,* river was *Kamby Bolong*; *Kin-tay* chopping wood for a drum when kidnapped)—Cousin Georgia—Kansas City, Kansas

language sounds like Mandinka; *ko* is *kora,* an old African stringed instrument; *Kamby Bolong* is likely Gambia River—Dr. Jan Vansina—Wisconsin

Kin-tay is pronunciation of *Kinte,* clan name going back to old kingdom of Mali—Dr. Philip Curtin—Wisconsin (on phone to Dr. Vansina)

Griots in back country tell Kinte family history; family villages of Kintes include Kinte-Kundah and Kinte-Kundah Janneh-Ya—Gambians in capital—Gambia (Africa)

Kinte clan began in Old Mali; one member, Kairaba Kunta Kinte, settled in Juffure in Gambia; his youngest son, Omoro, wed Binta Kebba; they had 4 sons; eldest, Kunta Kinte, disappeared soon after the king's soldiers came, when he was 16 and had gone to chop wood for a drum—Kebba Kanga Fofana (griot)—Juffure, Gambia

Col. O'Hare's Forces (British "king's soldiers") sent to James Fort in Gambia mid-1967—government records—Britain

Lord Ligonier under Capt. Thomas Davies sailed on the Sabbath, July 5, 1767, from Gambia River to Annapolis; cargo included 3265 elephants' teeth, 800 pounds of cotton, 32 oz. Gambian gold, 140 slaves—British shipping records—Britain

Lord Ligonier arrived in Annapolis Sept. 29, 1767; only 98 slaves survived—Annapolis Historical Society—Annapolis, Maryland

sale of slaves from Gambia River, Africa, announced—microfilm copy of *Maryland Gazette,* Oct. 1, 1767, p. 2—Annapolis, Maryland

4. Students might draw a line after *upriver,* the first comma, *ashore,* and the second comma. Accept reasonable alternatives; for example, students might include a comma after the first *village.*
   The travelers left their boat in Albreda.
   Juffure was the village where the *griot* lived.

5. Possible responses: They are about his own family. They prove his grandmother's stories, which fascinated him as a boy. They are a source of pride to him as an African American. They reflect the origins of so many African American families. They show the pain and suffering of slavery.

A Day's Wait

p. 33 Reading Check Students should circle *He is pale, he was shivering, and he looked as though it ached to move.*

p. 33 Stop to Reflect Students should circle *You better go back to bed* and *When he comes downstairs, the boy is dressed and sitting by the fire.* They may speculate that Schatz fails to obey because he is stubborn, does not want to be sick and refuses to admit that he is, and/or because he wants to show his father that he is strong and not some sort of weakling who takes to his bed as soon as he gets a cold.

p. 33 Reading Strategy *instructions:* lists that build information step by step; directions

p. 34 Literary Analysis Students might circle *dark circles under his eyes; lay still;* and *seems detached and listless.* Some students may divide the second circled item into two items and fail to circle one of the others, or circle three items all together.

p. 34 Stop to Reflect Accept all reasonable responses. Possible response: The boy thinks he is going to die and tells his father he need not stay to witness the painful experience.

p. 34 Stop to Reflect Some students may say that having an outdoorsman and sportsman for a father may make the boy want to be particularly brave and strong. Others may say that being familiar with hunting may make him more matter-of-fact about facing death.

p. 35 Reading Check He doesn't want anyone else to catch his illness. Students should circle *must not get what he has.*

p. 35 Literary Analysis Students should circle *he asks whether taking the medicine will do any good* and *he evidently isn't taking it easy.*

Accept all reasonable internal conflicts. Possible response: Schatz's inner struggle seems to be between his desire to face his illness bravely and his fear and worry about what will happen to him.

p. 36 Reading Strategy Students should circle *thermometers* and *kilometers*; heat or temperature.

p. 36 Literary Analysis Students should circle *relaxed* and *slack.* They may say that Schatz cries easily because he is relieved.

Review and Assess

1. The correct answer is *C.*

2. Students' wordings will vary. On the thermometers used in France, no one can live with a temperature of 44 degrees. So when Schatz heard the doctor say that his temperature is 102 degrees, he thinks he is sure to die.

3. Possible response: loving, patient, sympathetic, rugged

4. Schatz is (A) scared and (B) worried, BUT he tries to be (C) brave and (D) unselfish. Students may reversse the order of *A* and *B* and/or the order of *C* and *D.*

   Possible examples of (A) and (B): Schatz is pale; there are dark circles under his eyes; he is very stiff and tense; he seems detached and has trouble paying attention to his father's reading; he is evidently holding tightly onto his emotions; the next day he cries.

   Possible examples of (C) and (D): Schatz does not express his fears and holds tightly onto his emotions; he says he'd rather stay awake (i.e., to face death); even though it would be a comfort to have someone with him at this scary time, he tells father to leave because he knows it might bother the father to see his son die and orders people out of the room so that they don't catch the illness.

5. *evidently:* easily seen; clearly

   prescribed: ordered in writing; written in advance

   detached: unconnected

Was Tarzan a Three Bandage Man?

p. 41 Reading Strategy The correct answer is *A.* Students might circle some or all of the following: *pigeon-toed walker, walked pigeon-toed,* and *a painful form of . . .*

p. 41 Literary Analysis Students should circle: *"This is Jackie Robinson's walk,"* and *"He'd be faster if he didn't walk like that."* Students may find humor in the visual image of young Bill Cosby trying to walk pigeon-toed like Jackie Robinson or in the childish idea that imitating an admired athlete's style of walk would somehow reflect favorably on the person doing the imitating.

p. 42 Reading Strategy *emulate:* to admire and imitate

Students might circle [Bill and his friends] *wear a Band-Aid* and/or *the Band-Aid is just for show. . . .*

p. 42 Read Fluently Students should circle *sarcastic.*

p 42 Stop to Reflect The correct answer is *C.*

p. 43 Stop to Reflect Washington was a famous African American teacher, and the mother wants her son to concentrate more on his education and less on sports and neighborhood antics.

p. 43 Reading Check b. She will tell the father, and he will need not a mere bandage but stitches for his wounds.

p. 43 Literary Analysis Students should circle *Our hero worshipping was backwards.*

Review and Assess

1. Possible response: Bill and his friends admire the sports stars and want to be like them. Imitating the sports stars is a fad of sorts and is considered "tough" and "cool" among the boys' peers.
2. T: The mother thinks Bill's behavior is silly.
   F: The mother is a friend of Jackie Robinson's mother.

F: The mother thinks Bill's feet will fall off.
T: The mother has a good sense of humor.
F: The mother knows the names of all the popular sports heroes.

3. Suggested responses: Wearing the bandages does not really make anyone good at fighting. He is confusing the boys imitating the boxers with the actual boxers. He is confusing looking tough with being tough.
4. Suggested responses: Was the movie hero Tarzan tough and cool? Is the movie hero Tarzan worthy of imitation too?
5. Students should circle a *skin condition.*
6. *Purpose: to tell a funny, interesting story;* Possible examples: the boys imitating Jackie Robinson's pigeon-toed walk; the mother's remark, "He'd be faster if he didn't walk like that"; Bill imitating Buddy Helm's bowlegged walk; the boys wearing bandages to look like boxers; and so on.

   Purpose: to describe something important to him; Possible examples: Cosby indicating these athletes were "shining heroes" to him as a boy; showcasing his mother's wit or sense of humor; talking about what he did with his close friends of childhood (Fat Albert and the others).

   Purpose: to make a point about life or people's behavior; Possible examples: "Then, atheletes were sports stars even before they started to incorporate themselves"; "Our hero worshipping was backwards."

Unit 2

In Search of Our Mother's Gardens

p. 48 Stop to Reflect No. She worked past sundown, raising and caring for her family.

p. 48 Reading Strategy Students should circle *A.*

p. 48 Thinking Ahead Students should circle *B.* Students might explain that all the other choices are famous, celebrated people. In contrast, a poor woman who made quilts might be considered low.

p. 49 Literary Analysis No. Students should circle *our, mothers,* and *grandmothers.*

p. 49 Literary Analysis Possible response: She sees that her mother has given Walker her manner or style in addition to her stories.

p. 50 Literary Analysis The correct answer is *B.*

p. 50 Reading Check The correct answer is *C.* Students should circle *magic, magnificent, creativity,* and *art.*

p. 51 Reading Strategy The correct answer is *B. Intruded* means "interrupted." Students may say that the meaning of the root -trud- suggests that being intruded upon is like being pushed.

p. 51 Read Fluently The correct answer is *D*.

p. 51 Reading Check Students should circle *love of beauty* and *respect for strength*. The correct answer is *A*.

Review and Assess

1. She thinks they owe their creative spirit to the women who have lived before them.

2. Students should check *She and her husband worked hard . . .* and *No matter how plain their house. . . .*

3. The correct answer is *B*.

4. The correct answer is *D*.

5. Students may list: her mother's perseverance in planting a garden wherever she lived; her strength in caring for it; her ability to make it beautiful; and her ability to work hard for her family.

6. *-liter-: literate*/able to read; *literacy*/ability to read.

   -nym-: synonyms/words that mean the same thing; *antonyms*/words that have opposite meanings.

   -magni-; magnify/to enlarge; *magnificent*/large in beauty, wonder or power.

Seventh Grade

p. 56 Stop to Reflect Most students will say it is easier to study their native language because they begin with a stronger foundation. However, some students may note that the grammar and vocabulary of even a native language may be complex to learn.

p. 56 Reading Check The correct answer is *B*.

p. 56 Literary Analysis The correct answer is *C*. Possible response: He makes it seem as though the boys don't really understand that the models are scowling as a pose, not as a way of life.

p. 57 Read Aloud Possible response: Michael is Mexican but not good at Spanish; Victor is not good at Math. Victor is taking French.

p. 57 Think Ahead Possible response: It is possible that everything he imagines will not happen. It may not be his "lucky year."

p. 57 Reading Strategy Students may say *on the sly* means "sneakily." Students should circle *catch her eye*, on page 57. Catch her eye means "to get her attention by getting her to look at him."

p. 58 Literary Analysis Possible response: Students may like Victor because he is trying his best, but is not able to be as smooth as he wants.

p. 58 Stop to Reflect Possible response: No. The girls are probably staring because Michael looks strange.

p. 58 Literary Analysis Students may circle *pretended to read*, or *stretched out lazily in an attempt to disguise his snooping*. Students may circle parts of these phrases that get at the gist of the idea.

p. 59 Reading Check Possible response: They are not real words. Students should circle *to bluff his way out by making noises that sounded French*.

p. 60 Stop to Reflect Teresa might be able to help Victor in Math. Possible response: They may become friends.

p. 60 Reading Check The correct response is *D*. Students should circle *shame* and *love*.

p. 60 Stop to Reflect Victor goes to the library to learn French ahead of his classmates and ahead of Teresa.

Review and Assess

1. Victor signs up for French because Teresa was taking French, too.

   Victor is slow to leave homeroom because Teresa was still there, talking to the teacher.

   Victor goes outside during lunch because he thinks Teresa is eating outside.

   Victor pretends to know French to impress Teresa.

   Victor gets French books at the library because he wants to learn French so Teresa won't discover he does not speak the language.

2. Possible responses: Victor is embarrassed when he tries scowling. Victor is embarrassed when he says "Teresa" is a noun. Victor is embarrassed when he pretends to speak French.

3. Possible responses: Seventh grade is a time of fun, anxiety, uncertainty, or of a blooming interest in girls/boys, or of feeling self-conscious.

4. Possible responses: Amused: the incident of scowling; the boy's language when he tries to speak French. Understanding; the French teacher is kind to Victor; some of Victor's embarrassed, self-conscious feelings.

5. *Making a face* means moving the features on your face to show an expression.
   Catch her eye means "to get her attention by getting her to look."

Melting Pot

p. 65 Literary Analysis Students may circle *a close friend of my two boys.* This gives the essay an informal tone because it relates to the author's personal experiences.

p. 66 Reading Check Students should circle and number these words: (1) the old-timers; (2) the moneyed-professionals; (3) the old immigrants; (4) the new ones.

p. 66 Stop to Reflect Because she is "one of them."

p. 67 Literary Analysis Possible response: She probably likes them. She describes their reaction as they watch the glass workers. She describes *sitting with them and watching neighborhood activities.*

p. 68 Literary Analysis Students should mark *calamari* with *A.* Students should mark *sushi* with *B.* Students should mark *bait* with *C.*

p. 68 Reading Strategy 1. described in a very general way; 2. a very tense place; 3. two things that don't mix easily.

Review and Assess

1. People who call America a melting pot mean that the country's values and traditions are generated by the mixing of many different groups. No one culture retains its values—instead a new set of values and traditions comes from the mixing of cultures.

2. Students should check *It is most like a melting pot when people deal with each other person-to-person.*

3. Students should identify these conflicts: old-timers vs. young professionals; old immigrants vs. new immigrants.

4. Anna Quindlen is a young professional because she has a career and small children. She is an old-timer because she has lived in the community for a long time. She is an old immigrant because her grandparents immigrated to America.

5. *Taking over* means "taking control."

6. Possible response: Personal experience: Quindlen describes what it was like when she moved on to the block eight years earlier.
   Personal feelings: Quindlen defends her neighborhood.
   Informal language: half a dozen elderly men; I like you.
   Humor: The antiques store used to be a butcher shop.

The Hummingbird that Lived Through Winter

p. 73 Stop to Reflect Possible responses: Good point: They will feel comfortable among people who share customs and language. Bad point: They may not learn the new language or customs.

p. 73 Reading Check In the text, students should circle *wild and wonderful, plants, bushes,* and *trees.* In the minor column, students should circle *birds, butterflies,* and *bees.*

p. 74 Read Fluently Possible response: What color is the bird? Why does it shoot away? What does it eat?

p. 74 Literary Analysis Students should circle *wonderful, suspended,* and *most alive.* Student should draw boxes around *helpless, pathetic,* and *heartbreaking.* The correct answer is *D.*

p. 75 Literary Analysis Students may circle *signs of fresh life; the warmth of the room; the vapor . . . ;* or *the change.*

p. 75 Reading Strategy Students should draw a line between *rest* and *less.* Restless means without resting, or without being able to rest.

p. 76 Stop to Reflect Possible response: He means that people help all small animals, or that small animals need the protection of humans.

Review and Assess

1. Possible responses: 1. Dikran blows warm air on the bird. 2. He feeds it honey. 3. They let the bird go.

2. Possible response: Students may say that Dikran knows it is better for a bird to be free than for it to be house bound.

3. Students should place a check before the following statements: *He can barely see;*

He loves and respects nature; He respects the freedom of living things.

4. Students should place a check before the following statements. Each statement is followed by an appropriate explanation. *Hope or renewal/ He lives through winter. The fragile or delicate nature of life:* The tiny bird could have died. *The beauty and wonder of nature: His recovery is amazing; the birds in spring are beautiful.*

5. Hummingbird: a bird that hums. Helpless: Without being able to help. Heartbreaking: Something that breaks a heart; something that is painfully sad.

Unit 3

The Third Wish

p. 81 Reading Strategy (a) untangle. Students should circle *trying* and *entangled*.

p. 81 Literary Analysis Students should circle the words *a little man all in green*. The creature was freed from its prison.

p. 81 Literary Analysis Possible response: Mr. Peters expects three wishes because he knows the pattern of older fairy tales. Characters usually do not know what to expect.

p. 82 Reading Check Students should circle *he was a little lonely* and *had no companion for his old age.*

p. 82 Literary Analysis He gets his wish. He gets a wife almost instantly.

p. 83 Stop to Reflect Possible response: She may really be a swan.

p. 83 Literary Analysis (d) He knows what happens in fairy tales.

p. 84 Literary Analysis Students should circle *drives in the car* and *listen to the radio.*

p. 84 Read Fluently Possible response: Rhea is her swan-sister.

p. 84 Stop to Reflect Possible response: Mr. Peters may wish that he is together with his wife after he dies because he loves her so much.

p. 85 Literary Analysis Students should circle *no.* Students should circle the last sentence that describes Mr. Peters holding the withered leaf.

Review and Assess

1. He rescues a swan tangled in the weeds.

2. (b) He seems fed up with granting wishes and makes fun of human beings.

3. Possible response: His third wish was to be together in spirit with his wife. He knew she was still his companion.

4. Students should check *We are never comfortable . . . , Love sometimes means letting go . . . , What we wish for . . .* and *There are many different . . .*

5. In the first column students should list *three wishes; animals transforming;* and *unexpected outcomes.* In the second column students should list a *car; radio;* and *the offer of a trip around the world.*

6. The correct answers are *C* and *D*.

The Charge of the Light Brigade

p. 90 Literary Analysis The correct answer is *A*.

p. 90 Read Fluently The correct answer is *A*.

p. 90 Stop to Reflect The correct answer is *D*.

p. 91 Reading Check Students should answer *yes*. Students should circle *All that was left of them, Left of six hundred.*

Review and Assess

1. Students should check *They are riding . . . They are lightly armed . . . They are attacking.*
2. The correct answer is *A*.
3. Many of the soldiers are killed.
4. The correct answer is *B*.
5. On the first line students should write *cannon; them*. On the second line students should write *trapped*. On the third line students should write *battle*.
6. Fired on as frequently as rain drops in a storm.

The Californian's Tale

p. 96 Literary Analysis Students should circle *prospecting, pick, pan, horn,* and *strike.*

p. 96 Reading Strategy Students should circle the first sentence in the paragraph.

p. 97 Literary Analysis People were invited in and made welcome. Students should circle the last sentence of the paragraph.

p. 97 Stop to Reflect (c) He misses his own home.

p. 98 Reading Check (a) educated and a good storyteller. Students should circle *people who know things, and can talk—people like you.*

p. 98 Read Fluently Possible response: He may be lonely.

p. 99 Stop to Reflect Student should write *No*. Possible response: He may be embarrassed.

p. 100 Reading Check (b) thoughtful. Students should circle the entire paragraph to support their answer.

p. 100 Read Fluently disbelief or concern.

p. 100 Literary Analysis very; extremely.

p. 101 Literary Analysis Students should circle *fiddle, banjo, clarinet (p. 100), rattling dance-music,* and *big boots.*

p. 101 Literary Analysis Students should circle *right up the road.*

p. 101 Reading Strategy (a) Henry lost his mind when he lost his wife, and he gets worse on the anniversary of that loss. His friends play along to try to help him get through it.

p. 102 Stop to Reflect (d) all of the above

Review and Assess

1. (d) It is pretty and shows a woman's touch.
2. Students should write a *T* in front of *Henry talks about . . . , Henry lost his wife . . . , Henry's wife was well liked . . . ,* and *Henry's wife was an educated woman . . .* Students should write an *F* in front of *Henry's wife was an orphan* and *Henry's wife knew little about . . .*
3. The miners pretend she is coming home to help Henry through this rough time of the year.
4. (a) It could be lonely but those who were there were often kind and friendly.
5. First line: *friendly; folksy*. Second line: *colorful; descriptive*. Third line: *rural; homey*. Fourth line: *gathering together; playing musical instruments.*
6. Thirty-five years ago I panned for gold but I never found any.

Four Skinny Trees

p. 107 Reading Check (a) thin and scrawny. Students should circle *skinny* and *pointy.*

p. 107 Literary Analysis (b) If one person in a group loses his or her way, the whole group is affected.

p. 108 Reading Strategy (c) alone in a difficult world

Review and Assess

1. Both the speaker and the trees are skinny.
2. The speaker and the trees grow up in a poor city neighborhood.
3. Students should put a check in front of *strength, hope,* and *pride.*
4. First sentence: Students might write *Children do not belong in ghettos but often are raised there.* Second sentence: Students might write *Individual strengths are often hidden.* Third sentence: Students might write *Inner strength helps us reach high goals.*
5. Students should circle *(a) roots* and *(b) the trees' branches*

The Night the Bed Fell

p. 113 Reading Check Students should circle *it was wobbly and the heavy headboard would crash down on father's head in case the bed fell, and kill him.*

p. 113 Literary Analysis Students should circle *He thinks he needs to wake up every hour. Otherwise he might suffocate to death.*

p. 114 Reading Strategy Students should explain why they do or do not think it is significant.

p. 114 Reading Strategy The correct answer is (c).

p. 114 Reading Check Top Floor Attic: Mr. Thurber; Next Room: James and Briggs; In Hall: Rex, the dog; Across the Hall: Roy; Floor Below Attic: Mrs. Thurber and Herman

p. 115 Reading Strategy Students should explain what they think might happen. Yes. It is a significant event. It starts the chain of events.

p. 115 Stop to Reflect It's funny because the reason he uses the camphor is so that he can sniff it to revive his breathing because he is afraid he will stop breathing at night.

p. 115 Read Fluently Students should circle (b).

p. 116 Literary Analysis Students should circle the following: *He thinks the house is on fire; mother thinks he is trapped under his bed; "He's dying!" . . . "I'm all right!" Briggs yelled.*

p. 116 Reading Check Students should circle the following: *Father caught a cold.*

p. 116 Stop to Reflect Students should explain why they do or do not think it is funny.

Review and Assess

1. The correct answer is (a).
2. He does these things because he is afraid he will stop breathing at night.
3. Mother: She thinks her husband is trapped under the bed. Cousin Briggs:He thinks he is suffocating and everyone is trying to save him. Rex the Dog: He jumps on Briggs, thinking he is the culprit.
4. He probably exaggerated Briggs' fear of suffocation. The story of his Aunt Sarah leaving money for burglars outside her house might be an exaggeration. The story about his Aunt Gracie is probably an exaggeration when he says she piled shoes "about her house." The story of the dog jumping on Briggs might also be an exaggeration.
5. Students should check the following: The father goes up to the attic to sleep; Young James Thurber's cot collapses; The mother fears the attic bed fell and hurt or killed the father; Brother Herman yells to try to calm mother; Cousin Briggs pours camphor all over himself; Rex attacks Briggs; The father thinks the house is on fire and comes downstairs. Students should circle *Young James Thurber's cot collapses* as the event that causes all of the confusion.

All Summer in a Day

p. 121 Read Fluently Students should circle (a).

p. 121 Literary Analysis Students should circle the following: *Venus has known nothing but rain.*

p. 121 Reading Check They're the children of the men and women who came to Venus from Earth to set up a space colony.

p. 122 Reading Check Students should circle *nine.* They would have been two years old when they saw the sun before.

p. 122 Reading Strategy Margot: quiet and shy; William: bold and mean

p. 122 Literary Analysis Students should circle the following: *in the echoing tunnels of the underground city.*

p. 122 Stop to Reflect Possible answer: She only sings songs about the sun because she misses the sun and dislikes the rain.

p. 123 Reading Strategy Students should circle the following contrasts: *[Margot has] lived on Venus for only five years. Before that, she lived on Earth./The rest of the children have lived all of their lives on Venus. She remembers the sun./Because they were only two when they saw the sun,* *the don't remember it.* Possible answer: Margot's past experience might be considered a "crime" to the others because she is able to remember something they wish they could remember. They are probably jealous.

p. 123 Reading Strategy Students should circle the following: *Margot's parents are thinking of moving back to earth.* The children probably hate her for this because they are jealous.

p. 123 Reading Check Margot came to Venus five years ago, when she was four. She came from Earth.

p. 124 Reading Strategy Students should circle the following words: *protesting, pleading,* and *crying.* The other children are mean.

p. 124 Stop to Reflect Students should explain what they think will happen to Margot.

p. 124 Literary Analysis Students should circle *the jungle burned with sunlight.* The correct answer is (b) thick rain forest.

p. 125 Reading Check She cries because the raindrop means the sunlight is ending and the rain will start again soon.

p. 126 Stop to Reflect Students will probably say that she will feel very angry and sad.

Review and Assess

1. For seven years, it has rained constantly.

2. she is from Earth and remembers the sun; are mean to her; regret.

3. The correct answer is (b).

4. Students should check the following: Children can be mean to one another; Outsiders are often treated badly; If you are mean, you may regret it later.

5. 1. "Sometimes there were light showers; sometimes there were heavy storms; but always there was rain." 2. "She doesn't play games with the other children in the echoing tunnels of their underground city." 3. "It was the color of flaming bronze and it was very large. And the sky around it was a blazing blue tile color."

6. *Similarities:* Margot and her classmates 1. live on Venus 2. are nine years old 3. are eager to see the sun

Differences: 1. Margot remembers the sun. Her classmates do not remember the sun. 2. She has been living on Venus for only five years. Her classmates have been living on Venus their entire lives. 3. Margot did not get to see the sun because she was locked away in a closet. Her classmates went out and played in the sun.

The Highwayman

p. 131 Reading Check Students should write *night* on the line. Then, they should circle the following text: *The highways, or roads, had many inns where travelers stopped at night. Sometimes travelers were held up by robbers called highwaymen.*

p. 131 Stop to Reflect Students should circle (a). The details that point to the answer are *a French cocked-hat, a bunch of lace at his chin, a coat of claret velvet, breeches of brown doeskin,* and *a jeweled twinkle.*

p. 132 Literary Analysis He's probably jealous and dislikes the highwayman. He might try to get the highwayman in trouble.

p. 132 Reading Strategy The highwayman has probably robbed someone.

p. 133 Literary Analysis Students should circle the following: *they gag Bess and tie her to her bed by the window. They tie a gun called a musket to her, with the barrel below her heart.*

p. 133 Read Fluently The correct answer is (c).

p. 134 Literary Analysis The following words add to the suspense: *Nearer he came and nearer!; Her eyes grew wide for a moment; she drew one last deep breath.* Students might wonder if Bess will be able to let the highwayman know that the soldiers are after him.

p. 134 Literary Analysis He wants to go back to fight the soldiers because of what they did to Bess. Students should circle the following: *he spurred like a madman; with white road smoking behind him and his rapier brandished high.*

p. 134 Reading Check Bess shot herself while trying to sound off a gun shot to warn the highwayman that the soldiers were after him.

p. 135 Reading Check The correct answer is (c).

Review and Assess

1. He doesn't want anyone to see him because he is wanted by the law.

2. Highwayman: dashing, romantic, loyal; Bess: beautiful, romantic, brave, loyal; Tim: jealous.

3. The correct answer is (d).

4. The following details help build suspense: 1. Tied up and gagged, Bess desperately wants to warn her love of the danger that awaits him. 2. "The highwayman came riding/The redcoats looked to their priming." 3. "Nearer he came and nearer! Her face was like a light."

5. Tim probably told the authorities that the highwayman was at the inn because he likes Bess and is jealous of their love.

6. *Cause:* Bess pulls the trigger because she is trying to sound off a gun shot to warn the highwayman that the soldiers are waiting to get him. *Effects:* Bess kills herself. The highwayman hears the warning shot and rides away.

Amigo Brothers

p. 140 Think Ahead Students should circle *each youngster had a dream of someday becoming lightweight champion of the world.* Problems can develop in their friendship if they someday have to compete for a title.

p. 140 Reading Check What: division finals; When: seventh of August, two weeks away.

p. 140 Reading Strategy The wall is probably created by the tension they feel because they have to compete against each other.

p. 141 Literary Analysis Students should circle *Antonio nodded* and underline *Antonio.*

p. 141 Reading Check No. Students should circle *only one of us can win.*

p. 141 Read Fluently gotta: got to; don'tcha: don't you

p. 142 Literary Analysis Felix: he had figured out how to psyche himself for tomorrow's fight; Antonio: Antonio was also thinking of the fight/Antonio went to sleep hearing the opening bell for the first round. The narrator is omniscient or "all knowing."

p. 142 Reading Strategy Yes. His worry and concern over their friendship shows he cares.

p. 142 Stop to Reflect Students should explain what they think the boys are thinking.

p. 143 Reading Strategy The correct answer is (c). The words *He [Felix] missed a right cross as Antonio slipped the punch and countered with one-two-three lefts that snapped Felix's head back* help you make the inference.

p. 144 Literary Analysis Felix: Felix's legs momentarily buckled; Antonio: his long legs turned to jelly. The author uses their first names, rather than just "he" to make the shift in point of view.

p. 145 Reading Check Neither boy is winning.

p. 145 Stop to Reflect They probably keep fighting because they've become completely wrapped up in what they are doing and they don't hear the bell.

p. 145 Reading Strategy The correct answer is (d). Students should circle *No matter what the decision, they knew they would always be champions to each other.*

p. 145 Reading Check The announcer points to no one as the winner because the boys have already left the ring, arm in arm.

Review and Assess

1. The correct answer is (b).

2. How it brings them together: they worked out together and went running together. How it drives them apart: They have to compete against each other, and only one person can win.

3. Tall—A; short—F; dark—F; fair—A; boxes better when he comes in close—F; boxes more gracefully—A; has better moves as a boxer—F; keeps boring in on his opponent—F

4. Friendship is more important than winning.

5. Felix: 1. Felix knew they could not "pull their punches," or hold back when they fought 2. he had figured out how to psyche himself

   Referee: The referee was stunned by their savagery.

   Crowd: The fear soon gave way . . .

6. Antonio and Felix work very hard to fulfill their dreams about boxing; The Golden Gloves is an important tournament in the world of boxing.

Unit 5

Our Finest Hour

p. 151 Reading Check Students should circle the following words: *means sitting there in the studio and telling some stories into the camera and introducing the reports and pieces that other reporters do.* Students should circle (a) the main announcer.

p. 151 Literary Analysis Some problems will probably arise. The people who are usually in charge are away.

p. 152 Reading Strategy Students will probably circle the following text: *It was not the story I had introduced.* Students should circle answer (c).

p. 152 Literary Analysis They thought they had fixed the problem, but they had not. A political story from Washington, D. C. was supposed to be introduced, but pictures of people in France pretending to be dead to show the dangers of smoking came up on the monitor.

p. 152 Stop to Reflect Students should circle the following text: *since nobody in authority at CBS News, New York, had seen it or knew what was coming next, they decided to dump out of it.* Possible answer: People pretending to be dead might be disturbing to some people.

p. 153 Literary Analysis Students should circle the following: *French people pretending to be dead and myself, bewilderment and all.* The fact that he sees himself is funny because he's feeling bewildered by what is happening, he doesn't realize they are coming back to him, and then he sees himself with a look of bewilderment on his face.

p. 153 Read Fluently Students should circle (a).

Review and Assess

1. Students should circle answer (d).
2. Students should circle *calm* and *professional*.
3. No. His words are a follow-up to the fill-in producer yelling "What is going on?" so he was probably having fun with what had happened.
4. **Supposed to Happen:** He introduced his first report. **Actually Happened:** He saw himself on the monitor and then a different story was introduced. **Supposed to Happen:** He introduced a political story from Washington, D. C. **Actually Happened:** Pictures of people in France pretending to be dead to show the dangers of smoking came up on the monitor. **Supposed to Happen:** Osgood introduced a story about rafting. **Actually Happened:** Nothing happened on the monitor.
5. Any of the following details show that the author's purpose is mainly to entertain:
   - Osgood starts by explaining that he introduced his first report and then builds to make his point that a story came on that was not the story he introduced.
   - Then, Osgood explains that a political story from Washington, D. C. was supposed to be introduced, but pictures of people in France pretending to be dead to show the dangers of smoking came up on the monitor.
   - He explains how the monitor shows him with a bewildered look on his face.
   - He tells us how the fill-in producer screamed so loud "half of America" could hear him.
   - He ends his story by telling us the humorous way that the head of CBS responded to the incident.

Cat on the Go

p. 158 Literary Analysis Students should circle the following: *I went home for a blanket and brought 'im round to you.*

p. 158 Reading Strategy Students should circle answer (b). The words *terrible wound* show us that the cat is very badly hurt. The words *There's nothing anybody can do about . . . about that* also show us that it seems like a hopeless situation for the cat.

p. 159 Think Ahead Some students may think he will survive because his purrs are a positive sign.

p. 159 Reading Strategy Students should circle (a) try.

p. 159 Stop to Reflect He needs to sit still so that he can rest and heal.

p. 159 Reading Check The correct answer is (b).

p. 160 Literary Analysis He is playful and friendly.

p. 160 Reading Check Students should circle *odd* and *unusual*.

p. 160 Literary Analysis Students should circle *seemed to enjoy himself, enjoyed the slides*, and *was very interested in the cakes*.

p. 161 Read Fluently Students should circle *He's a natural mixer* and *cat-about-town*.

p. 161 Stop to Reflect Students should explain why they think he is named Tiger. Students might mention that tigers are in the cat family. Others might mention that tigers are very strong.

p. 161 Literary Analysis Possible answer: considerate and generous.

p. 162 Think Ahead Possible response: He's probably visiting an event in the area.

p. 162 Literary Analysis Students should circle *delight*. The correct answer is (a) She is warm and caring.

Review and Assess

1. The correct answer is *C*.
2. He purrs after being seriously injured. He likes to be a cat-about-town.
3. The Herriots are very sad about returning Oscar, but they also realize that he should be with his original owners because they had him first and they love him very much.
4. The correct answer is *B*.
5. Oscar the Cat: friendly and affectionate; James Herriot: skilled as a doctor and a good storyteller; Helen Herriot: caring
6. Oscar was always visiting people and places. Let's try this. The two boys screamed with excitement.

The Luckiest Time of All

p. 167 Reading Strategy Students should circle the following text: *somethin like the circus*.

p. 167 Reading Check Students should circle the following text: *wanted to join that thing and see the world*.

p. 167 Literary Analysis Students should circle the following text: *cutest one thing in the world next to you*. It is an exaggeration because she doesn't really mean that it's the cutest in the world, she is just stressing the point that she thinks it is a very cute dog.

p. 168 Literary Analysis Students should circle *I flew*. She probably exaggerates so that her great-granddaughter can appreciate the excitement of the moment.

p. 168 Stop to Reflect The traits Elzie seems to like are kindness and gentleness. Students should circle the following: *he had picked up that poor dog to see if he was hurt, cradlin him and talking to him soft and sweet*.

p. 169 Read Fluently Elzie says she is luckier than anybody for meeting her husband, but then in the last sentences she says that *most* of the time she thinks she's lucky. There are probably times when she's frustrated with her husband, so she's being funny when she says "Least mostly I think it."

Review and Assess

1. Students should circle two of the following words: adventurous, fun-loving, and shy. Adventurous: they want to join Silas Greene to see the world. Fun-loving: They want to join in on the excitement when they see the dancing dog and people throwing money for the dog. Shy: Elzie says she felt shy when she walked toward Amos.
2. Students should circle the following words: heroic, thoughtful, protective, nice.
3. It was unlucky because it hit the dog's nose and the dog chased her. It's lucky because the dog-chase led to her meeting her husband.
4. One example is when she calls the dog the "cutest one thing in the world next to you." Another example is when she refers to Amos as the "finest fast runnin hero in . . . Virginia." Another example is when she says the dog "lit out after me and I flew."
5. After all those years, she can look back and see how important that funny experience was in her life. She can realize how different life probably would have been for her if she had not had that experience. Certain moments probably stand out in her mind more than other

moments, so her use of hyperbole helps stress those particular moments and add more excitement to her story.

6. (c) spotted; (b) holding gently

How the Snake Got Poison

p. 174 Reading Check Students should circle *ladder*. The ladder is probably supposed to lead to heaven.

p. 174 Read Fluently Students should circle *Ah* for *I* and *de* for *the*.

p. 175 Literary Analysis The snake feels he needs protection so he won't be stomped on and so that his generation won't be killed off, but the small animals feel they need protection from the snake so he won't kill them and their generations.

p. 175 Reading Strategy Students should circle *B*. Students should explain why they agree or disagree.

p. 175 Stop to Reflect If the snake sees his enemy he will probably go after him.

Review and Assess

1. God gives the snake poison so that he'll be protected and so that his generation won't be killed off.

2. The correct answer is *C*.

3. The story couldn't end that way because in reality snakes are poisonous and have rattles.

4. The small animals complain that the snake's poison is killing their generations. The snake explains that he has to protect himself because all he sees is feet coming to step on him and he can't tell who is his enemy and who is his friend.

5. Students should check the following: *A snake's rattles protect small animals from the snake; All types of animals created by God deserve to remain on earth; Animals have special traits or abilities to help them survive.*

Unit 6

Rikki-tikki-tavi

p. 180 Reading Check Students should circle a *small furry animal that kills snakes*. The word *bungalow* is also explained in this paragraph. Students should put a box around the word *bungalow* and circle the words *one-story house*.

p. 180 Stop to Reflect Students should circle *Here's a dead mongoose. Lets have a funeral.* It is funny because Rikki was not dead.

p. 180 Literary Analysis (b) He is nosey. Students should circle *he is eaten up from the nose to tail with curiosity. The motto of all the mongoose family is "Run and find out.*

p. 181 Reading Check Students should circle *One of our babies fell out of the nest yesterday and Nag ate him.*

p. 181 Reading Strategy (b) they will fight. Students may write *The father says he will protect Teddy from snakes.*

p. 181 Literary Analysis (b) rising action

p. 182 Reading Strategy Rikki thinks he will fight Nag later.

p. 182 Reading Check Students should circle *It must be the head.* Possible response: Yes, because Rikki is a born snake killer.

p. 183 Literary Analysis Rikki will defeat Nag.

p. 183 Reading Strategy (a) try to kill Nagaina. Even with Nag dead, Nagaina is still a danger.

p. 184 Stop to Reflect Students should check *She is a concerned mother; She is angry . . . ,*

p. 184 Read Fluently (a) He wants to take her attention away from the family.

p 185 Literary Analysis Nagaina is killed by Rikki. Killing the last villain helps fix the problem.

p. 185 Literary Analysis He has become a hero and is welcomed by the whole family.

Review and Assess

1. Students should circle *brave, nosey*.

2. Mongooses are born to kill snakes; Rikki wants to protect Teddy from the cobra.

3. (d) He wants to clear the garden of deadly cobras.

4. 1. Nag eats a baby bird. 2. Nagaina sneaking up behind Rikki to do him harm. 3. Karait striking at Rikki.

5. The climax is when Nag is killed.

6. Students should write *We learn that Rikki is a natural predator of snakes; Rikki hears Nagaina mention the eggs are soon to hatch; Nagaina snuck up behind Rikki.*

After Twenty Years

p. 190 Reading Strategy Students should circle *the man* and *spoke*. Students should then use lines to separate the beginning and end of the sentence.

p. 190 Stop to Reflect The man wants to ease the concern of the police officer that he might be there for criminal reasons.

p. 190 Read Fluently Students should circle *Jimmy Wells, my best chum, and the finest chap in the world.*

p. 191 Reading Check Students should circle *to make my fortune.*

p. 191 Literary Analysis The police officer may be Jimmy Wells.

p. 191 Reading Check Students should circle *I've had to compete with some of the sharpest wits going to get my pile . . .*

p. 192 Literary Analysis Students should circle *with collar turned up to his ears.* This may mean the man is not Jimmy Wells.

p. 192 Stop to Reflect (c) Both a and b seem likely.

p. 193 Literary Analysis Most students will be surprised by this ending. The ending makes sense because it allows Jimmy to do his duty by having Bob arrested, while not making himself arrest his old friend.

Review and Assess

1. Bob and Jimmy agreed to meet at a specific time and place.

2. (b) They were close in childhood but have taken different paths in life.

3. Students should check *He wants to keep a promise . . . , He wants to show off . . . , He is curious . . .*

4. Jimmy is unable to arrest Bob himself because of the friendship and bond they once had.

5. Jimmy recognizes Bob as a criminal, the reader learns that Jimmy is the police officer, and Jimmy has another officer pose as himself to arrest Bob.

6. The police officer knows about the restaurant and when it was torn down; The police officer is probing Bob for details of his success out west.

7. Students should circle *a man leaned.* Students should draw lines between *store* and *a*, and between *leaned* and *with*. The man leaned in the doorway of a darkened hardware store. An unlit cigar was in his mouth.

Papa's Parrot

p. 198 Stop to Reflect Students should circle *Though* and *merely.* (b) Harry's

p. 198 Reading Strategy Students should answer yes. Harry is making friends and becoming interested in things other than the candy store.

p. 199 Literary Analysis Students should circle *embarrassed* and label it *D*. Students should circle *he keeps walking* and label it *I*.

p. 199 Reading Check Students should circle all words in quotation marks. Students should label *H* any phrase followed by *Harry said* or *Harry mumbled*. Students should label the other circled words *R*.

p. 200 Reading Fluently (a) annoyed

p. 200 Stop to Reflect His father

Review and Assess

1. Students should check *He has outgrown the store . . . , He and his friends now . . . , He is embarrassed . . .*

2. (d)

3. Harry learns that his father is lonely and misses him.

4. Students should write *Harry Tillian liked his papa.* Students should write *Mr. Tillian looked forward to seeing his son.*

5. Students should write *he keeps walking.* Students should write *Harry had always stopped in to see his father at work.*

6. Students should write *yes* or *no* and explain their responses.

Ribbons

p. 205 Read Fluently Students should circle *She's here! She's here!* and *"Paw-paw's here!"*

p. 205 Reading Check Students should circle *Chinese for grandmother.* Students should write *mother*

p. 205 Reading Strategy Students should circle *What's wrong with her feet?* Students might ask *Why is she sensitive?*

p. 206 Reading Check Ballet Lessons; her room

p. 206 Stop to Reflect Answers will vary.

p. 207 Literary Analysis Students should circle *Grandmother is a hero.*

p. 207 Reading Strategy Students might ask *Why didn't the mother explain the ribbons to the grandmother?*

p. 208 Think Ahead That something is wrong with Grandmother's feet.

p. 208 Reading Strategy Students should circle *What happened to your feet?* Students might ask *Was that very painful?*

p. 208 Literary Analysis (a) People try to spare their loved ones from pain.

p. 209 Literary Analysis Students should check *People will undergo . . . , People will do painful things . . .*

p. 209 Stop to Reflect The invisible ribbon is a bond between the women.

Review and Assess

1. Students should check *Grandmother is a brave woman . . . , Grandmother values freedom . . .*

2. (d) She can talk more with Ian, who has learned more Chinese.

3. Grandmother thinks the ribbons are for binding Stacy's feet.

4. (d) the loving family ties between Stacy, her mother, and Grandmother.

5. Students should check *Love and understanding . . . , We don't want those we love . . . , The best way to know a person . . .*

6. Students may ask questions such as *Why is grandmother so secretive? Because she is trying to shield her granddaughter. Why does grandmother treat Stacy differently than Ian? Because that is Chinese culture. What did grandmother's feet look like? Deformed.*

The Treasure of Lemon Brown

p. 214 Reading Check Students should circle *dark* or *angry.* Students should circle (b) His father won't let him join the Scorpions.

p. 214 Reading Strategy Answers will vary. *Is Greg afraid to be in the building?*

p. 215 Stop to Reflect Students may say that Greg's father was trying to encourage Greg to work hard.

p. 215 Read Fluently Students should circle (a) He fears being attacked.

p. 215 Reading Strategy Students will have varying questions.

p. 216 Reading Strategy Students will have varying questions. *How old is he?*

p. 216 Literary Analysis Students should circle *Every man got a treasure. You don't know that, you must be a fool!*

p. 216 Stop to Reflect Students should circle *No.* Students should circle *You got any money?*

p. 217 Think Ahead Answers will vary. *Greg will make scary sounds.*

p. 217 Read Fluently (c) proud

p. 217 Literary Analysis Students should circle *Brown felt like his son would be able to do something since he knew his father had.* (c) Greg's father telling how he studied hard to pass the postal test.

p. 218 Literary Analysis Students should circle (b) We often work harder for those we love.

p. 218 Stop to Reflect Lemon's experiences may allow Greg to realize the accomplishments of his father and will bring Greg and his dad closer together.

p. 219 Stop to Reflect Possible response: Greg smiles because he can now appreciate his father's lecture. He is looking forward to listening to his father.

Review and Assess

1. (d) He is blocks from home, and the rain is very heavy.

2. (c) They have heard that Brown has a treasure and want to steal it.

3. poor: homeless/lives in empty old building; dresses in rags

talented: got good reviews for playing harmonica and singing blues

loved family: traveled all over, working hard, to support his wife and son

proud: gave clippings of reviews of his performances to his son

sad: grieves for loss of wife and son

4. his old harmonica and clippings of old reviews of his performances

5. Students should put a check in front of *A person's achievements are a treasure that can be passed down* and *Just about everyone has a treasure of some kind.*

6. Possible question: What is Lemon Brown's treasure? Answer: an old harmonica he used to play when he performed, and clippings of old reviews of his performances

Possible question: Why does the treasure have special meaning to him? Answer: He gave it to his son, who treasured it and had it with him when he was killed in the war.

Possible question: What does Greg learn from Lemon Brown? Answer: to value his father's proud achievements and concern for Greg

Unit 7

I Am a Native of North America

p. 224 Reading Check The entire family lived in grandfather's house.

p. 224 Reading Check People learned to live with one another; learned to help one another; learned to respect the rights of one another.

p. 225 Reading Strategy Students should circle *They stripped the land and poisoned the water and air.*

p. 225 Stop to Reflect If we do not show love completely we are no better than the lowest of all animals. Answers will vary. Possible response: The ability to love is a special gift and if we choose not to use it we have refused the greatest gift of being human.

p. 225 Literary Analysis Without love we become weak.

p. 226 Stop to Reflect Answers will vary. In a perfect world this would make sense but it does not seem possible in the real modern day environment.

p. 226 Reading Strategy Students should write *Many young people have forgotten the old ways. They have been made to feel ashamed of their Indian ways.*

p. 226 Reading Check Native Americans must forgive the terrible sufferings the white society brought.

Review and Assess

1. Native American and White Society

2. Native Americans view nature as a gift that should be respected.

3. The author's idea of brotherhood is love and forgiveness.

4. Under *Native American Culture* students should write *People learn to respect the rights of their neighbors through communal living; People love and respect nature.* Under *White Society* students should write *People live near one another but do not know or care about their neighbors; People abuse nature.*

5. The author provided support for his main idea by explaining how well the Native American culture lived. He compares how the Native Americans used their natural resources to how the white society abused them.

All Together Now

p. 231 Reading Check Individuals can solve the race problem in America by being more tolerant.

p. 231 Reading Check No. People bring peace between races, not laws.

p. 231 Literary Analysis Students should underline *Each of us can decide to have one friend of a different race or background.*

p. 232 Reading Strategy Students should underline *Babies come into the world as blank as slates* and *Children learn ideas and attitudes from the adults*

p. 232 Literary Analysis Students should circle *Parents can actively encourage their children to be in the company of people* *who are of other racial and ethnic backgrounds.*

p. 232 Stop to Reflect It is easier to make small changes than it is to try to solve the whole problem.

Review and Assess

1. people
2. Civil Rights Act of 1964; Voting Rights Act of 1965. Laws cannot create tolerance; people's attitudes have to change.
3. The author means babies are innocent and can be taught anything by their parents and teachers.
4. The author is dedicated to bringing people together. She wants people to work towards racial peace.
5. Possible response: Do the supporting details make sense? Do they persuade me to accept the author's point of view? Students' responses to the second question may vary, but they should explain their answers.

How to Enjoy Poetry

p. 237 Literary Analysis Students should underline *When you really feel it, a new part of you happens, or an old part is renewed, with surprise and delight at being what it is.*

p. 237 Reading Check Things; actions; feelings

p. 237 Reading Check Poetry comes to you from outside you.

p. 238 Reading Strategy Students should underline *Poetry can describe the sun and stars in different ways and from different perspectives.*

p. 238 Literary Analysis Dickey explains how to begin writing poetry.

p. 238 Reading Strategy (b) It hints at the way a poem flows, or sounds, when you read it. Students should explain their responses.

p. 239 Literary Analysis Students should underline *Almost anything put into rhythm and rhyme is more memorable than the same thing said in prose.*

p. 239 Stop to Reflect Yes. Both reading and writing poetry help you to look at your own life differently. Reading and writing poetry help you make connections between things that you have never connected before.

Review and Assess

1. (c) poetry comes to you from outside you and something from within you must meet it
2. Giving to poetry means allowing yourself to get into the words and feel their meanings.
3. Rhythm and rhyme are important to poetry because they make the words more memorable and more pleasant to read.
4. Dickey explains that poetry can uncover a new part of you, and he explains how poetry comes to you from the outside.
5. 1. When you really feel poetry, a new part of you happens. 2. To understand poetry is to know it comes to you from outside. 3. You must make a gut connection with the poetry.

"The Chase" *from* An American Childhood

p. 244 Literary Analysis Students should circle *all out* and *Your fate . . . depended on your concentration and courage.*

p. 244 Reading Strategy The author wants the reader to know she enjoys competition and sports.

p. 244 Reading Check The black car stops because it was hit with snowballs.

p. 245 Reading Strategy Students should circle *He was in city clothes: a suit and tie, street shoes.* The purpose for including this information is to describe the challenge this driver took on when he decided to chase the kids in the snow.

p. 245 Literary Analysis Students should underline *You have to throw yourself into an activity with all of your energy if you want to win.*

p. 245 Stop to Reflect Students answers will vary.

p. 246 Literary Analysis Dillard's description of the events tells us she enjoys challenges and seeks excitement.

p. 246 Reading Strategy Dillard wants to show the level of difficulty and the toll the chase has taken on the pursuer.

p. 246 Literary Analysis Students should underline *The point was that he chased us passionately without giving up, and so he had caught us.*

p. 247 Reading Check Dillard feels the most satisfying thing about her experience is that she went all out and did her very best in a challenging situation.

Review and Assess

1. Dillard enjoys the competition and mental and physical aspects of football.
2. Dillard is outgoing. Dillard is competitive.

3. Dillard feels the man was a worthy opponent. She tells us this by describing how difficult the chase was for everyone involved.
4. A passage that entertains: *He ran after us, and we ran away . . . we were running for our lives.* A passage that teaches a lesson: *Then she realized that the man knew the same thing she did: You have to throw yourself into an activity with all your energy if you want to win.* A passage that explains something about the author: *Your fate . . . Nothing girls did could compare to it.*

Unit 8

A Christmas Carol: Scrooge and Marley, Act 1, Scenes 1 & 2

p. 252 Reading Strategy Students should respond with their own ideas of what a ghost looks like.

p. 252 Vocabulary (b) joke

p. 253 Vocabulary A poulterer sells poultry.

p. 253 Reading Check The story takes place on Christmas Eve, 1843.

p. 253 Read Fluently Make sure that students can pronounce all the words in the speech. Explain any words they don't understand.

p. 254 Reading Strategy Students should circle *ancient, awful, dead-eyed*

p. 254 Reading Strategy Students may say that Scrooge might jump or open his eyes and mouth wide.

p. 254 Reading Check He doesn't think his nephew should be merry because he is poor.

p. 254 Literary Analysis Bah! Humbug!

p. 255 Stop to Reflect (c) making money

p. 255 Reading Check Students should underline *But Scrooge rudely refuses.*

p. 255 Reading Strategy Students should draw a diagram that reflects the scene.

p. 256 Literary Analysis Students should circle *Cratchit smiles faintly.*

p. 256 Reading Check Cratchit gets one day off a year.

p. 256 Reading Check Cratchit wants to say Merry Christmas. Scrooge hates Christmas.

p. 256 Reading Strategy The scenery changes from an office to a street scene. Music is heard. People walk by.

p. 257 Literary Analysis Possible response: Scrooge is grumpy and snaps at passing boys. The other characters are happy and cheerful.

Review and Assess

1. Jacob Marley is Scrooge's former business partner. He is a ghost in this play.
2. Scenes 1 and 2 take place in Scrooge's place of business, a countinghouse.
3. Scrooge is stingy and he doesn't want to pay Cratchit for a day when he doesn't work.
4. *Things Scrooge Says:*
   Bah! Humbug!
   Every idiot who goes about with "Merry Christmas" on his lips, should be boiled with his own pudding, and buried with a stake of holly through his heart.
   Things Scrooge Does:
   He refuses to go to his nephew's for Christmas dinner.
   He refuses to give the kind men a donation for the poor.
5. *How he moves:* Possible response: He walks slowly, with a cane. He is bent over.
   His facial expressions: Possible response: He frowns. He says mean things under his breath. He tries to hit people with his cane.

A Christmas Carol: Scrooge and Marley, Act 1, Scenes 3–5

p. 262 Reading Check He sees Jacob Marley's face on the door knocker.

p. 262 Reading Strategy Students should circle *horrible to look at, pigtail, vest, suit as usual, drags an enormous chain, is transparent*

p. 262 Reading Check cash-boxes, keys, padlocks, ledgers, deeds, heavy purses of steel. Possible response: All Marley cared about in life was money, so he has to drag these things around as a punishment.

p. 263 Literary Analysis Students should draw a sketch of the scene as it is described.

p. 263 Reading Check He screams a ghostly scream and takes off his head.

p. 263 Stop to Reflect He did not care for other people during his life. All he cared about was money.

p. 263 Reading Strategy Students should use their imaginations to picture this figure. Possible response: A child with the head of an old man.

p. 264 Literary Analysis Students should circle the words *sir, really, please do understand*

p. 264 Literary Analysis Students should circle *panicked*

p. 264 Reading Strategy It is a snowy day in the country.

p. 265 Reading Check Students should underline *he thinks of the young caroler whom he shooed away from his office earlier that night. He says he wishes he had given him something.*

p. 265 Reading Check He thinks about Cratchit. He wishes that he had been kinder to him.

p. 265 Reading Strategy They describe how the boy Ebenezer is replaced by a man Ebenezer. The co-workers disappear and a young woman in mourning clothes appears.

p. 266 Reading Check money

p. 266 Reading Check The world is hard on people who are poor and it punishes people who try to be rich.

p. 266 Stop to Reflect He wishes that he had done things differently.

p. 267 Reading Check She is releasing him from marrying her.

p. 267 Stop to Reflect Answers will vary. Students should describe something happy that they want to see again.

p. 267 Reading Check The ghost of Christmas Past appears, Scrooge sees himself as a lonely boy in the schoolhouse. Scrooge sees his former boss and coworkers. Scrooge sees himself and a woman.

Review and Assess

1. Marley's ghost has to carry the chain because he didn't care for other people in life.
2. The Ghost of Christmas Past visits Scrooge after Marley leaves.
3. Scrooge as a young boy: Scrooge cries.
   Scrooge as a twelve-year-old boy: He says he loved his sister.
   Scrooge with his coworkers: He wishes he had been kinder to Cratchit.
   Scrooge with his fiancée: He yells "No!"
4. Scrooge was a lonely boy. Scrooge had a sister whom he loved. Scrooge was engaged at one time.
5. He panics.

Unit 9

The Cremation of Sam McGee

p. 272 Reading Strategy Students should underline *it stabbed like a driven nail.* The cold air is being compared to a driven nail as it stabs through the parka into the body.

p. 272 Reading Check Sam McGee was miserable because he was from the south and wasn't used to cold weather.

p. 272 Reading Strategy Students should circle *chilled clean through to the bone.*

p. 272 Reading Check Last remains refers to a dead body.

p. 273 Literary Analysis Sam dies from the cold.

p. 273 Stop to Reflect Possible response: The fire may warm Sam back to life.

p. 273 **Literary Analysis** Students should circle *snow* and *know*. Students should draw a box around *fear* and *near*. Student should draw arrows from *out* to *about*; from *dread* to *said*; from *cooked* to *looked*; and from *wide* to *inside*.

p. 274 **Literary Analysis** Students should check *Character*, *Setting*, and *Plot*. Sam the *character* is speaking, the cold *setting* is described, and the *plot* is covered by Sam speaking and the narration.

Review and Assess

1. unbearably cold
2. He is trying to earn money.
3. He promises to cremate Sam's body.
4. Sam felt so bad, the narrator felt obligated to keep his promise.
5. Sam McGee sitting up getting warm.
6. 1. setting: The cold Arctic. 2. characters: Sam McGee. 3. rhythm: Well he seemed so low that I couldn't say no.
7. Students should complete the *What it means* part with *it was unbearably cold; a very bright smile*; and *I tried not to be afraid.*

Annabel Lee

p. 279 **Reading Check** She died from the cold.

p. 279 **Literary Analysis** Students should circle *me, sea, chilling, killing*, and *Lee*.

p. 279 **Reading Strategy** The moon and stars remind me of Annabel Lee.

p, 279 **Literary Analysis** Students should read the bracketed lines aloud putting emphasis on the underlined words.

p. 280 **Stop to Reflect** 1. Lonely. 2. Angry. 3. Bitter

Review and Assess

1. The narrator blames the angels and the cold for Annabel Lee's death. The narrator believes the angels were jealous of the love between him and Annabel.
2. The narrator talks about the sea because the young lovers lived near the sea.
3. Students should underline *love, stronger far, love those, older, we, many, wiser,* and *we*
4. Students should list *beams/dreams,*

rise/eyes, sea/Lee, and *nighttide/bride/side* as the sets of rhyming words in the final stanza.
5. The moon and stars remind me of Annabel Lee.

Maestro

p. 285 **Reading Strategy** *Upturned* means to be facing upwards. Students should write the words *turned up*.

p. 285 **Reading Check** He hears his mother's voice.

p. 285 **Stop to Reflect** A song can be sung so beautifully that one might describe it as tasting great rather than sounding great. *Sweet on the tongue* is an example of this.

Review and Assess

1. The voice, the guitar, and the violin.
2. Sentimental, happy, proud.
3. Students should circle the word *strummed*.
4. Under *Clues that help Clarify*, students should write *in the air; to snare*. Beneath *Clarified Meaning*, students should write *to be tossed up in the air*.

The Village Blacksmith

p. 290 **Literary Analysis** Students should circle *his brawny arms are strong as iron bands*. This comparison tells us that the blacksmith has great strength.

p. 290 **Reading Strategy** Students should circle the words *he hears the parson pray and preach, he hears his daughter's voice*.

p. 290 **Reading Check** The blacksmith cries because he is remembering his wife who has passed away.

p. 291 **Stop to Reflect** Human lives often involve hard work under difficult circumstances and conditions. A hard fought life can be rewarding also like the work of the blacksmith.

Review and Assess

1. The blacksmith's life is difficult. His daily work involves dealing with extreme heat and lifting heavy materials.
2. Rough; large; strong.
3. His daughter singing reminds the blacksmith of his dead wife.

4. The correct answer is a furnace.
5. In the spaces under *Sense*, students should write *Sight; Touch; Sound*. In the spaces under *Sensory Language*, students

should write *Spreading chestnut tree; Strong as iron hands; He hears the parson pray and preach*.

Unit 10

Popocatepetl and Ixtlaccihuatl

p. 296 Reading Check Tenochtitlan

p. 297 Reading Strategy Students should read ahead to see if the Emperor makes wise decisions.

p. 297 Reading Check Students should underline *forbade her to marry*.

p. 297 Reading Check The Emperor trusted no one.

p. 298 Reading Strategy Answers will vary. The Emperor must have had wisdom to rule for so long. The Emperor never had wisdom if he forbade his daughter to marry.

p. 298 Reading Check As a reward, the emperor offers the hand of his daughter and the equal right to reign and rule Tenochtitlan.

p. 298 Literary Analysis Aztecs regarded warriors as heroes and war as a battle for honor.

p. 298 Reading Check The warriors report false news because they were jealous of Popo's success.

p. 299 Reading Check Ixtla dies because she believes her love has been killed in battle.

p. 299 Reading Strategy Student should read ahead to find details about Popo that make him more than an ordinary man.

p. 299 Literary Analysis The warriors could not have built the pyramid in one day. This is part of the folk tale that makes it sound miraculous.

p. 299 Reading Check He carried her body to the top of the pyramid and buried it under a heap of stones.

p. 300 Literary Analysis Students should check *Popo had two pyramids . . . , Popo stood next to Ixtla's . . .*

p. 300 Stop to Reflect No. This is an Aztec folk tale that was written as a fictional account of the mountains' origins.

Review and Assess

1. The emperor forbids them to marry.
2. By offering his daughter as a reward, he does not recognize her wishes.
3. Students should circle (a) The kingdom ends up with no ruler.
4. Ixtla dies because she believes the man she loves has been killed in battle.
5. Reading ahead sometimes helps you better understand what is happening earlier.
6. Possible responses: smoke in the memory of the princess; pyramids that change to volcanoes; Popo's decision to stand on top of the pyramid forever.

The People Could Fly

p. 305 Reading Strategy Students should underline *people who could fly; magic of flying; slavery; slave ships*, and *dark-skinned*.

p. 305 Reading Check The people are full of misery because they can't fly any more. They are miserable because they have been enslaved.

p. 305 Reading Check Some people have the special gift of being able to fly.

p. 306 Literary Analysis Students should circle the words *call him Toby; standin'*, and *Now*.

p. 306 Reading Check Sarah can't feed her baby because the overseer is watching.

p. 306 Reading Strategy Possible responses: violence; abuse; treating people and babies badly.

p. 307 Literary Analysis Students should underline *said so quickly* and *sounded like whispers and sighs.*

p. 307 Reading Check Possible response: The master wants to kill Toby because Toby is helping slaves escape.

p. 307 Reading Check The magic words are *buba yali* and *buba tambe.*

p. 308 Literary Analysis The correct answer is *B*.

p. 308 Stop to Reflect Most students will say it inspires hope because people find a way to save themselves from violence and pain.

Review and Assess

1. The people lose their wings when they become slaves.
2. Sarah tells Toby she must leave soon because she thought she would die.
3. Toby helps Sarah by chanting a spell and helping her fly.
4. Possible responses include: *say; hollerin',* and *Couldn't believe it, call him Toby; standin', Call her Sarah,* and *Now.*
5. *Life was painful and hard. They wanted to be free and they wanted to be safe.*

Demeter and Persephone

p. 313 Literary Analysis The events might describe volcanic eruptions.

p. 313 Reading Strategy Eros will shoot an arrow and someone will fall in love. Some students may predict that this love will stop the monsters from shaking the earth.

p. 314 Literary Analysis The Greeks say that people are hit by Eros' arrow and fall in love.

p. 314 Reading Check Students should underline *Eros shoots an arrow straight into Pluto's heart* and *a young woman gathering flowers.*

p. 314 Reading Check Persephone is the daughter of Demeter, the goddess of the harvest. Pluto kidnaps Persephone.

p. 315 Reading Strategy Possible response: Demeter might set the world on fire or destroy it.

p. 315 Literary Analysis The ancient Greeks believed that natural disasters were caused by the gods.

p. 315 Reading Strategy Students may predict that Zeus will save Persephone.

p. 315 Reading Check tasted food in the realm of the dead.

p. 316 Reading Check She likes things with fragrance. Jewels have no fragrance.

p. 316 Reading Strategy Students may predict that Persephone will be very unhappy or that she will die.

p. 316 Literary Analysis We have winter because Demeter doesn't allow things to grow while her daughter, Persephone, is with Pluto.

Review and Assess

1. Pluto takes Persephone to his kingdom because he is in love with her.
2. The correct answer is *C*.
3. Zeus solves the problem by asking Hermes to bring Persephone back.
4. When Persephone is on earth, there is spring and summer. When she is in the underworld the earth has fall and winter.
5. The myth of Demeter and Persephone explains the cycle of the seasons.
6. Possible responses: **Persephone:** *Prediction:* Students may have predicted she would die. *Outcome:* She did not die; but she was not completely happy either. **Demeter:** *Prediction:* Students may have predicted that Demeter would get Persephone back. *Outcome:* Demeter was able to get Persephone back for part of the year.

Icarus and Daedalus

p. 321 Reading Check Students should circle *a wonderful Labyrinth.*

p. 321 Reading Check It seemed impossible to leave because every ship was guarded.

p. 321 Reading Strategy Students should say what they think Daedalus will do.

p. 322 Literary Analysis He tries to teach Icarus how to use the wings safely.

p. 322 Reading Strategy If he doesn't remember his father's instructions he might be badly hurt or even die.

p. 322 Reading Strategy The heat of the sun could melt his feathers apart.

p. 323 Reading Check Students should underline the following: *The heat of the sun had melted the wax from his wings; the feathers were falling.*

p. 323 Stop to Reflect Students should say what they would do in the same situation.

Review and Assess

1. He is in Crete.
2. He plans to create wings so he can fly away.
3. He warns him not to fly too low or too high.
4. Icarus drowns at the end of the myth.
5. The myth teaches us the importance of being careful and cautious, and it teaches us to pay attention to others when they are teaching us how to do something that can be dangerous.

The following are some clues from the story: "For Icarus, these cautions went in at one ear and out by the other." / Icarus forgets all the instructions and soars as high as he can. / His father is way below him.

Answers to Part 2

"The Cat Who Thought She Was a Dog and the Dog Who Thought He Was a Cat" by Isaac Bashevis Singer

Use Context Clues (page 329)

1. c
2. d
3. b
4. a

"Two Kinds" by Amy Tan

Apply Word Identification Strategies (page 330)

Sample Responses:

1. tip and toes; meaning: walks on the tips of the toes
2. house and cleaning; meaning: cleaning the house
3. high and pitched; meaning: a pitch (or sound) that is high
4. ear and splitting; meaning: hurts (or splits) the ear
5. day and dreamed; meaning: dream during the daytime
6. show and piece; meaning: a piece that is shown off

from "Song of Myself" by Walt Whitman
"I'm Nobody" by Emily Dickinson
"Me" by Walter de la Mare

Read Poetry According to Punctuation (page 331)

Students might make notes that they do not pause at the end of a line with no punctuation, pause briefly at commas, pause briefly at ellipses and dashes, and pause longer at end punctuation.

"My Furthest-Back Person" by Alex Haley

Break Down Long Sentences (page 332)

Sample Responses:

1. Sentence: And when a main reading room desk attendant asked if he could help me, I wouldn't have dreamed of admitting to him some curiosity hanging on from boyhood about my slave forbears.

   Sentence broken into parts: A main reading room desk attendant asked if he could help me. I wouldn't have dreamed of admitting to him some curiosity. [The curiosity was] hanging on from boyhood about my slave forbears.

2. Sentence: Then, intensely, he queried me about the story's relay across the generations, about the gibberish of "k" sounds Grandma had fiercely muttered to herself while doing her housework, with my brothers and me giggling beyond her hearing at what we had dubbed "Grandma's noises."

   Sentence broken into parts: He queried me about the story's relay across the generations. [He queried me] about the gibberish of "k" sounds Grandma had fiercely muttered to herself while doing her housework. My brothers and I giggled beyond her hearing at what we had dubbed "Grandma's noises."

3. Sentence: The first native Gambian I could locate in the U.S. was named Ebou Manga, then a junior attending Hamilton College in upstate Clinton, N.Y.

   Sentence broken into parts: The first native Gambian I could locate in the U.S. was named Ebou Manga. [He was] then a junior attending Hamilton College in upstate Clinton, N.Y.

4. Sentence: I suppose I physically wavered, and they thought it was the hate; rustling whispers went through the crowd, and a man brought me a low stool.

Sentence broken into parts: I suppose I physically wavered. They thought it was the hate. Rustling whispers went through the crowd. A man brought me a low stool.

"The Third Level" by Jack Finney

Use Context to Determine Meaning
(page 333)

Sample Responses:

1. fear, war, worry and all the rest of it
2. a dozen men who looked just like me
3. pushing out new corridors and staircases like roots
4. tremendous trees whose branches meet overhead

"A Day's Wait"
by Ernest Hemingway

Reread (page 334)

Some of the behaviors that students may have questions about are:

1. When his father comes downstairs, Schatz is dressed, even though his father told him to go back to bed. On rereading the story, students might recognize that the boy was afraid of being sick.

2. Schatz does not follow what his father is reading to him. After rereading, students might realize that the boy is not listening because he is thinking about his illness.

3. The father goes outside for awhile. When rereading the story, students might recognize that the father was not very worried about his son's illness.

4. The boy refuses to let anyone come into the room to visit him. After reading the story again, students will probably recognize that the boy wanted to be alone to die.

"Was Tarzan a Three-Bandage Man?"
by Bill Cosby
"Oranges" by Gary Soto

Context Clues (page 335)

Sample Responses:

2. meaning: bad skin
3. meaning: bandages around the neck
4. meaning: trying to be like the injured
5. One possible sentence: Although baseball and football stars inspired us, our real heroes were the famous prize fighters, and the way to emulate a fighter was to walk around with a Band-Aid over one eye. Meaning: were our heroes

Unit 2

from *In Search of Our Mothers' Gardens* by Alice Walker

Ask Questions (page 336)

What I Know: Some students will focus on specific people they have known that work hard. Others might write about the motivations or lifestyles of hard workers.

What I Want to Know: Many students will wonder about the reason that some people work hard. Others might want to know how they can become hard workers themselves. Or, students may want to find out ways that they can avoid the kind of work they see some people do.

What I've Learned: Students may notice that many hard workers are so because they have no other choice in life, but that they also try to make things as beautiful as possible. Others will learn that work is not something to avoid—that there are certain pleasures that come from a hard-working life.

"Seventh Grade" by Gary Soto
"Melting Pot" by Anna Quindlen

Relate to Your Own Experience (page 337)

Students should record their ideas about what is happening in each scene. Student responses will vary based on their own experiences. Encourage students to relate their own experiences as much as possible.

"Fable" by Ralph Waldo Emerson
"Thumbprint" by Eve Merriam
"If—" by Rudyard Kipling

Paraphrase (page 338)

Sample Responses:

1. From Kipling—Poetic language: If you can dream—and not make dreams your master;/if you can think—and not make thoughts your aim. Paraphrase: If you can dream and think without making your own thoughts your main goal.

2. From Merriam—Poetic language: On the pad of my thumb/are whorls, whirls, wheels/in a unique design:/mine alone. Paraphrase: My thumbprint has its very own design.

3. From Emerson—Poetic language: If I cannot carry forests on my back,/Neither can you crack a nut. Paraphrase: I am not a mountain, but you are not a squirrel.

"Mother to Son"
by Langston Hughes
"The Courage That My Mother Had"
by Edna St. Vincent Millay
"The Hummingbird That Lived Through Winter"
by William Saroyan

Question (page 339)

Sample Responses:

Hughes: Students might understand worn stairs or wandering in the dark. They might not understand what a crystal stair is, and they might not understand the mother's tone.

Millay: Students will probably understand that the poet is praising her mother's courage and wishing that she had it. They might be confused by this image of the mother: "Rock from New England quarried;/Now granite in a granite hill."

Saroyan: Students will probably understand the old man's nature, and his love for living things. They may not understand why the man let the hummingbird go, or what the man means when he says that each bird is "our bird."

Unit 3

"The Third Wish" by Joan Aiken

Clarify (page 340)

Students may have a variety of questions about this selection. Some of the questions and answers might include:

1. What is causing the crying, struggling, and thrashing? After rereading, the students learn it is the swan.

2. Why does the swan look at the man with hate in his eyes? After rereading, students may be able to see that the bird was frightened.

3. Where did the little green man with a golden crown come from? After rereading, students should be able to recognize that the swan and the little green man are the same creature.

4. Why is Mr. Peters content in his old age? After finishing the story, students may see that his contentment came because he understood the swans and had loved Leita.

"A Boy and a Man"
by James Ramsey Ullman
from Into Thin Air
by Jon Krakauer

Predict (page 341)

Sample Responses:

"A Boy and a Man"

1. Rudi will be unable to save the man because the time it takes to get help will leave the man frozen.

2. Rudi will be able to save the man because he is so determined and willing to sacrifice his own comfort.

3. Rudi and Captain John Winter will climb the Citadel together as a way of honoring Rudi's father.

from *Into Thin Air*

1. The writer will be injured because of all the danger mentioned in the story.
2. The writer will be able to speed across the tower because he is so eager to do it, and because he loves the challenge.
3. Krakauer safely returns from Mount Everest because he survived to write his account.

"The Charge of the Light Brigade" by Alfred, Lord Tennyson
from Henry V, "St. Crispian's Day Speech" by William Shakespeare
"The Enemy" by Alice Walker

Reading Poetic Contractions (page 342)

1. Missing Letter or Letters: e; Full Word or Words: called
2. Missing Letter or Letters: e; Full Word or Words: remembered
3. Missing Letter or Letters: v; Full Word or Words: never
4. Missing Letter or Letters: e; Full Word or Words: accursed

"The Californian's Tale" by Mark Twain
"Valediction" by Seamus Heaney

Summarize (page 343)
Sample Responses:

1. Main events and details: Twain describes the lonely land around him. Summary: The land was so lonesome that the only sounds were those of insects.

2. Main events and details: Twain visits the cottage and finds it very pleasing compared to the experiences he's been through. Summary: Twain found a pleasing cottage and was happy to be away from the drudgery of the past weeks. The cabin was refreshing and homey.
3. Main events and details: Twain surveys the bedroom and notices many nice details. Summary: The bedroom was nicer than anything he had seen for a long time, with fine features.
4. Main events and details: Twain washes his face. Summary: As he washed his face and looked around the room, he found a picture.
5. Main events and details: The cottage owner tells Twain about his wife's return, and praises her beauty. Summary: The cottage owner praises his wife and can't wait for Twain to meet her, but he won't meet her because he is leaving.

"Stopping by Woods on a Snowy Evening" by Robert Frost
"Four Skinny Trees" by Sandra Cisneros
"Miracles" by Walt Whitman

Respond to Levels of Meaning (page 344)
The purpose of this exercise is to show how two different people can have different responses to a selection. Encourage students not to be shy in sharing their responses. Remind them that sharing responses can help both people to understand a selection better.

Unit 4

"The Night the Bed Fell" by James Thurber

Identify Causes and Effects (page 345)
Sample Responses:

1. Cause: Briggs fears that he will stop breathing in the night.
   Effect: He puts a glass of camphor by his bed.

2. Cause: Aunt Sarah Shoaf fears a burglar bringing chloroform.
   Effect: She piles her money, silverware, and other valuables outside her bed with a note.
3. Cause: Aunt Gracie Shoaf fears burglars.
   Effect: She throws shoes down the hall.

4. Cause: Narrator sleeps in a bad army cot.

   Effect: Cot crashes.

5. Cause: Cot crashes.

   Effect: Mother wakes and screams.

6. Cause: Mother screams.

   Effect: Herman wakes and shouts with mother.

7. Cause: Herman shouts.

   Effect: Briggs wakes up, thinking that he is suffocating.

8. Cause: Briggs wakes up, thinking that he is suffocating.

   Effect: Briggs pours camphor on himself, making the room smell terribly.

9. Cause: The room smells terribly.

   Effect: Briggs breaks open the window with his hand.

10. Cause: Briggs breaks open the window with his hand.

    Effect: Narrator wakes up, fearing he is in a bad situation.

11. Cause: Mother tries to get the door to the attic open.

    Effect: Father wakes up, fears the house is on fire, and yells, "I'm coming!"

12. Cause: Father yells, "I'm coming!"

    Effect: Mother thinks he's talking to God and is dying.

13. Cause: Dog doesn't like Briggs.

    Effect: Roy has to hold the dog down.

14. Cause: Father comes downstairs.

    Effect: Mother weeps.

15. Cause: Father wanders around in the night.

    Effect: Father catches a cold.

"All Summer in A Day"
by Ray Bradbury

Picture Setting and Actions (page 346)
Sample Responses:

See: Rain, "the drum and gush of water, with the sweet crystal fall of showers and the concussion of storms so heavy they were tidal waves come over the islands."

Hear: Rain, "they always awoke to the tatting drum . . ."; No rain, "the silence was so immense and unbelievable that you felt your ears had been stuffed or you had lost your hearing altogether."

Feel: Warmth of the sun, "But they were running and turning their faces up to the sky and feeling the sun on their cheeks like a warm iron; they were taking off their jackets and letting the sun burn their arms."

Smell: "The door slid back and the smell of the silent, waiting world came in to them."

"The Highwayman" by Alfred Noyes
"The Real Story of a Cowboy's Life"
by Geoffrey C. Ward

Identify Causes and Effects (page 347)
Sample Responses for "The Highwayman":

1. Cause: The Highwayman comes to see Bess.

   Effect: The Highwayman promises to return to get her.

2. Cause: The horsekeeper overhears.

   Effect: He warns the authorities.

3. Cause: King George's men come to the inn.

   Effect: Bess is captured.

4. Cause: Bess gets her hand on the gun so she can warn the Highwayman.

   Effect: She kills herself to save him.

5. Cause: The Highwayman returns to avenge Bess's death.

   Effect: He is killed by King George's men.

Sample Responses for "The Real Story of a Cowboy's Life":

1. Cause: The cowboys traveled through dusty ground.

   Effect: They would rinse their mouths to clean out the dirt.

2. Cause: One jittery cow would act up.

   Effect: An entire herd would stampede.

3. Cause: The herds ruined settlers crops and brought disease.

   Effect: The cowboys and settlers weren't friendly.

4. Cause: Herds came to their destination.

   Effect: Cowboys would relax in town.

"Justin Lebo" by Phillip Hoose
"The Rider" by Naomi Shihab Nye
"Amigo Brothers" by Piri Thomas
"The Walk" by Thomas Hardy

Make Inferences (page 348)

Sample Responses:

1. In "Amigo Brothers," students might infer that the boys are great friends because they do not want to hurt each other in the fight.
2. Readers of "The Walk" might infer that the speaker was able to enjoy himself because he does not think of his old companion as being left behind.
3. In "Justin Lebo," students may infer that Justin is goodhearted because he wants everyone at the boys' home to have a bike and because he works hard to make it happen.
4. Students may infer from "The Rider" that the speaker is lonely because she wonders if biking can eliminate loneliness and she is riding a bike herself.

Unit 5

"Our Finest Hour"
by Charles Osgood

Distinguish Fact From Opinion (page 349)

Sample Responses:

1. Opinion. The words "easy enough" and "most of the time" show that this is a personal opinion.
2. Fact. You could prove this by finding the reporter and the story.
3. Fact. You could prove this by looking at the piece after the commercial.
4. Opinion. The terms "all in all" and "not the finest" express personal feelings and cannot be proven.
5. Opinion. The term "really great impression" cannot be defined or proven—it expresses personal opinion.

"Cat on the Go" by James Herriot

Understand Bias (page 350)

Sample Responses:

1. He found the cat a pleasant creature.
2. He was a generous pet owner and had probably already taken in strays.
3. He was hoping to find the cat.
4. He wanted to know that the cat would be okay.
5. Herriot is kind and gentle.

"The Luckiest Time of All"
by Lucille Clifton
"Father William" by Lewis Carroll
"The Microscope" by Maxine Kumin
"in Just—" by E. E. Cummings
"Sarah Cynthia Sylvia Stout Would Not Take the Garbage Out"
by Shel Silverstein

Recognize Author's Purpose (page 351)

Sample Responses:

2. "and eddieandbill come/running from marbles and piracies and it's/spring"
3. "We ought to ship him off to Spain/He says he's seen a housefly's brain."
4. "At last the garbage reached so high/That finally it touched the sky."
5. "But, now that I'm perfectly sure I have none [brain],/Why, I do it again and again."

"Zoo" by Edward Hoch
"The Hippopotamus" by Odgen Nash
"How the Snake Got Poison"
by Zora Neale Hurston

Evaluate an Author's Message (page 352)

Sample Responses:

2. We often treat things that are different from us as a commodity.
3. We view things from our own perspective, but often fail to think of things from other perspectives.
4. People treat you differently depending on whether you are a friend or an enemy.

Unit 6

"After Twenty Years"
by O. Henry

What Happens Next? (page 353)

Students may write predictions after the following events:

1. The man walks up to the policeman.
2. The man tells the policeman that he is supposed to meet his old friend Jimmy here.
3. The man pulls out a diamond-studded watch.
4. The policeman leaves.
5. "Jimmy" shows up.

   Encourage students to compare their predictions with what actually happens.

"Rikki-tikki-tavi"
by Rudyard Kipling

Predict (page 354)

Students may write the following predictions:

1. The mongoose will become a friend to the family because they choose to take care of him when he is nearly dead.
2. Rikki-tikki-tavi will save the family from a snake because the father mentions how safe the mongoose is, and how the mongoose could defend Teddy from a snake.
3. Nag will cause further trouble for the family and the mongoose because he has eaten the baby bird.
4. The mongoose will defeat Nag because nag is afraid of him.
5. Nagaina will kill Teddy or the mongoose as revenge for the death of Nag.

   Encourage students to compare their predictions with what actually happens.

"Papa's Parrot" by Cynthia Rylant

Identify with a Character (page 355)

Encourage students to explore their own feelings by writing a detailed diary entry.

"Suzy and Leah" by Jane Yolen

Make Inferences (page 356)

Sample Responses:

Paragraph beginning with the words "Today I walked"

Detail #1: "A line of rickety wooden buildings"

Suggests: The refugee camp has poor accommodations.

Detail #2: "Just like in the army"

Suggests: The refugees are treated as if they are part of the war.

Detail #3: "A fence lots higher than my head. With barbed wire on top."

Suggests: The refugees are kept like prisoners because people fear they may escape.

Paragraph beginning with the words "I put on the blue dress"

Detail #1: "I put on the blue dress."

Suggests: Leah has nothing else to wear.

Detail #2: "The color reminded me of your eyes and the blue skies over our farm before the smoke from the burning darkened it."

Suggests: Leah is homesick, remembering her life before the war.

Detail #3: "I had no mirror until we got to the school"

Suggests: The conditions in the refugee camp aren't very good.

"Ribbons" by Laurence Yep
"The Treasure of Lemon Brown"
by Walter Dean Myers

Ask Questions (page 357)

Sample Responses:

1. "Ribbons." Question: Why is there a break after Dad stops the ballet lessons?

   Answer: The break shows a passage of time and the narrator's perspective.

2. "The Treasure of Lemon Brown." Question: What is the purpose of the third paragraph (beginning "Greg had sat in the small, pale green kitchen")?

Answer: It gives the reader some history and context without telling all the background.

3. "The Treasure of Lemon Brown." Question: What is the purpose of the final paragraph?

Answer: It concludes the story by giving a hint about Greg's feelings at the end.

"Stolen Day"
by Sherwood Anderson

Identify with the Characters (page 358)

Sample Responses:

1. Some students might talk about the boy's age and his relationship with his family. Others might talk about his school situation.

2. Many students will be able to identify with a fear of being sick, especially fear that comes from seeing other sick people.

3. Students will probably identify with the boy's longing for his mother's affection or his jealousy over her care for the drowned child.

4. Some students will understand the boy's love of fishing, but others may not be able to identify with it. A lot of students will share his concerns about health and family.

5. Some students will identify more with the boy's family—the teasing siblings and the busy mother, for example. Others may suffer from a permanent health condition and might identify most with Walter.

Unit 7

"How to Enjoy Poetry"
by James Dickey

Recognize the Organization (page 359)

Sample Responses:

1. Understand that poetry comes from outside you, but requires something inside you to live.

2. Don't let the poet write down to you; read up to him.

3. Remember that poetry is new to each reader.

4. Start simply.

5. Open yourself as wide as you can.

6. Read the list of images and think about your own life.

7. Think about the rhythm.

8. Try writing poetry yourself.

9. Try to understand how the world interacts with words

10. Recognize connections between things.

"No Gumption" by Russell Baker
"The Chase" from *An American Childhood* by Anne Dillard

Understand the Author's Purpose (page 360)

Sample Responses:

1. "I loved to pick through trash piles and collect empty bottles, tin cans with pretty labels, and discarded magazines. The most desirable job on earth sprang to mind. 'I want to be a garbage man.'"

2. "There were two filling stations at the intersection with Union Avenue, as well as an A&P, a fruit stand, a bakery, a barber shop, Zuccarelli's drugstore, and a diner shaped like a railroad car."

3. "My idea of a perfect afternoon was lying in front of the radio rereading my favorite Big Little Book *Dick Tracy Meets Stooge Viller*."

4. "We smashed through a gap in another hedge, entered a scruffy backyard and ran around its back porch and tight between houses to Edgerton Avenue."

5. "The oldest two Fahey boys were there— Mikey and Peter—polite blond boys who lived near me on Lloyd Street . . . Chickie McBride was there, a tough kid, and Billy Paul and Mackie Kean too, from across Reynolds, where the boys grew up dark and furious, grew up skinny, knowing, and skilled."

6. "Some boys taught me to play football . . . Best, you got to throw yourself mightily at someone's running legs. Either you brought him down or you hit the ground flat out on your chin, with your arms empty before you. It was all or nothing."

"Nolan Ryan" by William W. Lace

Set a Purpose for Reading (page 361)

Sample Responses:

Question 1: Who is Nolan Ryan?

Question 2: Why is he called a Texas treasure?

Question 3: What is Ryan like?

Question 4: Does Ryan have any records?

Answer 1: Nolan Ryan is a great major-league baseball pitcher.

Answer 2: He is a successful player with an admirable lifestyle. He is modest and uncomplicated.

Answer 3: He is a balanced person with interests and commitments beyond baseball. He takes care of his health and his family.

Answer 4: Ryan holds almost 50 major league records, including strikeouts and no-hitters.

"Rattlesnake Hunt" by Marjorie Kinnan Rawlings
from *Barrio Boy* by Ernesto Galarza
"I Am a Native of North America" by Chief Dan George
"All Together Now" by Barbara Jordan

Identify the Author's Main Points (page 362)

Sample Responses:

from *Barrio Boy*

Main point: Entering a new situation can be frightening.

Supporting Details: 1) The day the speaker enrolls, he and his mother have to go into the building without knowing exactly what to expect. 2) Ernesto has to sit in the front row.

"I Am a Native of North America"

Main point: Real love is the only thing that can heal cultural divides.

Supporting Details: 1) The speaker's father grew up in a house of love and learned to love people. 2) Our spirits feed on love.

"Rattlesnake Hunt"

Main point: Facing your fears is the best way to conquer them.

Supporting Details: 1) The author goes on a rattlesnake hunt even though she is afraid. 2) The author learns about how rattlers work.

"All Together Now"

Main point: We need to build a more tolerant society.

Supporting Details: 1) History shows that racism continues. 2) Children can be taught to be tolerant and to enjoy people who are different from themselves.

Unit 8

"A Christmas Carol: Scrooge and Marley" Act I by Charles Dickens dramatized by Israel Horovitz

Picture (page 363)

Sample Responses:

1. Stage Direction: A ghostly bell rings in the distance. MARLEY moves away from

SCROOGE, now, heading D. again. As he does, he "takes" the light: SCROOGE has disappeared into the black void beyond.

How it Helps Me Picture the Play: Scrooge is a dark character and his mystery continues.

2. Stage Direction: We see SCROOGE'S clerk, BOB CRATCHIT, who sits in a dismal tank

of a cubicle, copying letters.

How it Helps Me Picture the Play: Bob Cratchit's work situation is dreary and unending.

3. Stage Direction: SCROOGE will walk alone to his rooms . . . There will be occasional pleasant greetings tossed at him. SCROOGE, in contrast to all, will grump and mumble.

How it Helps Me Picture the Play: Scrooge's movement and his grumpiness contrast with the cheerful, spirited people around him.

4. Stage Direction: SCROOGE fastens the door and walks across the hall to the stairs . . . he checks each room; sitting room, bedrooms, slumber-room. He looks under the sofa, under the table: nobody there.

How it Helps Me Picture the Play: Scrooge lives in a large house, but there is nobody there with him.

5. Stage Direction: Outside the window, specters fly by, carrying money-boxes and chains. They make a confused sound of lamentation.

How it Helps Me Picture the Play: The scene is spooky, and Scrooge is haunted by it.

"A Christmas Carol: Scrooge and Marley" Act II by Charles Dickens dramatized by Israel Horovitz

Question (page 364)

Sample Responses:

1. Students might not understand why Scrooge is so hateful. As they read the play, they will understand his past, and the reasons for his misery.

2. Students might not understand why the ghosts keep appearing to Scrooge. As they read, they will understand that the ghosts are used to help Scrooge understand the spirit of Christmas.

3. Students might not understand why the ghost of Christmas Present takes Scrooge to the Cratchit's home. As they read, they will see that Tiny Tim's condition will change Scrooge's heart.

4. Students might not understand how Bob Cratchit can drink a toast to the cruel Scrooge. As readers keep reading, they see that Bob Cratchit has a heart that is kind enough to include Scrooge.

5. Students might not understand how Scrooge can save the situation for Tiny Tim. As they read, they will understand that the ghosts still give Scrooge the chance to change his ways and Tiny Tim's outcome.

The Monsters Are Due on Maple Street by Rod Serling

Predict (page 365)

Sample Responses:

1. Students might predict that the play will deal with strange events based on the fifth dimension because of the narrator's comments at the beginning of the play.

2. Students might predict that the monsters will destroy the humans based on the lack of electricity and phone service after the meteor.

3. Students might predict that Tommy will communicate with the monsters since he is the one that believes that they are real from the beginning.

4. Students might predict that Goodman is one of the aliens because he didn't pay attention to the meteor, and his car is the only one in the neighborhood that starts.

5. Students might predict that the people themselves are the real monsters since they are so quick to judge Goodman.

6. Students might predict that the dark approaching figure is going to be a friend rather than a monster based on the paranoia that everyone is feeling.

Unit 9

"The Cremation of Sam McGee" by Robert Service
"Washed in Silver" by James Stephens
"Winter" by Nikki Giovanni

Identify the Speaker (page 366)
Sample Responses:
2. He can't deny a request from a friend.
3. He is loyal to his dying friend.
4. Though he never spoke it, he was unhappy about carrying McGee's body.
5. He is worn out, but he perseveres.
6. He is sensitive to hearing his friend's body burn.

"Seal" by William Jay Smith
"The Pasture" by Robert Frost
"Three Haiku" by Matsuo Bashō, translated by Daniel C. Buchanan

Read According to Punctuation (page 367)
Sample Responses for Stop at a Period:

I'm going out to fetch the little calf that's standing by the mother. ("The Pasture")

On sweet plum blossoms the sun rises suddenly. (Haiku 1)

On that nameless mountain lie thin layers of mist (Haiku 2)

Temple bells die out. (Haiku 3)

Sample Responses for Pause at a Comma or Hyphen:

Back up he swims past Sting Ray and Shark, out with a zoom, a whoop, a bark; ("Seal")

Quick-silver quick, softer than spray, down he plunges and sweeps away ("Seal"

I shan't be gone long.—You come too. ("The Pasture")

Sample Responses for Read with Emphasis at an Exclamation Point:

He plops at your side with a mouthful of fish! ("Seal")

Look, a mountain path! (Haiku 1)

A perfect evening! (Haiku 3)

"Martin Luther King" by Raymond Richard Patterson
"Annabel Lee" by Edgar Allen Poe

Paraphrase (page 368)
Sample Responses:
2. His passion was so great that he had to follow it.
3. He showed the suffering world how great a man can be.
4. She died. OR Her dead ancestors took her to be with themselves.
5. The angels were jealous of our love and that's why they took her.
6. The bright stars remind me of the eyes of Annabel Lee.

"Full Fathom Five" by William Shakespeare
"Onomatopoeia" by Eve Merriam
"Maestro" by Pat Mora

Listen as You Read Poetry (page 369)
Sample Responses:
2. the sounds of the bell ringing ding-dong
3. the repetition of the s sound 6 times
4. the repetition of the sh sound 4 times
5. the repetition of the short i sound 6 times
6. the repetition of the g sound 3 times

"Fog" by Carl Sandburg
"Life" by Naomi Long Madgett
"Loo-Wit" by Wendy Rose
"The Village Blacksmith" by Henry Wadsworth Longfellow

Respond to Poetry (page 370)
Students may agree or disagree with the poets' ideas, but encourage them to give reasons for their response. Responses should include personal experiences that relate to each poem.

"Popocatepetl and Ixtlaccihuatl"
by Juliet Piggott

Predict (page 371)

Sample Responses:

Prediction 1: The Princess Ixtla will marry Popo.

Why It May Happen: They love each other.

What Actually Happens: She dies because she thinks he has been killed in a battle.

Prediction 2: Popo will defeat the enemy tribes.

Why It May Happen: He is a fine warrior.

What Actually Happens: He defeats the enemy tribes.

Prediction 3: The Princess Ixtla will die.

Why It May Happen: She is very sick because she believes Popo is dead.

What Actually Happens: The Princess dies and her mournful lover buries her at the top of a mound of stones.

"The People Could Fly"
by Virginia Hamilton
"All Stories are Anansi's"
by Harold Courlander
"The Lion and the Statue" by Aesop
"The Fox and the Crow" by Aesop

Recognize Storyteller's Purpose (page 372)

Sample Responses:

1. The storyteller's purpose is to show the suffering of the slaves, and the way they dealt with it. Students might learn more about conditions on a plantation.

2. The storyteller's purpose is to show how the spider became the owner of all stories. Students might learn about the kinds of animals in Western Africa.

3. The purpose of the storyteller is to teach the lesson that sometimes people represent reality the way they want it to be. Students might recognize that they do this themselves sometimes.

4. The storyteller's purpose is to teach the lesson that flatterers aren't always trustworthy. Students might realize that they sometimes use flattery for the wrong reason.

"Phaëthon, Son of Apollo"
by Olivia Coolidge
"Demeter and Persephone"
by Anne Terry White
"Icarus and Daedalus"
by Josephine Preston Peabody

Predict (page 373)

Sample Responses:

1. Students might predict that something bad will happen to Phaëthon because he is prideful and insists on being the best at everything. Others might insist that his strength will keep him from harm.

2. Students might predict that Persephone will return to her mother forever. Others might predict that she will have eaten with Pluto and will be unable to escape him.

3. Students might predict that tragedy will come to Icarus because of carelessness that his father warns him against.